ABOUT THE AUTHOR

James Fulford is a Fellow of The Institute of Chartered Accountants in Ireland. He obtained first place in Ireland in the pre-final examinations and, since qualification, has studied commercial law and, more recently, computing.

Based outside Belfast, James is a regular contributor to the Institute's professional journal, *Accountancy Ireland*, as well as being a partner in both a computer consultancy firm and an accountancy practice. He started his career in a large local accountancy practice. After qualification he joined an international practice, with responsibility for technical and quality control matters, and later moved to the accounts department of a sole practitioner.

THE ACCOUNTANT'S GUIDE TO ADVANCED EXCEL

James Fulford

Oak Tree Press

Dublin

Oak Tree Press
Merrion Building
Lower Merrion Street
Dublin 2, Ireland

A catalogue record of this book is
available from the British Library.

ISBN 1-86076-126-7

Printed in Ireland by Colour Books Ltd.

CONTENTS

Contents

Acknowledgements

This book, like the one before it, is the result of a lot of hard work and effort by a long list of people. My apologies in advance to anyone not specifically mentioned.

Firstly, I would like to thank everyone at Oak Tree Press, the publishers, for their continued professionalism and hard work. My gratitude goes to the production manager, Jenna Dowds, in particular. Her patience with all of the screen shots is very much appreciated. I thought I was making life easier and, as always, it didn't quite work out that way.

Secondly, I would again like to acknowledge the impact my fellow members of the Institute of Chartered Accountants have had in forming my persona as a professional accountant. I will not embarrass them by listing them individually, but, by analysing the strengths of each, I believe I have benefited greatly.

Thirdly, because of the nature of this book, there must be a word of gratitude to Peter Wright, the author of *The Beginner's Guide to VB* by Wrox Press. His ability to write an interesting and informative book on a subject that could so easily be dry and off-putting has, itself, been an inspiration. Whilst VB is not covered in detail in *The Accountant's Guide to Advanced Excel*, it forms a necessary background to the production of the Random Data Generator etc. in order for a substantial and meaningful tutorial to be designed.

Fourthly, a special mention to Jack Kennedy for his input and, above all, particular thanks for his life-saving backups and unending enthusiasm.

And finally, I would like to thank my wife Margaret, without whose support this book would not have been possible.

James Fulford
April 1999

Dedication

To Alan, Alison and Margaret.

The "A" team

PRELUDE

In the beginning there was work . . . And there still is!

This is your first day. You arrive at reception where I meet you. "Welcome to Joe Bloggs Inc! As you know I am the Financial Controller of the group, and you will be responsible for Bloggs Wholesalers Co., one of the subsidiary companies . . ."

Just then, John Smith comes in and interrupts me. "James, I need you to . . ." He notices the new face: "Oh. Hello um . . . Yes. You are . . . the new accountant. That's right. Anyway, James, I have set up a meeting on Thursday with production, sales and marketing, and I want you to get some figures for us to look at. This situation has me edgy . . ."

He was referring to Thingies. A couple of years ago we had started importing Whatsits, which John had predicted would be the biggest thing since Widgets. And he was right. Sales had exceeded all expectations, even his, and Joe Bloggs Inc. had expanded rapidly. We now make Whatsits under licence, and export them as well as wholesaling them locally.

But then competitors in the Far East started to make Thingies, and we were in a whole new ball game. There is nothing to worry about yet, but when John starts talking about being edgy he wants information, and he wants to know all of the angles.

The meeting on Thursday will be important, with key company members attending. Some are comfortable with figures, but most aren't.

And the computer system doesn't help. The company grew too fast, and the system hasn't kept up. Everyone is complaining that they cannot get the information they need. We are costing an upgrade, and I am pulling together the information needs of the various departments for the programmers. However, in the meantime . . .

I know what. Why don't you work with me for the next couple of days? You can watch me query the system and pull everything together in Excel. I will explain everything as I go along, then you will be able to pick up your new job more easily.

Two days should be plenty of time for what we want to do . . .

INTRODUCTION

This book is the second in *The Accountant's Guide* series, and builds on the knowledge gained in the first book, *The Accountant's Guide to Excel*, extending it into areas not relevant to starting out with Excel. To recap, the contents of the first book are shown below:

- **Understanding Windows**:
  The hardware
  Directories
  Clipboard, Cut, Copy and Paste
  Printing, Saving, Opening.

- **Excel Functionality**:
  A review of the program in its broader context
  The screen
  The toolbars and menu
  AutoSave, Formatting, Dates etc.
  Using the keyboard and mouse
  Autofill.

- **Spreadsheet Design**

- **Building Spreadsheets**:
  A high volume processing model
  A front end calculator model
  An accounts and projections model.

If you want to learn any or all of these aspects, or have not received any formal training in Excel, you will probably benefit from working through *The Accountant's Guide to Excel* before building on that foundation with this book.

WHO IS THIS BOOK FOR?

This book is written from the perspective of those who need to use a spreadsheet as an analysis tool to slice and dice figures, to see trends and patterns in the financial results (whether historic or projected), and to assist in the preparation of reports and presentations based on these results.

It is written very much from the perspective of the accountant, and is not a book for statisticians, engineers or mathematicians.

Specifically, it will suit:

* Auditors and accountants in public practice
* Accountants in industry
* Accountants in government departments and the public sector
* Trainee accountants
* Non-accountants, suitably experienced in finance
* Business degree students.

WHAT IS COVERED IN THIS BOOK?

This book covers the "what if . . ." and "did you know . . ." aspects of analysing the financial figures, and summarising the raw data into alternative perspectives of the same source information.

This is achieved by building on the case study used in *The Accountant's Guide to Excel* and using the case study to explain the issues involved, including how to use Excel to prepare the initial analysis of the raw data.

As an accountant, not only are you expected to understand and interpret figures, you must be able to communicate with non-financial members of the management team. This book therefore also looks at the presentation of the "new" information discovered.

The book is split into five distinct sections. They are:

Section 1

This section includes a recap of spreadsheet design, including layout and insertion of comments, and reviews the Auditing Toolbar. Programming basics are considered, and Excel VBA and macros are used to build a flexible spreadsheet "what if" model. A pre-built random data generator is included at the end of the section.

Section 2

This section describes databases, and explains how to use Excel's data Tools, including filtering and sorting data, summarising data using PivotTables, reviewing a range of possibilities with Data Tables, finding answers with Solver and presenting a range of spreadsheet answers with Scenario, using in-built functions for forecasting.

Section 3
This section reviews PowerPoint, and explains how to prepare a slide show presentation. The report contents for Section Four are established.

Section 4
This section broadens out the Whatsit model, lists some questions, uses scenarios, goal seek, pivot tables, conditional formatting and starts to change the way we look at results covering statistical analysis, extrapolation, charting the results, etc., thus broadening the perspective.

Section 5
This section covers other Excel issues, including consolidation, and a summary chapter to close the book.

Appendices
These include:
* Guidance notes for the Whatsits Sales Data Generator used in Section 4
* Copies of The PowerPoint Pro-formas used in Section 3
* Details about the Spreadsheets included with this CD.

WHAT IS NOT COVERED IN THIS BOOK?

Excel is a vast program, and there are many aspects that you, as an accountant, will never need to learn.

Of the areas that are within your remit, there are advanced Power User aspects that may be useful to you in your specific circumstances, and aspects which are considered to be fundamental building blocks that must be learnt by everyone before branching off into detailed elements of the program.

Specifically, this book does not cover the "basic" matters referred to in *The Accountant's Guide to Excel*, especially as regards how to use the Windows program, how to print, and how to open, save, and close files. Knowledge of the Excel menu structure and toolbar is explained in that book, and the knowledge is, therefore, assumed here. Other areas of knowledge assumed are: how to format cells; the distinction between text and numbers, and, how to use Object Linking and Embedding, and the difference between them. Knowledge of basic functions, their structure, and the interaction of several functions within the one statement is also assumed.

For Power Users, this book does not cover detailed Visual Basic Programming — including programming conventions — or Access databases, programming and design.

Both of these aspects are multidiscipline matters that require consideration to be given to screen "front ending" as well as using database queries, forms and reporting. Each topic is a book in itself.

HOW TO GET THE MOST FROM THIS BOOK

You will gain more from Excel if you practice, and you will gain more from this book if you follow the exercises on your own PC.

All of the models built in this book are included on the enclosed CD-ROM so that you can review them "live".

To access the files directly, follow the steps below:
1.   From Excel, choose Open from the file menu
2.   In the Open File dialogue box, change to the CD drive (usually D)
3.   Search for the appropriate file, and click on it to select it. Double-click to open, or choose the Open button.

The CD-ROM is read only. If any amendments are made to the file and you wish to keep the updated file you will have to save it to your hard drive (usually C:). You cannot save it on the CD.

If you prefer, any or all of the files can be copied to your hard drive by using Explorer. To do this:
1.   Start Explorer and select the CD drive
2.   Whilst holding down the Control key, select the file(s) with the mouse. The selected files are highlighted in blue
3.   With the mouse cursor on one of the files, right click and select Copy
4.   Change to the hard drive (usually C:), select the appropriate folder, and right click the mouse. Choose Paste.

The more you put into using this book, the more you will get from it. Good luck on your road to Power User status!

Section One

CONTROLLING SPREADSHEETS: OVERVIEW

In this section we want to set the scene in terms of how we want to use Excel – how we define its use will impact on how we design the spreadsheet layout, the controls we build in, the number of cells we want to use per sheet, when we will use a second sheet etc.

We will therefore look at:
• Spreadsheet design
• Auditing spreadsheets
• Programming basics
• Excel VBA and macros.

We need to be confident that we can control Excel, and lay out the spreadsheet in a meaningful and sensible way.

We want our audience to have complete confidence in the spreadsheet models we present, and consequently have complete faith in our professionalism and professional judgement.

When we present our documents to the Board we want to be confident that we are:
• Accurate in our modelling
• Presenting the information in a slick and cohesive manner
• Logically moving from scenario to scenario
• Using formats for extracting and displaying trends and outcomes that are readily understood by the audience — some of whom will not be as comfortable with figures as we are.

The better our presentation, the more management will concentrate on our message, and the less they will be distracted by the medium. And that will reflect well on us.

Chapter One

STARTING POINT

The better the foundations, the stronger the house.

This chapter reviews the knowledge we assume you have already acquired. This will allow us to move into Excel at speed in the subsequent chapters and clarify things as early as possible.

If you need to revise or update your knowledge in the areas identified below, please do so now. The more complete your knowledge of the "basics" the easier it will be to add further knowledge later.

THE "BASICS"

The problem with describing something as basic is that it may not be basic at all. The more accurate description is The Fundamentals. These are listed below:

Understanding the Hardware

- This requires you be familiar with the equipment, including the keyboard and the mouse.
- In addition you must be familiar with the input of information with the keyboard or mouse as the preference takes you, and the feedback provided by Windows and Excel (in terms of the style of mouse cursor during certain operations, such as AutoFill).
- Be aware of the types of memory, the use of Shadow Memory, and the Swap File on the hard drive.
- Understand drive-naming conventions.

Windows

- Understand Folder (or directory) structure and file addresses. Be familiar with using Explorer.
- Understand printing and Print Manager. Understand Clipboard and Object Linking and Embedding.

Excel

- Be familiar with the screen layout.
- Know how to customise the Toolbar.
- Be aware of the difference between running commands from the toolbar and accessing the menu.
- Know how to use the File Open Common Dialog Box, and how to Save As a different file format.
- Know how to access Excel functions.
- Be able to work with cells — Copy, Edit, Paste, Paste Special.
- Be able to work with sheets — Move, Copy, Rename, Named Ranges.

With this in mind we will now recap on the issues involved in spreadsheet design and layout.

RECAP OF SPREADSHEET DESIGN

When we start with a fresh spreadsheet several questions immediately arise:

- Where do we want to place the input area?
- Where will we place the calculation area?
- What will the front end (output area) look like?
- How many sheets do we want to use? When will we start a new one?

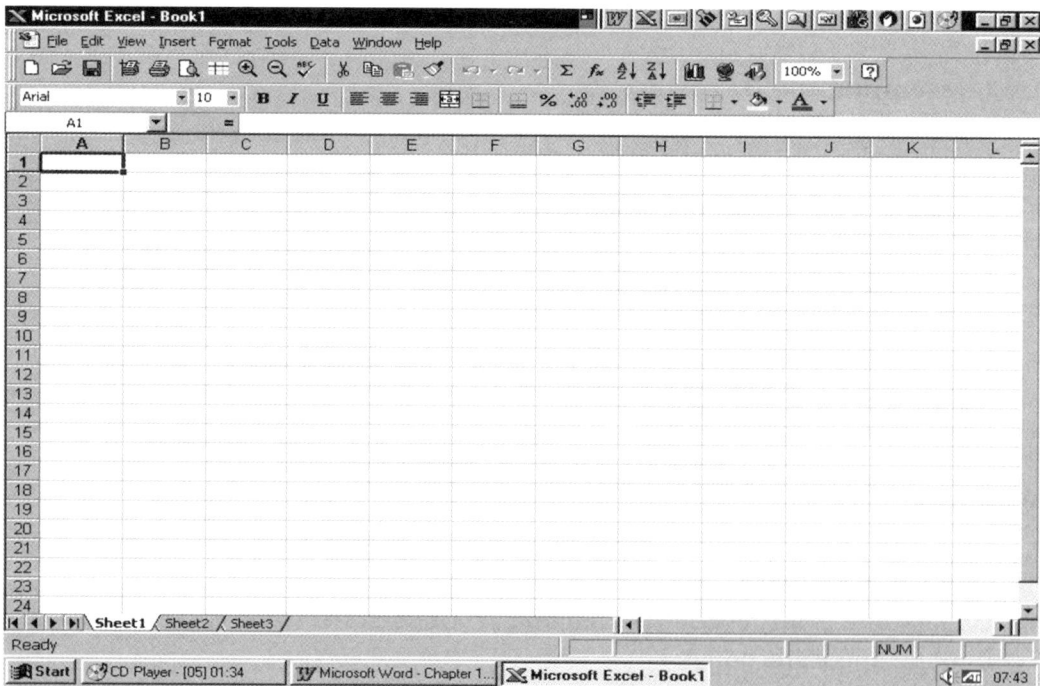

The answers to these questions are related back to the purpose of the spreadsheet. There are three broad types of spreadsheet:

- Figures intensive (for example, cash flow projections)
- Clerical intensive (for example, volume processing of sales invoices)
- User interface type (i.e. user input/output screens for non-technical people)

The mix of "back end/front end" sophistication is different for each type of spreadsheet. However, irrespective of the categorisation, the starting point is to define certain criteria that will apply to all spreadsheets. The full list of questions we must ask are noted below:

General Background Questions

- What file name will we use? It must be meaningful.
- Where will the spreadsheet be saved? On C: drive, floppy disk, network file server?
- Which file format will we save the file in? Excel '97, '95, 5.0 etc.?
- Who will use the spreadsheet? You, more junior staff, a qualified accountant, a Power User . . . ?
- How often will the spreadsheet be used? Will it be a "throw away" spreadsheet or will you want to use it for months or years, again and again, (a "template" spreadsheet)?
- What is the spreadsheet to be used for? How complicated is the issue we are reviewing?
- How important is it (professional indemnity, job security, etc.). The more important, the greater the need for a proper trail.

Design Issues

- What period is covered in the spreadsheet? How many years? What are the break periods?
- Should annual projections be split one year per sheet, or all years on one sheet?
- What is the reporting period?
- The detailed workings may give monthly information. However, is the final report shown as an annual total?
- What will the final report look like? How many pages? Condensed or full size? How will it fit in to the rest of the report? Charts? Tables?
- Which headings will be pasted into the final report from the spreadsheet? Are they to be bold? Which typeface?

Sheet Layout

- What are the main components of the spreadsheet?
- What links are there between sections, and what information exists in each section?
- How is information to be grouped on sheets? Is all of the detail on one sheet, or grouped (for example, by date) and split across several sheets?

Screen/Paper Layout

- What width of columns will be used — especially for headings?
- Which formats will be used to display dates etc?
- Are negative numbers in brackets? What rounding off will be used?

Answering these questions properly, and thereby addressing the issues involved, will ensure a rounded, professional, spreadsheet solution is implemented, balancing the sophistication of the model with the time required to develop it.

In **Chapter Two** we will look at the auditing tools provided in Excel for tracing errors in spreadsheets, and consider how best to prepare a physical trail through a spreadsheet.

Chapter Two

AUDITING SPREADSHEETS

Seeing is believing.

THE NEED FOR AUDITING

It is very easy to quickly produce quite complex spreadsheets, with formulae, linked cells, and summaries. Checking that all of the formulae are correct, linked to the correct input areas, and properly summarised can actually take longer than the initial preparation, and to this end ensuring that a logical design and a proper physical trail exists is of great benefit.

In addition Excel includes Auditing Tools which colour-code the information on the screen, further enhancing the checking process.

The purpose of this chapter is, therefore, to explore the Auditing Tools provided, and to demonstrate good spreadsheet design in practice.

THE AUDITING TOOLS

The auditing tools are accessed from the menu; click on Tools, Auditing. A drop down menu appears as can be seen on the next page.

It is generally better to display the toolbar (last option in the menu), in order to have all of the tools readily available.

The auditing tools are:
- Trace Precedents
- Remove Precedent Arrows
- Trace Dependents
- Remove Dependent Arrows
- Remove All Arrows
- Trace Error
- New Comment
- Circle Invalid Data
- Clear Validation Circles.

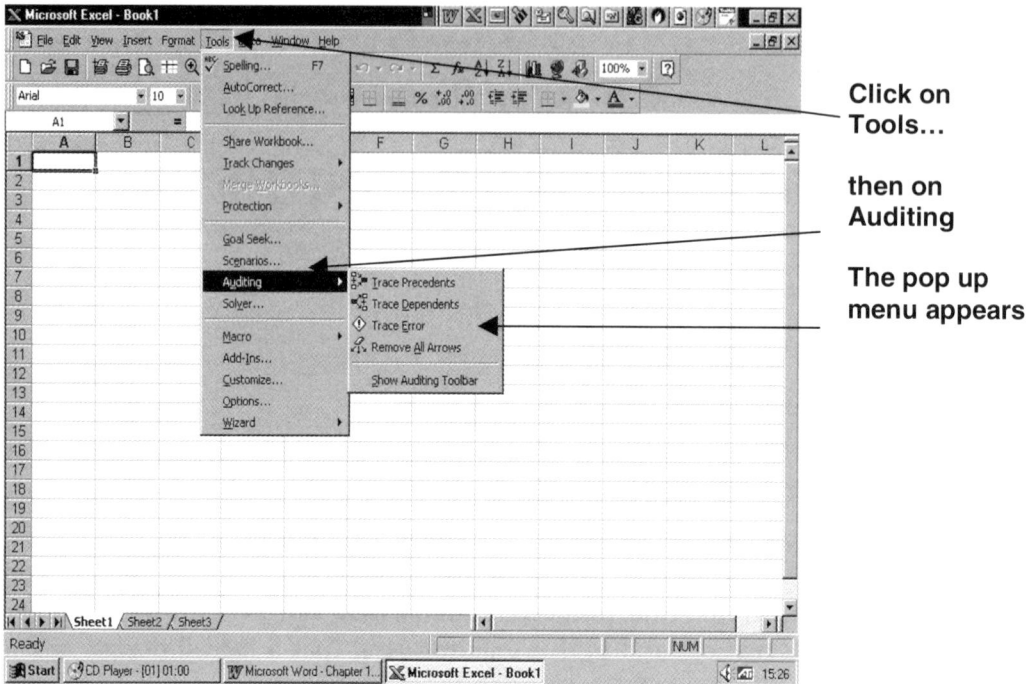

In broad terms, then, the tool is expected to be used by both the designer of the spreadsheet (tracing features), and by others within a group (comments and circling to highlight invalid data). Of course, you can use all of the tools if you are highlighting errors, but are not fixing them at this time.

We will practice using the tools.

EXAMPLE SPREADSHEET

Start Excel, and enter the following in Sheet 1.

Cell A1	Sales	**Cell D1**	5000		**Cell A3**	Purchases	**Cell A5**	GP
Cell B5	25%	**Cell D3**	=D1*(1-B5)					

The spreadsheet looks like this (the audit toolbar is activated).

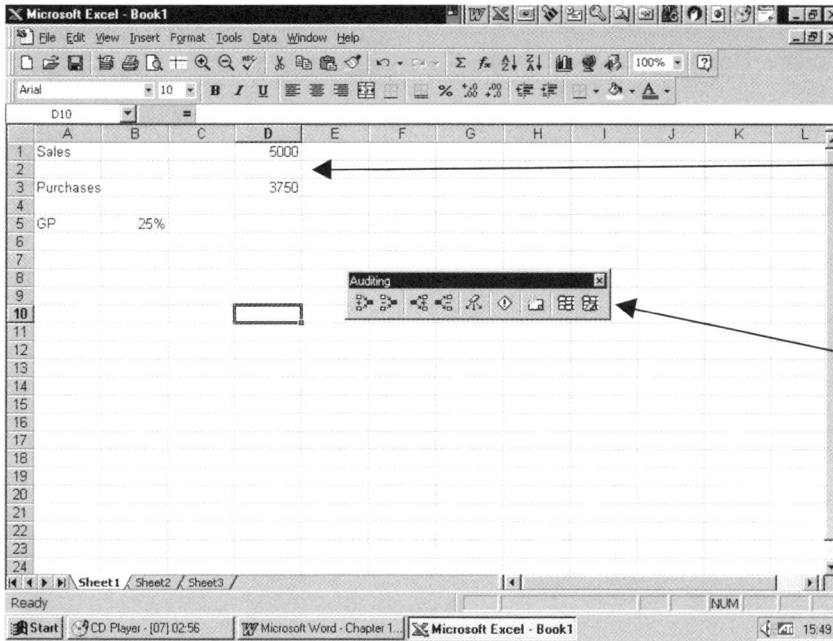

Figures and formula are entered

The Auditing Toolbar is active

Highlight cell D1 and click on Trace Precedents. Nothing happens, and the computer beeps — the figure is not dependent on anything else; it is input directly.

Click on Trace Dependents. A blue line appears, pointing from D1 to D3, showing that D1 affects D3.

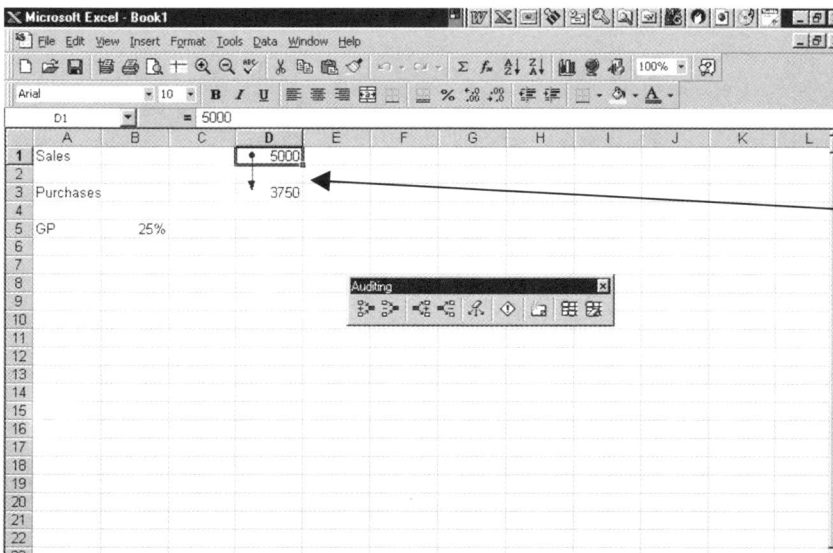

Audit Line traces from D1 to D3

Erase the line by clicking the erase button. Now make cell D3 active, and click on Trace Dependents. Nothing happens, and the computer beeps — the figure does not affect anything else on the spreadsheet.

Now click on Trace Precedents. Two blue lines appear, one from D1, and one from B5.

**Click on
Trace
Precedents**

**Two lines
appear**

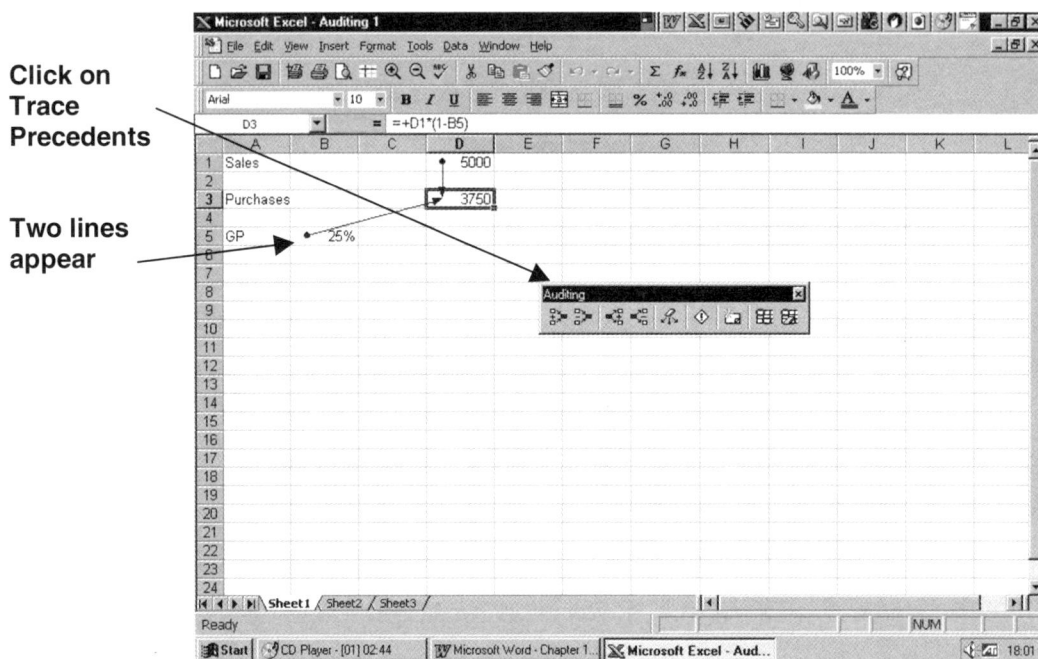

The tracing facility can also be used to trace further back through the cells. However, it does become complicated. Enter the following:

Cell D5	=D1-D3	**Cell A7**	Expenses	**Cell A8**	Wages
Cell A9	Commission	**Cell B9**	5%	**Cell C8**	5000
Cell C9	=D1*B9	**Cell D11**	-SUM(C8:C10)	**Cell A13**	Net Profit
Cell D13	=SUM(D5:D11)				

The spreadsheet is saved as **Auditing 1.xls** on the CD, and it is shown below.

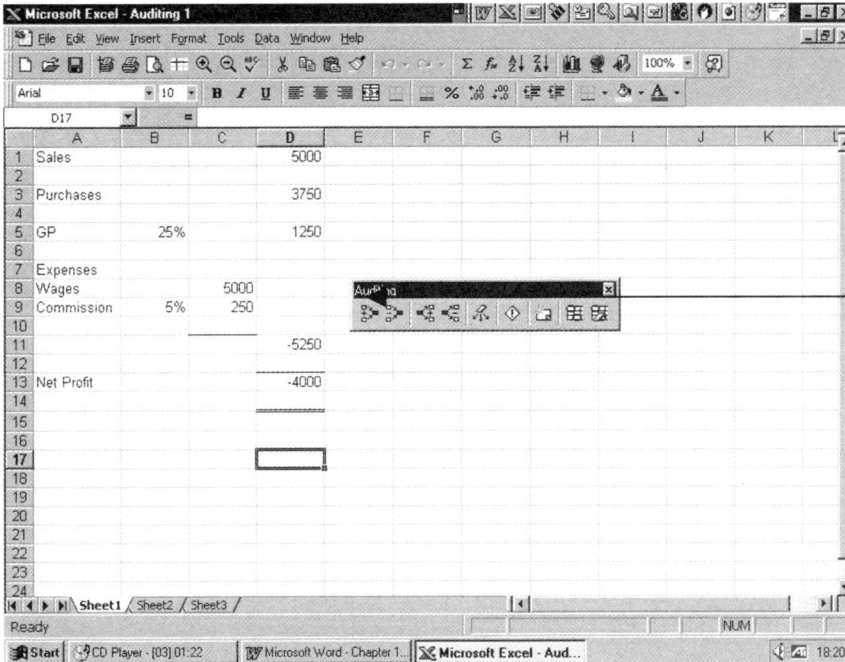

The spreadsheet is not complicated or difficult to follow

Now, select cell D13, and click on Trace Precedents. Keep clicking, and with each successive click the audit tool traces one back. When all items have been shown the computer beeps.

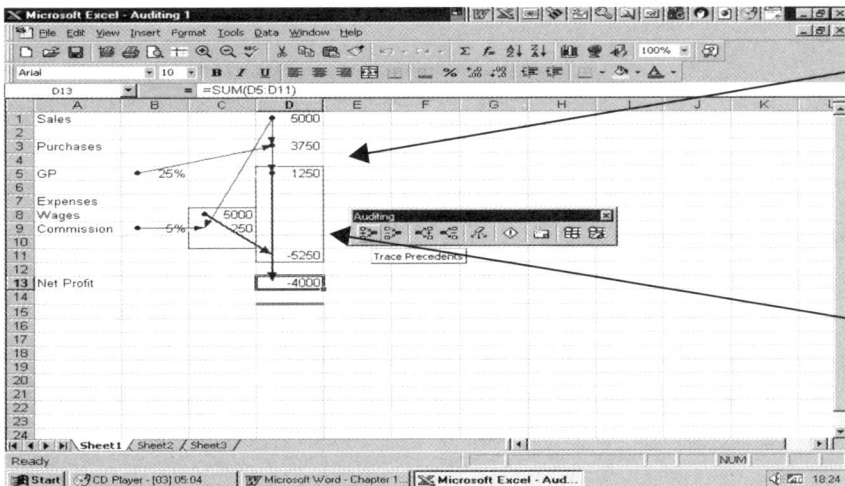

The number of arrows begins to look complicated

Note the boxes to show Sum ranges

If the items being highlighted are off screen the line still shows as before, but the spreadsheet must be scrolled to see it. This is shown in Sheet 2 on Auditing 1.xls on the CD.

If the cell being referred to is on another sheet a dashed line appears, with a small spreadsheet icon. Double clicking the dashed line brings up the Go To dialog box.

Reference to another sheet

Double click on the dashed line and...

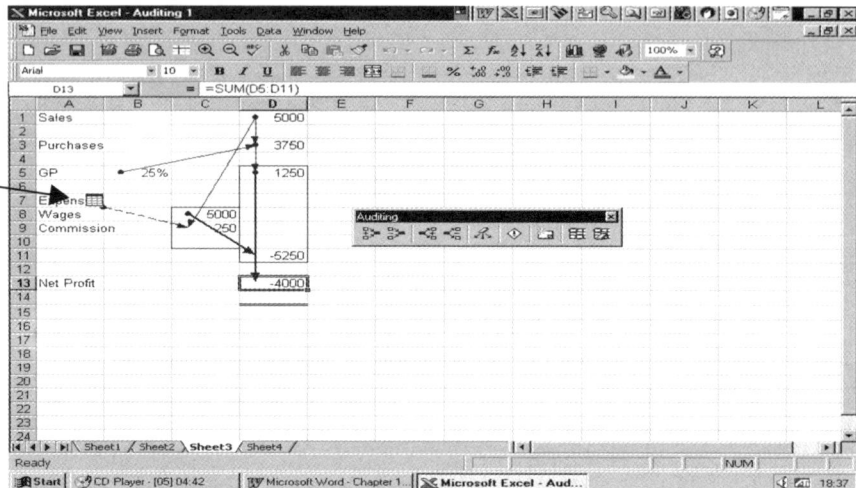

...the Go To dialog box appears. Select the reference and click OK

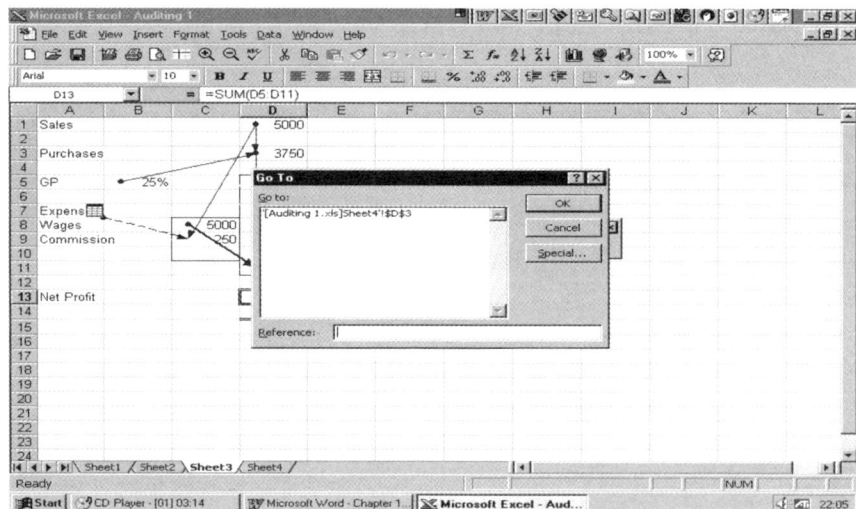

TRACE ERROR

The next button on the Auditing Toolbar is Trace Error. This is really a filtered Trace Precedents button.

We will use the previous example, and cause an error to arise. The commission is based on Sales multiplied by the commission percentage. Change cell B9 to "R" (text) instead of a value. The error message #VALUE is displayed in three places.

Activate cell D13, and click on Trace Precedents several times. The screen looks like this. This is saved on Sheet 1 of **Auditing 2.xls** on the CD.

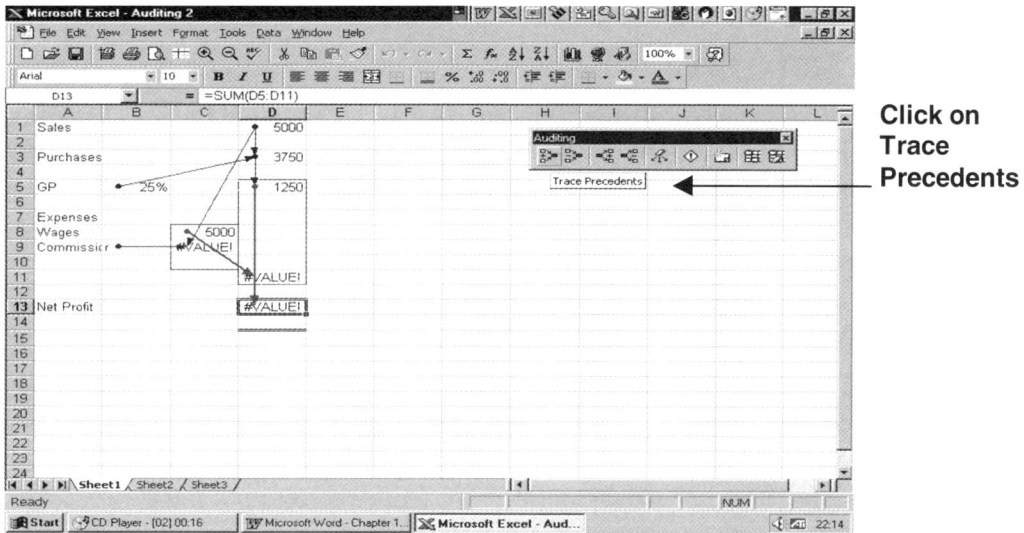

Click on Trace Precedents

A mixture of red and blue lines appears, but the source of the error is not immediately apparent.

Clicking Trace Error instead produces the following screenshot. This spreadsheet is saved as Sheet 2 on **Auditing 2.xls**.

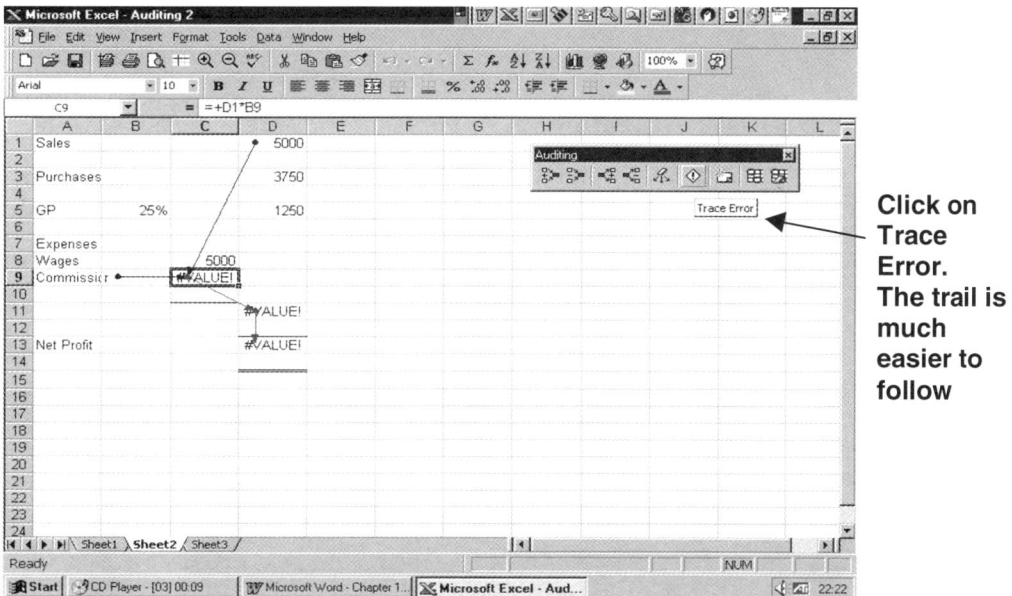

Click on Trace Error. The trail is much easier to follow

The source of the error is much easier to identify.

NEW COMMENT

The next button on the Auditing Toolbar is New Comment. Using Comments was covered in *The Accountant's Guide to Excel*.

CIRCLE INVALID DATA

The next button on the Auditing Toolbar is Circle Invalid Data. This is a database function, and is used to highlight errors in lists, to easily identify entries that do not correspond to the correct data type or value, as specified when the database was first set up.

We will be reviewing databases and Excel functionality in Section Two.

ALTERNATIVES

The Auditing Tools are useful. However, they are limited in their usefulness because, irrespective of how sophisticated they are, they cannot make up for poor spreadsheet design in the first place. The file **Auditing 3.xls** is based on the accounts and projections spreadsheet built in *The Accountant's Guide to Excel*, except it is incomplete, and it contains some (minor) errors. See how well you can follow the spreadsheet structure by using the auditing tools.

The alternative to using the auditing tools is to build error checking into the spreadsheet and to have a full trail of figures to explain how summaries are produced. This makes "desk checking" much easier.

As a general rule, auditing tools are useful, but they will not make up for deficiencies in design.

NEXT

In the next chapter we look at creating paper trails on the spreadsheet.

Chapter Three

DESK CHECKING SPREADSHEETS

Tracing without greaseproof paper . . .

In order to ensure we create our spreadsheets to an agreed pattern and consistency the second thing we need to review is creating a proper trail of information in the spreadsheet. This technique was covered in depth in *The Accountant's Guide to Excel*, when building the spreadsheets used there, so this chapter is a short recap, tailored specifically for the types of spreadsheet we are using here.

Depending on the type of spreadsheet, its size and complexity, and the type and number of formulae used the amount of audit trail required to be built in will vary.

The trail, including comments, step by step figures and results, and highlighting is always a matter for personal judgement. However, let us set some parameters to work from.

NO TRAIL

Start Excel and select Insert, Function from the menu.

Select Financial in the left-hand box, and DB in the right hand box, then click OK.

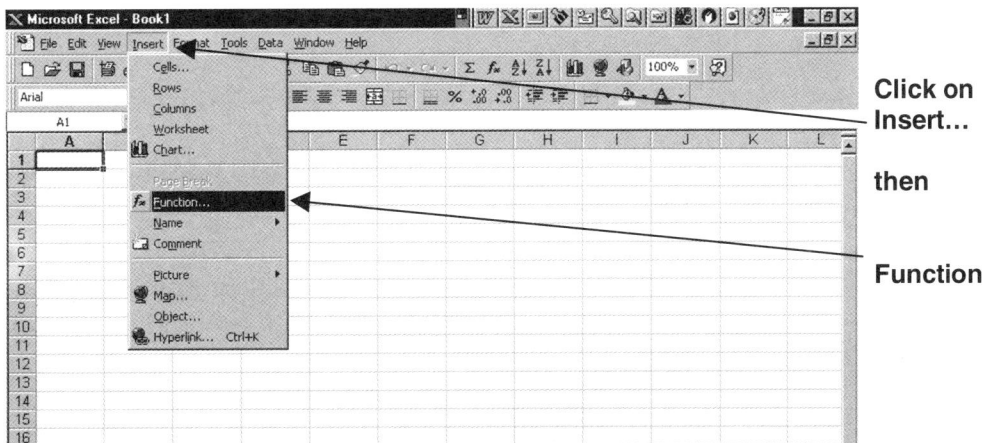

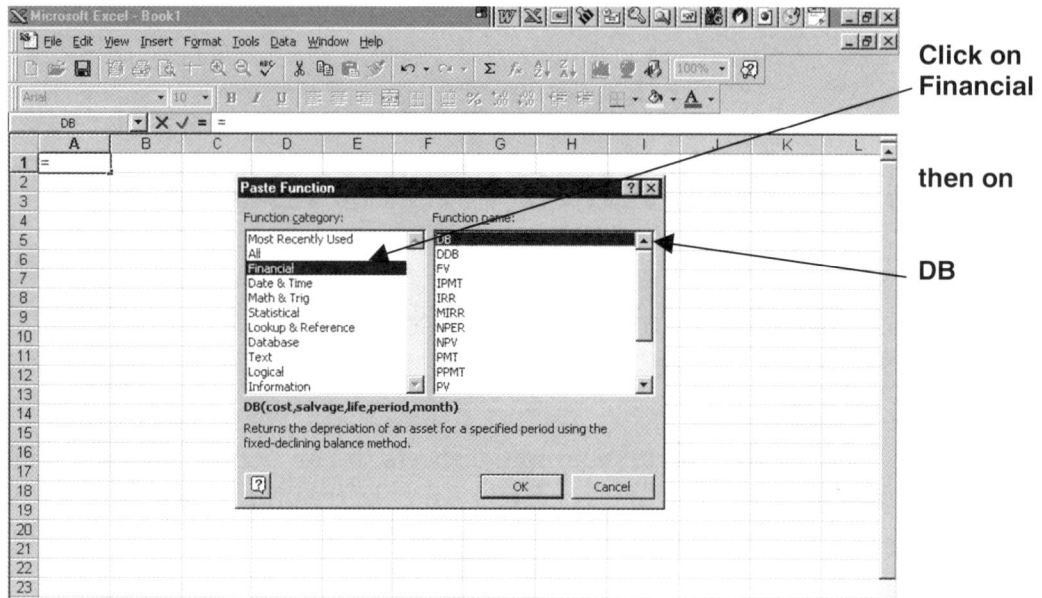

An input box appears. Enter 5000 for cost, 1000 for salvage, 5 for life, and 4 for period, and click OK. The spreadsheet looks like this. The cell displays the result but, is that informative?

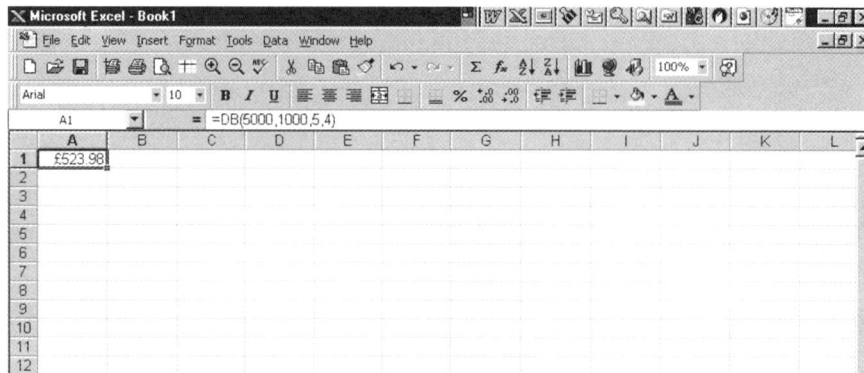

AUDIT TRAIL

The result is displayed, but the details, in terms of cost etc. are only shown in the cell. We will make it more informative if we include notes and information about the calculation.

We would therefore want to give the asset details in the calculating part of the spreadsheet, and then carry forward the calculated result by linking the cell forward. The amended spreadsheet therefore looks like this:

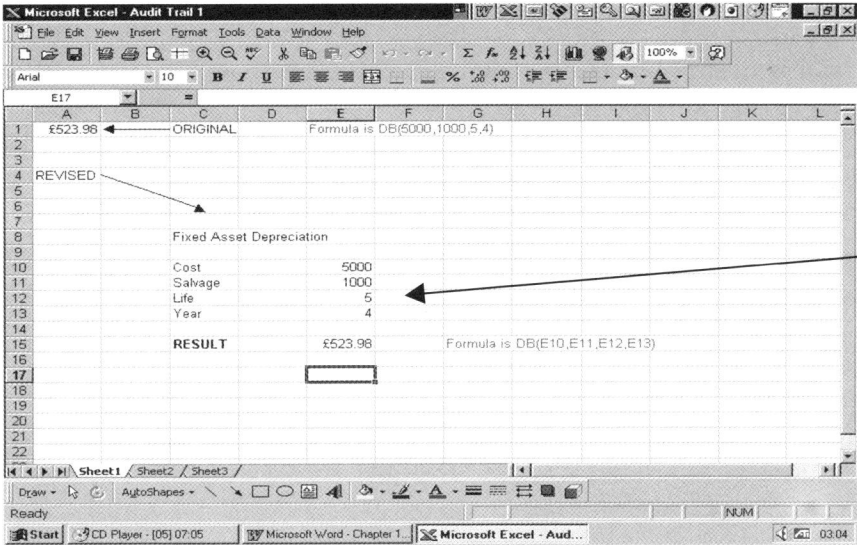

The full details used in the formula are shown in the spreadsheet

This is saved on the CD as **Audit Trail 1.xls**. Note that when the formula input box displays the cell reference is given, not the value. This has the added advantage of being able to update the result by changing cells E10 to E13 as appropriate.

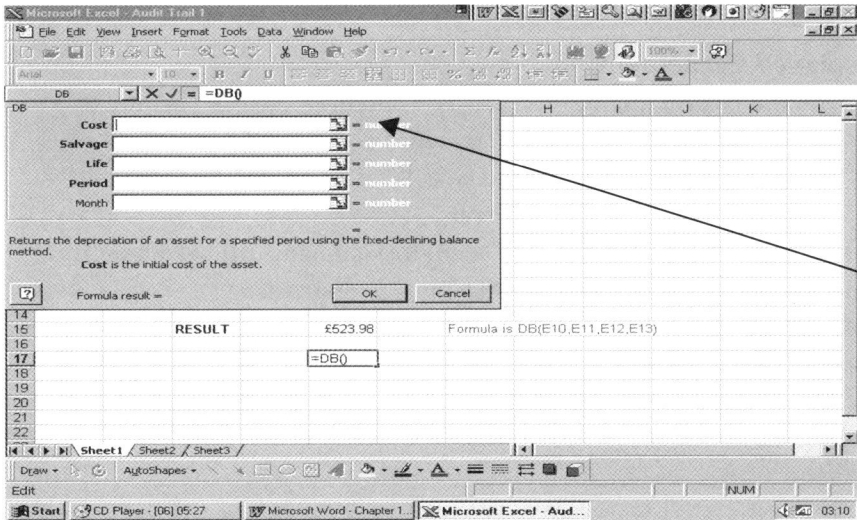

Click on the icon. The input box is minimised, and the cell can be selected with the mouse

Generally, if a built-in formula is to be used you should annotate the spreadsheet.

COMMENTS

The expanded trail is useful, but there may be factors that have a bearing other than the cold facts of cost, salvage value etc.

If, for example, a reminder of why the useful life is only five years would be useful there are three possible ways to display our notes:

- Type them directly into a cell
- Add a comment that is displayed permanently
- Add a comment that is only displayed when the cell is highlighted.

The advantages and disadvantages of each are set out below:

ADVANTAGES	DISADVANTAGES
Direct Entry Into a Cell	
It is quick and easy to enter	If there are a lot of notes it clutters the screen
It is easily seen, especially if the font is in colour	If notes are long they may extend beyond the relevant area of the spreadsheet
	The cell display can be truncated if cells to the right are not empty
Comment Displayed Permanently	
The yellow background box highlights the comment	The box obscures the cells below. If comments are only added at the end some cell contents may be hidden in error
It is not truncated if cells to the right are not empty	Too many comments all permanently displayed is distracting
The font size is small, which minimises the size occupied by the comment	
Comment Displayed When Highlighted	
Space saving. Each cell with a comment has a small red triangle in the right hand side	Too many hidden comments do not assist the user in following the documentation in a logical manner
It is not truncated if cells to the right are not empty	Hidden comments are unsuitable for warnings etc.
The font size is small, which minimises the size occupied by the comment.	

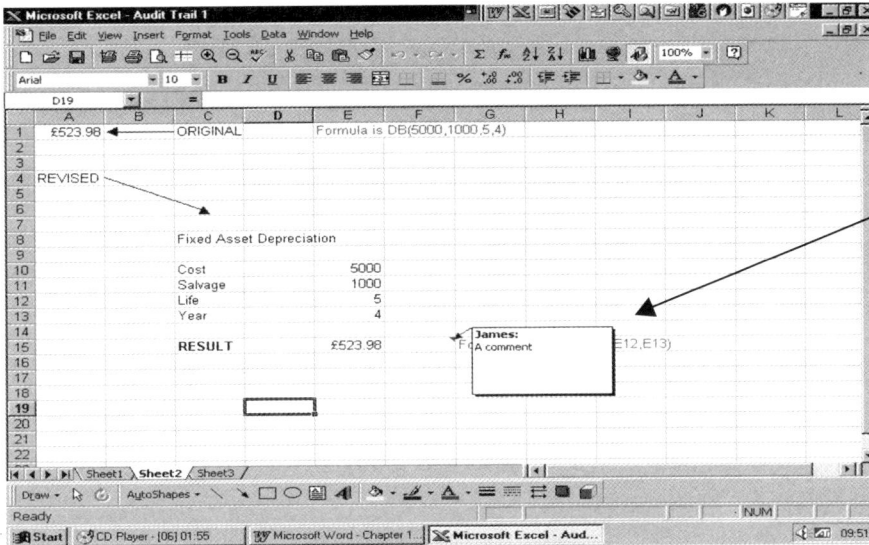

The above spreadsheet is saved as Sheet 2 of **Audit Trail 1.xls**. You should use a combination of the three methods, depending on the circumstances.

ADDING COMMENTS

Having reviewed the options, we will now explain the steps relevant to adding comments. Start Excel. Make cell C4 active, and right click. Select Insert Comment from the drop down menu.

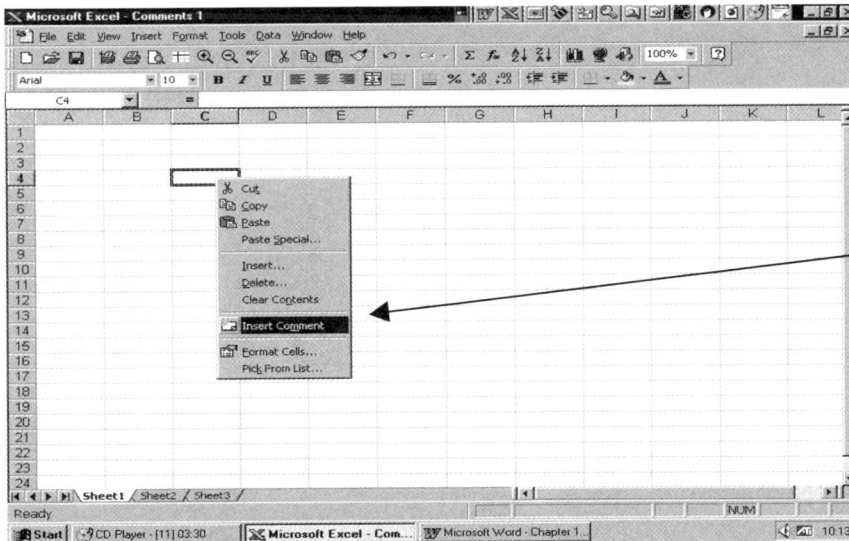

Now type the comment "This is a comment", deleting the heading automatically inserted. Click outside the comment to finalise it.

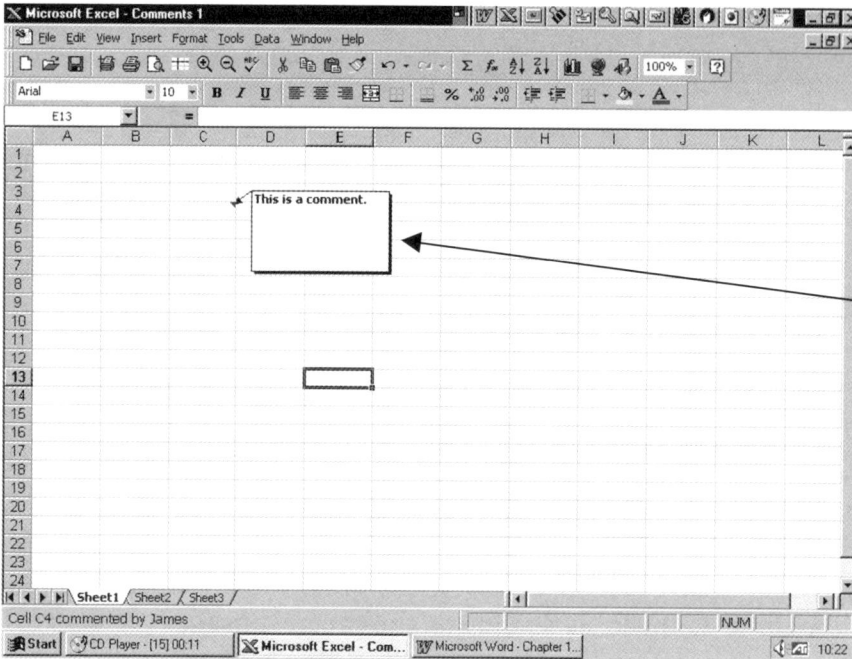

The comment appears when the mouse moves over cell C4, and is hidden at other times

If we make cell C4 active and right click, an amended menu appears. This replaces Insert Comment with three choices — Edit Comment, Delete Comment, and Show Comment. Highlight Show Comment.

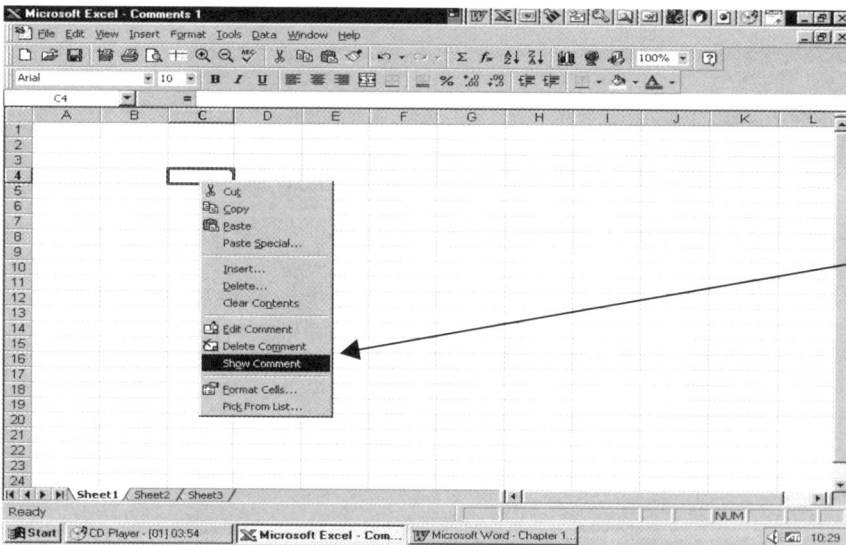

With cell C4 active, right click and select Show Comment

The comment is now permanently displayed, whether the mouse is near the cell or not. The choice of hidden and permanently displayed is on a cell by cell basis, so the style of annotation can be amended to suit.

Make the comment at cell C4 display permanently, and then add a hidden comment to cell D11. The spreadsheet is saved on the CD as **Comments.xls**.

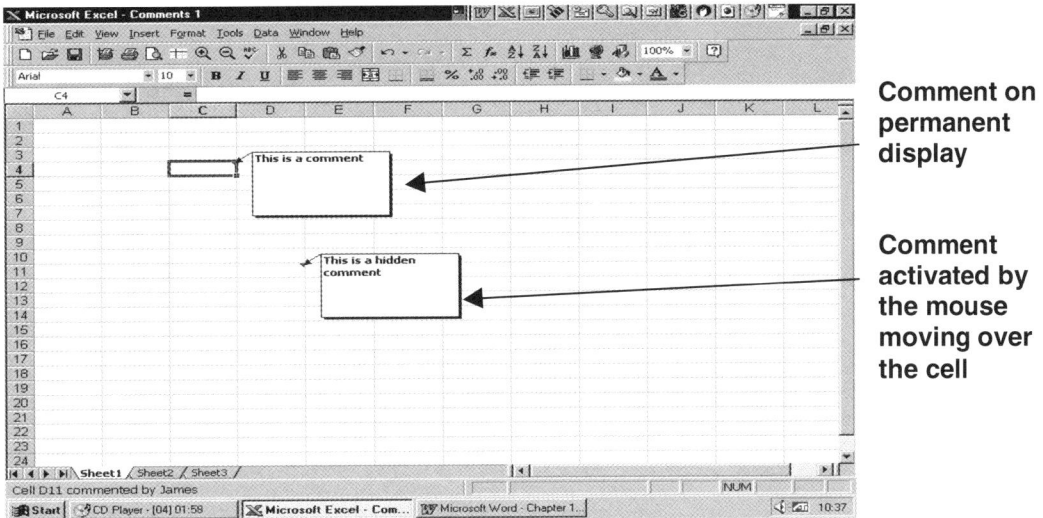

Comment on permanent display

Comment activated by the mouse moving over the cell

SUMMARY

Although, there are tools to assist in locating errors in spreadsheets, a full layout will provide a trail that can be desk checked, with comments to document the trail. All of this is "back end", because it is for our use only, not for the executive meeting at which we will be presenting our findings. But it will save us time in the long run, and will give us faith that there are no errors in our modelling, and speed up finding any that exist. It will also allow us to amend and update the model as new information comes to light, or as new complications are built in.

NEXT

That concludes our brief review of audit trails in spreadsheets. In the chapters that follow, we look at using programming to facilitate the ease of use of our spreadsheet, and consider how we might use it in our final presentation.

Chapter Four

PROGRAMMING

Oh dear . . .

Programming as a name and as a concept seems to possess two qualities — it creates a lot of fear, and it gives a high impact, highly professional polish to spreadsheets when done properly.

However, books on programming are hundreds of pages long, and as accountants we do not have the time, background, skills, knowledge, or desire to program as such.

What we want to do in this chapter is give some background about programming in order to put Excel programming using VBA (Visual Basic Applications) in context, and to identify those aspects that are of interest to us, and to isolate the areas that are not.

VISUAL BASIC

Visual Basic is a full programmer's Windows version of Basic, written by Microsoft. Originally each part of the Microsoft Office suite of software had its own unique version of Visual Basic, called Applications Edition — so there was an Excel VBA edition, an Access VBA edition etc. Each version was slightly different and thereby unique.

Visual Basic grew from these different flavours of VBA to become an all-encompassing program. Excel still comes with Excel VBA Edition provided free, but we will use the Visual Basic program here to explain what is involved in the programming process, and then draw this back to what we want to achieve with Excel VBA.

WHAT IS WINDOWS PROGRAMMING?

At its simplest, Windows programming involves drawing command buttons etc. on the screen, and then adding code to the buttons. Clicking on the buttons activates the code and it runs. If there is no code, it is just a picture on the screen.

The screen shot below is taken from Visual Basic, and explains the main areas involved in programming.

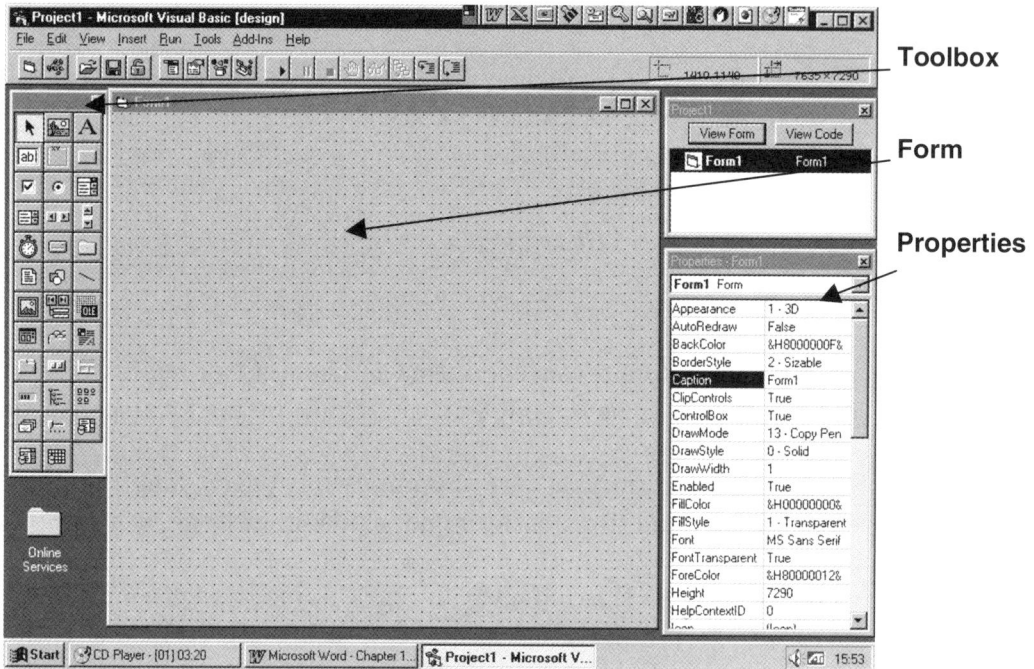

TOOLBOX

The toolbox contains the buttons for drawing the command buttons, option buttons etc. on the form.

FORM

This is the blank palette on which everything is drawn, and it becomes the screen background.

PROPERTIES

Everything drawn on the form from the toolbar has its own properties — size, position, colour, font for text appearing in the control etc.

EVENTS

When something happens, in terms of user input, this is called an event. In our simple context this would normally be the clicking of a command button. This starts the code to run, and we are then controlling the processes and output without any further user input needed. It could be described as "Macros without the walls".

In the context of Excel examples of events are:
- A command button to move to the next sheet
- Option buttons, to choose different scenarios — pessimistic, realistic and optimistic
- A message box to warn or advise the user.

In this context the only differences between the VB form and the Excel spreadsheet are:
- The VB form is plain, whilst the spreadsheet has a grid
- The controls must stay within the confines of the form, whereas in Excel the user can scroll out of the assigned area, and thereby lose the buttons.

When a command button and option buttons are placed on the form it looks like this.

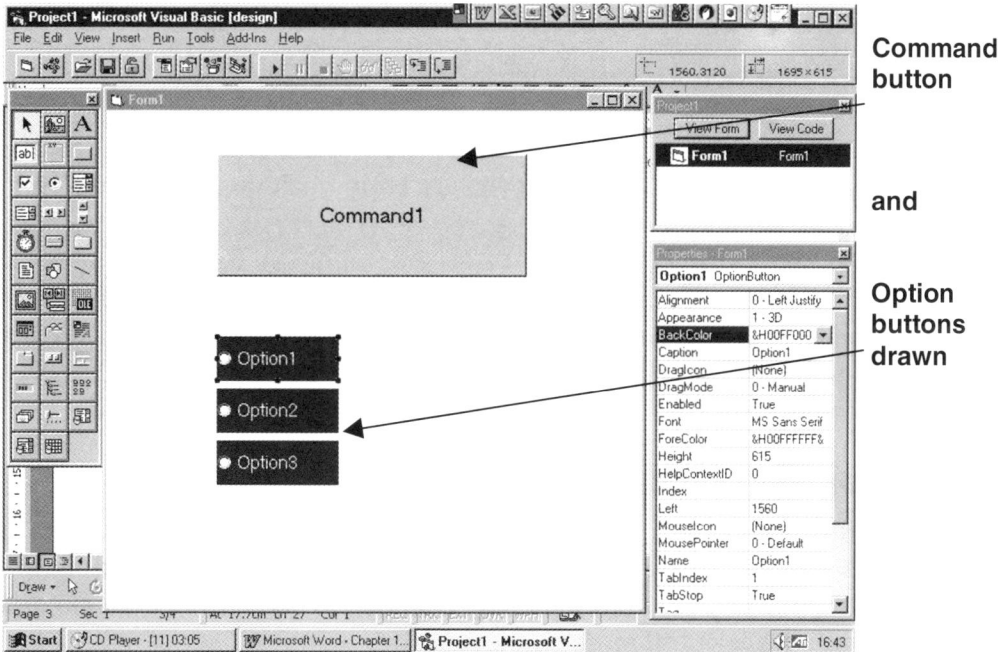

In Excel the equivalent screen looks like this.

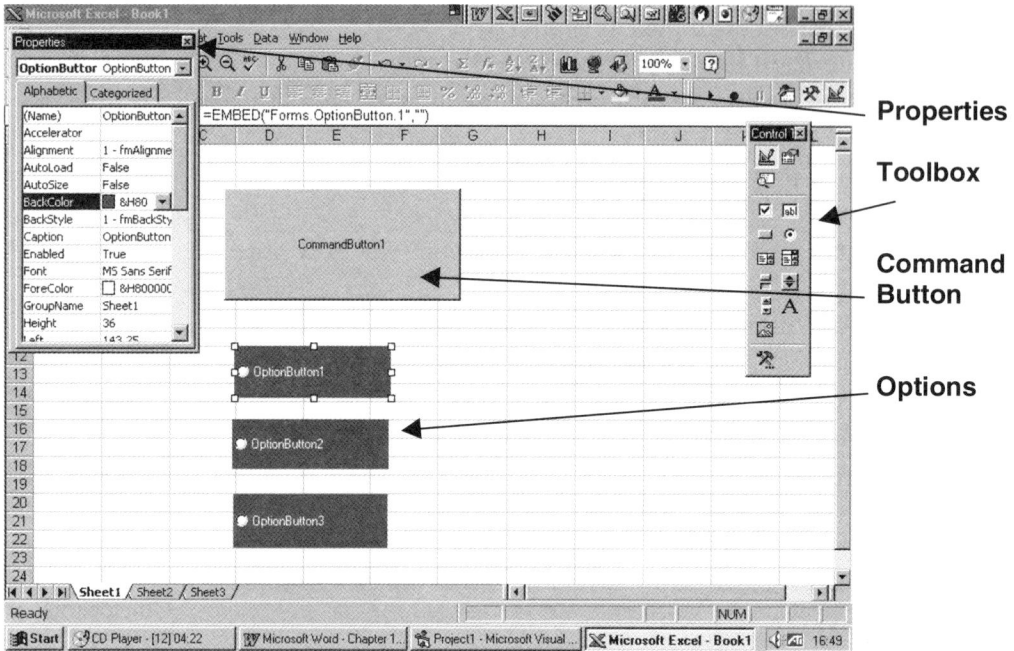

There is much less screen clutter, and the amount of control available on the Properties dialog box, and the range of tools, are both much more restricted than the VB version.

However, the same principles apply to programming in Excel Visual Basic Applications Edition as in Visual Basic proper. The fact that VB has more tools in the toolbox, and a more structured presentation of the project — with a Project Window for co-ordinating the development of the forms, and an easier interface for adding code to the controls — is one of convenience rather than content.

PROGRAMMING CONVENTIONS

In the following section we will look very briefly at what is involved in programming a simple form — an input area for a figure to be entered by the user, an output area which multiplies the number by two, and a Command Button to activate the calculation.

In a spreadsheet this can be completed in moments, because there are no procedures to set up — this has already been done as part of the Excel program. In VB the tools must be selected and drawn, and then coded.

For an accountant, time is money, and there must be very good reasons for taking this longer route.

In programming everything must be done from the beginning. Nothing is pre-set, and therefore everything must be defined.

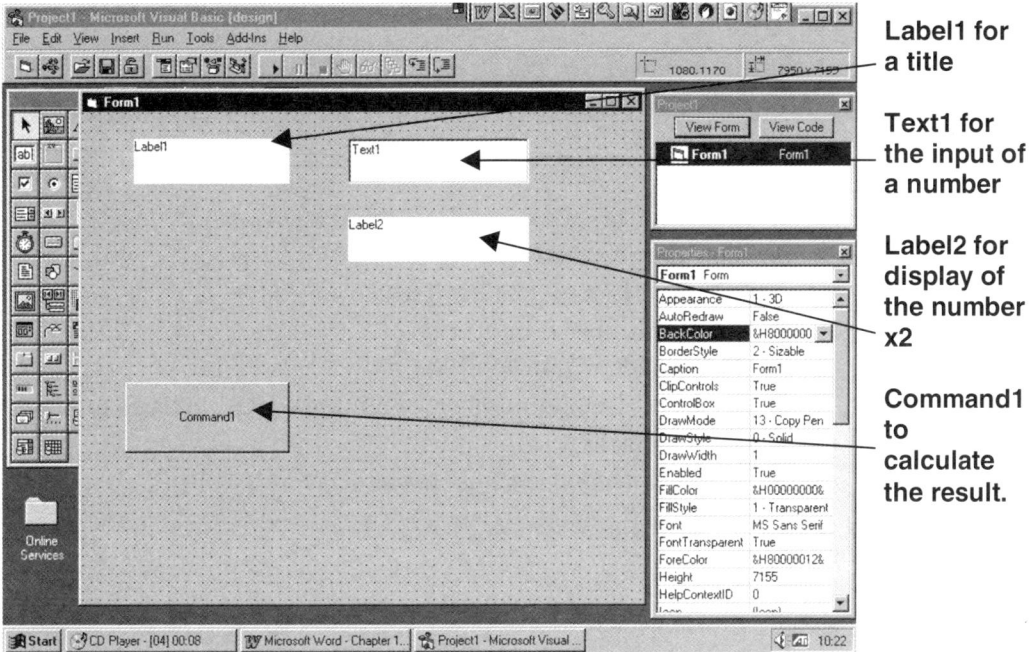

The steps are:

- The caption for Label1 must be changed to "Input the number here"
- The default text for Text1 must be changed to a blank
- The default caption for Label2 must be changed to a blank
- The caption for the Command Button must be changed to Calculate.

The program does not know what type of input Text1 will receive — text, numbers or alpha numeric. The program must first of all define the input as a number, and then perform a calculation, namely multiply the number by two. The result must then be displayed as the caption in Label2.

This is controlled by pressing the Command Button, so the code is attached to the Command1, not Text1 and not Label2.

Writing the code is dealt with on the next page.

CODING THE FORM

The number that the user places in Text1 must be defined as a number. The amount of memory allocated to the task must also be decided, so we must choose between:

Integer	A whole number between −32768 and 32767
Long	A whole number between −2,147,483,648 and 2,147,483,647
Single	A decimal number from −3.402823E38 to 3.402823E38
Double	A very large decimal number, or a number with a large number of decimal places
Currency	A decimal with four decimal places

We will use Long.

The first line of code is therefore:

        Dim UserNumber As Long.

DIM is used to advise VB that we are defining something.

UserNumber is a name chosen by us to identify what has been input to the textbox Text1.

As Long sets the precision of our calculation. This means that if the user inputs 13.2 the answer will display as 26, not 26.4.

The second line of code is:

        Dim Result As Long.

DIM as above.

Result is a name chosen by us for the answer to UserNumber multiplied by 2.

As Long as above.

The third line of code is:

        UserNumber = Text1.Text.

This advises the program where it can find the number we are interested in.

The fourth line of code is:

        Result = UserNumber * 2.

This advises the computer of the calculation to perform.

The fifth line of code is:

        Label2.Caption = Result.

This tells the program to change the Label2 caption to the same text as the result.

The program is fully written out below.

```
Dim UserNumber As Long
Dim Result As Long
UserNumber = Text1.Text
Result = UserNumber * 2
Label2.Caption = Result
```

This does not include any error trapping, to accommodate the user putting in text instead of numbers.

As you can see, everything must be set out step by step. With error trapping every eventuality must be considered — numbers too big or too small, text instead of numbers, changing focus back to the text box for the next entry... the list can become almost endless.

EXCEL PROGRAMMING

A large part of the hard work is already taken care of by Excel — figures or text are entered into cells, and Excel interprets it correctly. Formulae are also easily added.

In this context therefore, what we are trying to achieve in Excel VBA is automation. We want to take advantage of all of the programming features already built into Excel, rather than have to redefine number precision etc. and we want to continue to generate output into the cells, rather than into labels or textboxes.

CONCLUSION

We have looked at programming in outline here, in order to provide background as to what it is, and to explain that, without a very broad knowledge base of programming, care must be taken before rushing headlong to use it.

There are aspects of programming that are of great benefit, as we will see in the next two chapters, and a knowledge of programming is useful background knowledge to bring to bear. However, in the next two chapters we will be using macros principally for coding. In this chapter we are trying to allay concerns that using macros is an easy, and somehow second best option, and that "real" accountants are more macho than that.

If you do want to learn programming, there are many excellent books on the subject. My favourite starter book is *The Beginners Guide to VB* from WROX Press.

Chapter Five

EXCEL VISUAL BASIC APPLICATIONS EDITION (I)

The real stuff!

We will now practise with Excel VBA, in order to learn how to use the programming features. We will use Macros where possible in order to have the VB coded automatically, and code directly where this does not work.

DISPLAY THE VB TOOLS

First of all we need to activate the VB tools. Start Excel and, with the mouse in the toolbar area right click and select Visual Basic from the drop down menu.

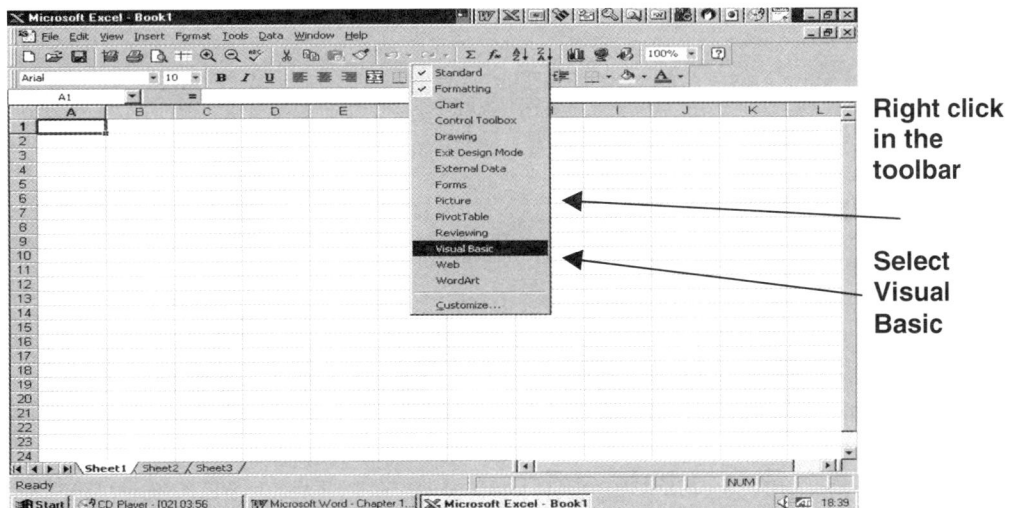

The VB toolbar is displayed. If it floats in the spreadsheet area drag it to the toolbar and drop it there. The tools available are:
- Run Macro
- Record Macro

- Resume Macro (dimmed)
- Visual Basic Editor
- Control Toolbox
- Design Mode.

We want to work with the Control Toolbox, so click on it, and then drag the toolbar up to become a third line in the toolbar area, rather than have it floating in the spreadsheet area.

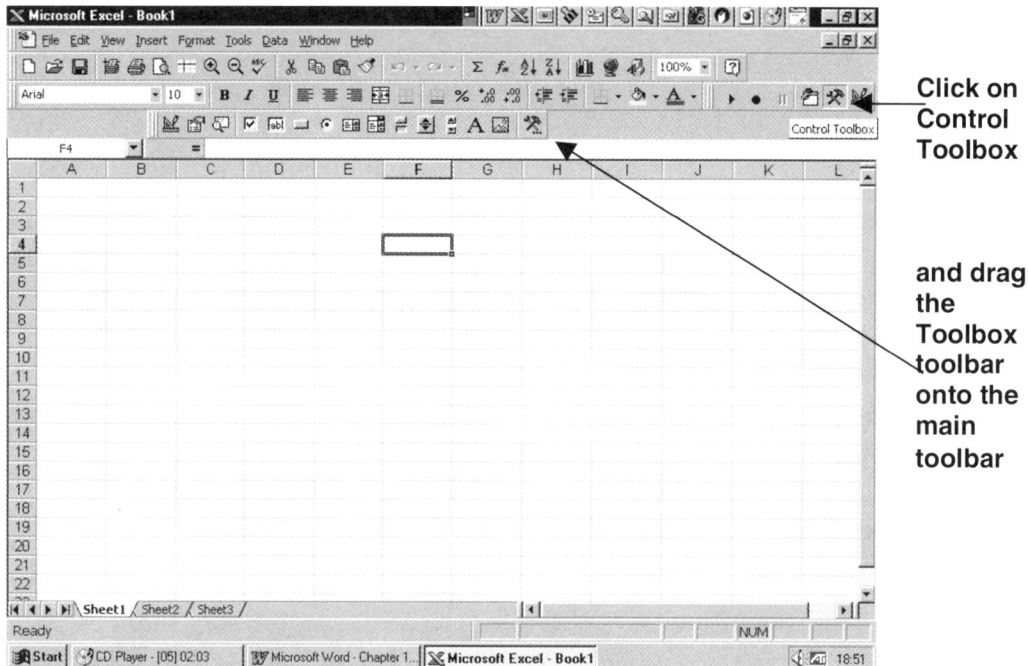

Click on Control Toolbox

and drag the Toolbox toolbar onto the main toolbar

WITH EXCEL VBA YOU CAN . . .

What do we want to do? Let's consider the possibilities.

When we make our final presentation to senior management we will want to look at various options and scenarios. We will want to move from one scenario to another smoothly. We will want to include charts and graphs as appropriate.

We could use Option Buttons for the different scenarios, and Command Buttons to move from one section of the spreadsheet to another.

We could use Command Buttons to load different data sets, and to update charts and graphs.

We will look at each in turn.

OPTION BUTTONS

We want to set up three buttons, for Scenario 1, Scenario 2 and Scenario 3.

Click on the Option Button icon in the toolbar, and move the mouse to the bottom of the spreadsheet. Hold down the left mouse button and drag out a rectangle shape. Release the mouse and the Option Button control is finished. It can be dragged around the spreadsheet if it is not quite where you intended it to go.

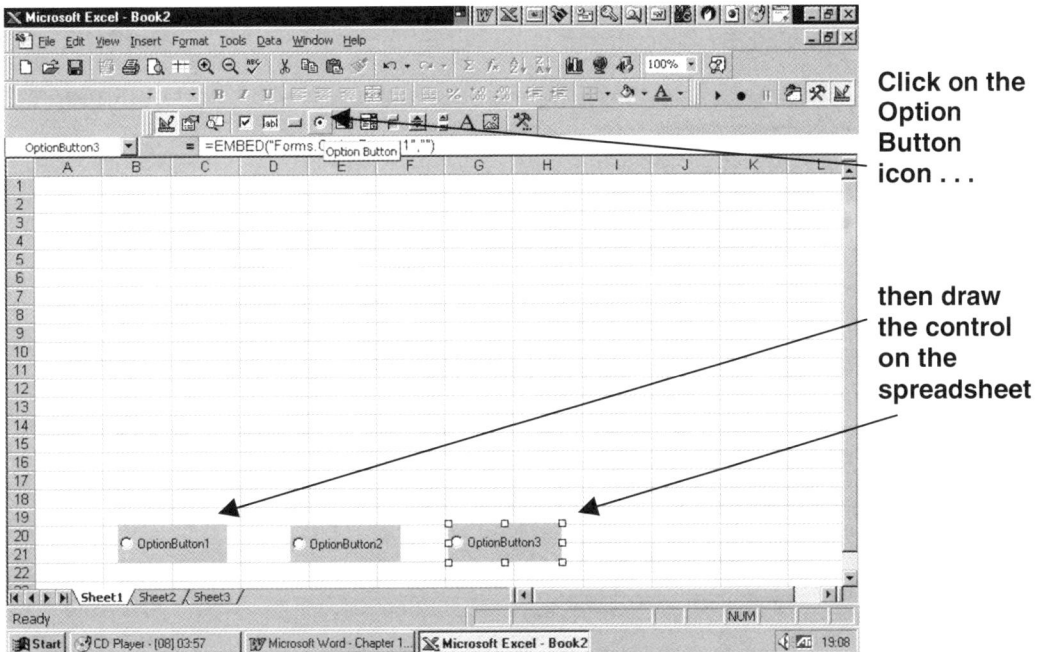

Click on the Option Button icon . . .

then draw the control on the spreadsheet

CHANGE THE NAMES ON THE BUTTONS

By default the buttons give a name which is the same as the control name. To change the first name to Scenario 1 select the button and right click. Select OptionButton Object, then Edit.

The name in the control is activated, and can now be replaced. Repeat this for the other two buttons.

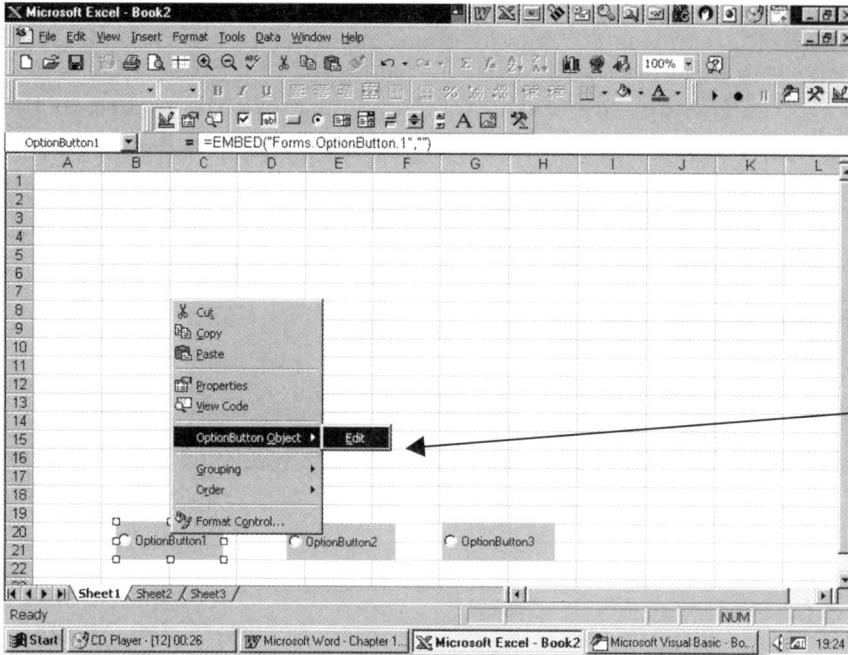

Right click...

select OptionButton Object...

then Edit

The buttons should look like this once they have been changed.

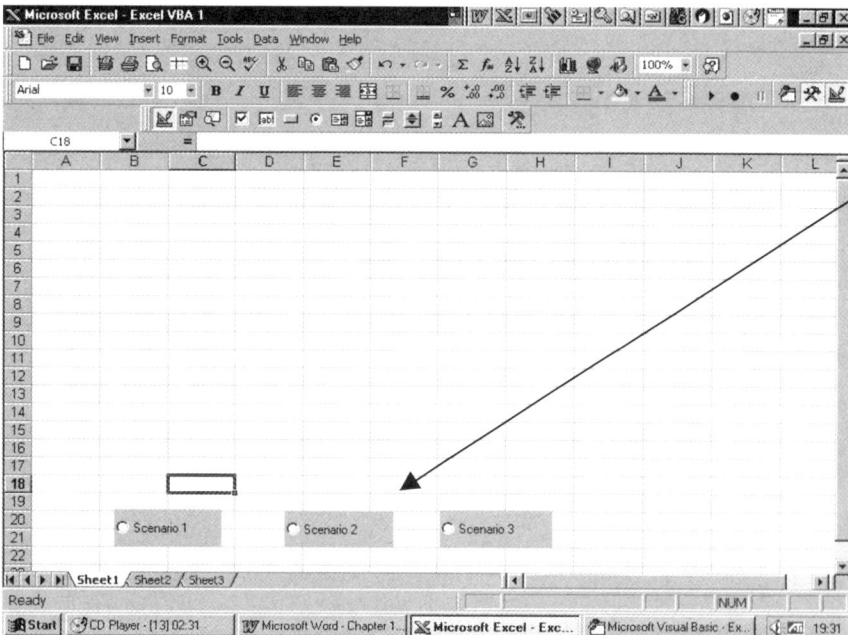

The buttons are now re-labelled

ENTER SALES ETC.

Enter the following into the spreadsheet.

Cell C2	Sales	Cell F2	10000
Cell C4	Purchases	Cell F4	=F2*F8
Cell C6	Gross Profit	Cell F6	=F2-F4
Cell C8	GP %	Cell F8	40%

The spreadsheet looks like this. It is saved on the CD as **Excel VBA 1**.

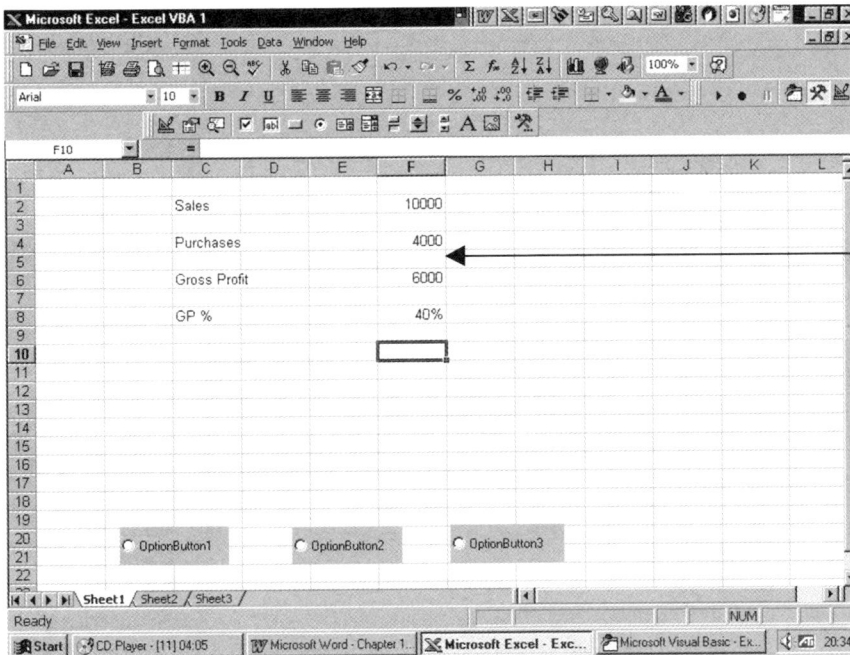

The entries are made in the spreadsheet

CREATE A MACRO

The option buttons are going to work as follows; Scenario 1, GP% 40%; Scenario 2, GP% 50%; Scenario 3, GP% 60%.

In order to find the VB code we want we will create a macro for one scenario, and then adjust it accordingly. Click on the Record Macro button in the toolbar. The Record Macro dialog box appears, with detail about the macro that is about to be created and a default name, usually Macro1. Accept the default name, then click OK.

Click on cell F8 and enter 40%, then press Return. Click on the Stop Recording button.

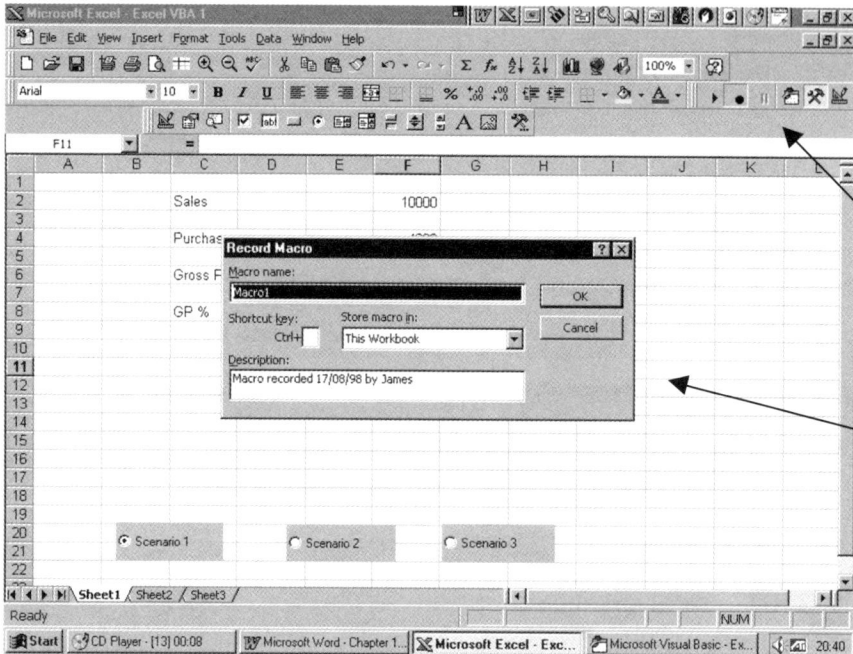

Click on Record Macro

The Record Macro dialog box appears

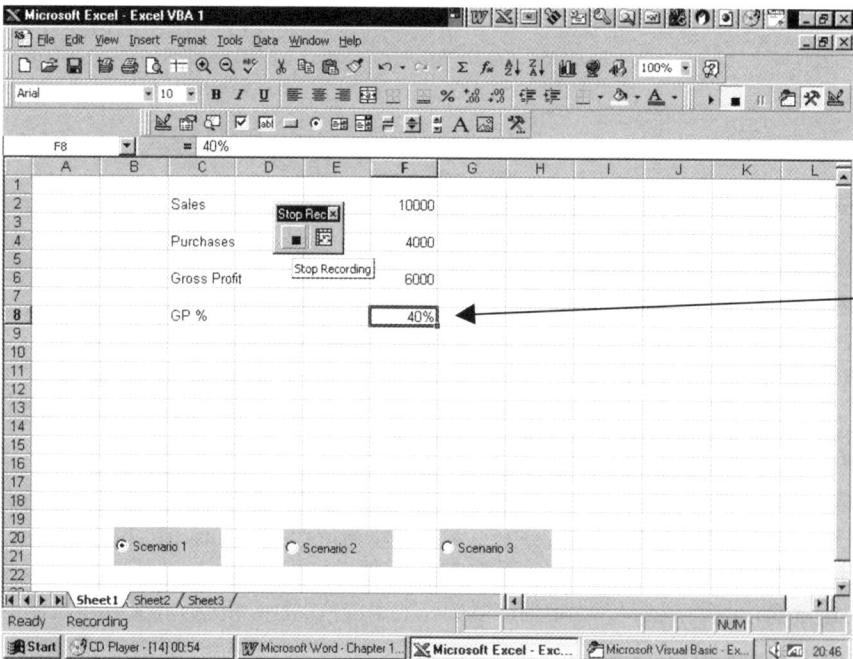

Click in cell F8, enter 40% and then click on Stop Recording

RUN THE MACRO

We want to check that the Macro operates correctly, so we will run it. Change the cell contents to 60% so that we can see the change when the Macro inserts 40% in the cell.

To run the Macro click on Run Macro, select the Macro name and click Run.

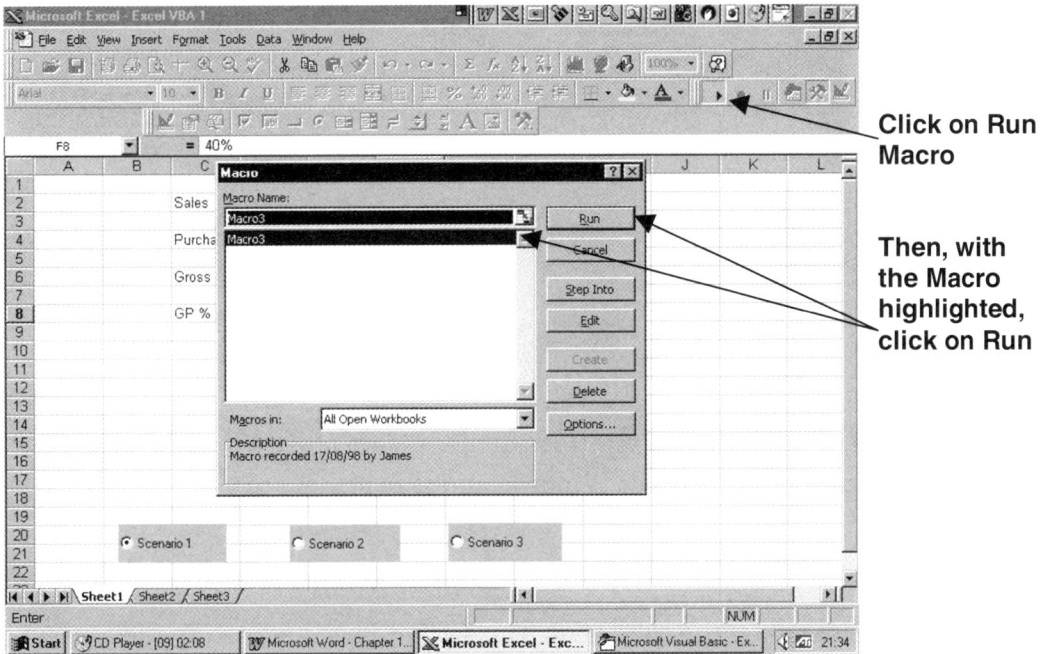

Click on Run Macro

Then, with the Macro highlighted, click on Run

The Macro should be working correctly. If it is, click on Run Macro again and, with the Macro highlighted, click on Edit.

The Visual Basic program starts, and the code for the Macro is shown.

The screen shot on the next page shows the code. The spreadsheet is saved on the CD as **Excel VBA 1.xls.**

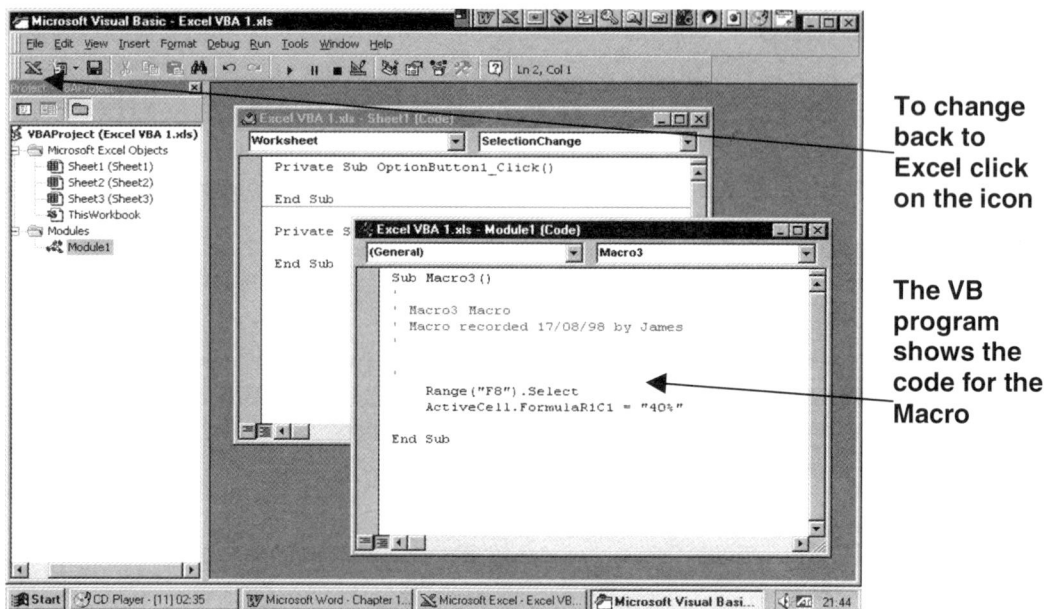

THE VISUAL BASIC CODE

The VB code is shown in the Code Window, and it reads:

    Range("F8").Select
    ActiveCell.FormulaR1C1 = "40%"

The first line is selecting the cell at F8. The second line is adjusting the contents of the cell to 40%.

The code is ready to copy into the code section of the Scenario 1 option button. The only variation for the other option buttons will be to change the percentage to 50% and 60% respectively.

In the Code Window highlight the text and press Ctrl+C to copy it. Double click on Sheet1 (Sheet1) in the Project Window, and paste it in to each option button (Ctrl+V to paste).

The three scenario buttons now work — clicking each button changes the GP% to the correct amount, and it means that the three scenarios can be discussed in a meeting and the spreadsheet can be changed seamlessly.

The file is saved on the CD as **Excel VBA 1.xls**.

**Click on
Sheet1
(Sheet1)**

**The Code
Window
changes**

**Select Option
Button1 etc,
and paste in
the code,
changing the
% figures**

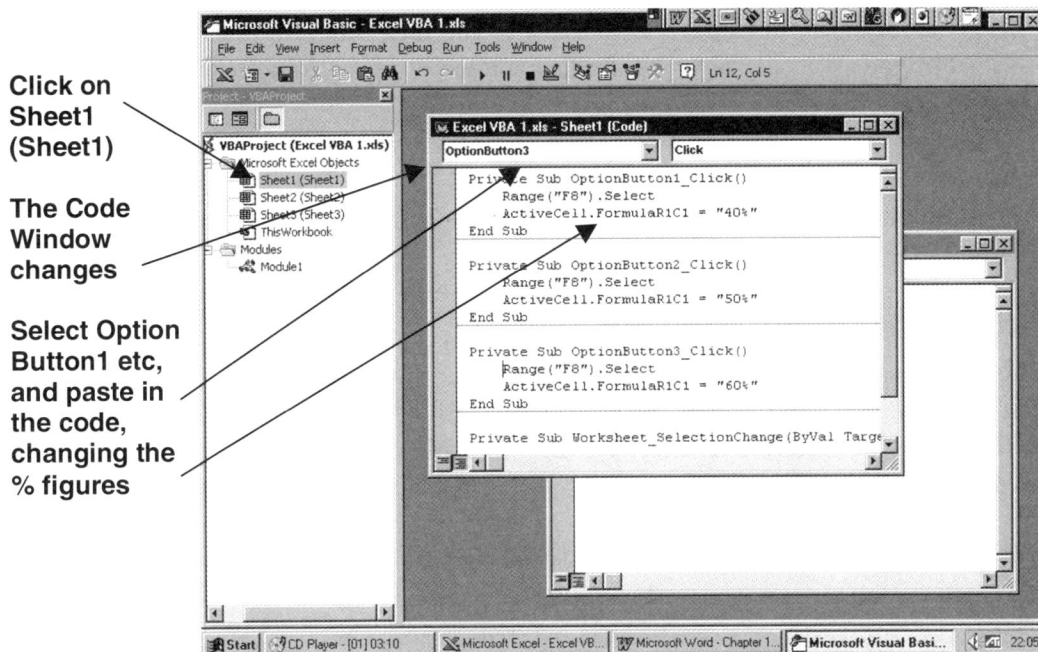

ADDITIONAL CODING

It would improve the spreadsheet's appearance if we add the scenario name to
the display when the relevant option button is clicked. We will add the title to
cell C1 and, in order to highlight it, we will display it in colour.

We already know how to enter the name into the cell from the previous macro:

```
Range("C1").Select
ActiveCell.FormulaR1C1 = "Scenario 1"
```

If you run another macro for the code for setting the colour it should, depending
on your selections, be similar to this:

```
With Selection.Font
    .Name = "Arial"
    .FontStyle = "Bold"
    .Size = 10
    .Strikethrough = False
    .Superscript = False
    .Subscript = False
    .OutlineFont = False
    .Shadow = False
    .Underline = xlUnderlineStyleNone
    .ColorIndex = 38
End With
```

This gives all of the parameters relevant to the font, including those that are not being changed. We only want to set the colour, so if we remove the non-relevant ones we are left with:

    With Selection.Font
        .FontStyle = "Bold"
        .ColorIndex = 38
    End With

AN ALTERNATIVE COLOUR

The colour selected above is taken from the palette available. Any mix of colour can be chosen by using the RGB (Red, Green, Blue) formula instead.

To access details about this, or other formula, review Help in the Excel VB module.

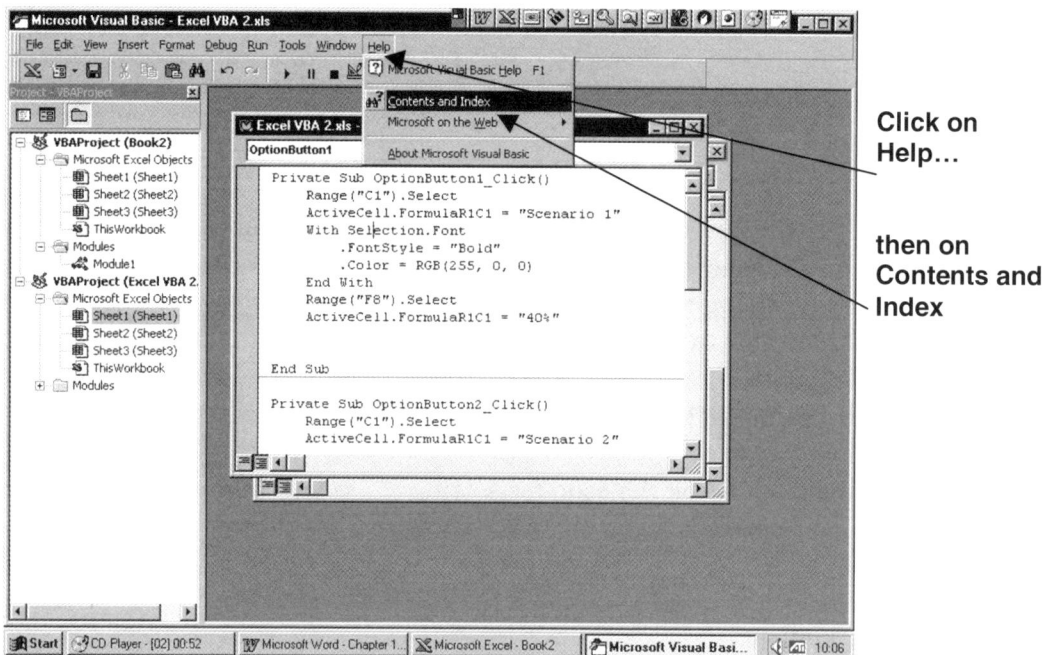

When the Help screen starts select the Index tab and type in "Colo".

There is a filter that searches as each letter is input, and this should highlight topics. Remember that spelling is American, so colour is actually color.

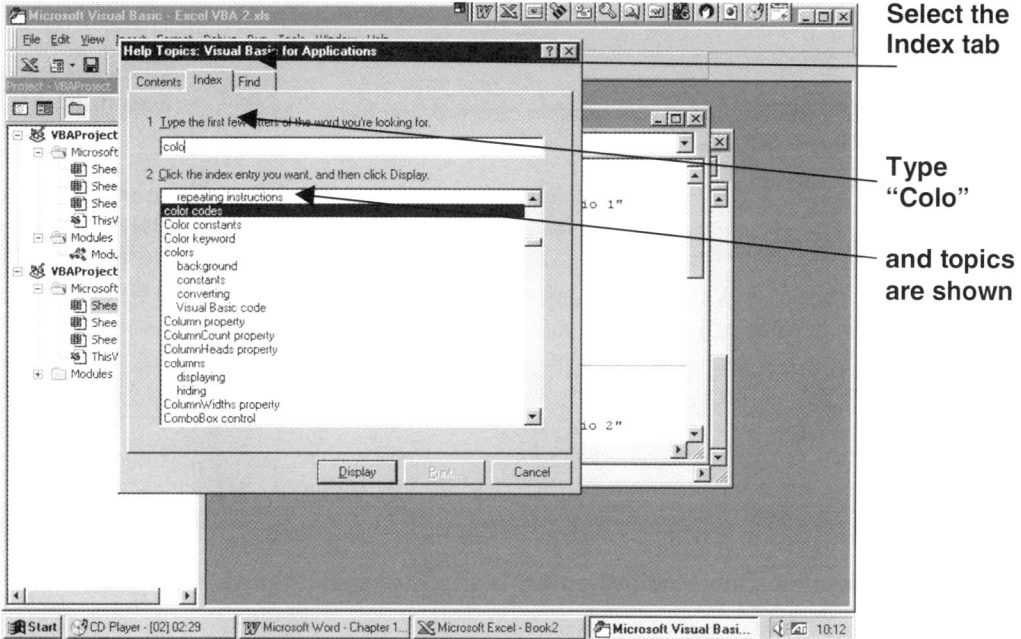

Select the
Index tab

Type
"Colo"

and topics
are shown

Select Color Codes, then RGB Function.

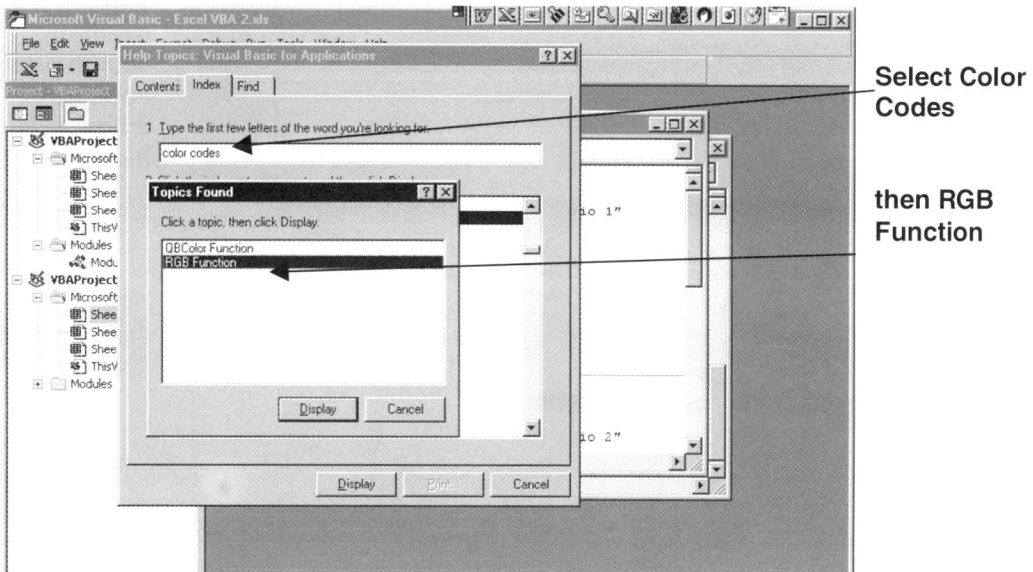

Select Color
Codes

then RGB
Function

The Help file is displayed. Read this for background, then select Example at the top of the Help screen.

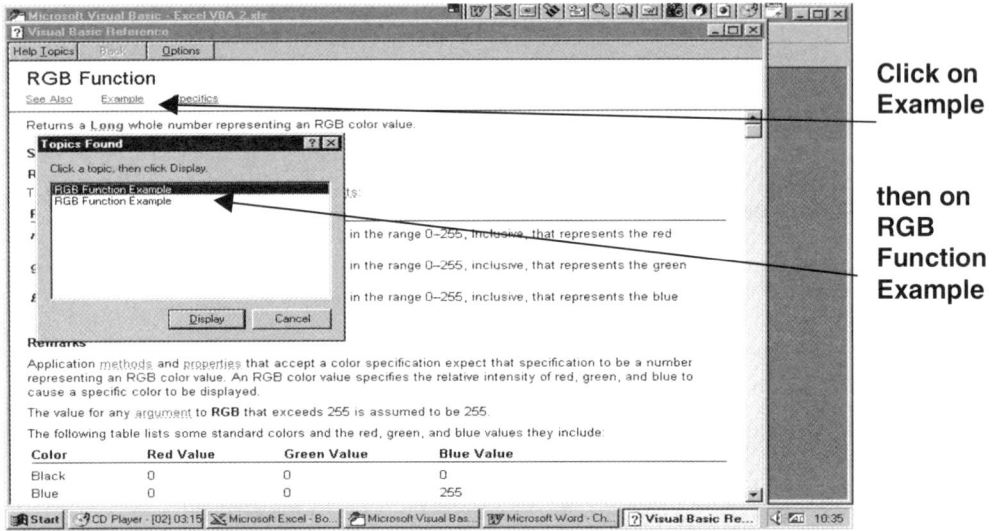

Click on Example

then on RGB Function Example

The example given is shown below, suitably highlighted.

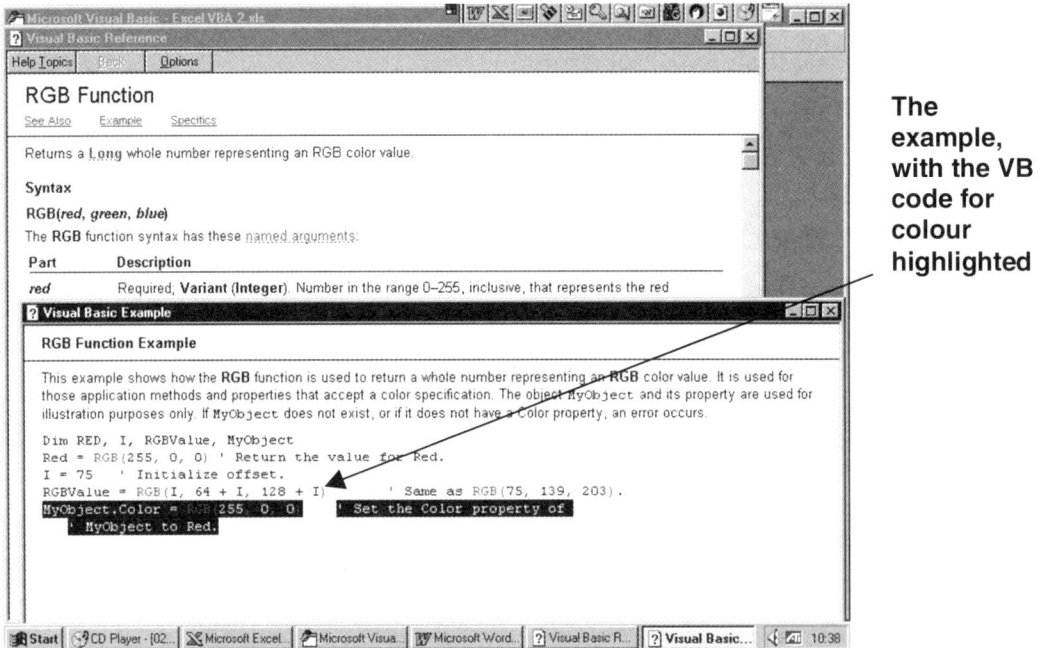

The example, with the VB code for colour highlighted

The highlighted VB code reads:

MyObject.Color = RGB(255, 0, 0)

[Set the Color property of MyObject to Red]

The portion above, which is in square brackets, is text explanation. The code part we are interested in is:

```
MyObject.Color = RGB(255, 0, 0)
```

In our code MyObject is replaced with Selection, so the code in our spreadsheet becomes:

```
With Selection.Font
    .FontStyle = "Bold"
    .Color = RGB(255, 0, 0)
End With
```

You can access Help at any stage, and amend the code generated by the macro by inserting alternative code if desired.

THE ORDER OF PLAY

The only other thing to mention is the order in which the code is executed.

Start **Excel VBA 2.xls** and click on Scenario 1, then Scenario 2, and then Scenario 3. In the first two cases the title is written first, then cell F8 is made active, and the contents are written in. In the last case this is reversed.

The code in the first two instances is:

```
Range("C1").Select
    ActiveCell.FormulaR1C1 = "Scenario 1"
    With Selection.Font
    .FontStyle = "Bold"
    .Color = RGB(255, 0, 0)
End With
Range("F8").Select
    ActiveCell.FormulaR1C1 = "40%"
```

In the third instance it is:

```
Range("F8").Select
    ActiveCell.FormulaR1C1 = "60%"
Range("C1").Select
    ActiveCell.FormulaR1C1 = "Scenario 3"
    With Selection.Font
    .FontStyle = "Bold"
    .Color = RGB(0, 0, 255)
End With
```

Setting the proper order makes the cell containing the GP% active, which helps to highlight it. The GP% is the important part of the scenario, not the title, so it will make the spreadsheet look more professional and less clumsy.

NEXT

In order to keep this chapter short we will finish here, and we will look at Command Buttons etc. in the next chapter.

Chapter Six

EXCEL VISUAL BASIC APPLICATIONS EDITION (II)

More of the same . . .

In **Chapter Five** we looked in detail at Option Buttons, and how to code them. In this chapter we want to broaden this out to consider Command Buttons, Check Boxes, Drop Down Lists (Combo Boxes) and Toggle Buttons etc.

CHECK BOXES

Option Buttons are linked to each other, and only one can be active at any one time. Check Boxes work independently of each other, and they are useful for performing "what if" type calculations.

We will build a spreadsheet, combining Check Boxes with the Option Buttons we built earlier.

SPREADSHEET EXAMPLE

In the spreadsheet we want to calculate sales, gross profit, advertising expenses and net profit, and then flex it for:

- Changes in gross profit percentage
- We will/will not advertise on television
- We will/will not advertise by post
- We will/will not use telephone sales.

Set up a spreadsheet as follows:

Cell D1	Sales	**Cell E1**	Cost	**Cell E2**	Of Advert.
Cell A4	Television Advertising	**Cell A5**	Postal Advertising	**Cell A6**	Telephone Sales
Cell D4	60%	**Cell D5**	30%	**Cell D6**	25%
Cell E4	40%	**Cell E5**	20%	**Cell E6**	40%
Cell A9	Base Sales in units	**Cell A10**	Selling price per unit	**Cell A12**	Additional sales in units
Cell D9	20000	**Cell D10**	2	**Cell A13**	=A4
Cell A14	=A5	**Cell A15**	=A6	**Cell D13**	=D4*D9
Cell D14	=D5*D9	**Cell D15**	=D6*D9	**Cell F4**	Sales
Cell F6	Purchases	**Cell F8**	Gross Profit	**Cell J8**	GP%
Cell I4	=(D9+D13+D14+D15)*D10	**Cell I6**	=I4*(1-K8)	**Cell I8**	=I4-I6
Cell K8	50%	**Cell F10**	Expenses	**Cell F11**	=A4
Cell F12	=A5	**Cell F13**	=A6	**Cell I14**	=SUM(H11:H13)
Cell F16	Net Profit	**Cell I16**	=I8-I14		

The spreadsheet is saved on the CD as **Excel VBA 3.xls.**

The Option Buttons have been set up as before, except that the coding has been changed to reflect the revised positioning of the GP% cell, and no heading is displayed. The spreadsheet is shown below.

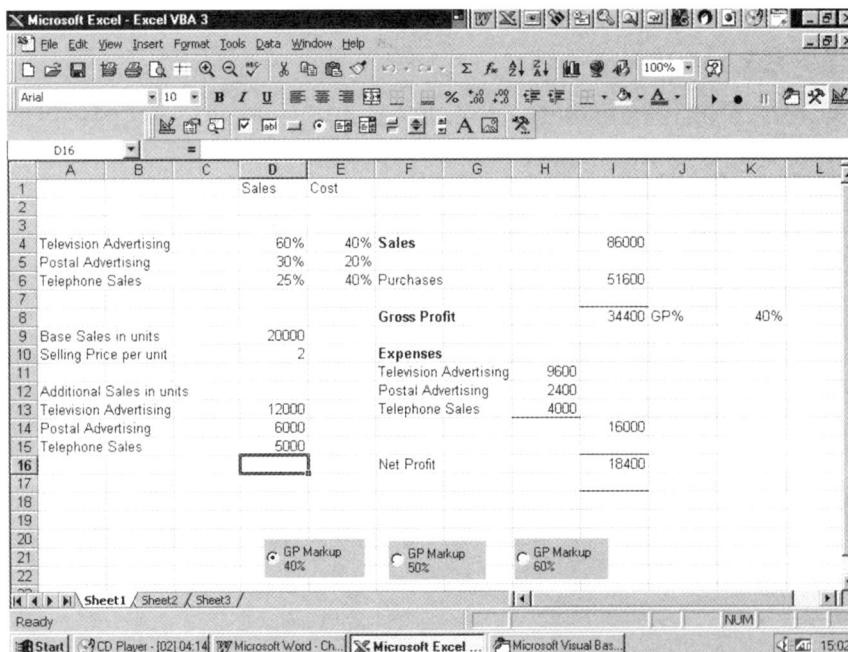

The spreadsheet as per the table over, with Option Buttons included

DRAW THREE CHECK BOXES

We need to draw three Check Boxes on the screen, one for amending Television Advertising, one for amending Postal Advertising, and one for Telephone Sales.

Click on the Check Box icon in the toolbox, and draw the Check Box from cells B19 to C19.

The screen will look similar to the one shown below. The spreadsheet is saved on the CD as **Excel VBA 3.xls**.

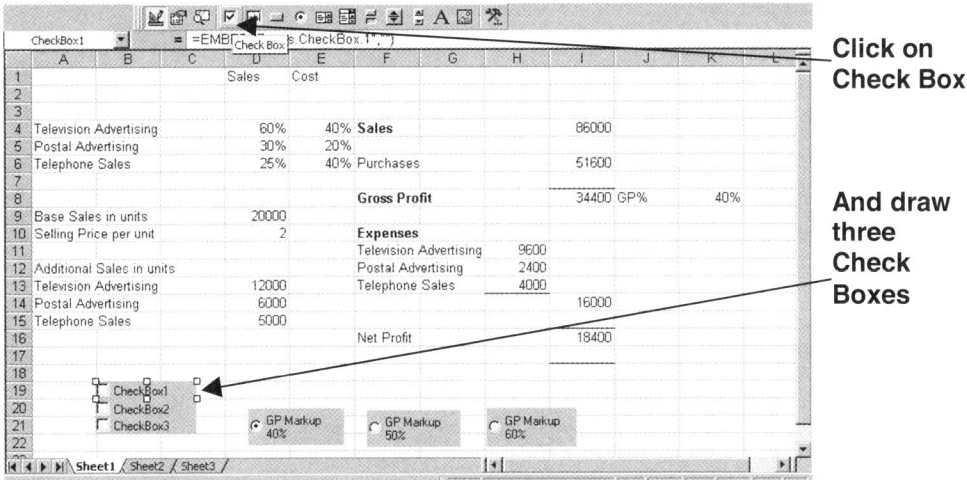

Click on Check Box

And draw three Check Boxes

AMEND THE TITLE IN THE CHECK BOX

At present the Check Boxes are labelled CheckBox1, CheckBox2 and CheckBox3. We need to re-label them, and the procedure is the same as for re-labelling the Option buttons — click on Design mode button if necessary, highlight the Check Box, right click and select CheckBox Object, Edit.

CODING THE CHECK BOX

The Check Box returns one of two results — True (value of 1) or False (value of 0). We do not therefore code the Check Box as such; we set the parameters to those required.

To set the parameters we need to activate the Properties dialogue box. Click on the Properties icon in the Toolbox.

The Properties dialogue box allows different properties to be set. We are interested in setting the property for the following items:

Linked Cell

TV Advertising	C13
Postal Advertising	C14
Telephone Sales	C15

We will set the value (true or false) at run time by clicking the box. Click on Exit Design Mode in the toolbox, and then click on the checkboxes. Cells C13 to C15 display True or False as appropriate. The spreadsheet is saved on the CD as **Excel VBA 4.xls**.

Click on the Properties icon

The Properties dialogue box appears

Enter C13 etc.

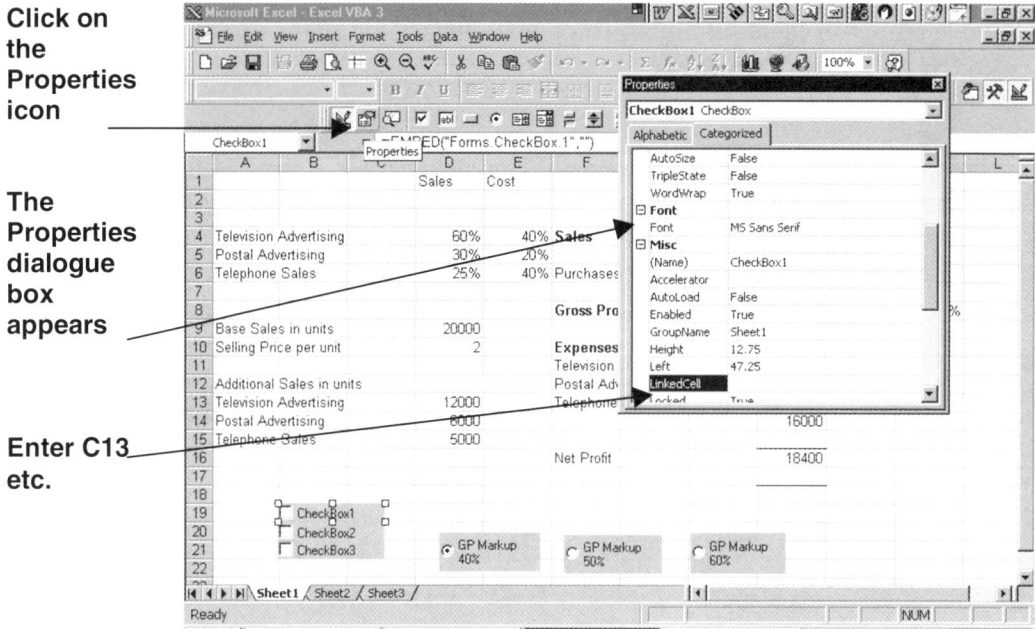

AMEND SALES FORMULAE

The sales formulae need to be adjusted to pick up the true or false state. Change cell D13 from =D9*D4 to =D9*D4*C13. Amend cells D14 and D15 accordingly. The revised spreadsheet looks like this.

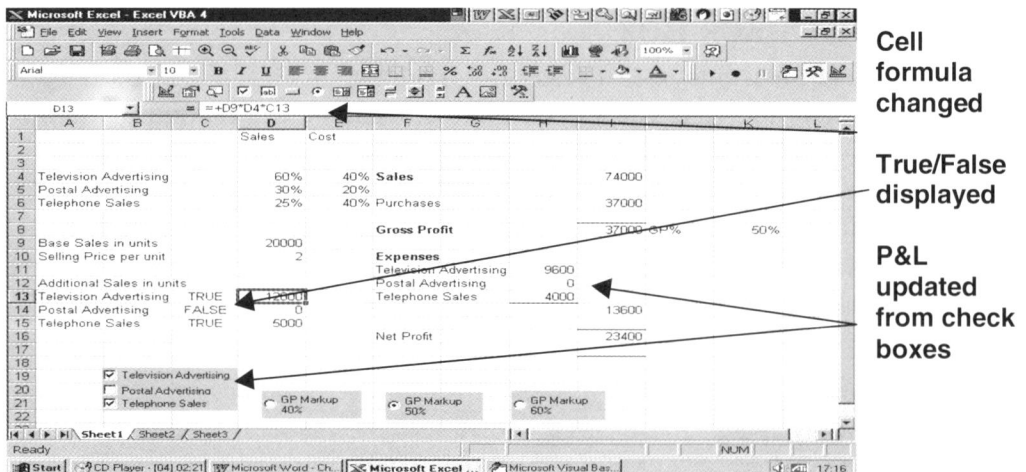

Cell formula changed

True/False displayed

P&L updated from check boxes

The full working version is saved on CD as **Excel VBA 4.xls**. If we were using this spreadsheet in practice, we would hide column C and reposition the Option Buttons accordingly.

SPIN BUTTON

The next button we will review is the Spin Button. By clicking on it we can change the value of a cell in the spreadsheet, thereby flexing results easily.

We will add a Spin Button to the spreadsheet **Excel VBA 4.xls**. Open the spreadsheet.

Click on the Spin Button icon in the Toolbox, and draw the Spin Button in cell C9.

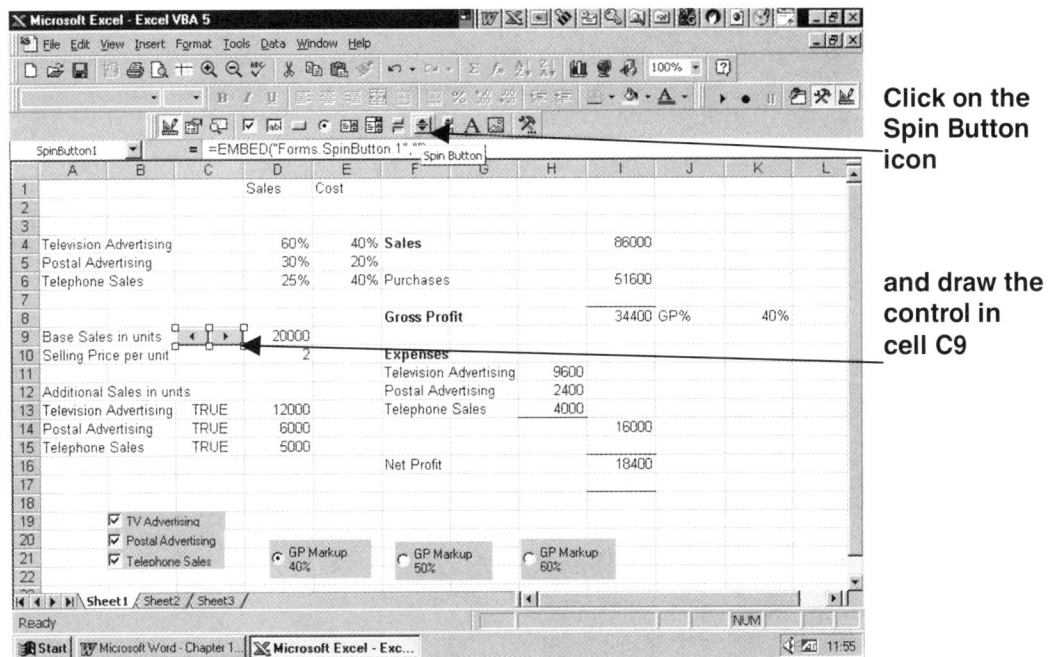

Click on the
Spin Button
icon

and draw the
control in
cell C9

The Spin Button works by assigning a maximum and minimum value to the button, and then linking it to a cell in the spreadsheet. These criteria are set through the Properties dialogue box, accessed in the same way as for the Check Box.

Set the criteria as follows:

     Linked Cell D9
     Maximum 35000
     Minimum 10000
     Small Change 1000
     Value 20000

Click on Exit Design Mode, and click on the button — it changes the Base Sale number of units sold, which affects the number sold with advertising initiatives, all of which feeds into the Profit and Loss Account.

The other controls — the GP% option buttons and the Check Boxes — still work, and we can now quickly review the results of a range of scenarios.

The Spin Button changes the units sold

Option Buttons are selected

Check Boxes are turned on and off...

and the P&L is updated

The spreadsheet is saved on the CD as **Excel VBA 5.xls**.

SCROLL BAR

The Scroll Bar works in a similar way to the Spin Button, except it has a slider bar between the two arrows.

In our spreadsheet, in order to conserve space we have chosen to use the Spin Button. In different circumstances we may decide the Scroll Bar would look better.

COMMAND BUTTON

The Command Button draws a button similar to those available in Access etc., but without any coding attached. They are useful for controlling movement around the spreadsheet — back and forward, going from one sheet to another in a controlled way, or moving to different areas within the one sheet.

If we do use Command Buttons in this way buttons must be provided in each location, in order to ensure the user does not navigate to an area, only to find he cannot navigate back from it.

The code for the Command Button is found by recording a macro for the action that we want to achieve, in exactly the same way that we coded the Option Buttons earlier.

The CD contains the spreadsheet **Excel VBA 6.xls** with Command Buttons pre-coded. Open the spreadsheet and review the code used.

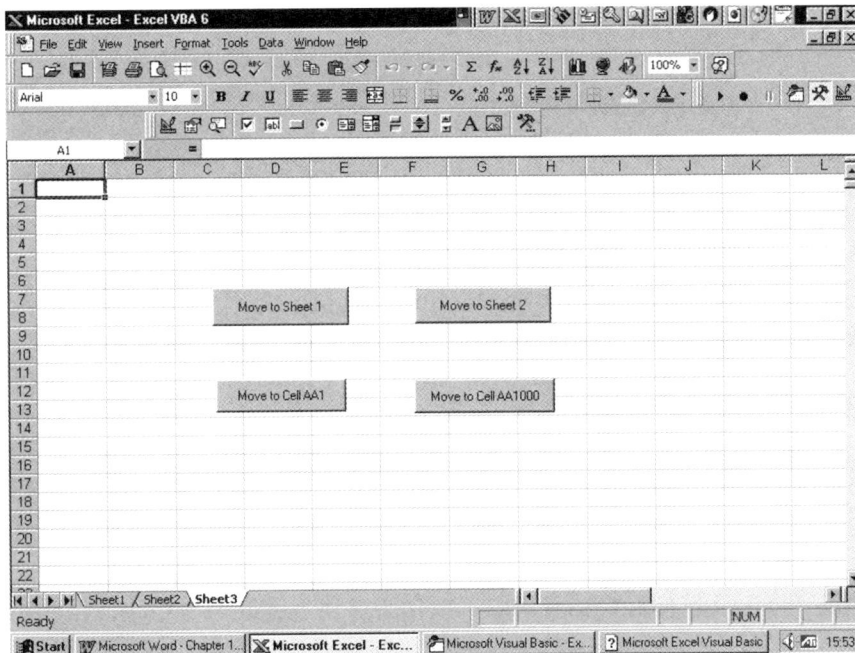

Sheet 3, with Command Buttons to other sheets and within the same sheet

CODING

If you checked the spreadsheet, you will have noticed that the coding for the command buttons has been achieved differently.

Command Button on Sheet 1
        Code   Call Macro 1

This calls the Macro statement, rather than using code directly. This means code does not have to be retyped.

If this method were used throughout, several different macros would need to be recorded in order to provide the proper code for each button.

Command Button on Sheet 2:

```
Code              Sheets ("Sheet1").Select
                  Dim myRange As Range
                  Set myRange = Worksheets ("Sheet1").Range ("A10")
                  myRange.Select
```

The code activates cell A10 once Sheet 1 has been selected.

Command Button on Sheet 3 (Move to AA1):

```
Code              Range("AA1").Select
```

The worksheet is already active, so it does not need to be selected.

EXCEL VBA CODING VS. MACROS

The VB code generated for a macro may not achieve the correct result if the code is used in the buttons directly, and changes may need to be made.

In general it will be easier and quicker to record macros. However, once programming skills have been learnt it is more efficient to code directly into the buttons. In addition, certain tasks can only be achieved by coding directly, as they cannot be recorded in a macro.

TOGGLE BUTTON

The Toggle Button is similar to a Check Box — click it to toggle it on, click again to toggle it off.

TEXT BOX

This displays text in the box and, if linked to a cell in the spreadsheet, the cell updates as each keyboard character is pressed.

The spreadsheet **Excel VBA 7.xls** illustrates how it will work. For demonstration purposes a further cell calculates, based on the linked cell value, which is itself based on input to the text box.

Note that if alpha characters are entered the calculating cell displays an error message.

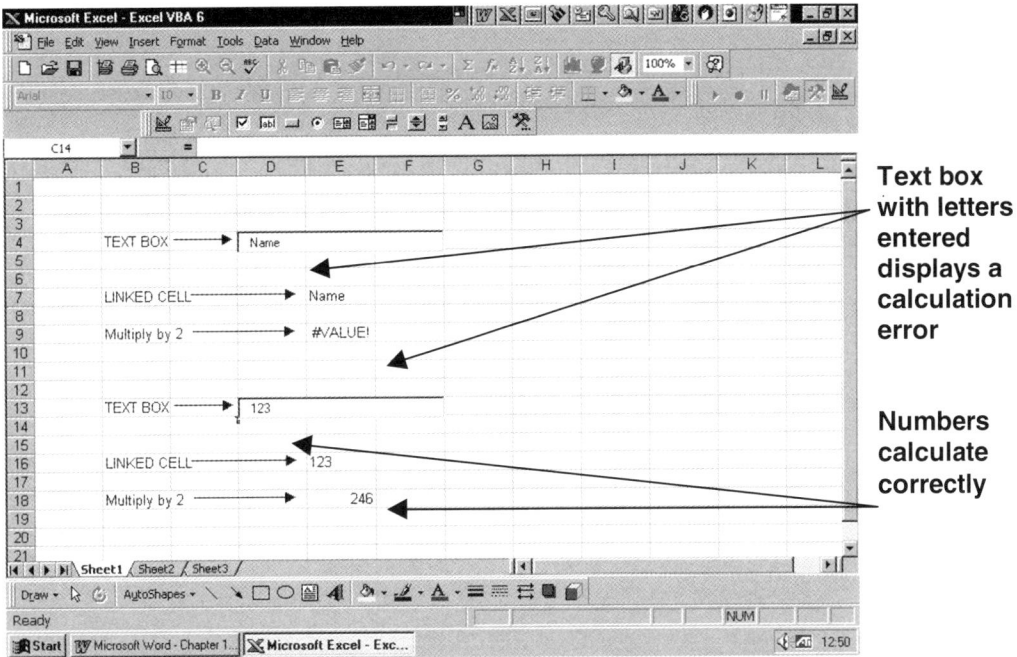

The Text Box is accepting user input in a range of formats and, unless we code the text box for error trapping as regards type of input, this could impact severely on the rest of the spreadsheet.

The Text Box would therefore be best left to being used in a fully programmed environment.

From a practical point of view, there is little advantage to be gained in entering data into a text box and linking from it to a cell.

LIST BOX AND COMBO BOX

The List Box allows a range of items to be listed and, when it is linked to a cell in the spreadsheet, the chosen item appears in that cell.

The Combo Box is a combined Text Box and List Box — the user types in the text box part, and the entry is chosen from the list contained in the drop down section. The list can be accessed by clicking on the down arrow.

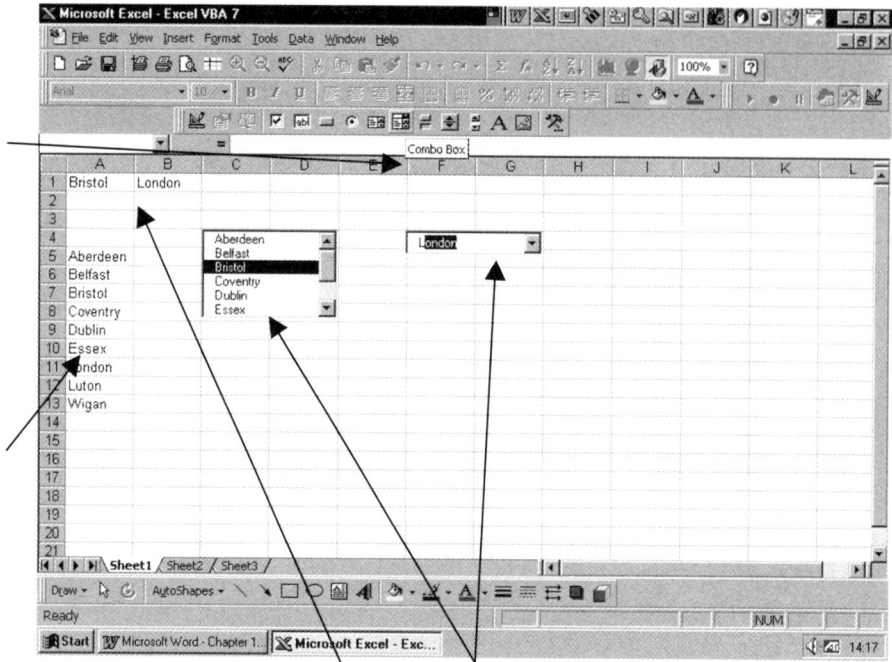

Click on Combo or List Box icons and draw the box

Fill in a range of cells to provide the names

Set the properties of the Combo and list boxes, and set the linked cell.

Combo and List Boxes are usually used in a database environment, and it also requires programming. We will not use them here.

LABELS AND IMAGES

These are used to provide enhanced impact to the screen shots, although they do obscure the cells underneath, so their use must be properly controlled.

We will not use them here.

NEXT

As a final chapter we will look at a program written to generate random sales data, to draw together the use of macro recording and the full structured language of VB.

Chapter Seven

RANDOM DATA GENERATOR

Figures shaken, not stirred.

In the next section we look at databases and data and how to summarise and present it. In order to make it a useful exercise we will need a substantial block of data to practice with.

In order to avoid having to type it in manually, a program is saved on the CD called **Pivot Table Random Number Generator.xls** which generates random sales data for us to work with.

For those interested, this chapter explains how the program was written, in order to explain some of the issues involved in programming, and also to demonstrate how easy programming can be, and how useful it can be to ourselves, if done at a basic enough level.

THE ANSWERS WE WANT TO GENERATE

We want to generate four thousand records of sales information. We will summarise the data in pivot tables, so we cannot use a simple repetition algorithm because the results would be predictable and there would be nothing "new" to discover in the analysis such as:

- How is the sales team performing?
- How well are sales performing across the range of goods?
- Are sales different in the different geographical areas? By value? By volume?

SPREADSHEET LAYOUT

The above refers to the summarisation of the data. The original details, line by line, will cover:

- Sales Invoice number
- Date
- Location
- Sales person
- Number of items sold — small, medium and large
- Value.

With the headings set up the spreadsheet looks like this.

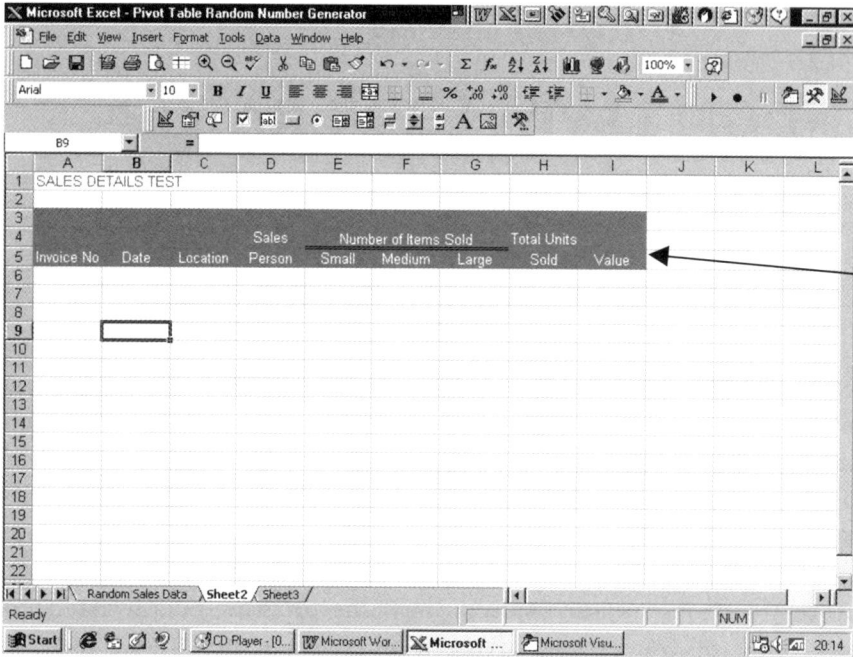

The headings are set up. Green shading is used to highlight them

An additional heading has been inserted, to act as a physical check that the number of units is correct. This is covered in the coding section below.

DRAW A COMMAND BUTTON

Next, a command button is drawn on the spreadsheet. This button will control the generation of the data, so a title of "Insert Random Data" is entered on it.

It is positioned above and to the left of the headings so that, if we freeze the pane and scroll down, the button is not lost from sight.

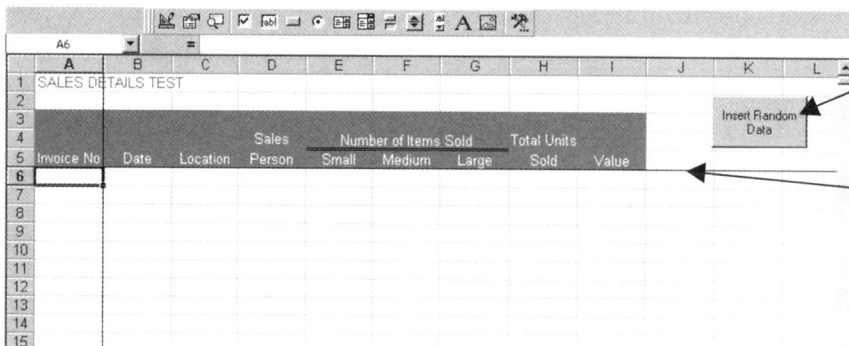

The command button is above the Freeze Panes line

Now we are ready to code the button. However, run the program first in order to see how it works in practice. Depending on the speed of your machine it may take a few minutes to generate the data, especially the Sales Value.

CODING

You can now call up the code and check it. The code is explained below.

OVERALL STRUCTURE

The code is split into distinct sections:
- Definitions
- Parameters
- Message boxes, to offer the option of not proceeding
- Blanking out of the existing data
- Data insertion in column A
- Data insertion in column B
- Data insertion in column C
- Data insertion in column D
- Data insertion in column E
- Data insertion in column F
- Data insertion in column G
- Data insertion in column I
- Data insertion in column H is not directly generated by the code.

Definitions

The definitions section defines what each of the parameters is, and the number value that is stored for that parameter. The items defined as Integer, for example, will only store whole numbers.

Parameters

The parameters section gives the values of items used later in the program – the number of transactions set up (DataSize = 4000), the selling price of the small goods (SellingPriceSmall = 40), medium sized goods (SellingPriceMedium = 75) and the large goods (SellingPriceLarge = 102).

Messages

The message boxes are coded with the message that is to be displayed, the type of buttons presented (OK and Cancel), a title and an exclamation label in the second message box.

Blanking Out Existing Data

This is done primarily to act as physical proof that the data has been re-populated.

Data Insertion in Column A

This is where the programming differs fundamentally from how we would physically enter the transactions.

If we entered the data manually we would put in the sales invoice, then the date of the transaction, the location etc. and complete each transaction individually.

However, because each column contains different types of data, from a programming point of view it is easier to deal with each type as a block. We therefore populate all of column A, then all of column B etc.

Looping

All of the columns are populated in the same way: the code runs and fills the cell, then the cell below is activated and the code re-runs. This re-running is called a loop, and it runs for the number of times defined in the parameter Datasize, noted above (four thousand in this case).

Cell Formatting

Column B is interesting, because the dates are calculated as the starting date of 35796 plus 1 to give the next date (35797) etc.

The cells in column B in the spreadsheet are pre-formatted to display the number as a date, and the column correctly shows dates.

Randomising the Data

The formula for column B is:

DateSold = 35796	Date 1 January 1998
NewDateSold = 1	Reset the counter
CellRow = 6	
CellColumn = 2	Define the first cell
For Newline = 1 To DataSize	Loop from 1 to 4000
Cells(CellRow, CellColumn).Value = DateSold	Cell value is the date number
CellRow = CellRow + 1	Move the cell down 1
If NewDateSold = 8 Then	After 8 dates are inserted then
DateCheck = (100 * Rnd)	Generate a random number between 0 and 1, then multiply it by 100

If DateCheck > 30 Then	Check if the random number is more than 30. If it is then...
DateSold = DateSold + 1	Increase the date by 1 day
End If	End the check of the random number calculation
End If	End the check if over 8
NewDateSold = NewDateSold + 1	Add one to the date when the previous loop is exited
If NewDateSold = 9 Then	If the counter is now 9 then...
NewDateSold = 1	Reset the counter to 1
End If	End the check
Next	Repeat the loop

The random number is started after eight dates are inserted, so there will always be at least eight sales per day. However, there is potentially no upper limit. In the spreadsheet on the CD there are twenty-four sales on 4 January.

This random number generation followed by value checking is used in the subsequent columns in order to flex the data in an unpredictable way, giving the data a "lifelike" quality.

Column H

The sales in columns E, F and G are randomised, to range from zero to five. It is possible that sales of all three types will be zero, and code therefore checks the cross tot of sales units. If it totals zero, one is inserted in the Small Units column.

CONCLUSION

Having a large amount of randomised data is very helpful for practising with Excel's in-built functions, and generating this with code is a very efficient and cost-effective way to produce it.

There are other practical uses for simple programs. The object of this chapter is to demonstrate that it may be beneficial to you to learn even basic programming, beyond the use of macros.

However, it is very much a personal decision.

NEXT

That concludes this section. We have looked at auditing spreadsheets, layout, programming and macros, and have seen how on screen presentation can be improved.

In the next section we will look at data and its summarisation, including the use of pivot tables. To this end, we will use the Random Data Generator discussed here.

Section Two

INFORMATION: OVERVIEW

Information is the highly-processed product obtained from manipulating and summarising raw data. In this section we are looking at how to gather information, and how to use Excel to view the information in different ways.

We will therefore look at:

- Databases
- Pivot Tables
- Goal Seek
- Scenarios
- Conditional Formatting.

In order to understand data we need to know something about databases, and Excel's database functionality. We also need to be able to understand pivot tables, and how they can help in interpreting results, and highlighting queries.

We will learn and practise these skills here, so that, later in the book, we can prepare the analysis of the actual and projected Whatsits results, ready for our meeting.

Chapter Eight

DATA TO INFORMATION

Knowledge is power. Information is money.

As a broad definition, data is the term usually reserved for the basic details entered into a system. It is unprocessed, in the sense that it has not been summarised into useful and meaningful information.

Data mining is then the process of digging deep into the system to find the meaningful details that lie hidden.

To a certain extent there is a blur in the use of, and distinction between, the terms data and information. For our purposes we will use data to mean the bulky detail, and information to mean the summarisation and analysis of that data. Information is an overview of the detail.

We must understand what data is and how it exists in order to understand how to process it into information, and how to make that information meaningful to us in our particular circumstances.

DATABASES

A database is the repository for all of the raw data. Knowledge of databases will help you to understand the summarisation of the data later.

Databases, as with most things, are full of terminology. The diagram below shows how a database is built.

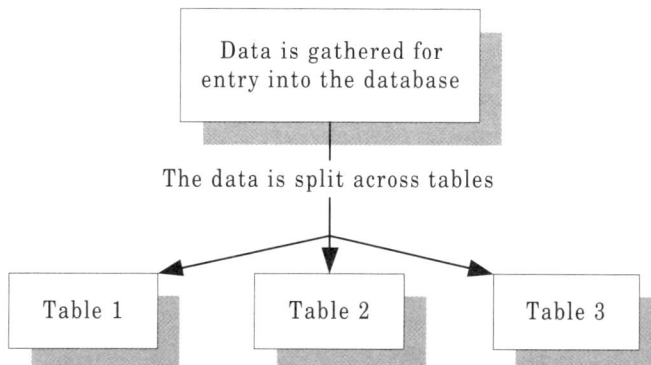

```
        ┌─────────────────────┐
        │  Data is gathered for│
        │  entry into the database│
        └─────────────────────┘
                   │
                   ▼
       The data is split across tables
                   │
        ┌──────────┼──────────┐
        ▼          ▼          ▼
   ┌─────────┐ ┌─────────┐ ┌─────────┐
   │ Table 1 │ │ Table 2 │ │ Table 3 │
   └─────────┘ └─────────┘ └─────────┘
```

What is the significance of the tables? They are the key to the power of the database and the reason why so much useful and easy analysis of data is possible.

The diagram can be expanded, to show how the data is then drawn forward to produce the information.

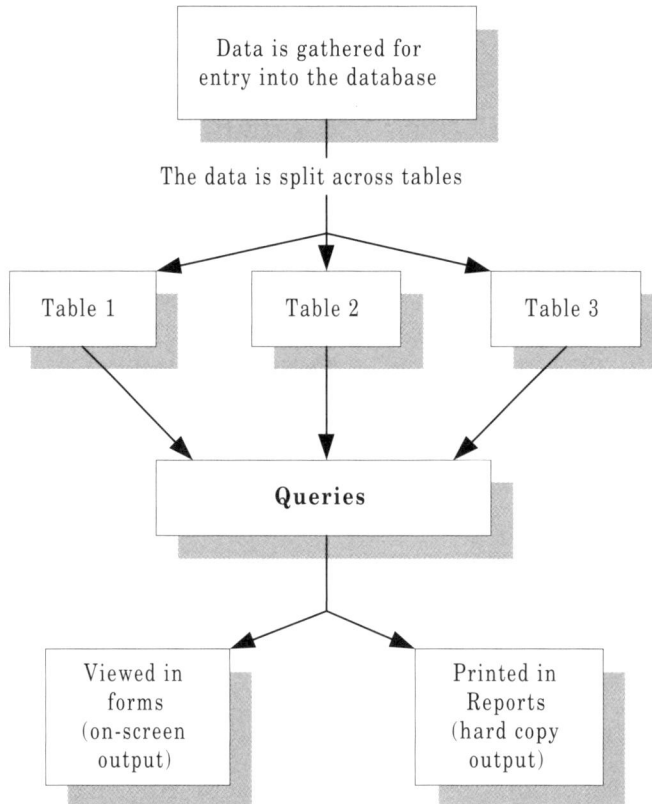

```
            ┌─────────────────────┐
            │ Data is gathered for│
            │ entry into the database│
            └─────────────────────┘
                     │
       The data is split across tables
          ┌──────────┼──────────┐
          ▼          ▼          ▼
     ┌────────┐ ┌────────┐ ┌────────┐
     │Table 1 │ │Table 2 │ │Table 3 │
     └────────┘ └────────┘ └────────┘
          │          │          │
          └──────────┼──────────┘
                     ▼
            ┌─────────────────────┐
            │      Queries        │
            └─────────────────────┘
                     │
              ┌──────┴──────┐
              ▼             ▼
       ┌───────────┐ ┌───────────┐
       │ Viewed in │ │Printed in │
       │   forms   │ │ Reports   │
       │(on-screen │ │(hard copy │
       │  output)  │ │  output)  │
       └───────────┘ └───────────┘
```

The full process shown by the diagram is explained in words below. We will assume it is a customer database in our company, Joe Bloggs Inc.

Data is Gathered

The database must be updated with new entries as we acquire new customers, or as details change for existing customers (they move address, incorporate etc.).

The details are entered on a company-produced Standard Input Form, and the form is used to enter the data onto the computer screen.

The Database is Updated

The entry is validated by the clerk as having been input correctly, and the database is updated with the new customer details. The data is put into the appropriate tables by the database.

Table Structure

Why split the data across several tables? Why not keep everything together? If data was static there would not be a problem — the reason why tables are used is to minimise the corrections that need to be made to the database to keep it up-to-date and accurate.

First of all we will look at the limitations of a one-table structure in our database.

THE SINGLE TABLE DATABASE

We are recording customer details. The Standard Input Form contains details of Customer A, and we enter her name, address, credit card details and first order details.

The next customer is entered, and the next, and the next . . .

Customer A orders again. We have to input all of the details about the customer again, as well as details of the goods ordered.

The next customer entry is made, and the next, and the next.

Customer A changes address. The next order records all the details correctly. Do we re-input the new address into the previous database entries, or leave them at the old (wrong) address?

The next customer entry is made, and the next, and the next.

Customer A gets married and changes her name and address. She places an order. Do we re-input the new name and new address into the previous database entries, or leave them at the old (wrong) address, and the previous surname?

The next customer entry is made, and the next, and the next.

Multiple Orders

If Customer A orders five different types of goods at once, we will need to input full details (name, address, credit card details, goods ordered etc.) five times.

Querying the Database

The sales team wants to do a mail shot to advertise a special offer, and they want a mailing list of customers. How many times will Customer A appear, and how will we know which entry is correct?

How much duplication of input is there to ensure the database is always accurate and up to date?

THE TWO-TABLE DATABASE

By adding one extra table and linking them things simplify greatly.

The first table includes the standing data — name, address, credit card details; the second shows the one-off data — the sales order.

The first table includes a unique customer reference, and the order includes the same unique reference. Running a query will use this unique reference to link the sales order and the customer.

When Customer A places her next order the name, address etc. are displayed on screen already. The clerk updates the address, and the detail in the first table is changed.

Multiple Orders

If Customer A orders five different types of goods at once, the screen can be set to show the two tables separately. The five entries in table 2 can be input without changing the customer details displayed.

Querying the Database

The sales team wants to do a mail shot to advertise a special offer, and they want a mailing list of customers. How many times will Customer A appear, and how will we know which entry is correct?

This time the mailing list is only drawn from table 1. There is only one entry for Customer A, and it is the most up to date information we have available.

FURTHER TABLES

At its most basic the two-table structure is all that is needed. A tighter database arises if there is a table of products and prices, and a table for customer discounts. After that, it depends on the type of queries we are wanting to run, and therefore how the data has to be summarised — if the links between data are not established we cannot relate one set of information to another.

Therefore, if there is no link between the customer name and the date of the last order, the sales team will not know if the customer is "live".

In addition, it depends on whether the database is isolated from the rest of the company. The orders table may be related to a production table to co-ordinate between production and sales, the production table will be related to a suppliers table for the ordering of goods etc.

Database Queries

Storing data in a database is not of itself important. What is important is the ability to query the data and provide analysis of relationships so that, for example, the sales team can contact the relevant customers. The information need that the database is required to answer will determine how the information is stored.

Building the queries in the database is one solution.

Exporting the data to Excel and using the in-built functionality is a powerful and easy alternative.

EXCEL

Excel is a spreadsheet, not database software. But, what is a database?

In *The Accountant's Guide to Excel* we defined a spreadsheet as: "A scratchpad used to record text and numbers in a variety of formats".

A natural progression is to use the functionality to manipulate the cell contents (the text and numbers) and re-organise them alphabetically or in number order, to display only those cells with one attribute etc.

This is approaching our view of a database.

Combine this with the functionality of Excel — Internal Rate of Return, Goal Seek, Scenarios etc. and the data moves into 3D.

In order for the data to become 3D we need more background on understanding Excel in context, and therefore what can, and cannot (easily) be done.

The most important aspect from our perspective is that we do not want any "work around" solutions. If Excel cannot easily achieve what you want, you should identify it and ask the company's programmers to assist.

EXCEL DATABASE EXAMPLE

We will now look at a simple database in Excel. Start Excel and open the file **Excel Database 1.xls.**

The screen looks similar to this. Note that the icons on my screen have been customised to suit my needs — your set of icons may be slightly different.

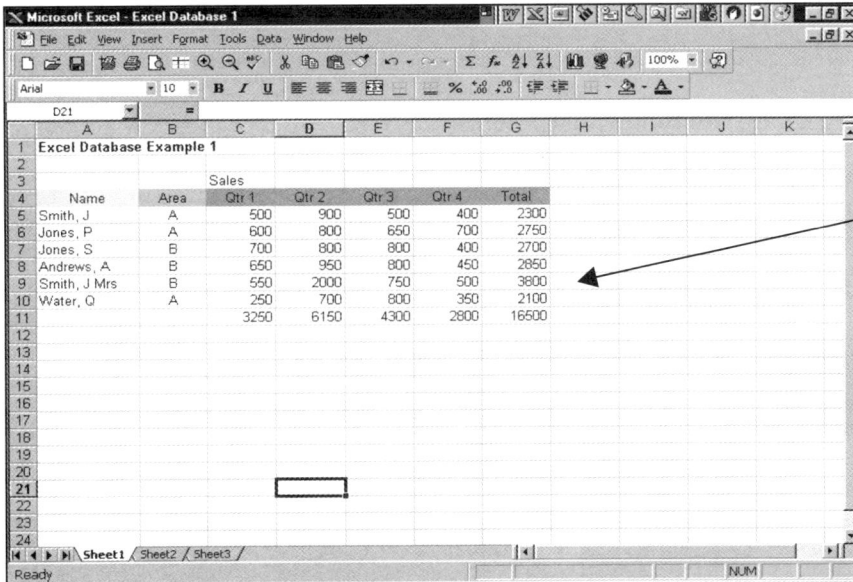

The data table we are working with

You should already know how to format the text, colour the cells, centre the cell contents etc. as necessary.

The data in the table is not in any particular order – the names are not in alphabetical order, and the sales by area are not kept together. The figures are therefore more difficult to interpret than otherwise.

We will sort the figures. Black out the table (mouse drag, or use F8 and the arrow keys). Select Data, Sort from the menu. The screen looks like this.

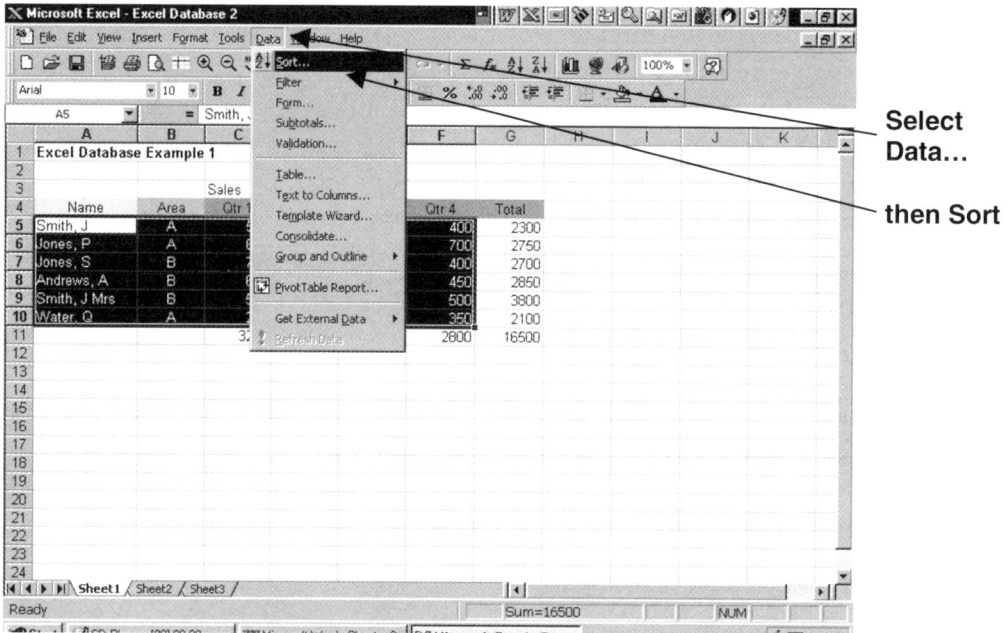

Select Data...

then Sort

Selecting Sort brings up the following screen.

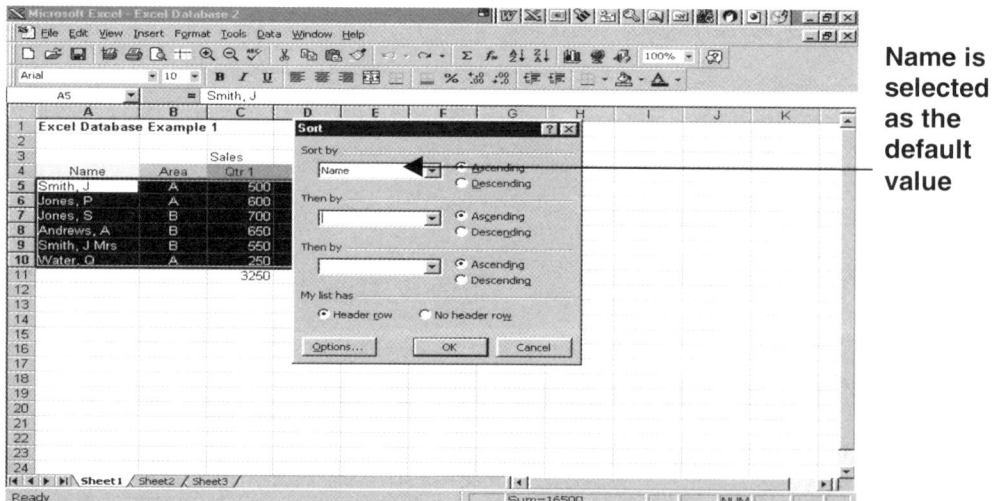

Name is selected as the default value

The default chosen by Excel is to sort by name only. Try this first, and note the results — the Areas are not grouped together in the table.

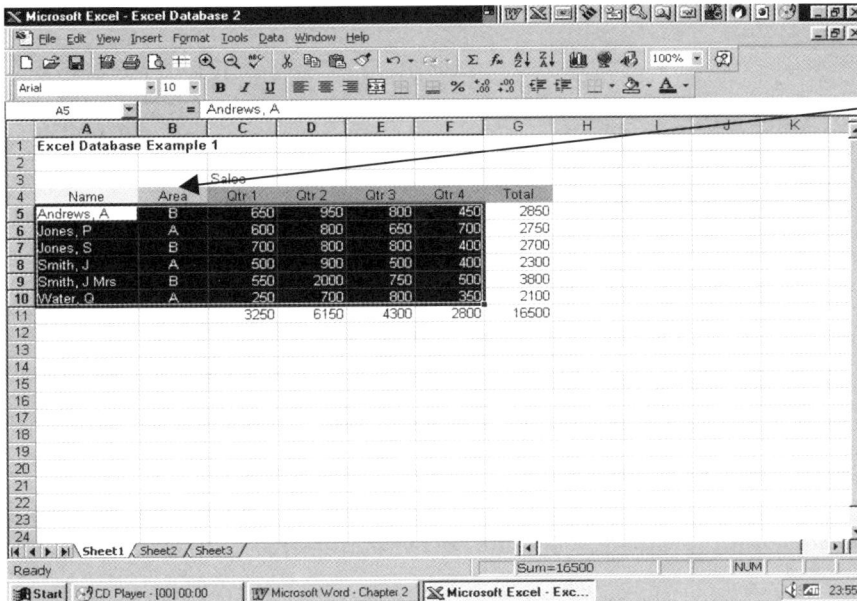

The sort has not grouped the Area codes

Next, select Sort by Name, then by Area. Click on the down arrow on the second drop down box and select Area.

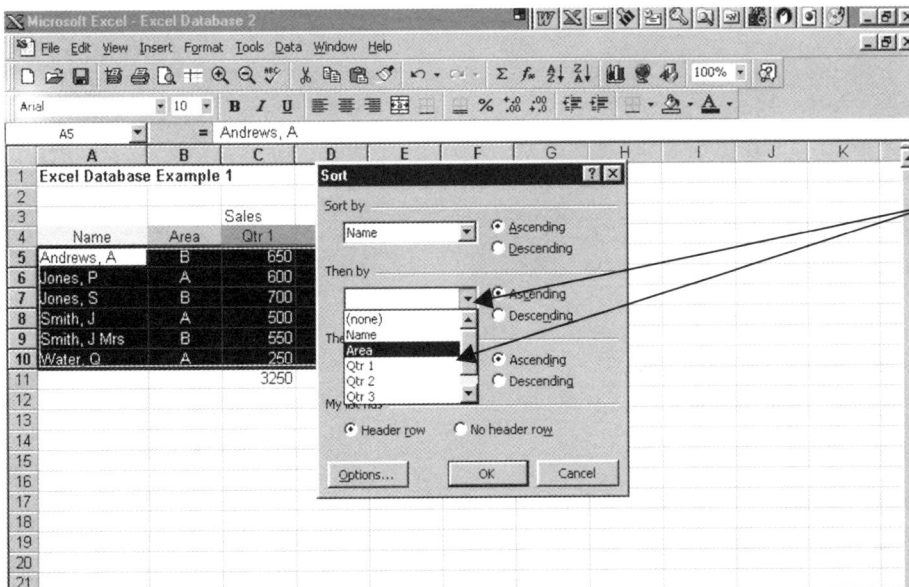

Select Area in the second drop down box

The revised sort looks like this.

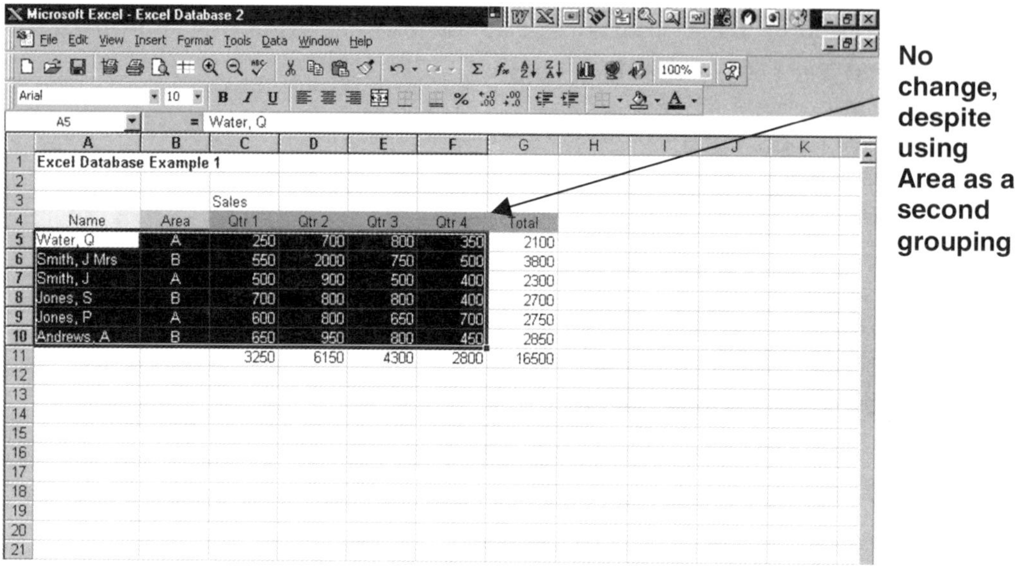

No change, despite using Area as a second grouping

To get the result we want, we have to sort by Area first, then by Name. The final result is shown below, and is saved as **Excel Database 3.xls**.

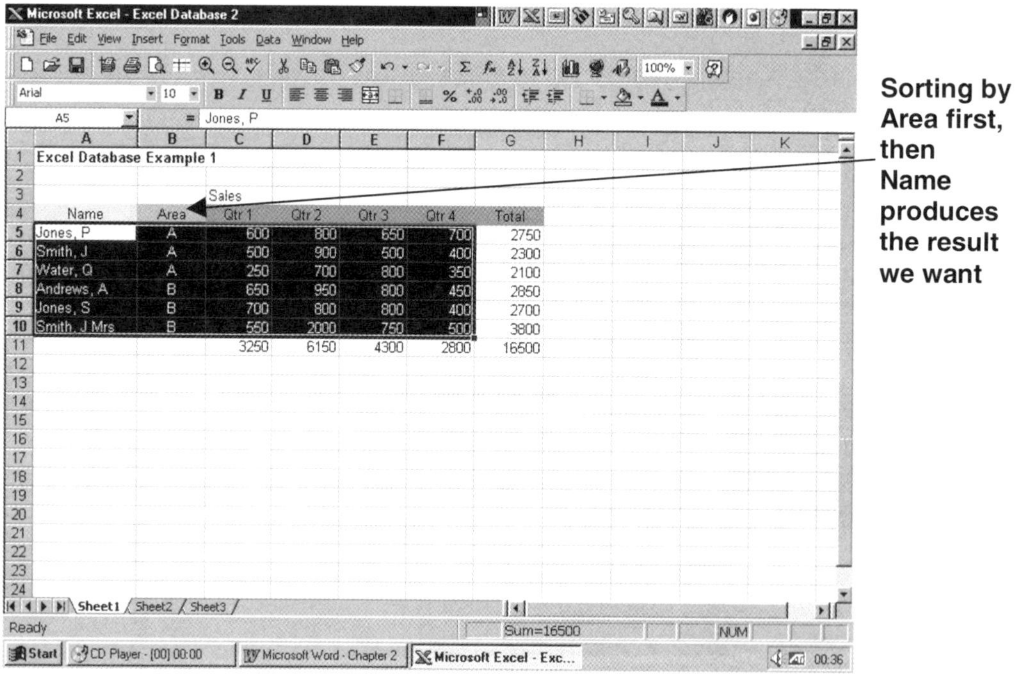

Sorting by Area first, then Name produces the result we want

In English our sort was "Display the sales team in alphabetical order by area". In Excel the English is more accurately stated as "Within each area, display the sales team in alphabetical order".

Now the data is starting to look intelligible.

FILTERING

A further improvement can be made when viewing the data. If we want to review a long list of transactions and highlight only those transactions that fulfil one (or more) criteria, we can filter the data.

We will demonstrate using Filter with the spreadsheet **Filter 1.xls**.

Open the spreadsheet and, with a cell within the data list active, select Data, Filter, AutoFilter from the menu.

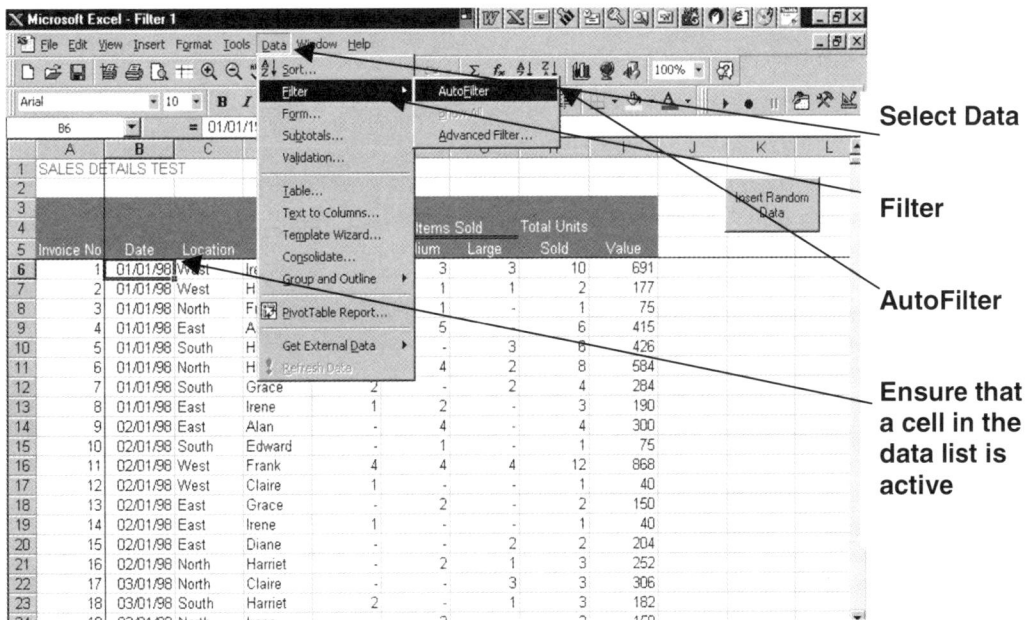

A list of drop down arrows appears in the headings section. Select the arrow in the Sales Person column, and choose Irene.

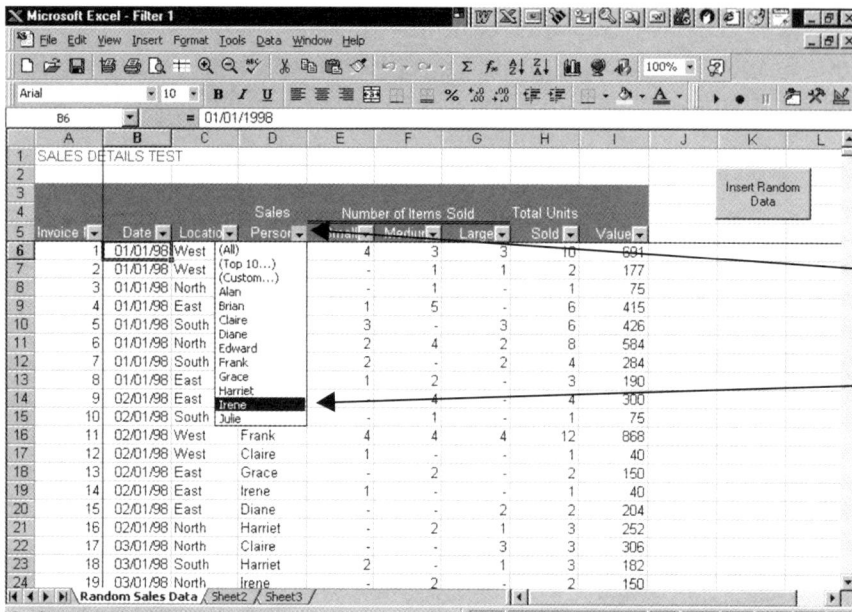

A list of sales made by Irene is shown. All other sales are hidden.

Now click on the down arrow at Location, and select West. Only those sales by Irene AND in location West are displayed.

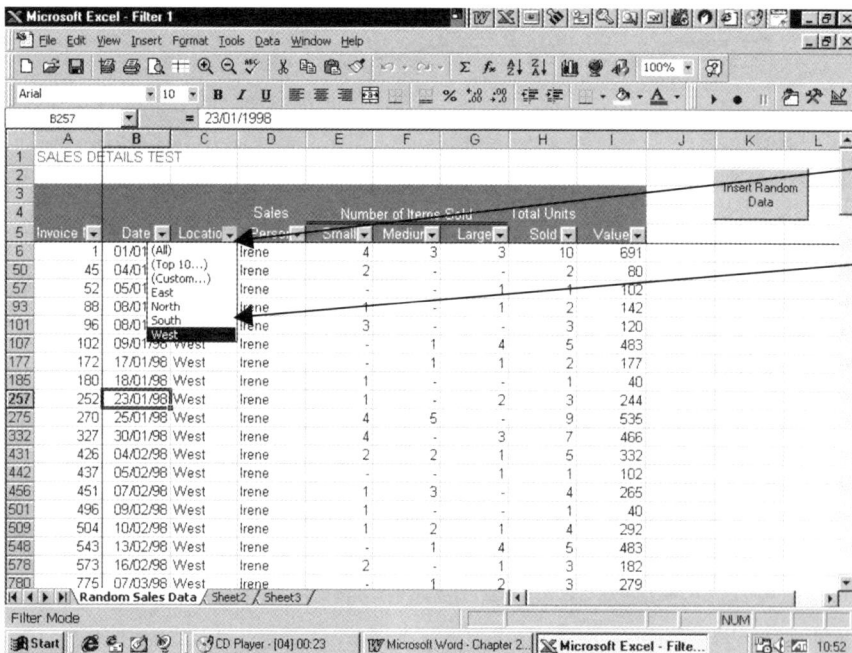

Further filtering can continue as required. To see all of the occasions when she sold only large items, select the filter for nil sales of small and nil sales of medium.

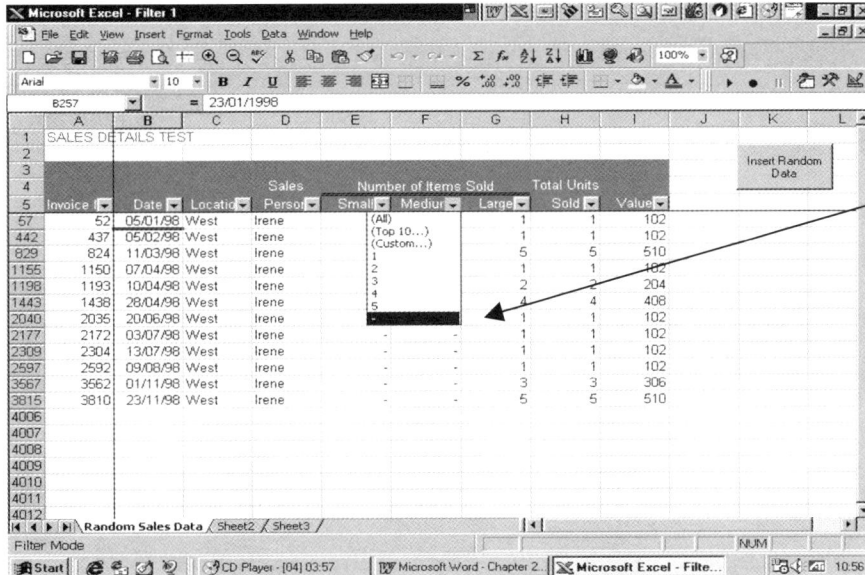

Filter out sales of small and medium, to leave sales of large

ADVANCED FILTER

The advanced filter option allows more than one criterion to be selected in each heading. The list can therefore be filtered for two sales personnel in one area, achieving sales in excess of a set value in a month.

The spreadsheet **Filter 2.xls** is used to demonstrate the technique.

In order to allow the criteria to be specified, the data has been moved down to A15. Copy the label headings to row 4, and below the relevant headings type the criteria to show sales by Irene and Harriet with a value over £500.

Copy the labels

Enter the criteria below the relevant label

Ensure there is a space before the data list

With a cell in the data list active, select Data, Filter, Advanced Filter. The following dialog box appears.

The Advanced Filter dialog box appears.

The list range is entered automatically

The options are:
* Filter the list in place
* Copy to another location
* Unique records only

Filter in place acts like the AutoFilter used previously, hiding the non-relevant items.

Copy to another location will create a copy of the relevant entries, allowing further manipulation of the data without affecting the original.

Unique records filters out duplicates.

If the Copy to another location option button is selected the third input box becomes activated.

We will filter in place. Place the cursor in the Criteria range input box, and then click on the icon on the right hand size to minimise the box. Click and drag to select the cells from A4 to I6, and release the mouse button. The dialog box is restored.

Click OK, and the filter is applied.

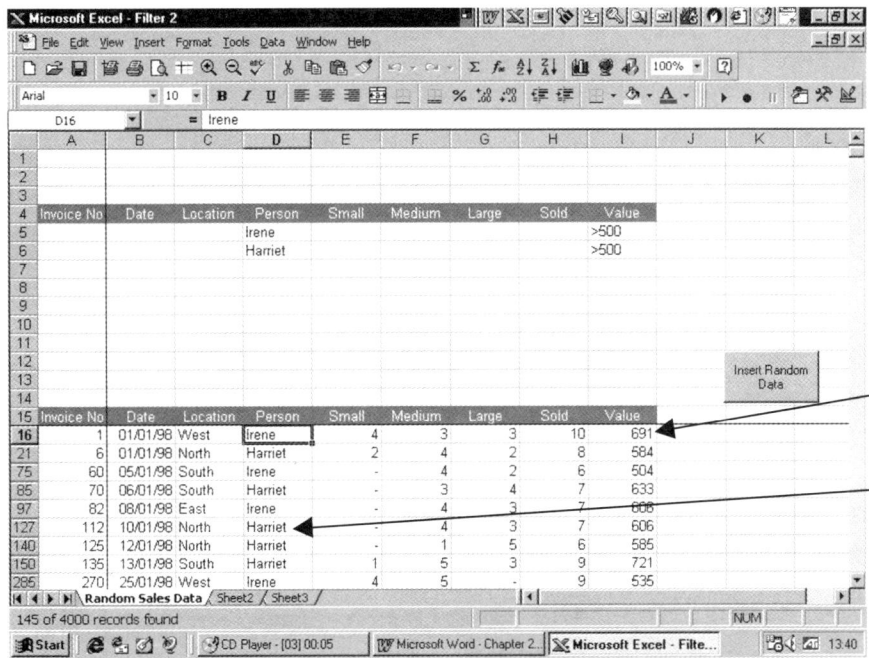

The filter has been applied

Only items over £500 for the two sales staff are shown

It is not necessary to have a heading in the criteria section unless filter items are entered. However, if they are omitted and a new filter is applied, the criteria range would then need to be re-specified.

CUSTOM FILTERS

The final aspect of filtered lists, which combines the AutoFilter facility used initially with the more flexible multi-filter aspects of the Advanced option is Custom Filter.

Open **Filter 3.xls**, and apply AutoFilter as previously. In the Names column click on the down arrow, and choose Custom from the list.

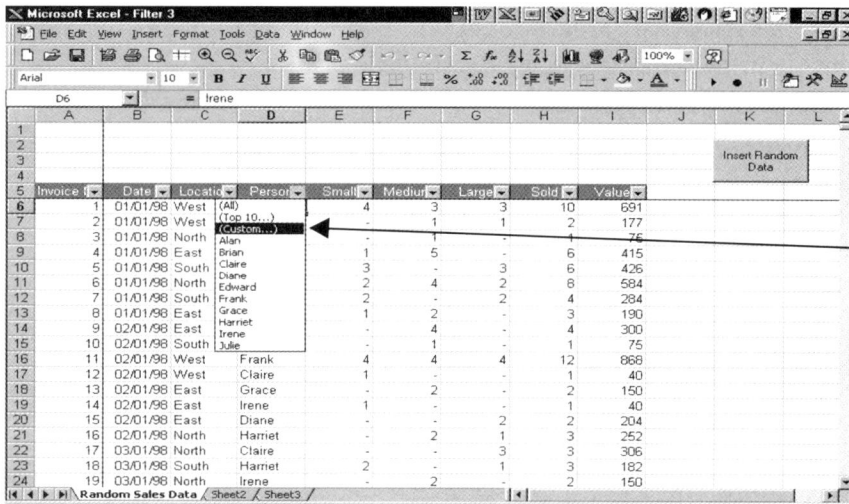

Select Custom from the list

The following dialog box appears. Select "equals" as the entry in the two left boxes, and click on the "or" option button. Enter "Irene" and "Harriet" in the two boxes on the right, or click the down arrow and choose them from the list. Click OK.

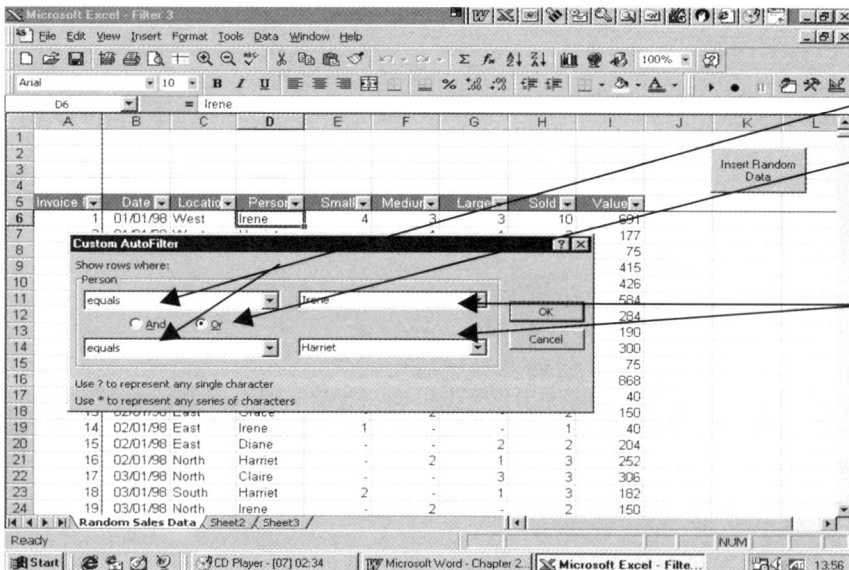

Select "equals"

and "or"

and enter "Irene" and "Harriet"

Filtering is a quick and easy way to investigate figures, and to highlight only those items that are of interest. However, to obtain a summarised overview of the data requires us to use PivotTables.

NEXT

In order to keep the chapters short we will break here. In the next chapter we will look at PivotTables.

Chapter Nine

EXCEL DATA TO EXCEL INFORMATION

A dictionary provides meaning to words.
Excel provides meaning to figures!

In this chapter we are going to look at pivot tables to see how to summarise data in order to be able to obtain an overview of the results. Pivot tables are usually run as advanced database queries from within the database; however, by running it from within Excel we do not have to rebuild queries each time we run a different pivot table perspective. In addition, drag and drop ensures quick and easy manipulation.

We will use a set of randomly generated sales information to practice our analysis techniques.

BACKGROUND

The spreadsheet **Pivot Table 1.xls** contains a copy of the random data generator program, and 4000 entries have already been generated.

The background to the data is as follows:
- The sales cover the period from 1 January 1998 to 10 December 1998
- There are four geographical sales areas; North, South, East and West
- There are ten sales staff; Alan, Brian, Claire, Diane, Edward, Frank, Grace, Harriet, Irene and Julie
- There are three types of goods sold — small, medium and large
- The sales prices of the goods are; small £40, medium £75 and large £102.

We want to find out:
- What are the monthly sales totals?
- How do the sales staff compare to each other?
- Do we have the same market penetration in each area?
- Which items are selling better — small, medium or large?

We will build the pivot tables, and look at the results.

WHAT IS A PIVOT TABLE?

A pivot table summarises the results from a large table of data, but it does a lot more. It allows easy manipulation of the data to check the detailed analysis of that specific query, and views of the data are easily changed.

By looking at the information in different ways it allows different perspectives to be taken on the underlying transactions, so that meaningful decisions can be taken.

PREPARING A PIVOT TABLE

Pivot tables are set up with the help of a PivotTable Wizard, which is accessed from the Data part of the menu.

Rename Sheet2 on the spreadsheet **Pivot Table 1.xls** to Pivot Table, then click on Data, PivotTable Report on the menu.

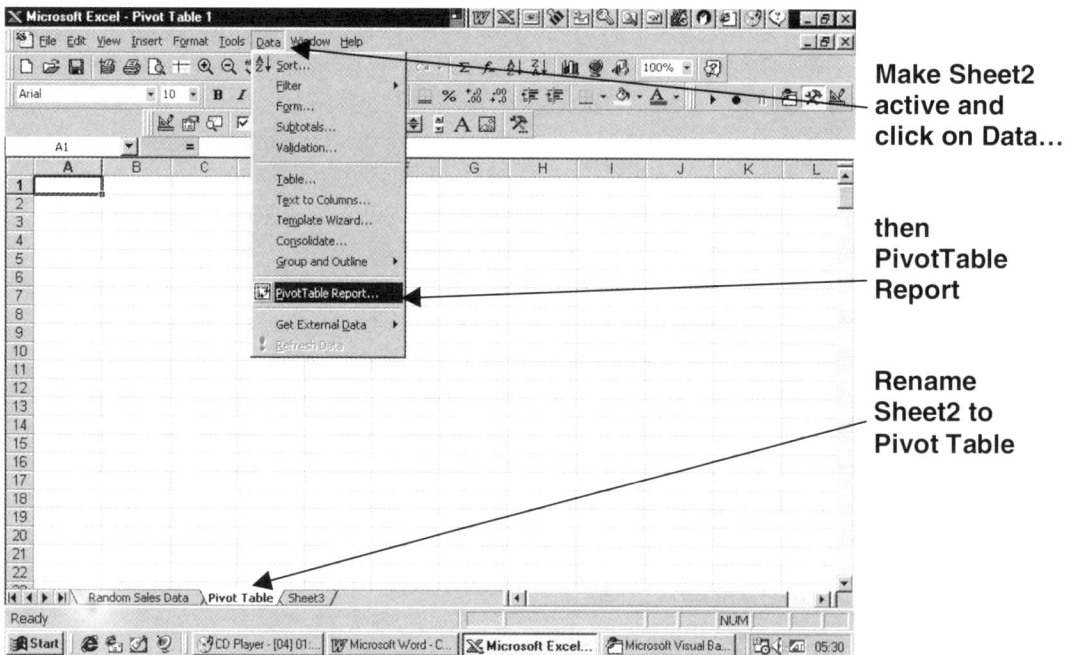

The Wizard starts, and the first step appears. The choices given are:
- Excel list or database
- External data source
- Multiple consolidation ranges
- Another PivotTable (this is greyed out, because at present there are no other pivot tables set up).

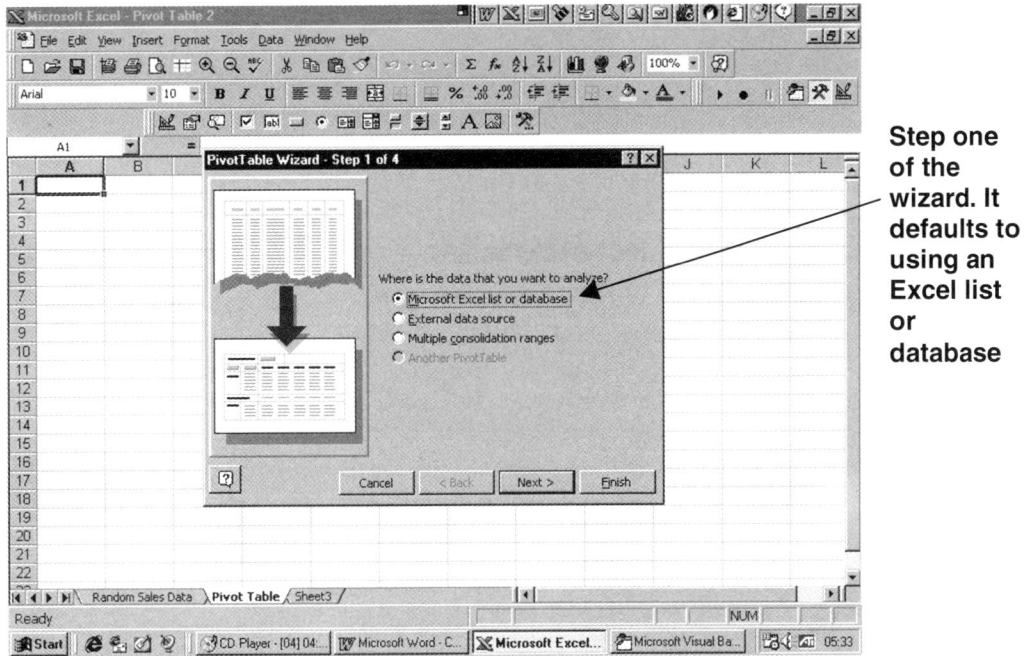

Step one
of the
wizard. It
defaults to
using an
Excel list
or
database

If the data were not already in Excel there are two choices – either export the information to Excel from the database (Access for example), or import the information into Excel. In order to do the latter Microsoft Query must be installed. Generally, it will be easier to export the data to Excel first, and then work on it.

Multiple Consolidation Ranges is used to select several different blocks of cells within Excel, for example if there are separate spreadsheet pages, one for each geographical area.

Click on Next.

The screen changes to that shown below. Click on the sheet Random Sales Data to activate it.

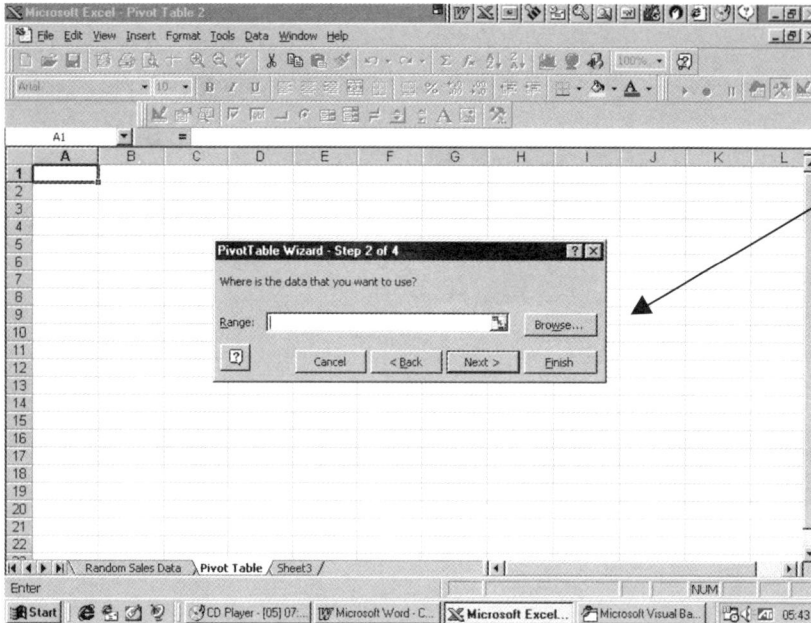

Step 2

Click on the sheet Random Sales Data to see the range we want to select

Select the cells from A5 to I4005. This selects the labels for the spreadsheet, as well as the data.

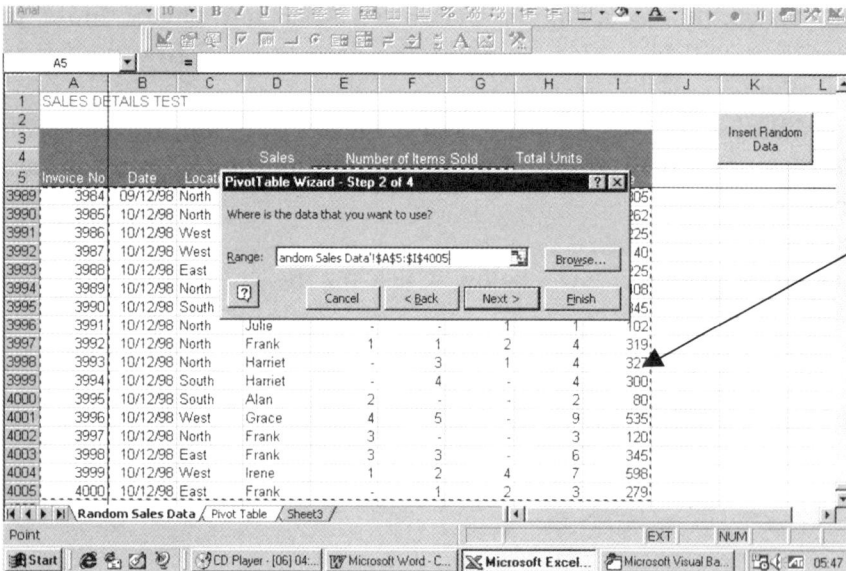

The range is selected

Click in A5, press F8 then click in I4005

Click on next. The screen changes to

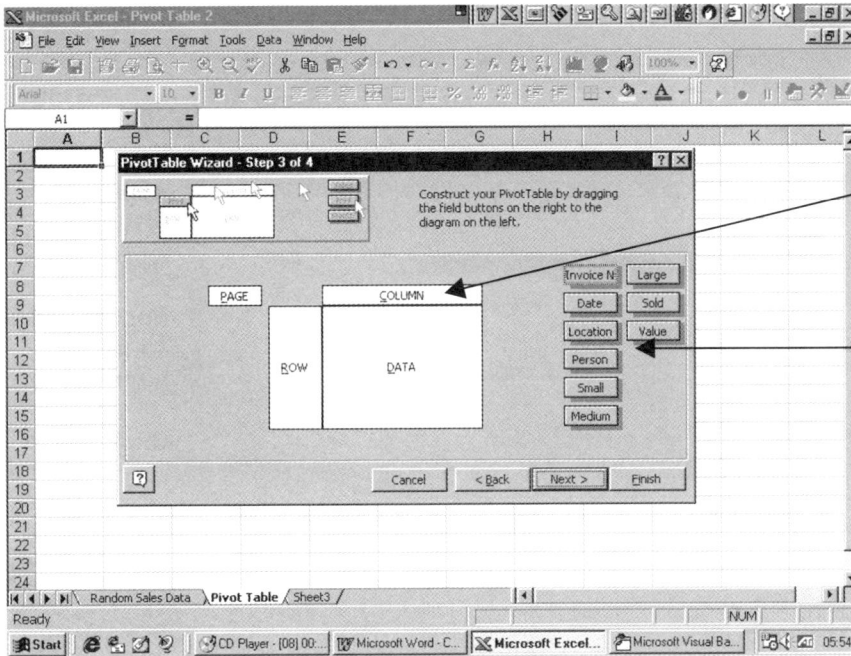

The PivotTable format is shown.

The headings in cells A5 to I5 are shown

We can now decide how we want to summarise our 4000 transactions. Drag Person to Row, Location to Column, and Value to Data.

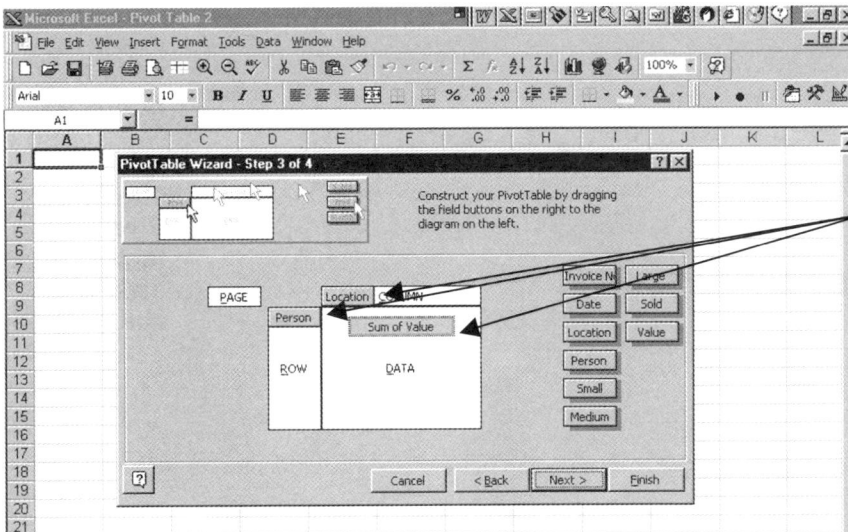

The three items are dragged across

The final step is to confirm where the table is to display. The reason for using a blank sheet is we know that we will not be accidentally overwriting information.

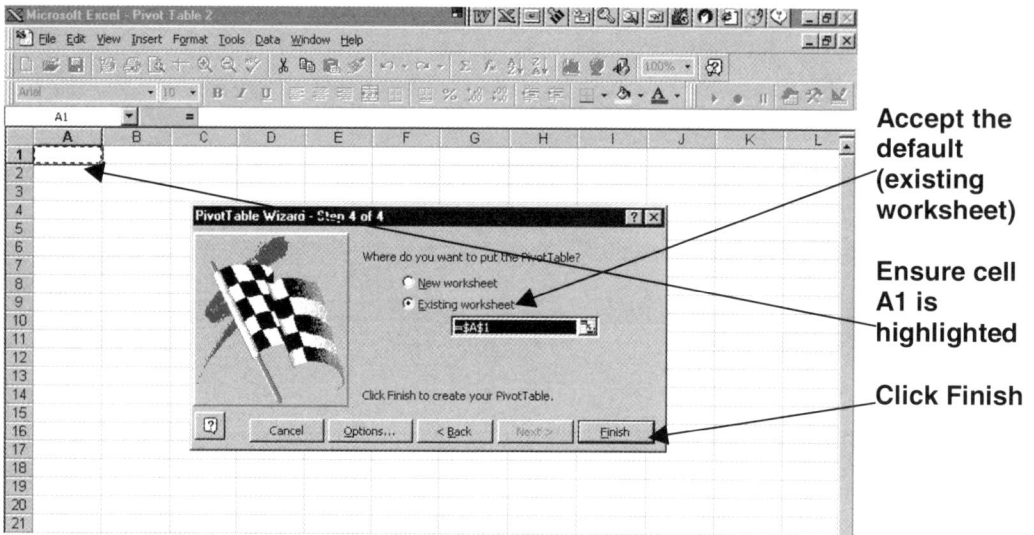

Accept the default (existing worksheet)

Ensure cell A1 is highlighted

Click Finish

The pivot table is produced.

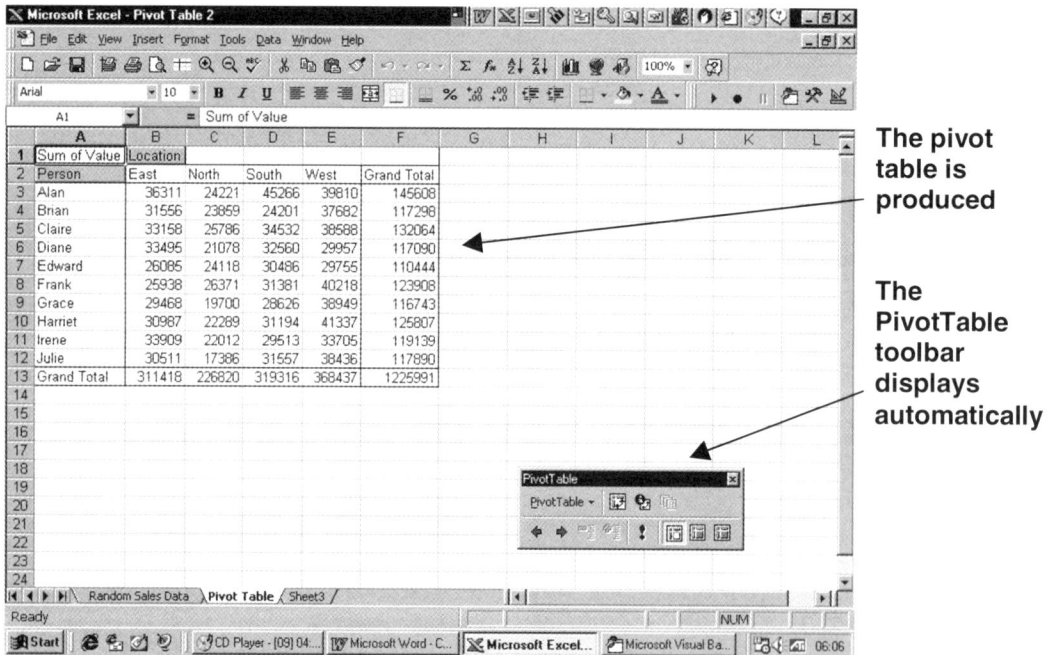

The pivot table is produced

The PivotTable toolbar displays automatically

This summarises the sales by person, and the sales by location. In order to finish this view of the data we will present it in a chart, and then manipulate the data analysis.

Ensure that one of the cells in the pivot table is active, then click on Insert, Chart in the menu. The screen looks like this.

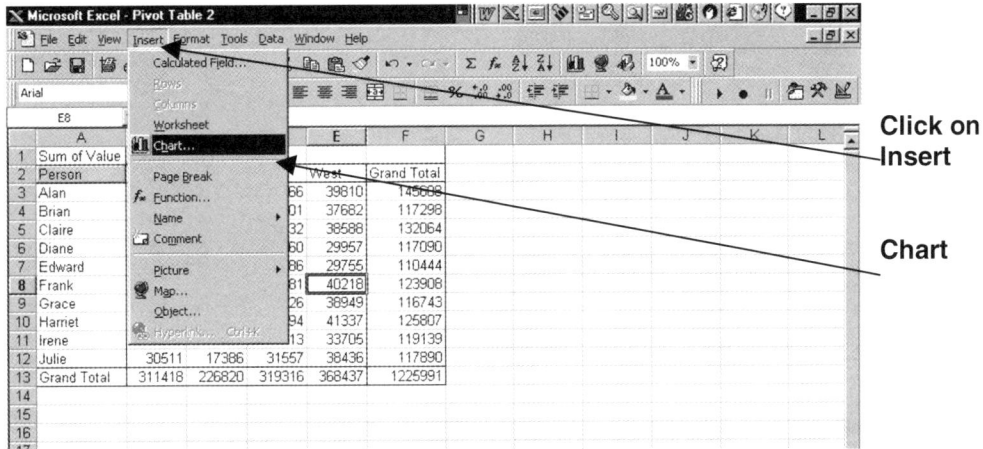

Click on Insert

Chart

The Chart Wizard starts. Select the first style.

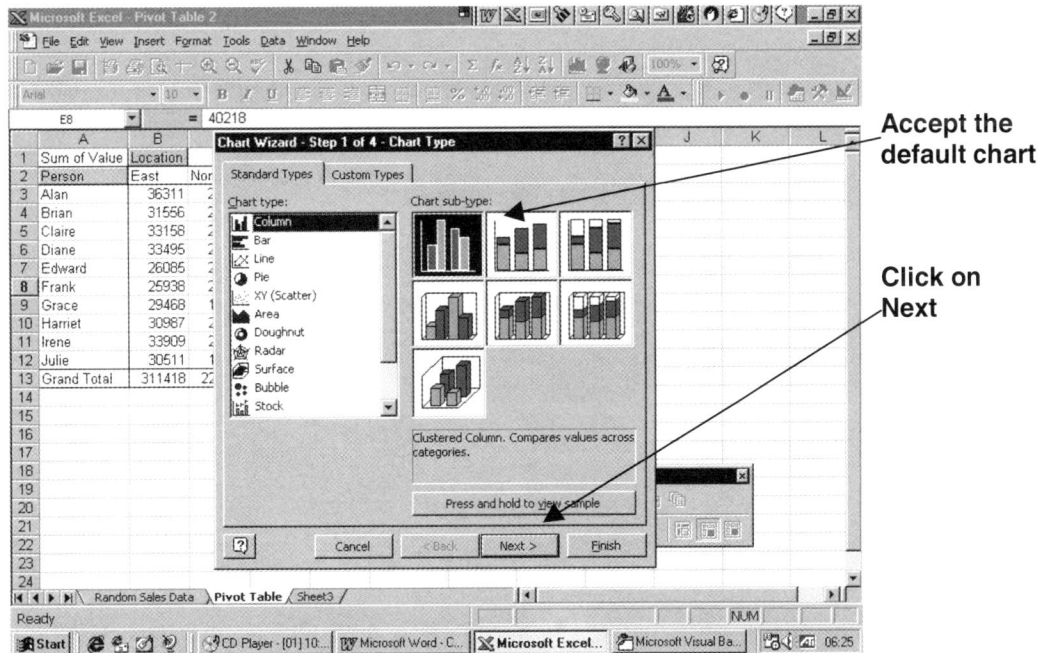

Accept the default chart

Click on Next

The default sets the data range as = 'Pivot Table'!$A$2:$F$13. This includes the Grand Total, so adjust the formula to read = 'Pivot Table'!$A$2:$F$12.

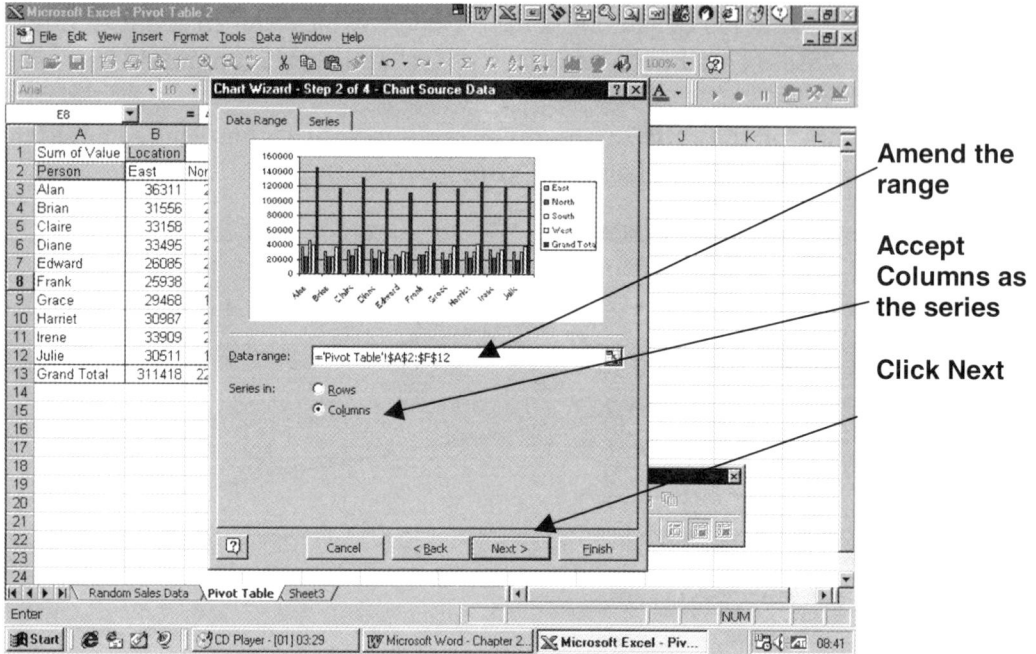

Enter "Sales by Employee" as the title, "Employees" for the X-axis and "Amount" for the Y-axis.

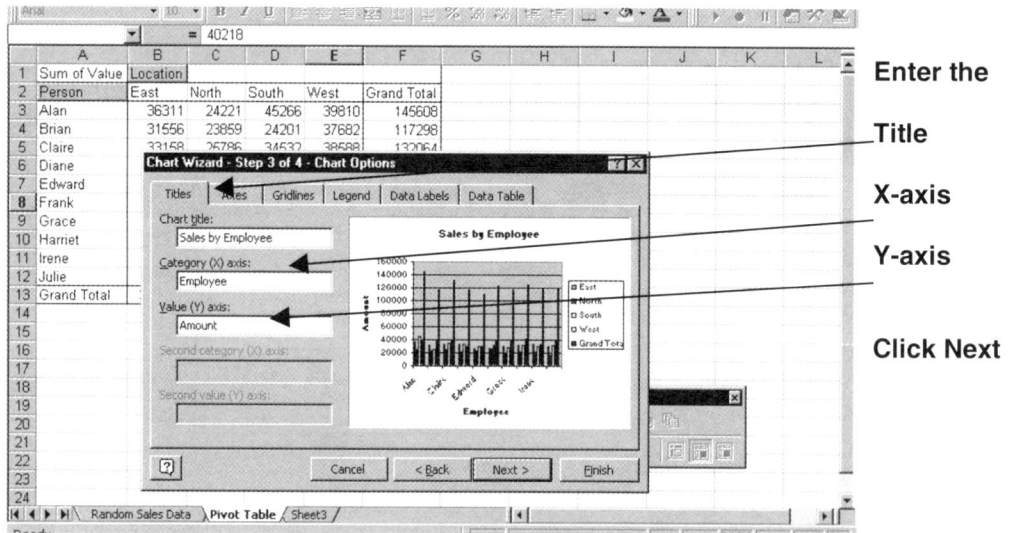

Select the option button for placing the chart on a new sheet, and call it "Pivot Table Chart".

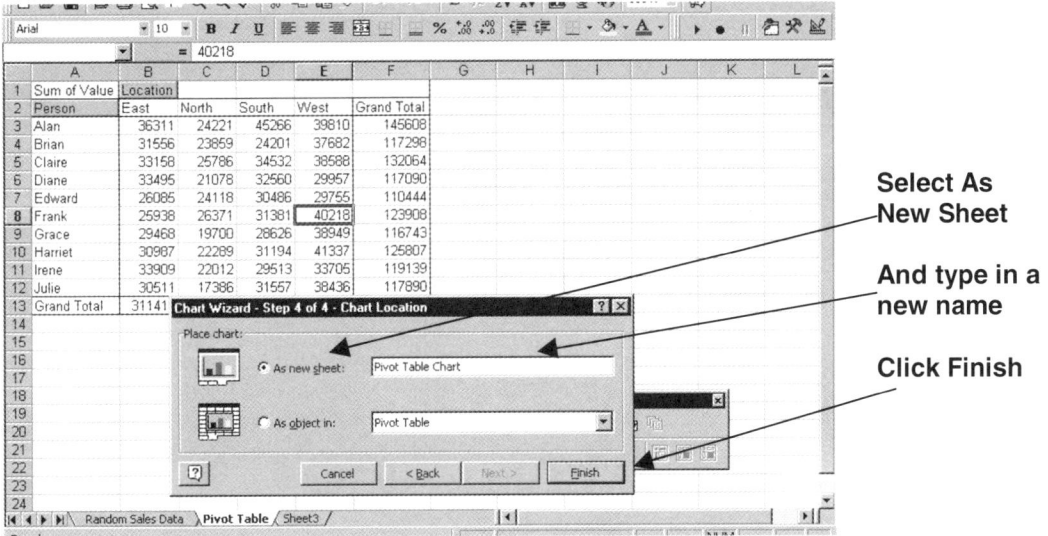

	A	B	C	D	E	F	G	H	I	J	K	L
1	Sum of Value	Location										
2	Person	East	North	South	West	Grand Total						
3	Alan	36311	24221	45266	39810	145608						
4	Brian	31556	23859	24201	37682	117298						
5	Claire	33158	25786	34532	38588	132064						
6	Diane	33495	21078	32560	29957	117090						
7	Edward	26085	24118	30486	29755	110444						
8	Frank	25938	26371	31381	40218	129908						
9	Grace	29468	19700	28626	38949	116743						
10	Harriet	30987	22289	31194	41337	125807						
11	Irene	33909	22012	29513	33705	119139						
12	Julie	30511	17386	31557	38436	117890						
13	Grand Total	31141										

**Select As
New Sheet**

**And type in a
new name**

Click Finish

The chart is displayed in a new sheet.

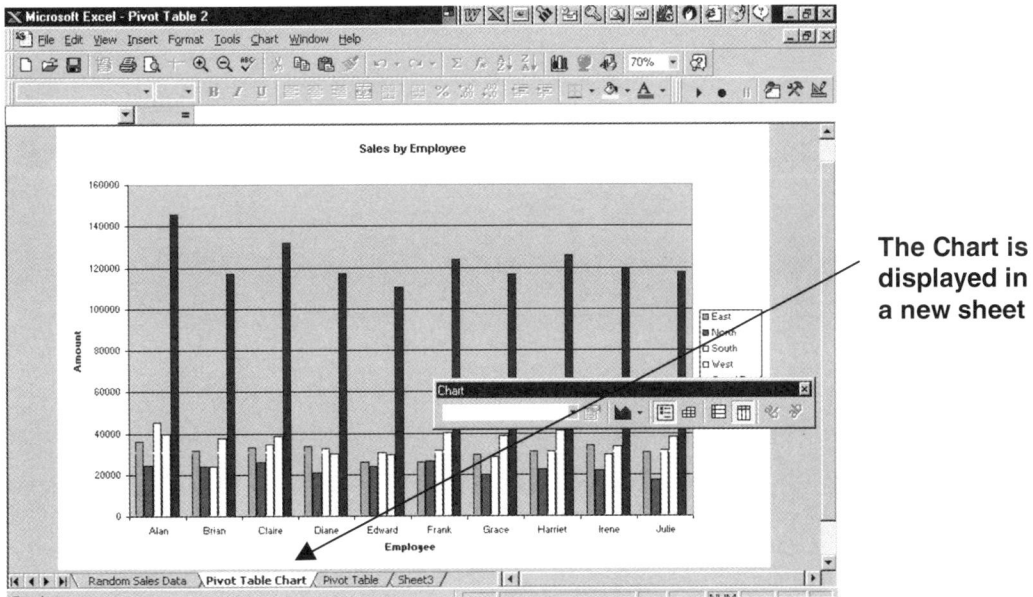

**The Chart is
displayed in
a new sheet**

The charting toolbar is covered in depth later.

NEXT

We have seen how to prepare a reasonably straightforward view of the sales data, suitably summarised.

Next we want to create some more sophisticated views, and to use drag and drop. However, we will finish this chapter here, in order to keep it short.

Chapter Ten
MORE PIVOT TABLES

Look at it like this . . .

In the last chapter we started summarising the data in a PivotTable. In this chapter we want to answer the questions posed in that chapter, and to see how else we can use the PivotTables.

The questions we posed were:

- What are the monthly sales totals?
- How do the sales staff compare?
- Do we have the same market penetration in each area?
- Which items are selling better — Small, Medium or large?

We know from the first pivot table what the sales total is. We have also compared the sales staff as regards value of sales.

We will prepare a PivotTable based on number of items sold, irrespective of value.

SALES BY VOLUME

Open the spreadsheet **Pivot Table 3.xls** and move to cell AA1 on the PivotTable sheet. Click on Pivot Table Wizard and set up a new pivot table.

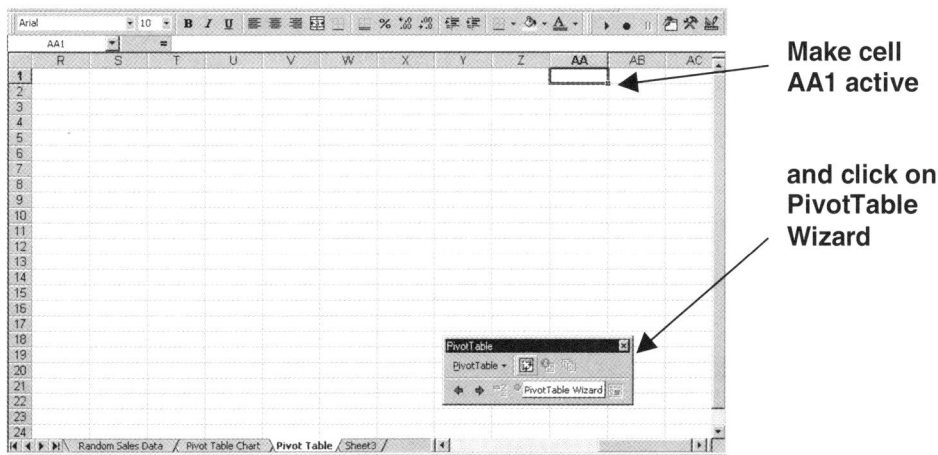

Make cell AA1 active

and click on PivotTable Wizard

Select Another PivotTable from the screen, then select the name of the pivot table.

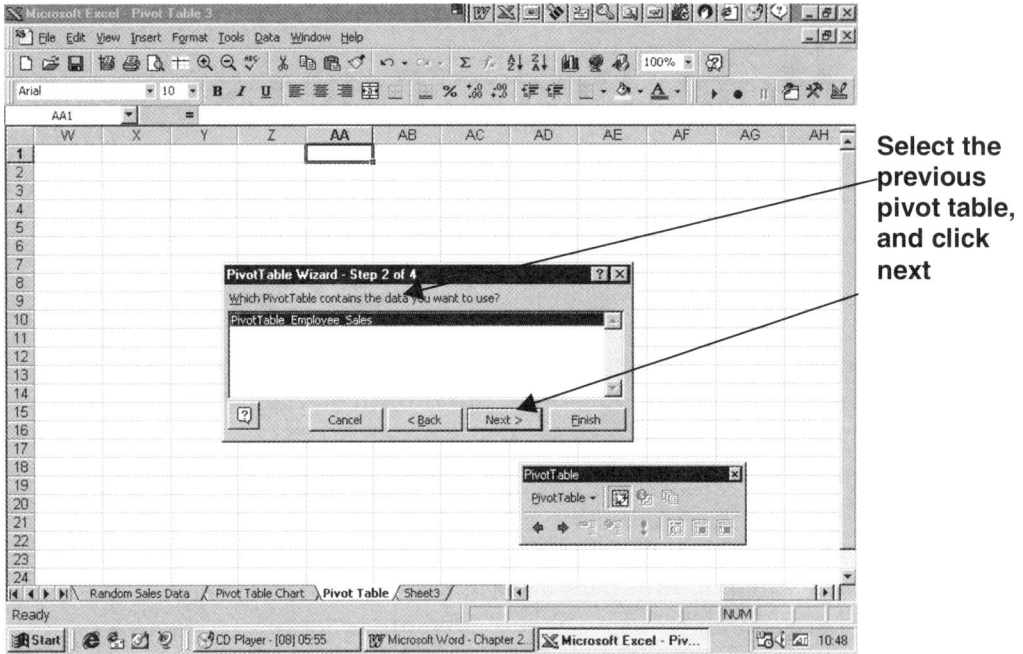

Select the previous pivot table, and click next

This time, the row is Person, the column is location, but we drag Small, Medium and Large into the data area. The description automatically changes to Sum of Small etc.

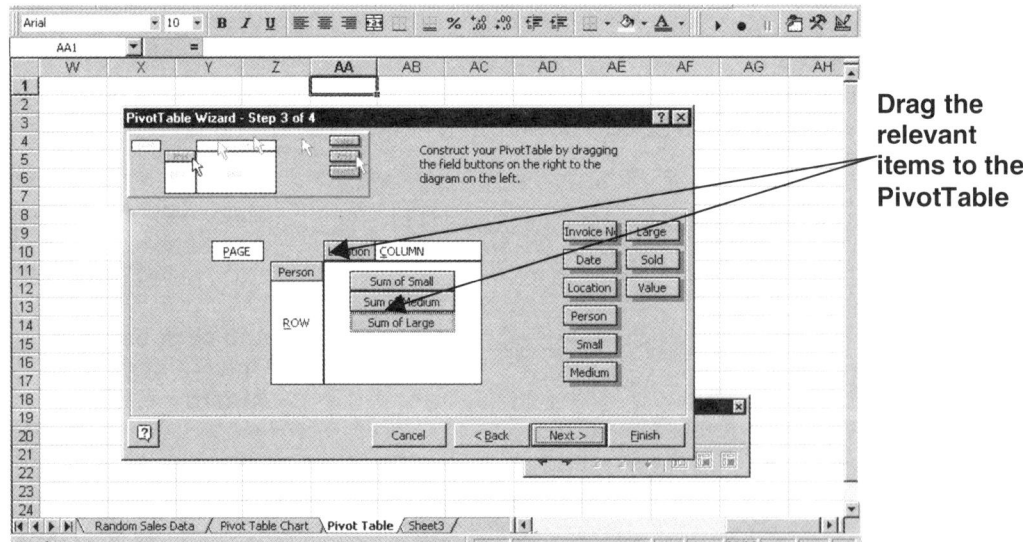

Drag the relevant items to the PivotTable

Click on Next, then Finish. The spreadsheet is shown below, and is saved on the CD as **Pivot Table 3.xls.**

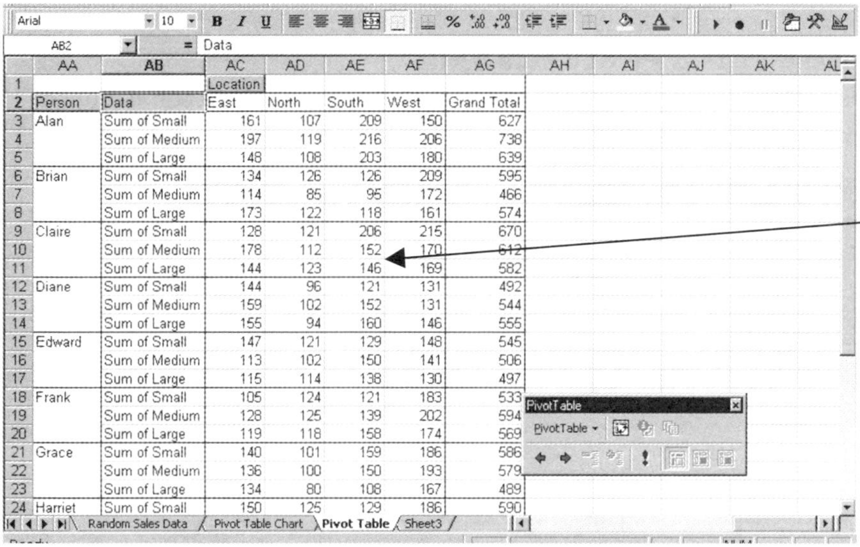

		Location				
Person	Data	East	North	South	West	Grand Total
Alan	Sum of Small	161	107	209	150	627
	Sum of Medium	197	119	216	206	738
	Sum of Large	148	108	203	180	639
Brian	Sum of Small	134	126	126	209	595
	Sum of Medium	114	85	95	172	466
	Sum of Large	173	122	118	161	574
Claire	Sum of Small	128	121	206	215	670
	Sum of Medium	178	112	152	170	612
	Sum of Large	144	123	146	169	582
Diane	Sum of Small	144	96	121	131	492
	Sum of Medium	159	102	152	131	544
	Sum of Large	155	94	160	146	555
Edward	Sum of Small	147	121	129	148	545
	Sum of Medium	113	102	150	141	506
	Sum of Large	115	114	138	130	497
Frank	Sum of Small	105	124	121	183	533
	Sum of Medium	128	125	139	202	594
	Sum of Large	119	118	158	174	569
Grace	Sum of Small	140	101	159	186	586
	Sum of Medium	136	100	150	193	579
	Sum of Large	134	80	108	167	489
Harriet	Sum of Small	150	125	129	186	590

The new PivotTable, showing number of units sold

The same information expressed slightly differently is achieved by dragging the heading Data and dropping it beside the heading location. This is saved on the CD as **Pivot Table 4.xls.**

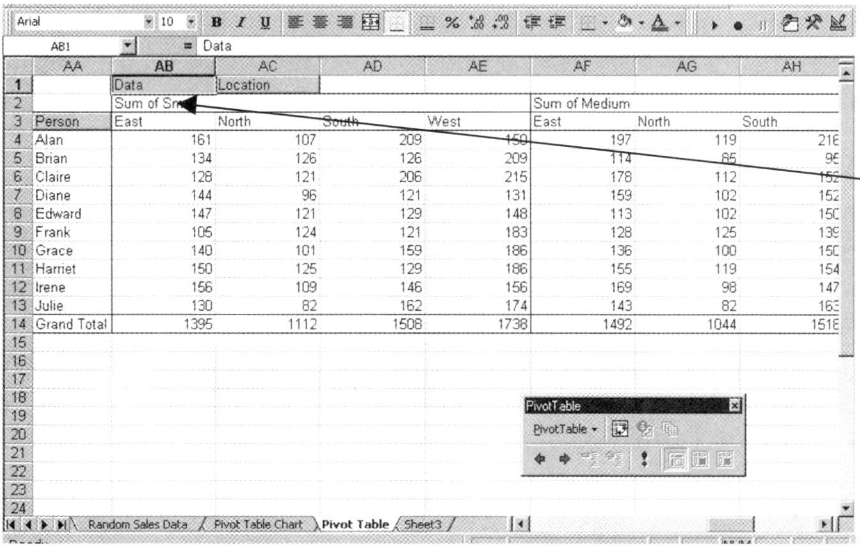

	Data	Location					
	Sum of Sm				Sum of Medium		
Person	East	North	South	West	East	North	South
Alan	161	107	209	150	197	119	216
Brian	134	126	126	209	114	85	95
Claire	128	121	206	215	178	112	152
Diane	144	96	121	131	159	102	152
Edward	147	121	129	148	113	102	150
Frank	105	124	121	183	128	125	139
Grace	140	101	159	186	136	100	150
Harriet	150	125	129	186	155	119	154
Irene	156	109	146	156	169	98	147
Julie	130	82	162	174	143	82	163
Grand Total	1395	1112	1508	1738	1492	1044	1516

The Data heading is dragged to Location and dropped.

The results have been "pivoted", giving the table its name.

Finally, as an alternative presentation, drag the heading Data and drop on the far side of location. The data is reorganised, so that instead of showing Sum of Small for the four regions, then Sum of Medium etc. it displays All Sales in East (Small, Medium and Large), then All Sales in North etc.

This is saved on the CD as **Pivot Table 5.xls.**

Note that the Data heading is dragged on top of Location, and then dropped. If it is dragged into column AD and it is dropped, nothing happens.

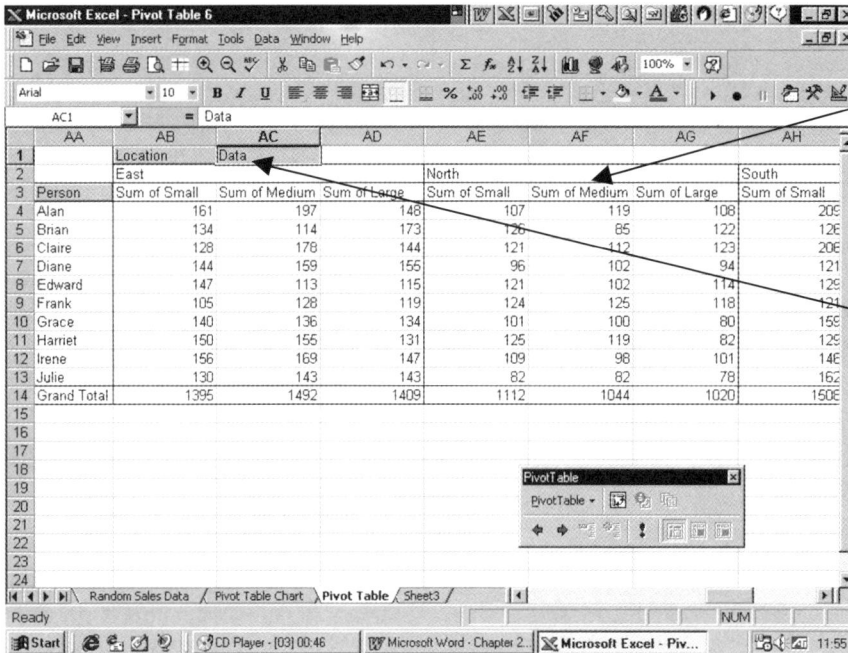

Another view of the information

Data is to the right of Location this time

TOTALS AND DATES

We can see the daily sales for each employee and in total. Set up a new PivotTable on Sheet Three at cell A1. Rename the sheet Pivot Table 1.

Drag the employee name into the Row, the Value into the Data section, and Date into the Page section, on the left of the PivotTable.

The PivotTable is shown below. Any date can be selected from the drop down list, and a daily total of sales is displayed, split between the various staff. It is saved on the CD as **Pivot Table 6.xls.**

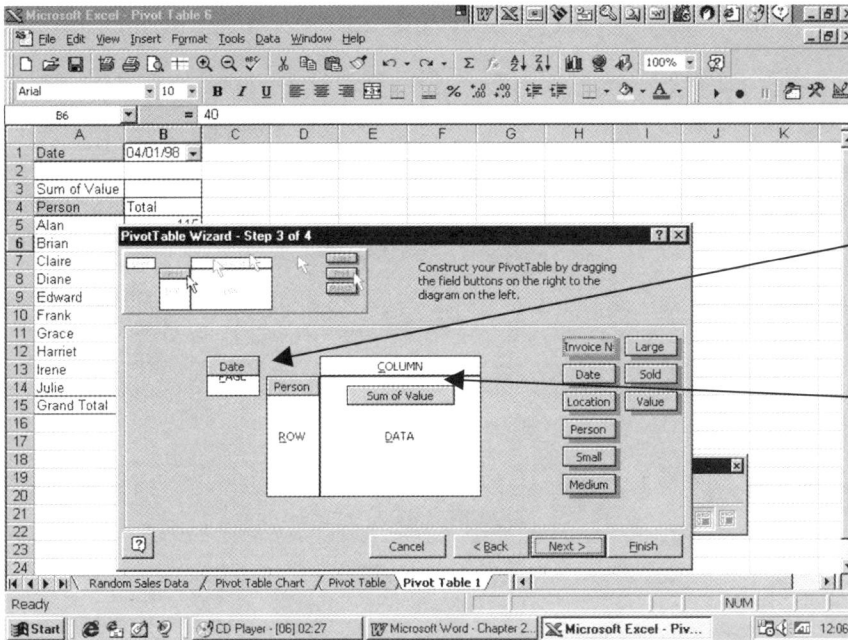

Drag Date to
the Page
section

Note there is
nothing in
the Column
section

The PivotTable shows daily sales totals, after selecting the date from the drop
down list.

Alternatively, the Date heading can be dragged on top of Person and dropped,
and the Person heading can be dragged to cell A1 to work the same way the Date
filter worked previously.

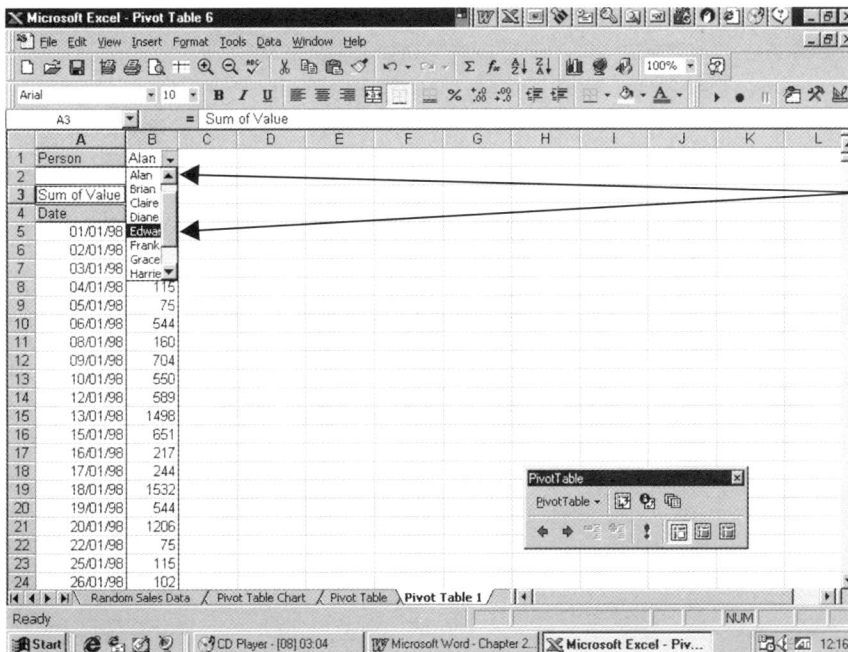

Dragging the
headings
from one to
the other
creates a
daily sales
report by
person

Now that we have a daily sales report we will summarise it into a monthly sales report.

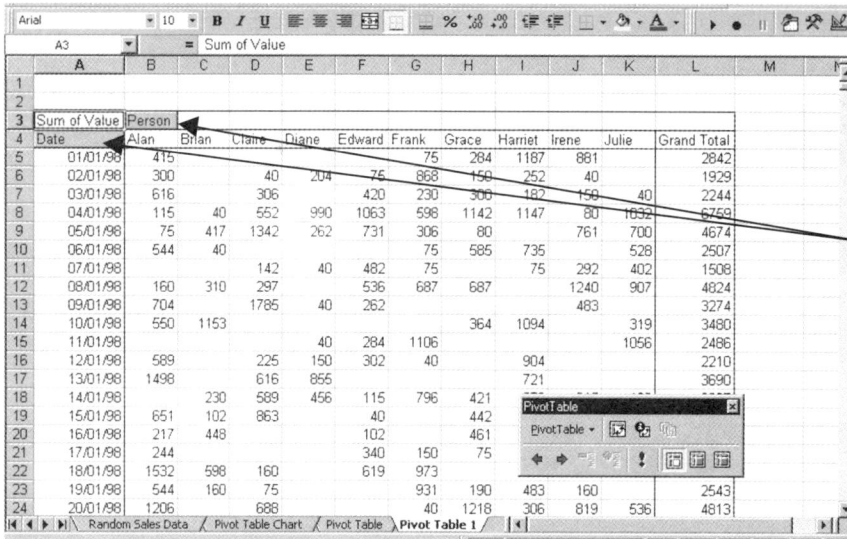

Date	Alan	Brian	Claire	Diane	Edward	Frank	Grace	Harriet	Irene	Julie	Grand Total
01/01/98	415					75	284	1187	881			2842
02/01/98	300		40	204	75	868	150	252	40			1929
03/01/98	616		306		420	230	300	182	150	40		2244
04/01/98	115	40	552	990	1063	598	1142	1147	80	1032		6759
05/01/98	75	417	1342	262	731	306	80		761	700		4674
06/01/98	544	40				75	585	735		528		2507
07/01/98			142	40	482	75		75	292	402		1508
08/01/98	160	310	297		536	687	687		1240	907		4824
09/01/98	704		1785	40	262				483			3274
10/01/98	550	1153				364	1094			319		3480
11/01/98				40	284	1106				1056		2486
12/01/98	589		225	150	302	40		904				2210
13/01/98	1498		616	855				721				3690
14/01/98		230	589	456	115	796	421					
15/01/98	651	102	863		40		442					
16/01/98	217	448			102		461					
17/01/98	244				340	150	75					
18/01/98	1532	598	160		619	973						
19/01/98	544	160	75			931	190	483		160		2543
20/01/98	1206		688			40	1218	306	819	536		4813

The Date and Person labels are dragged to their respective sections

Click on a date in January. The entire line is highlighted. Next, click on the Group arrow in the PivotTable Toolbar

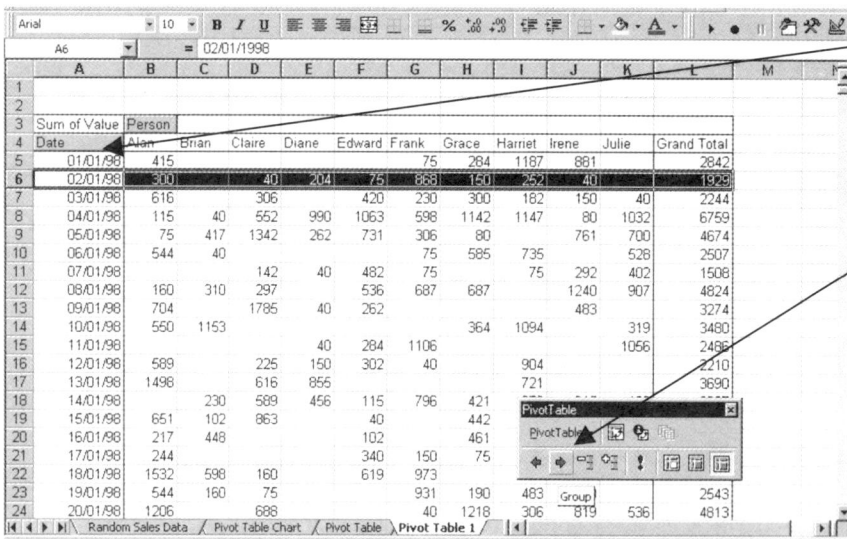

Date	Alan	Brian	Claire	Diane	Edward	Frank	Grace	Harriet	Irene	Julie	Grand Total
01/01/98	415					75	284	1187	881			2842
02/01/98	300		40	204	75	868	150	252	40			1929
03/01/98	616		306		420	230	300	182	150	40		2244
04/01/98	115	40	552	990	1063	598	1142	1147	80	1032		6759
05/01/98	75	417	1342	262	731	306	80		761	700		4674
06/01/98	544	40				75	585	735		528		2507
07/01/98			142	40	482	75		75	292	402		1508
08/01/98	160	310	297		536	687	687		1240	907		4824
09/01/98	704		1785	40	262				483			3274
10/01/98	550	1153				364	1094			319		3480
11/01/98				40	284	1106				1056		2486
12/01/98	589		225	150	302	40		904				2210
13/01/98	1498		616	855				721				3690
14/01/98		230	589	456	115	796	421					
15/01/98	651	102	863		40		442					
16/01/98	217	448			102		461					
17/01/98	244				340	150	75					
18/01/98	1532	598	160		619	973						
19/01/98	544	160	75			931	190	483		160		2543
20/01/98	1206		688			40	1218	306	819	536		4813

Click on a date...

then on Group

The Grouping dialog box appears. Change the Ending At date to 31/1/98 and then recheck the Ending at box — otherwise only one month is displayed.

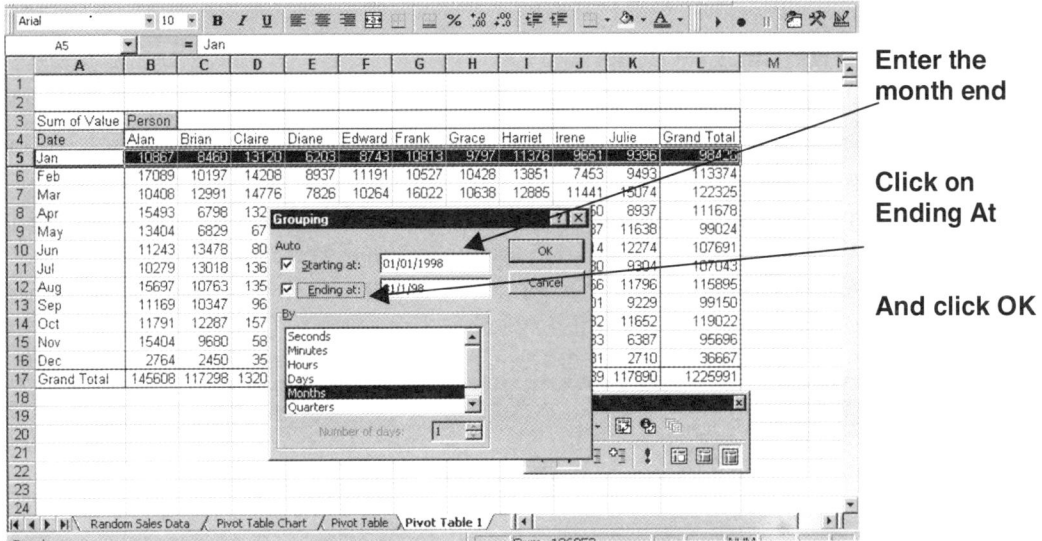

Enter the month end

Click on Ending At

And click OK

The final list looks like this:

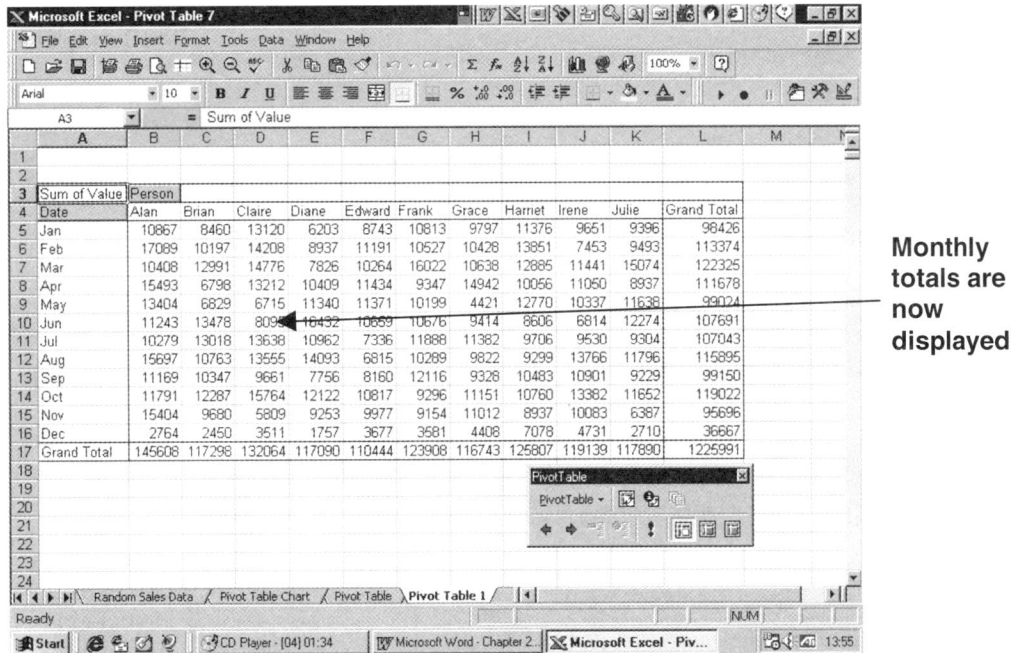

Monthly totals are now displayed

The spreadsheet is saved on the CD as **Pivot Table 7.xls**.

Equally, we could have summarised the figures quarterly if we had wanted, and by volume instead of value.

The quarterly sales volume figures are shown in **Pivot Table 8.xls** on the CD.

THE PIVOTTABLE TOOLBAR

That is enough examples of how we can rearrange our views of the data. We will now look at the tools provided in the toolbar, and see the options available to us when designing or changing a PivotTable.

If we are going to use the toolbar regularly it would be helpful to display it on the toolbar section instead of having it floating in the spreadsheet viewing area.

Drag the toolbar into the toolbar area, and drop it in place. In the screen shot below it is placed beside the VB Toolbox toolbar.

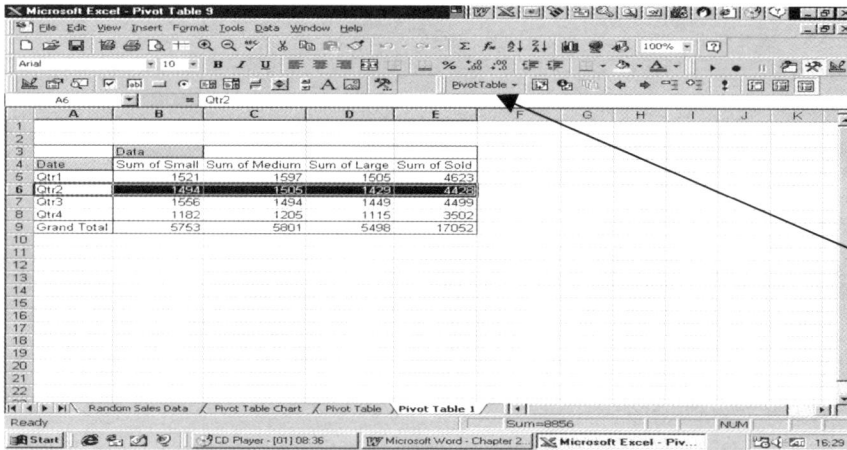

Drag the PivotTable Toolbar and drop in the toolbar area

The toolbar contents are reviewed in the order they appear above.

PIVOT TABLE DROP DOWN MENU

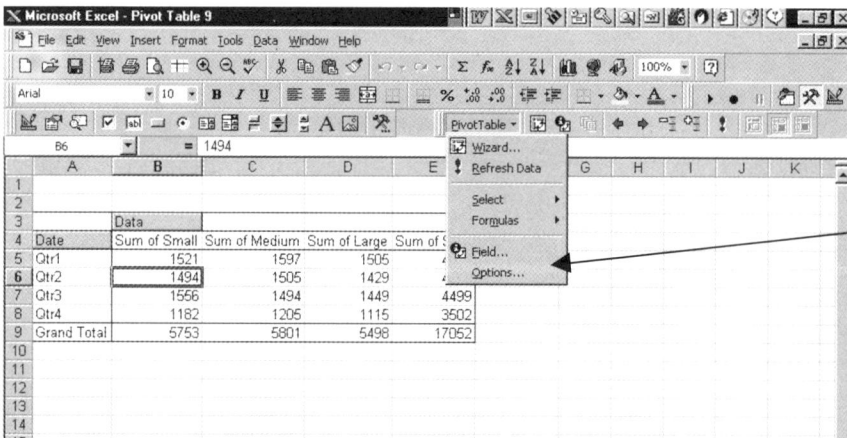

Clicking on the icon displays the drop down menu

If the active cell is in a PivotTable all options on the drop down menu are available

WIZARD

The first item in the drop down menu is the Wizard. We have used this before, when creating a PivotTable.

REFRESH DATA

The second item is Refresh Data. The pivot table will not automatically update if the source data changes. Open **Pivot Table 9.xls**. This contains the same pivot details as before, but the random Data has been re-run.

The SUM formula has been entered below the bottom of the data section of the Random Sales Data sheet, at cells E4007 to H4007, and the formula ='Random Sales Data'!E4007 etc. has been entered in the Pivot Table 1 sheet in order to display the correct totals below the Pivot Table.

The totals are different.

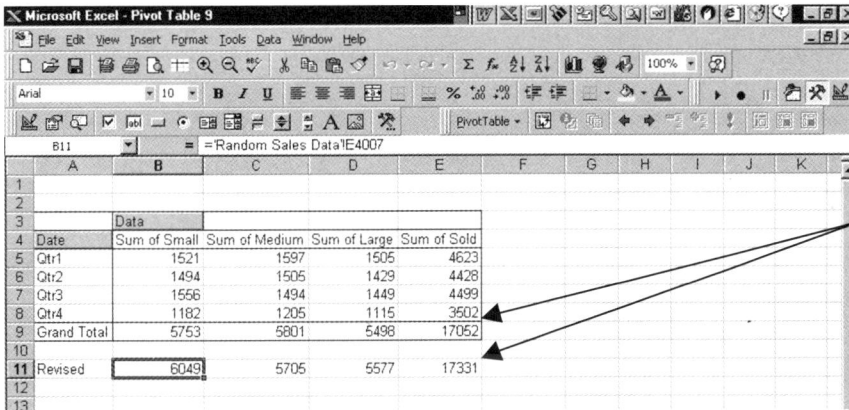

The source data has been amended, but the table did not update

With a cell in the pivot table active, click on the Refresh Data icon.

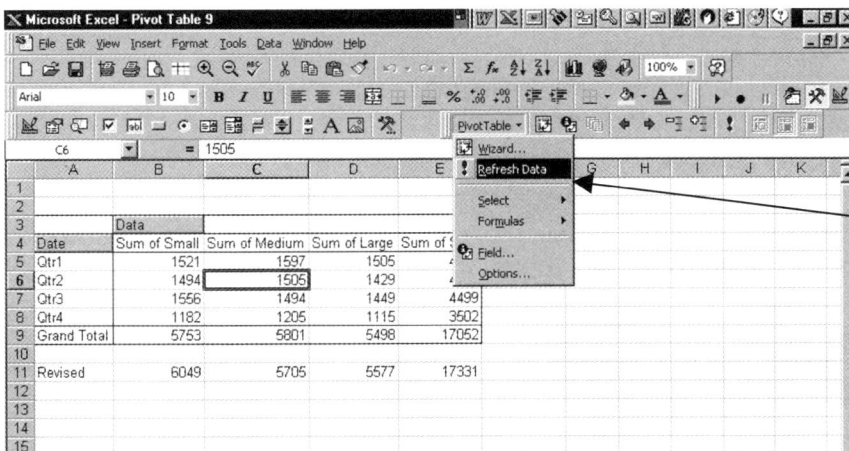

Click on Refresh Data

A warning appears, advising that the table has changed.

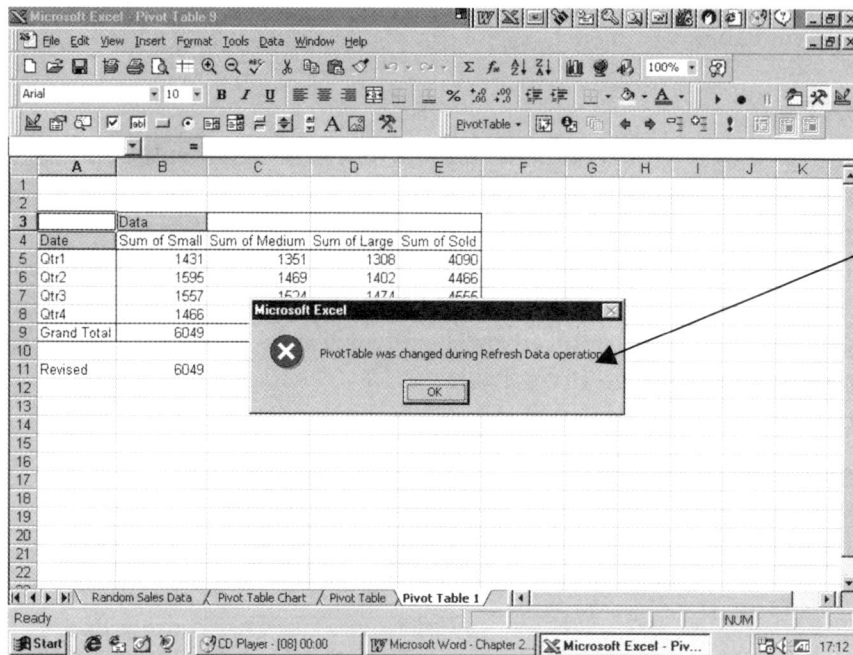

The message advises that there was an adjustment to the pivot table

SELECT

The next item on the drop down menu is Select. Highlighting it activates a sub-menu, which contains the following:

Label	To select the label
Data	To select the data in the table
Label and Data	To select both
Entire Table	To select the entire table
Enable Selection	To allow the selection of a type across a range.

Once the item in the table is selected the wizard can be launched. Double clicking the table will activate a menu offering a changed view of the data etc.

These options are useful if the PivotTable shows product sales in each area. The data etc. is then selected across the range. The screen below shows an example. It is saved on **Pivot Table 10.xls**, as the PivotTable sheet.

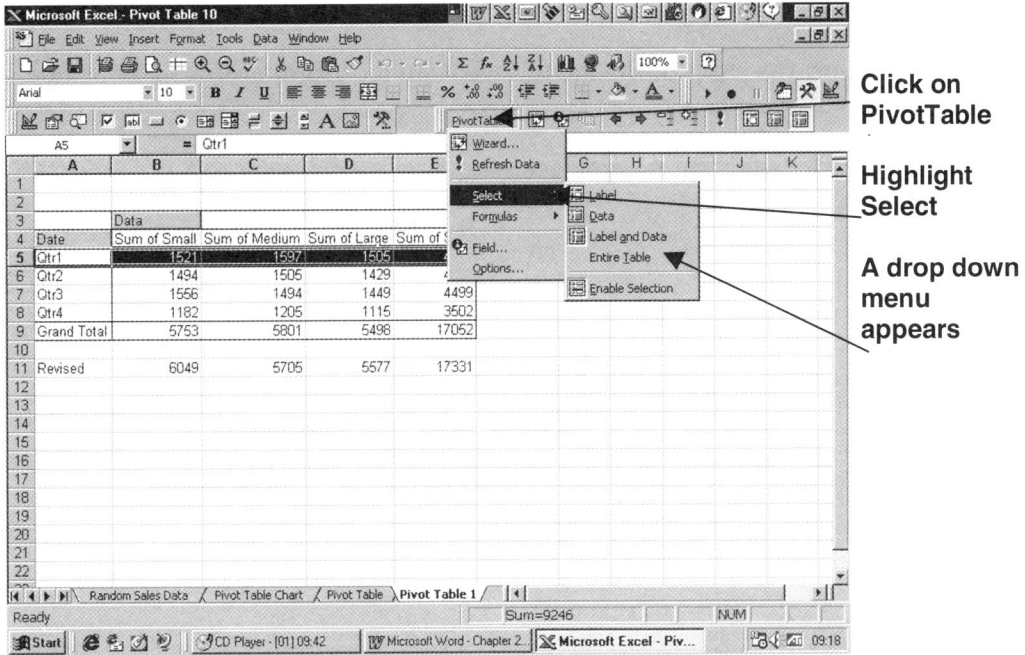

By clicking Enable Selection, the items are selected across a number of headings.

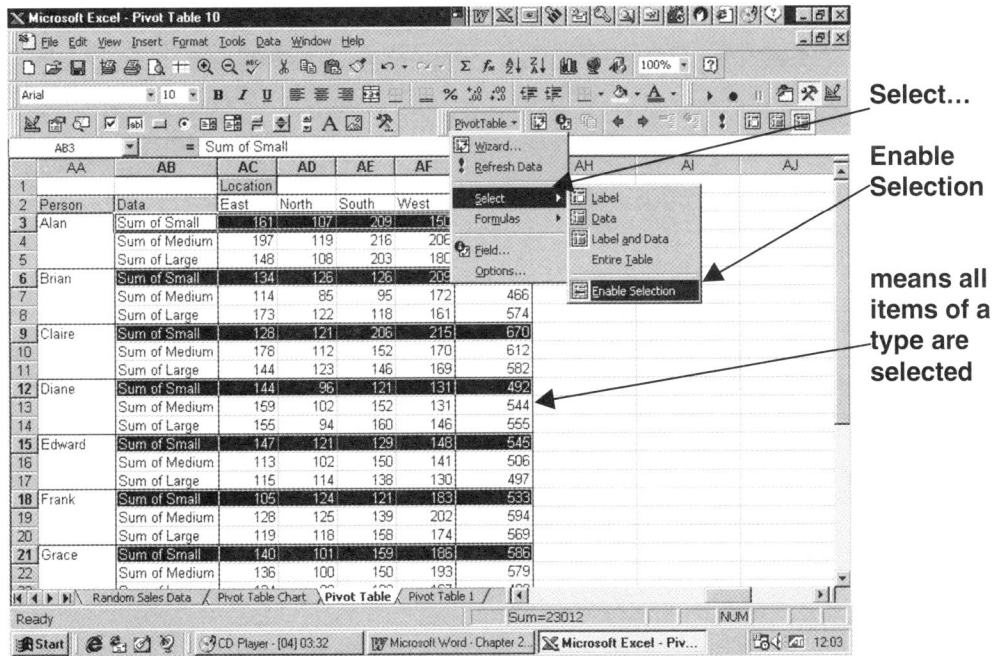

FORMULAS

The next item on the drop down menu is Formulas. Highlighting it activates a sub menu.

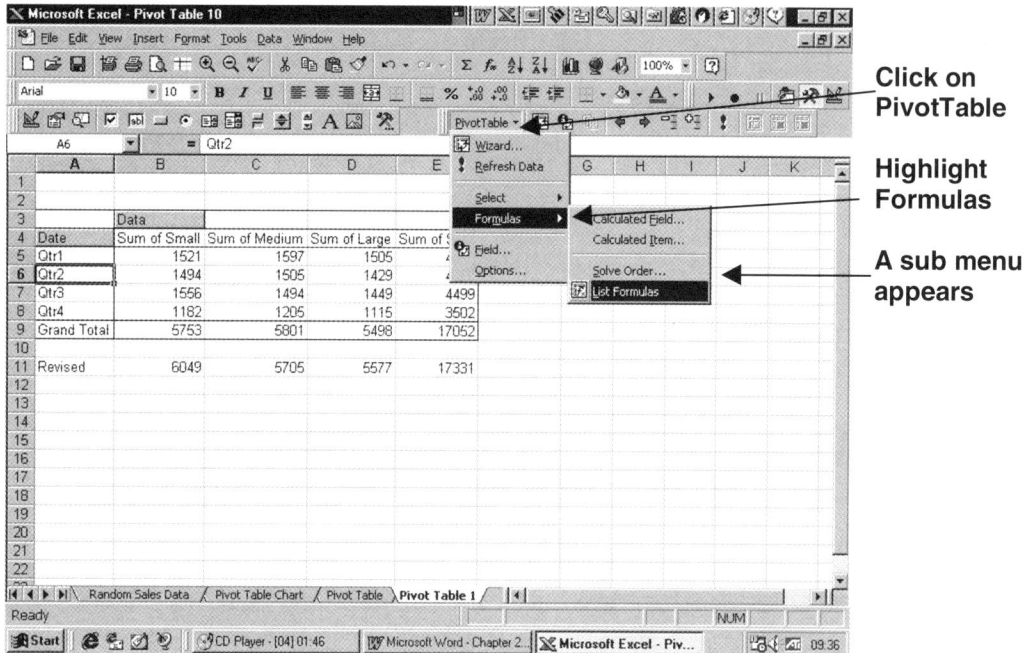

The menu options are:

    Calculated Field...
    Calculated Item...
    Solve Order...
    List Formulas.

We will enter a calculated field in a pivot table, to demonstrate its use. Open **Pivot Table 10.xls** and select the Pivot Table tab.

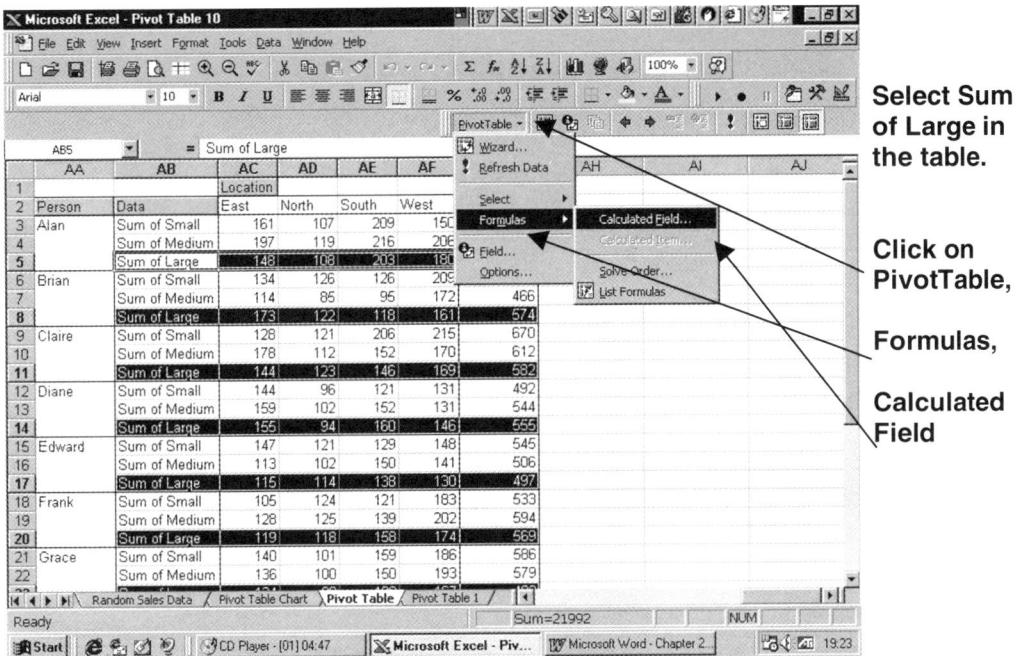

Select Sum
of Large in
the table.

Click on
PivotTable,

Formulas,

Calculated
Field

The Insert Calculated Field dialog box appears.

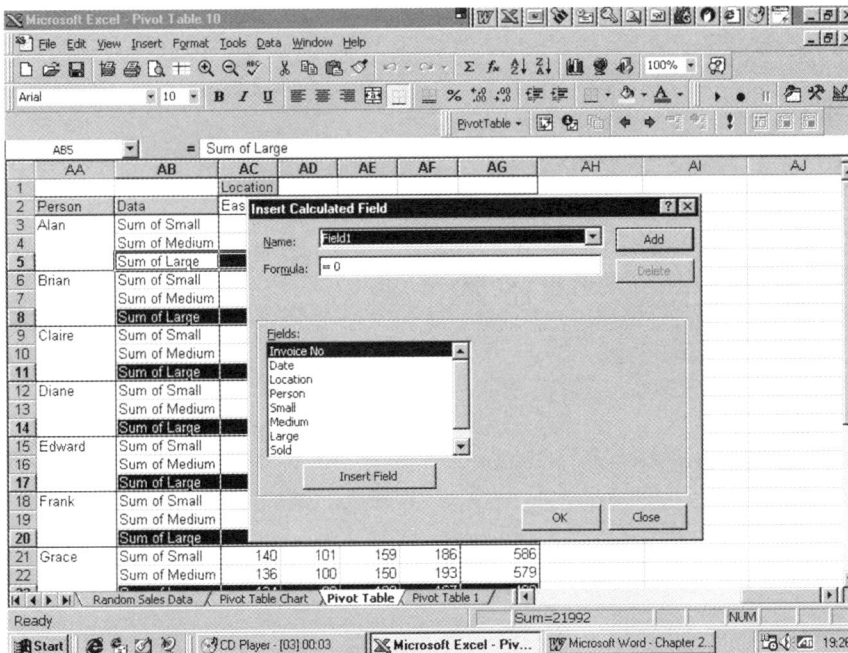

Replace the name Field1 with Total Units Sold.

The Formula box shows = 0.

Highlight Small in the list box below, and click Insert Field.

Press +

Highlight Medium in the list box below, and click Insert Field.

Press +

Highlight Large in the list box below, and click Insert Field.

Click OK.

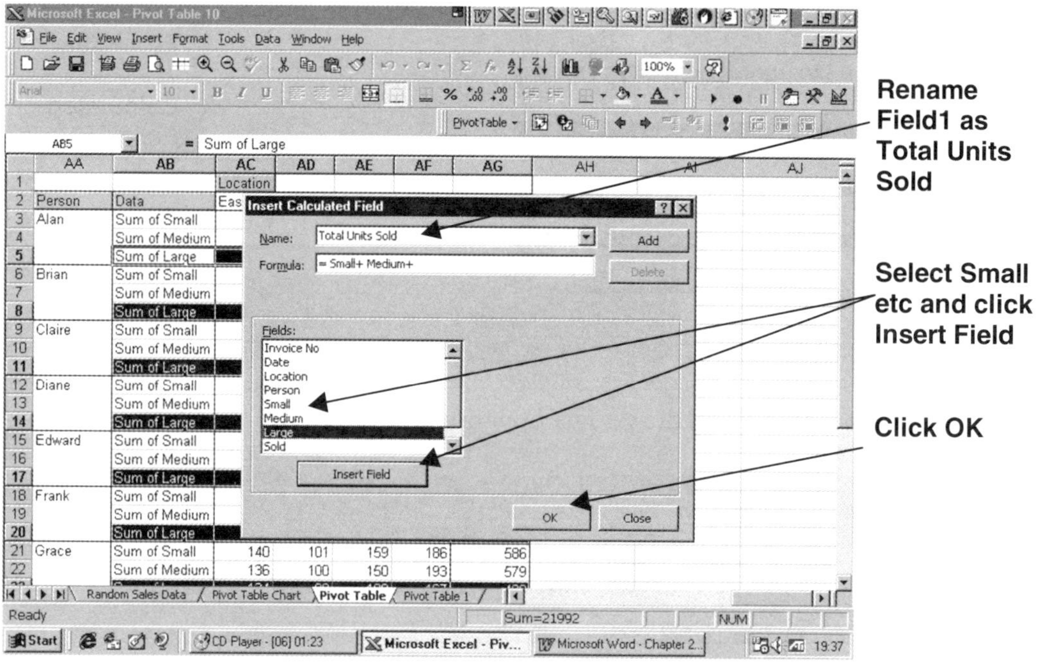

The new field is entered. It totals the units sold in each location for each person, and produces a grand total at the end of the pivot table.

	AA	AB	AC	AD	AE	AF	AG
1			Location				
2	Person	Data	East	North	South	West	Grand Total
3	Alan	Sum of Small	161	107	209	150	627
4		Sum of Medium	197	119	216	206	738
5		Sum of Large	148	108	203	180	639
6		Sum of Total Units Sold	506	334	628	536	2004
7	Brian	Sum of Small	134	126	126	209	595
8		Sum of Medium	114	85	95	172	466
9		Sum of Large	173	122	118	161	574
10		Sum of Total Units Sold	421	333	339	542	1635
11	Claire	Sum of Small	128	121	206	215	670
12		Sum of Medium	178	112	152	170	612
13		Sum of Large	144	123	146	169	582
14		Sum of Total Units Sold	450	356	504	554	1864
15	Diane	Sum of Small	144	96	121	131	492
16		Sum of Medium	159	102	152	131	544
17		Sum of Large	155	94	160	146	555
18		Sum of Total Units Sold	458	292	433	408	1591
19	Edward	Sum of Small	147	121	129	148	545
20		Sum of Medium	113	102	150	141	506
21		Sum of Large	115	114	138	130	497
22		Sum of Total Units Sold	375	337	417	419	1548

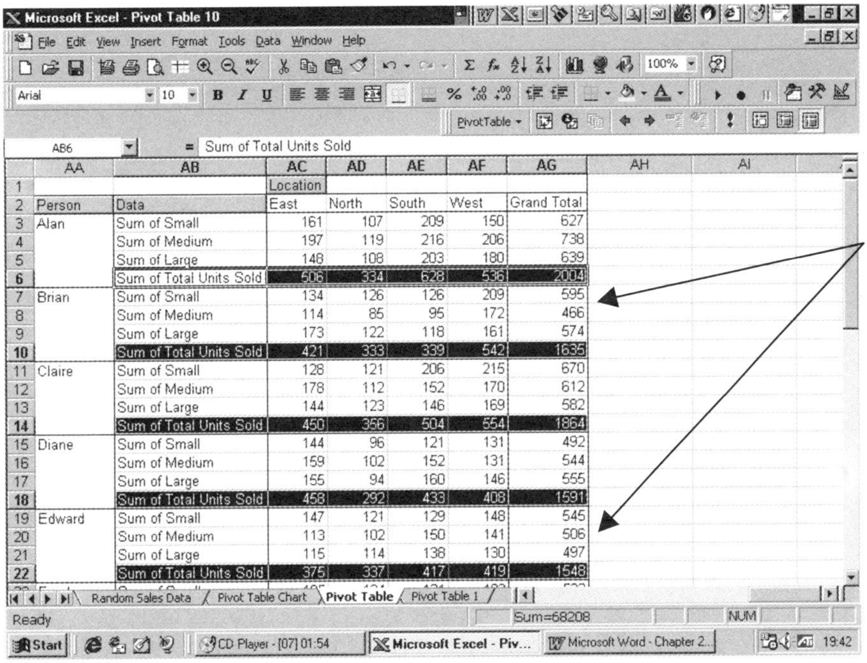

The total of the units is calculated and displayed

The other options within the sub menu relate to calculating for an item, changing the order of calculation within the formulae established, and inserting a new sheet to display the order of calculation in writing.

The spreadsheet is saved as **Pivot Table 11.xls**.

NEXT

Pivot tables are an excellent way of summarising large amounts of data. However, in the next chapter we look at ways of preparing and reviewing projected data.

Chapter Eleven

Data Tables

It could be this, or this, or this . . .

Pivot Tables are an excellent way of summarising a large amount of data, and for seeing relationships that may not otherwise be apparent. But what about projections? For these we need Data Tables.

What is a Data Table?

Normally we would think of projections of sales as a best, worst, expected situation. Data Tables allow a large number of permutations to be summarised in one table, so that a broader perspective can be taken.

Marketing Budget Example

A simple example will demonstrate the table.

The sales team is looking at the marketing budget. At present we spend £20,000, sell 1000 units at £50 each, and the marginal cost of producing the items is £20.

If they increased the marketing activity by £20,000 they think they should sell a further 500 units — at best a further 1000, at worst another 250.

Is it worth pursuing?

Step 1

First of all, set up the above details into a Profit and Loss format. It is saved on the CD as **Data Table 1.xls**.

Set up the initial details in a simple Profit and Loss format

Step 2

Set up the row and column headings for the values we want to compute. In this case we will set up the table at AA1 etc. as follows:

Cell AA1	Sales Example	**Cell AA3**	Data Table
Cells AB5 to AJ5	AutoFill the cells, starting at 20000 in steps of 4000. End value is £52000	**Cells AA6 to AA21**	AutoFill the cells, starting at 1000 in steps of 100. End value is 2500

The range is extended beyond that originally given so that the sales team can consider the results outside their original Best/Worst/Expected guesses.

Step 3

At the intersection of the rows and columns (cell AA 5) enter the formula = E14. The cell therefore shows the Net Contribution per the Profit And Loss Account in A1 etc.

In order to distinguish it in the table the cell has been formatted to display blue.

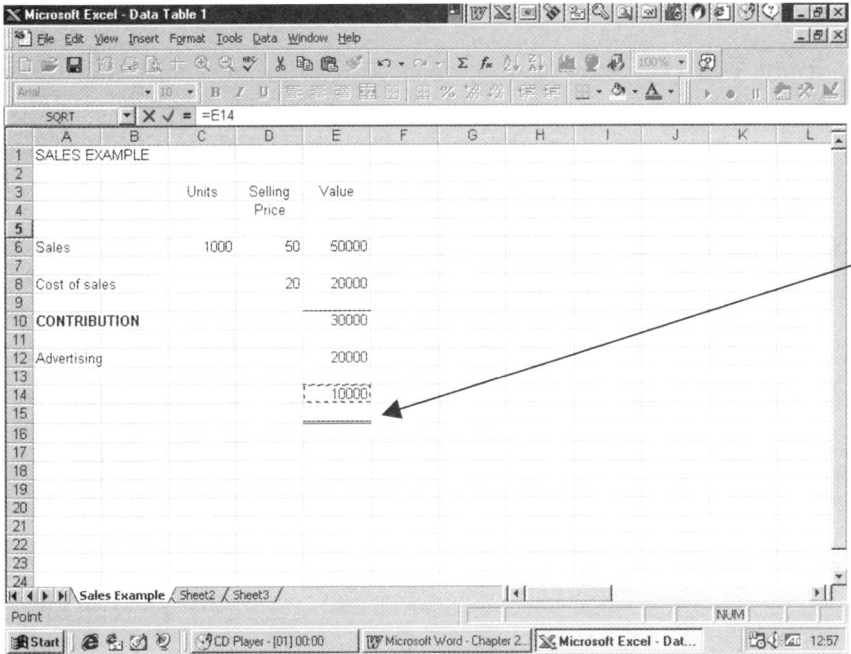

In cell AA5
type = then
press
Ctrl+Home

Then select
cell E14 and
press return

Step 4

Select all cells in the table — in this case cells AA5 to AJ21. Select Data from the menu, then Table.

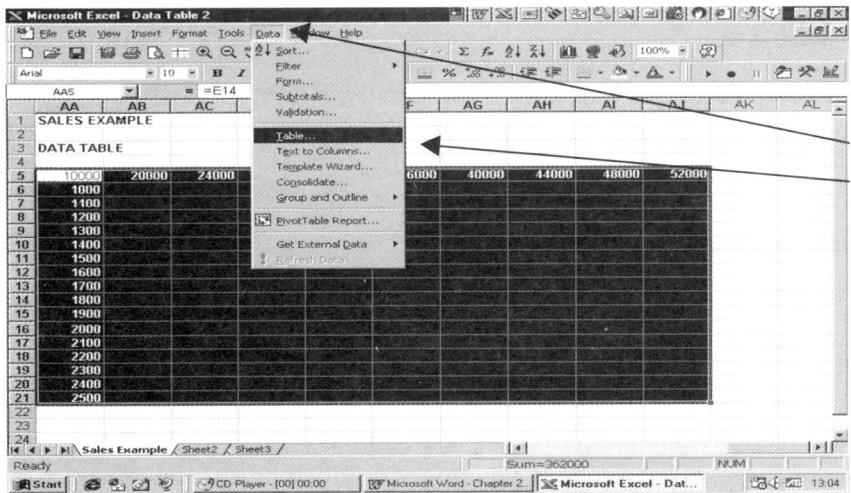

Highlight
the cells,
then select
Data…

… Table

Step 5

Select the row input cell (i.e. advertising) from the original Profit and Loss Account (cell E12), and the column input cell (i.e. units sold) at cell C6. Notice that the cell references are entered as absolute addresses. Click on OK, and the table is populated. It is saved on the CD as **Data Table 2.xls**.

The table is generated.

Net contribution at a range of marketing costs and a range of units sold can easily be read off

Step 6

The table is now completed, and the sales team can consider "what if" variations. However, to make the table even easier to read, formatting the results is a great benefit.

CONDITIONAL FORMATTING

First of all, we want to highlight all instances where the net contribution is actually less than we are achieving at present. We want to display in red all figures that are less than £10000.

Highlight the table results (NOT the headings), then select Format from the menu, then Conditional Formatting.

The Conditional Formatting dialogue box appears. Click on the down arrow in the box that contains the word "between". A list of formulae appears. Select "Less Than".

Click in the next box to activate it, and click on cell AA5 (value 10000) to select it.

This sets the criteria for the cells. Next we want to select the type of formatting we want to use.

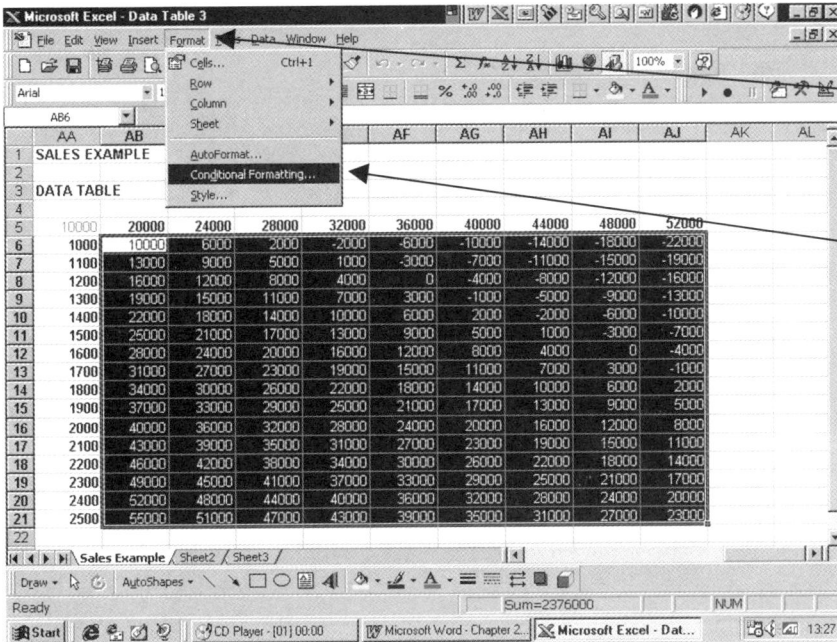

Highlight the table figures, then select Format, then Conditional Formatting

Choose italic for the font style, and red as the colour.

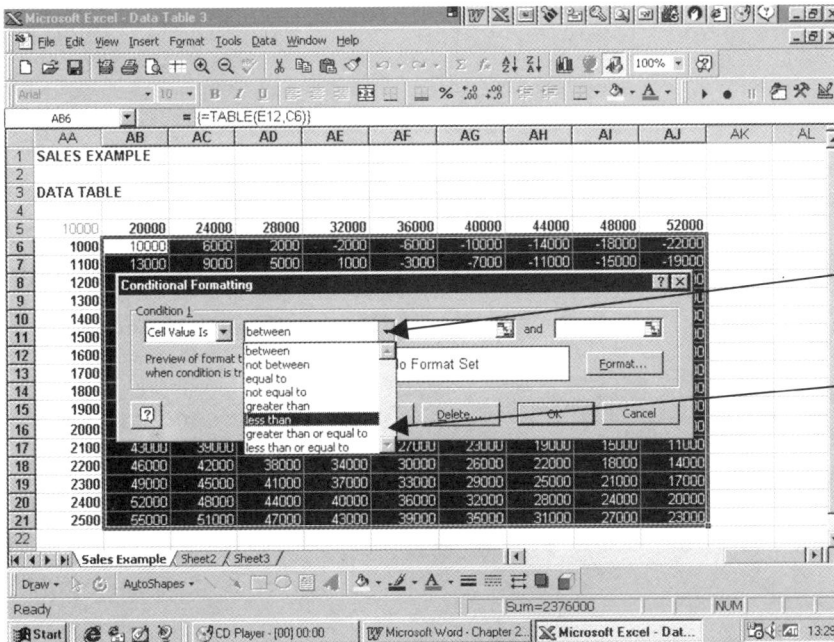

The Conditional Formatting dialogue box is displayed.

Select the drop down arrow

and choose Less Than

The spreadsheet is saved as **Data Table 3.xls** on the CD.

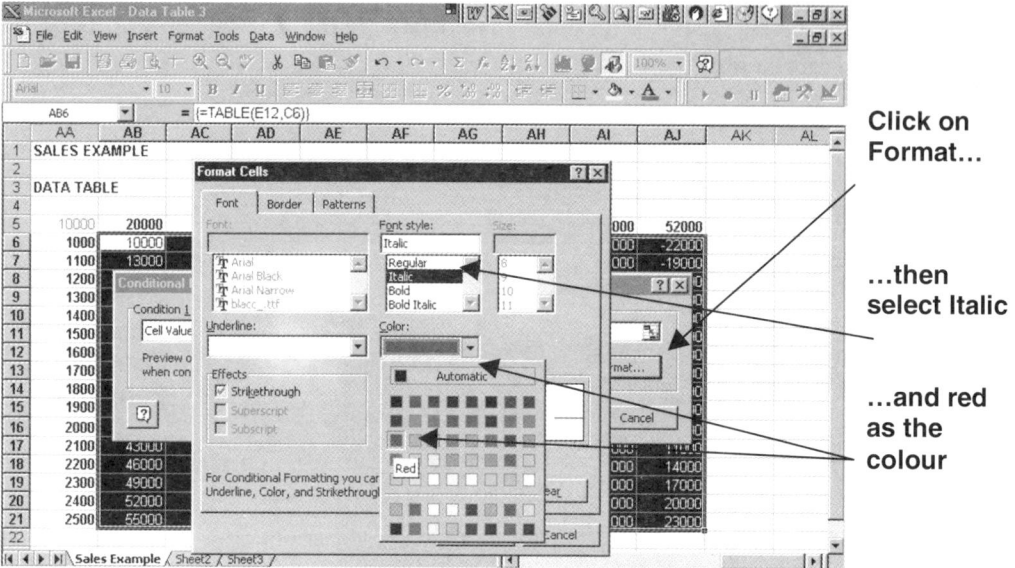

Click on
Format...

...then
select Italic

...and red
as the
colour

What else can we achieve or improve?

First of all, we will format to display negative figures (i.e. net deficits) in brackets. Select all cells in the table, and right click. Select Format Cells . . .

In the Number tab select custom, and amend the format for displaying negative numbers from #,##0;-#,##0 to #,##0__;(#,##0);Nil. This shows the negative figures in brackets, and displays the word Nil if the cell contents are zero.

Next, move (drag and drop) the table to AB5, add headings for Advertising and Units, put arrows to show the extent of the range, and fill in the cells with yellow.

The spreadsheet is saved on the CD as **Data Table 4.xls**.

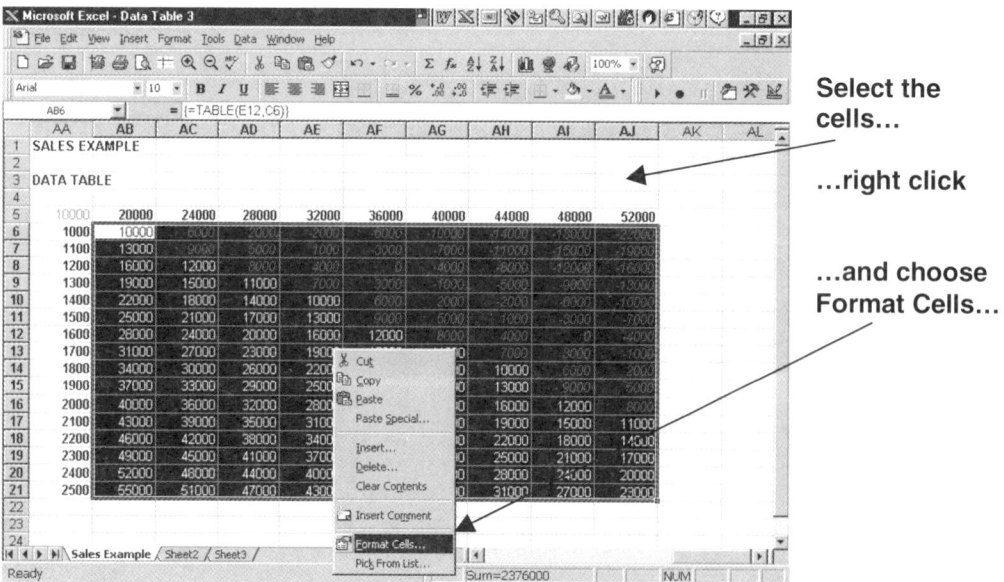

Select the
cells...

...right click

...and choose
Format Cells...

Microsoft Excel - Data Table 4

File Edit View Insert Format Tools Data Window Help

Arial   ▼ 10 ▼   **B** *I* U

AD7   = {=TABLE(E12,C6)}

	AA	AB	AC	AD	AE	AF	AG	AH	AI	AJ	AK	AL
1	SALES EXAMPLE											
2												
3	DATA TABLE											
4			Advertising									
5		10000	20000	24000	28000	32000	36000	40000	44000	48000	52000	
6	Units	1000	10,000	6,000	2,000	(2,000)	(6,000)	(10,000)	(14,000)	(18,000)	(22,000)	
7	Sold	1100	13,000	9,000	5,000	1,000	(3,000)	(7,000)	(11,000)	(15,000)	(19,000)	
8		1200	16,000	12,000	8,000	4,000	Nil	(4,000)	(8,000)	(12,000)	(16,000)	
9		1300	19,000	15,000	11,000	7,000	3,000	(1,000)	(5,000)	(9,000)	(13,000)	
10		1400	22,000	18,000	14,000	10,000	6,000	2,000	(2,000)	(6,000)	(10,00)	
11		1500	25,000	21,000	17,000	13,000	9,000	5,000	1,000	(3,000)	(7,000)	
12		1600	28,000	24,000	20,000	16,000	12,000	8,000	4,000	Nil	(4,000)	
13		1700	31,000	27,000	23,000	19,000	15,000	11,000	7,000	3,000	(000)	
14		1800	34,000	30,000	26,000	22,000	18,000	14,000	10,000	6,000	2,000	
15		1900	37,000	33,000	29,000	25,000	21,000	17,000	13,000	9,000	5,000	
16		2000	40,000	36,000	32,000	28,000	24,000	20,000	16,000	12,000	8,000	
17		2100	43,000	39,000	35,000	31,000	27,000	23,000	19,000	15,000	11,000	
18		2200	46,000	42,000	38,000	34,000	30,000	26,000	22,000	18,000	14,000	
19		2300	49,000	45,000	41,000	37,000	33,000	29,000	25,000	21,000	17,000	
20		2400	52,000	48,000	44,000	40,000	36,000	32,000	28,000	24,000	20,000	
21		2500	55,000	51,000	47,000	43,000	39,000	35,000	31,000	27,000	23,000	
22												
23												
24												

Sales Example / Sheet2 / Sheet3 /

Ready   NUM

Start   CD Player - [00] 00:00   Microsoft Word - Chapter 2...   Microsoft Excel - Dat...   14:43

Annotations:
- Headings added
- Cells formatted to show red if less than 10,000
- Negative figures in brackets
- Zero displays as Nil

FURTHER FORMATTING

This level of formatting is probably sufficient. However, one more possibility to consider is highlighting those values that are "cost effective". If we take the view that we will not spend an extra £1 on advertising unless we expect to generate an extra £1 of net profit, we will therefore avoid the risk of spending money on advertising without an appropriate level of reward.

To complete this task we must complete additional conditional formatting.

Highlight the cells in the table and select Format from the menu, then Conditional Format. The dialogue box appears as before, and the boxes are already completed.

Select Add>> and a second line of (empty) input boxes appears. Select "Greater Than" and in the formula section choose cells AB5, then +AC5 -AC5.

The formula appears in the input box as =$AB$5+$AC$5-$AC$5. In English it reads "Contribution at beginning, plus advertising in row AC5, minus advertising in row AC5".

Change the formula to =$AB$5+AC$5-$AC$5. This reads "Contribution at beginning, plus advertising in THIS row, minus advertising in row AC5".

The finished spreadsheet is saved on the CD as **Data Table 5.xls**.

The sales/advertising levels that meet the "value for money/risk vs. reward" target we set are displayed in green. The sales/advertising levels that result in a contribution level at least equal to the level that we are achieving to date, but are below our "value for money/ risk vs. reward" target, are displayed in black. And the sales/advertising levels that equate to a fall from our present contribution levels are displayed in red, with negatives in brackets.

We could have used cell fill colours as well, instead of just font colour.

NEXT

In this chapter we have explored another highly effective means of analysing a range of outcomes. The proper presentation of these results, in terms of conditional formatting and cell formatting is visually very useful.

In the next chapter we look at Solver.

Chapter Twelve

SOLVER

And remember: You can't exceed this, or this, or this . . .

A data table is useful for looking at a range of possible outcomes in a two dimensional sense. Its purpose is to quickly refer to the broad options of "what if" and then to hone down the number of alternatives.

A more complicated model can be built using Solver. This allows constraints to be built into the model and, as before, we will build a model in order to explain how to use it.

PRODUCTION EXAMPLE

In the database we built in **Section One** we had three products for sale — Small, Medium and Large. In this example we assume that the Sales Team are being asked to push the most profitable line in order to maximise profit.

However, the amount of machine time required to produce each item is different, a minimum amount of each type must be produced, the amount of finance available is limited . . .

The full details are listed below.

Types of goods	Small, Medium, Large
Selling prices	£40, £75, £102
Variable costs	£15, £35, £45
Machine time	10, 17, 27
Maximum machine hours available	30,000
Minimum sales of each type	25% of the total production
Maximum sales of each type	500, 750, 750
Maximum total cost of sales	£40,000
Objective	**Maximise the Total Contribution**

Step 1

Set up the above details in a spreadsheet. It is saved on the CD as **Solver 1.xls**.

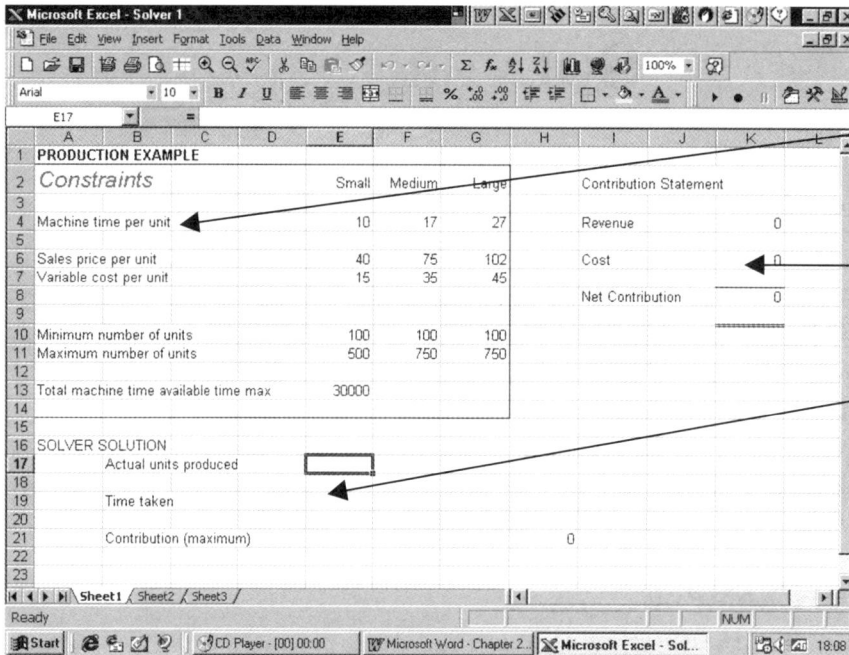

A table of the parameters is set up...

... a contribution statement...

...and a section for the output of the Solver answers

Step 2

Start Solver. Select Tools from the menu, then Solver.

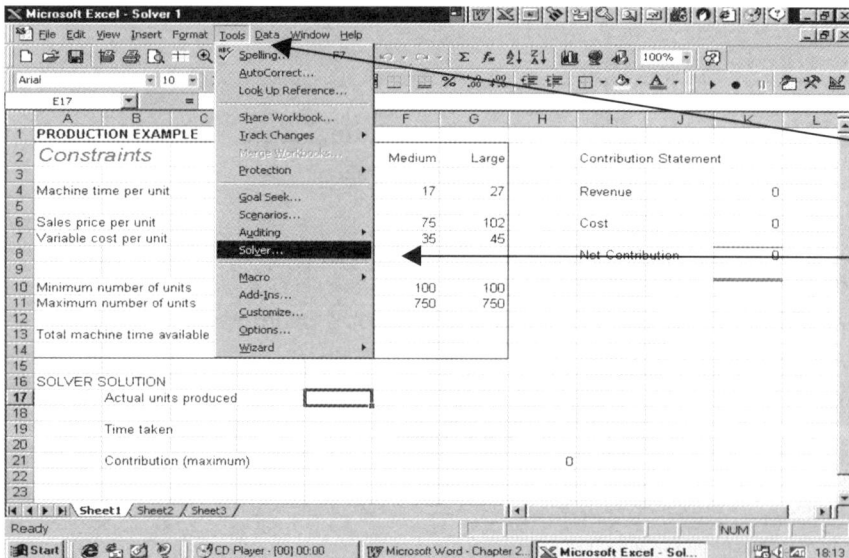

Click on Tools

Solver

Step 3

Solver starts, and we select the cells with the parameters etc. The first cell to select is the Target Cell. This is the Net Contribution in cell K8. Absolute references are entered when it is selected with the mouse.

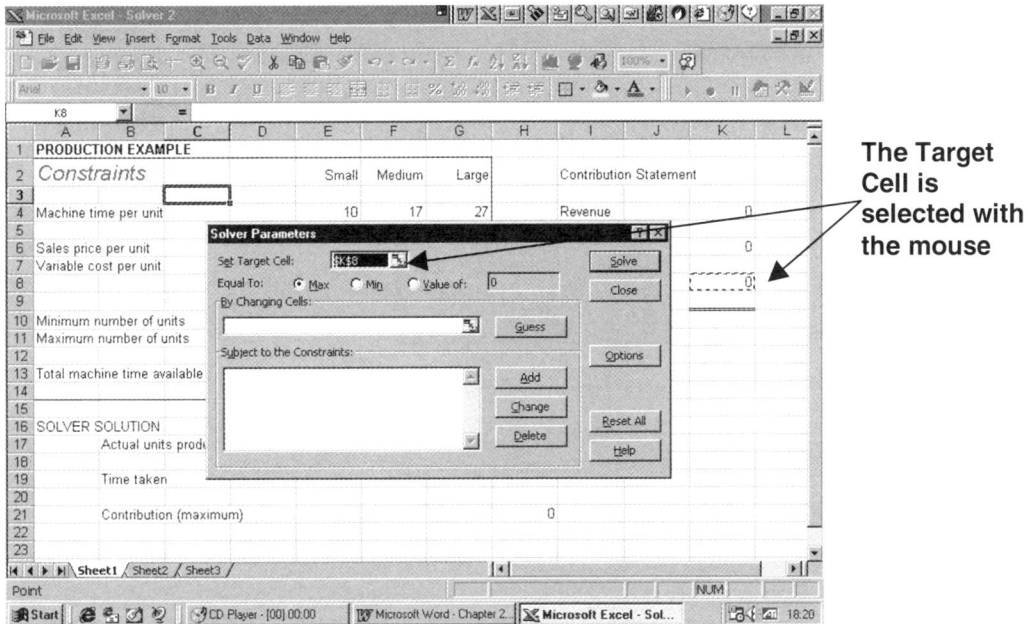

The Target Cell is selected with the mouse

The next input box to complete is By Changing Cells. Minimise the box and click and drag to select cells E17 to G17. Absolute cell references are entered automatically.

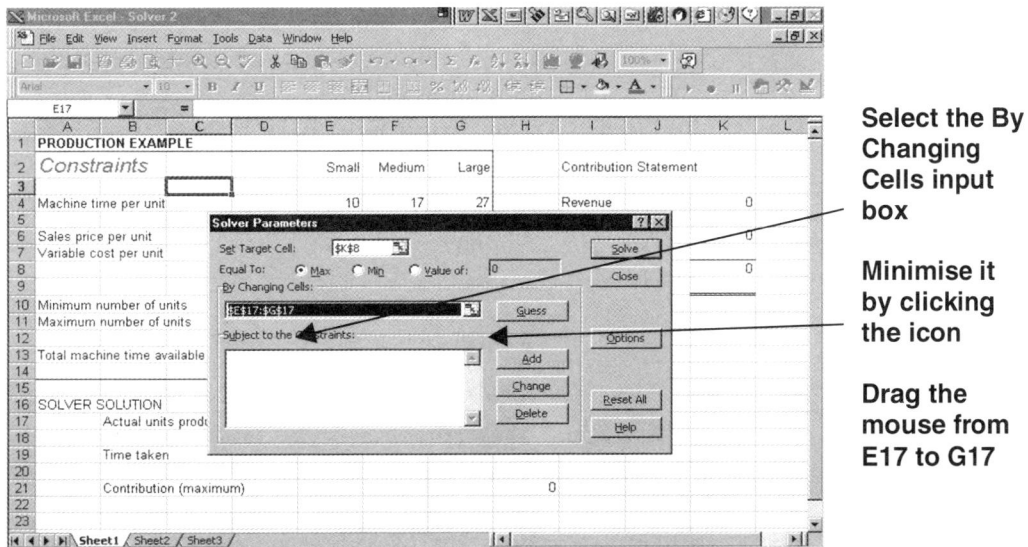

Select the By Changing Cells input box

Minimise it by clicking the icon

Drag the mouse from E17 to G17

We will now define the constraints. Click on Add. An input box appears for setting up the criteria.

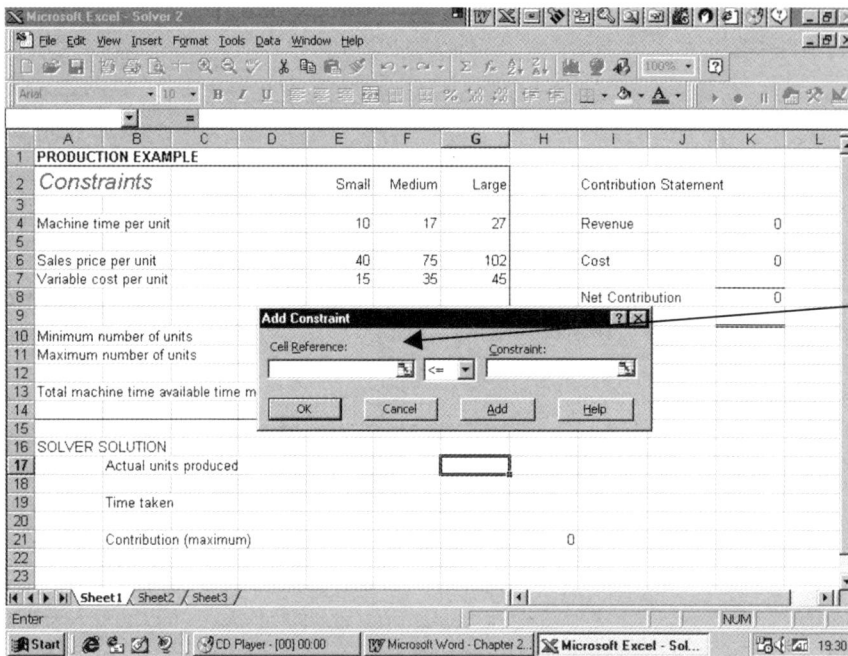

The Add button was pressed. The Add Constraint input box appears

The various constraints we want to enter are given below.

Cell Reference	Sign	Constant	English
$E$17	< =	$E$11	Small units is less than or equal to the maximum allowed
$E$17	=	Integer	The answer must be in whole numbers
$E$17	> =	$E$10	Small units is more than or equal to the minimum allowed
$E$17	> =	$H$17/4	The answer must be at least ¼ of the total units
$F$17	< =	$F$11	As above
$F$17	=	Integer	As above
$F$17	> =	$F$10	As above
$F$17	> =	$F$17/4	As above
$G$17	< =	$G$11	As above
$G$17	=	Integer	As above
$G$17	> =	$G$10	As above
$G$17	> =	$H$17/4	As above
$H$19	< =	$E$13	As above
$K$6	< =	40000	Variable cost is less than or equal to 40000

The completed spreadsheet is saved on the CD as **Solver 2.xls**. Run the program and check the result. It should show Small 497, Medium 323 and Large 472 units. The total contribution is £52,249.

Change the number of machine hours available to 22500 (cell E13). Re-run Solver. The revised numbers are Small 498, Medium 500 and Large 334 units. The total contribution is £51,488.

REPORTS

Finally, when running Solver you will have noticed that three reports are available; Answer, Sensitivity and Limits.

Three reports are available once Solver has calculated the result

The Sensitivity and Limits reports are not available if Integers is used. In order to demonstrate the reports a copy of the Integer sheet has been taken, and the Integer constraints have been removed.

The spreadsheet is saved on the CD as **Solver 3.xls**.

NEXT

That concludes Solver. Next we will look at Scenarios.

Chapter Thirteen

SCENARIOS

Now! Try changing this, and this, and this . . .

In **Section One** we looked at using Excel VBA to change GP percentages etc. As an alternative, we can store pre-set parameters and change our model by using Excel's Scenarios.

The main difference between Scenarios and VBA is that Scenarios changes the variables in a predefined way, with no user input, whereas VBA allows all permutations to be considered "live". Which method is best in any given circumstance will be a matter for your professional judgement.

Once again, we will use an example in order to explore the facility.

PROFIT AND LOSS ACCOUNT EXAMPLE

In this example we will set up a small profit and loss account, and then set down different criteria for GP percentage, overheads etc.

The details are listed below:

Sales	101,023
Cost of Sales	50%
Wages	30,014
Rent	10,000
Rates	3,729
Telephone	2,179
Stationery, Advertising and postage	7,155
Insurance	1,333
Repairs	651
Depreciation	10,184
Bank Interest and Charges	5,487

The spreadsheet is saved on the CD as **Scenario 1.xls**.

Note that there is a formula in cell A21, which reads =IF(F21<0, "Net Loss", "Net Profit"). This will print Net Loss if the figure in cell F21 is negative, and Net Profit if the figure is zero or positive.

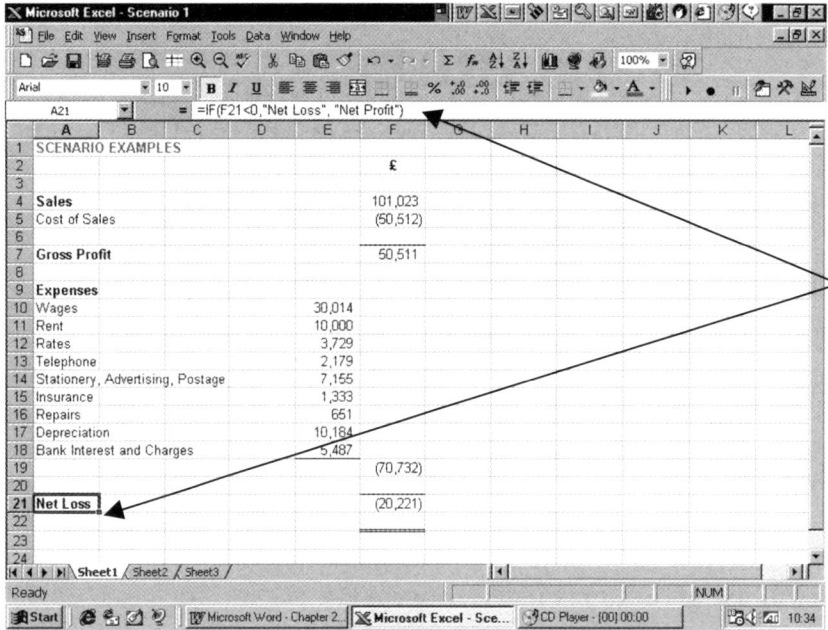

The Profit and Loss Account has been set up

Note the formula in cell A21

Step 1

ALWAYS save the original scenario, otherwise it will be lost. Select Tools from the menu, then Scenarios.

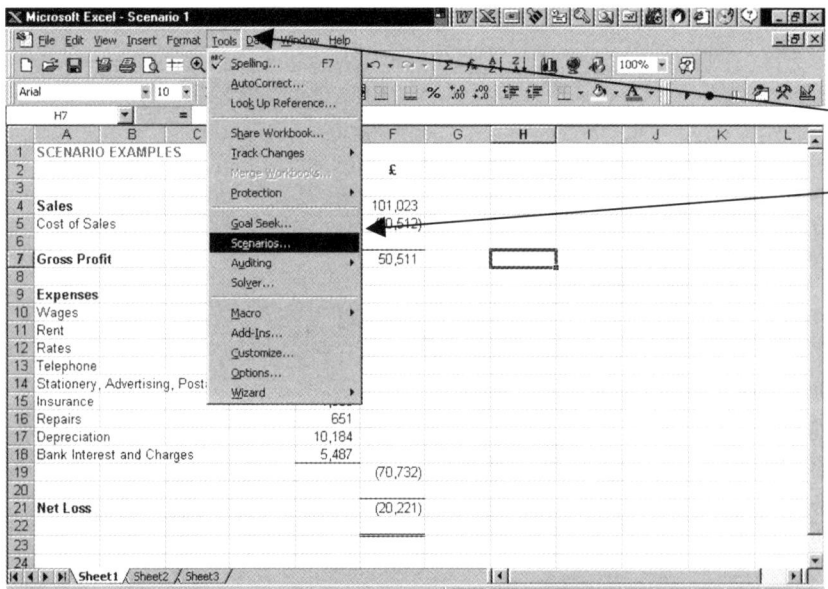

Select Tools...

Scenarios...

Step 2

The following dialog box appears. Click on Add.

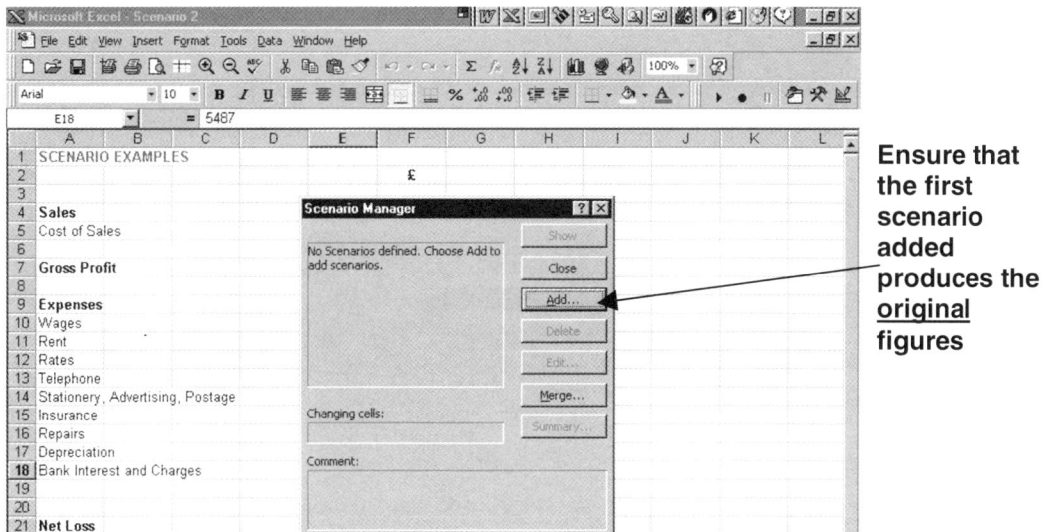

Ensure that
the first
scenario
added
produces the
<u>original</u>
figures

Step 3

Type the name (i.e. Original) in the Scenario Name input box, and click on the
icon to choose the cells.

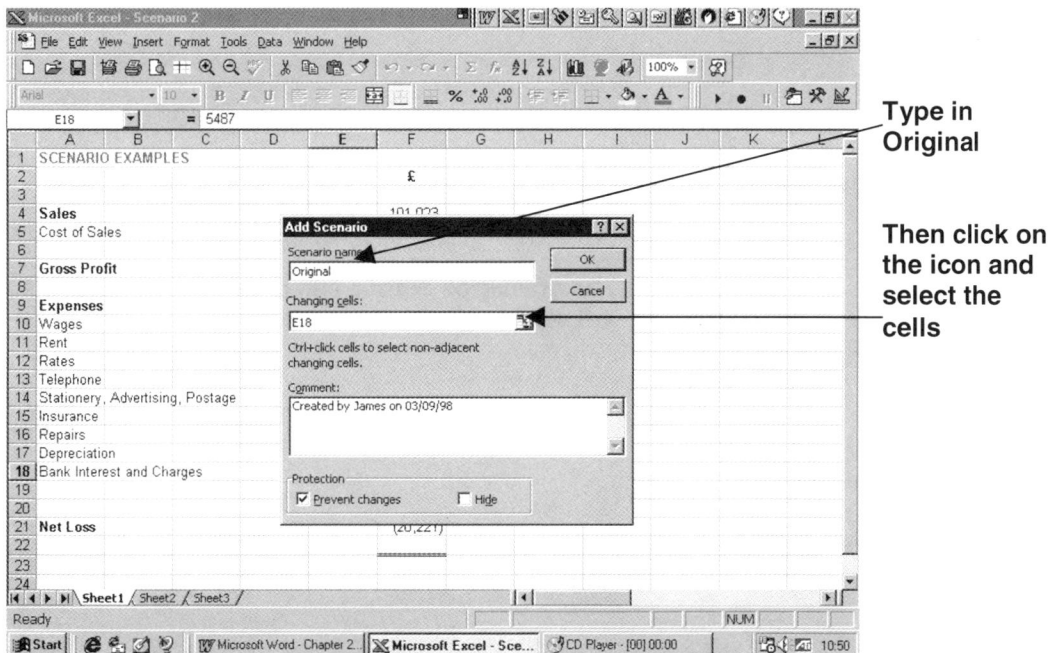

Type in
Original

Then click on
the icon and
select the
cells

Step 4

The dialog box shrinks to reveal the cells. The first cell is chosen by clicking in cell F4. Hold down Ctrl and select cells E10 to E18. All cells selected have a flashing dashed line around them.

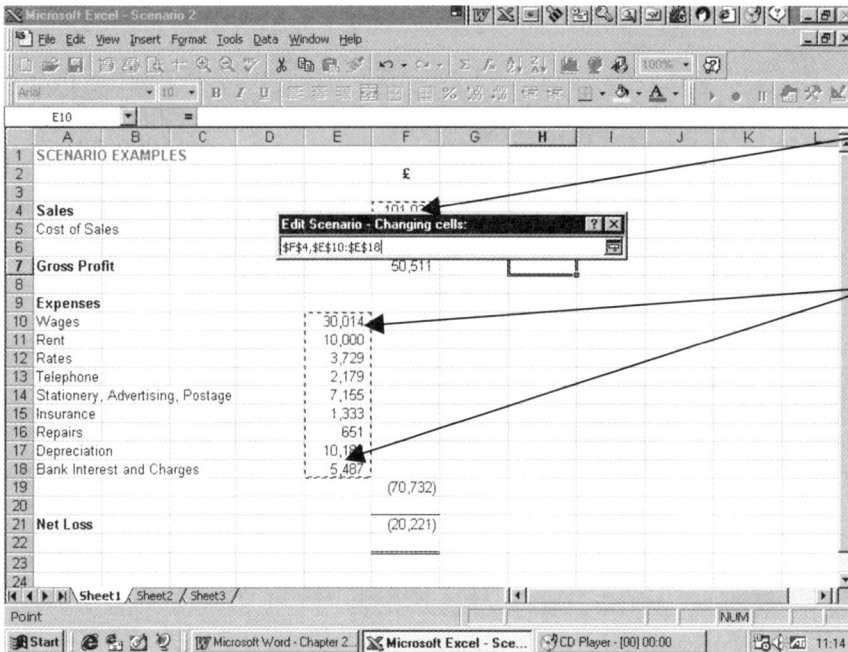

Click on cell F4

Hold down Ctrl and select E10 to E18 with the mouse

Step 5

Press Return and the cells are selected.

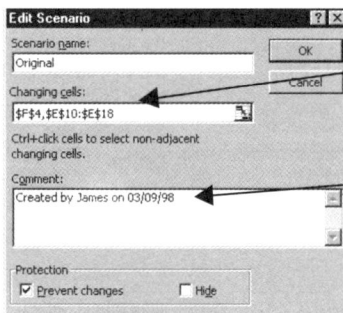

The cells are entered in the dialog box

The scenarios author and date are also entered automatically

Click on OK, and the values are ready to be entered.

Step 6

Scenario cells and their values are displayed.

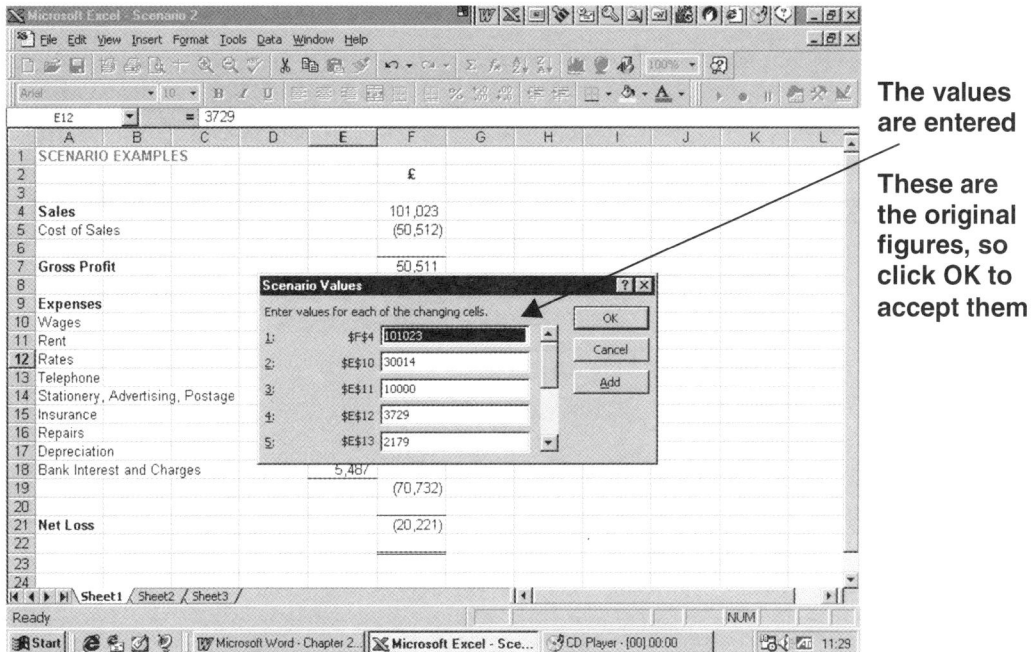

The Scenario is completed. To run the scenario click on Show. The spreadsheet is saved on the CD as **Scenario 2.xls**.

We will now set up another scenario. Sales will increase by 10%, wages by 5% and advertising by £1,000.

Complete the above steps as before, and name the scenario "Sales+10%; Wages+5%; Advertising+1000".

In the Scenario Value dialog box the present figures are shown. Change the figures as follows:

Cell	Original Entry	Revised Entry
$F$4	101023	=101023*1.1
$E$10	30014	=30014*1.05
$E$14	7155	=7155+1000

The spreadsheet is shown below.

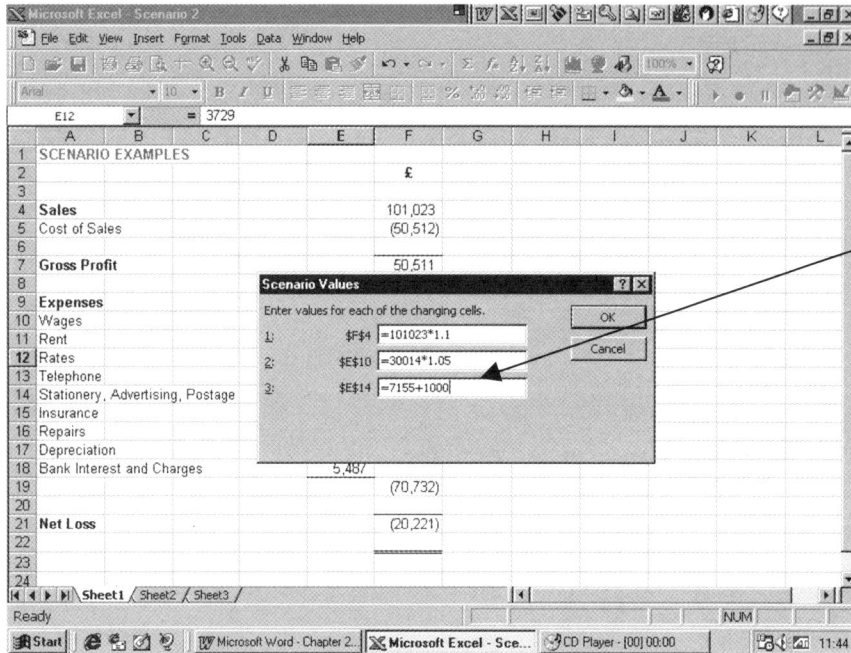

**Enter the
new figures
or formulae
in the
Scenario**

When OK is displayed a warning message appears.

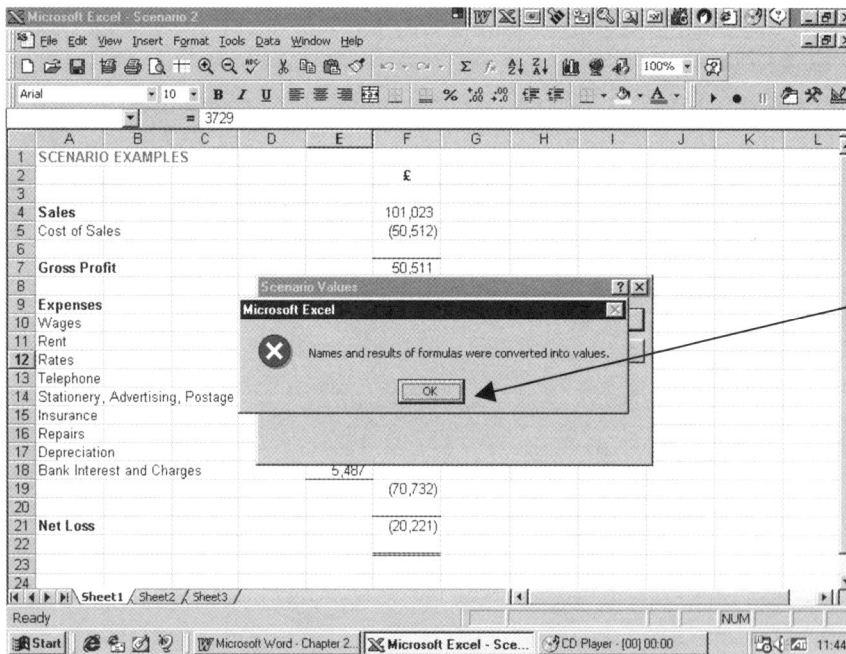

**The warning
message
appears**

Click OK

The warning states that any formulae will be converted to values. This means that formulae can be used to set the value initially, when the scenario is being run, but it avoids the error of running the same scenario twice, and applying the percentage change to the revised, instead of the original figure.

The scenario now appears in the Scenario Manager dialog box.

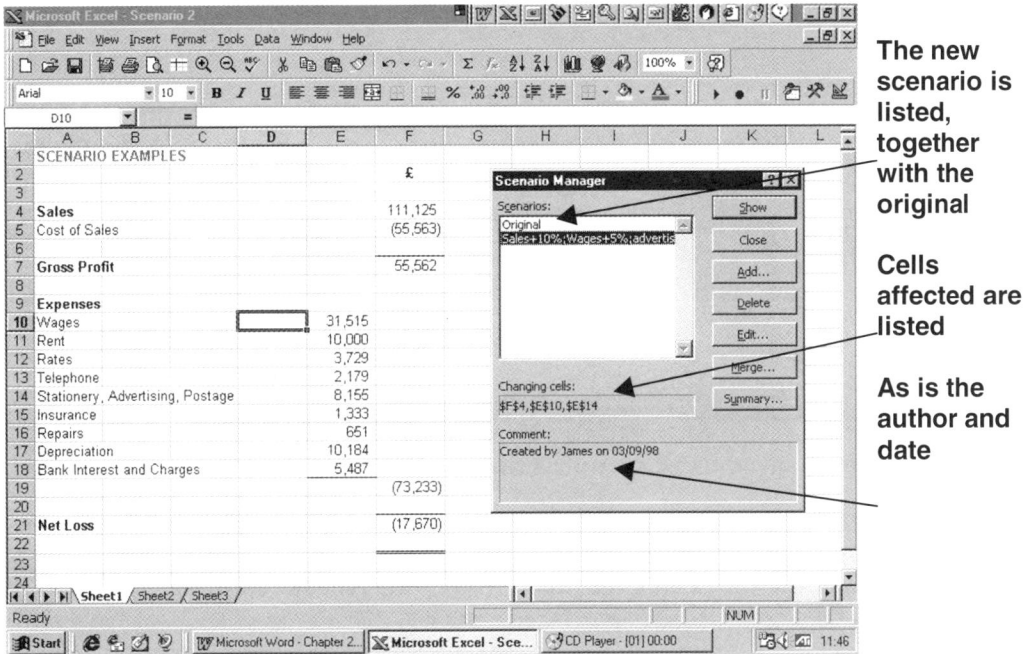

The new scenario is listed, together with the original

Cells affected are listed

As is the author and date

The spreadsheet is saved on the CD as **Scenario 3.xls**.

That concludes the preparation of scenarios. There are two further items to mention as regards the Scenario Manager. Clicking on the Summary button (at the bottom of the dialog box) reveals two options — prepare a Scenario Summary Report, and produce a Scenario Pivot Table Report.

These reports are produced as additional sheets in the existing workbook, and provide information for reviewing what is happening in the currently selected scenario, compared to the original scenario as set up.

When producing the reports, make sure that the relevant cell is highlighted — in this case, Net Profit at cell F21.

The spreadsheet is saved as **Scenario 4.xls**.

NEXT

In the next chapter we look at presenting the spreadsheet results graphically in
Chart form.

Chapter Fourteen

CHARTING

Look at it this way . . .

We have looked at how to present information on spreadsheets, and how to look at different views of the results — by using VBA, Scenarios and other things that change the cell contents, and pivot tables, filtering and things that summarise or draw out information hidden in the detail.

However, the fundamentals, in terms of on screen presentation, are the same.

In the next few chapters we will review charting, and the options available to presenting information graphically.

In all cases it is a matter of professional judgement as to whether one particular method of presentation is better than another. It depends largely on the audience.

CHARTING DATA

In order to demonstrate the charting capabilities, we will use the data generated in **Filter 3.xls**. It has been saved again as **Charting 1.xls**, so that any work we complete does not impact on the original.

Open **Charting 1.xls**. The filter has been cancelled, and a pivot table has been prepared in the sheet labelled Pivot Table.

We will chart with this pivot table

	A	B	C	D	E	F	G	H	I	J	K	L	M
1	Sum of Value	Person											
2	Date	Alan	Brian	Claire	Diane	Edward	Frank	Grace	Harriet	Irene	Julie	Grand Total	
3	Jan	10867	8460	13120	6203	8743	10813	9797	11376	9651	9396	98426	
4	Feb	17089	10197	14208	8937	11191	10527	10428	13851	7453	9493	113374	
5	Mar	10408	12991	14776	7826	10264	16022	10638	12885	11441	15074	122325	
6	Apr	15493	6798	13212	10409	11434	9347	14942	10056	11050	8937	111678	
7	May	13404	6829	6715	11340	11371	10199	4421	12770	10337	11638	99024	
8	Jun	11243	13478	8095	16432	10659	10676	9414	8606	6814	12274	107691	
9	Jul	10279	13018	13638	10962	7336	11888	11382	9706	9530	9304	107043	
10	Aug	15697	10763	13555	14093	6815	10289	9822	9299	13766	11796	115895	
11	Sep	11169	10347	9661	7756	8160	12116	9328	10483	10901	9229	99150	
12	Oct	11791	12287	15764	12122	10817	9296	11151	10760	13382	11652	119022	
13	Nov	15404	9680	5809	9253	9977	9154	11012	8937	10083	6387	95696	
14	Dec	2764	2450	3511	1757	3677	3581	4408	7078	4731	2710	36667	
15	Grand Total	145608	117298	132064	117090	110444	123908	116743	125807	119139	117890	1225991	
16													
17													
18													
19													

THE CHARTING TOOLBAR

Right click in the toolbar, and activate the Charting toolbar. Most of the icons are greyed out, because they are not available until after a chart has been prepared, and it is being edited.

The first step is to decide what it is that will be presented in a chart. At present the table shows monthly totals, and the annual totals of each person and the monthly total of the company for all employees.

We will chart the annual turnover achieved by each member of staff. Start the Chart Wizard, which is on the Standard Toolbar.

Click on Chart Wizard to prepare a chart

Right click and activate the chart toolbar

Select Chart Type Column, and Chart sub-type Clustered Column.

Select Column . . .

and in sub type select Clustered Column

Click Next

Click Next. Step 2 defaults to the entire range for data, and to columns.

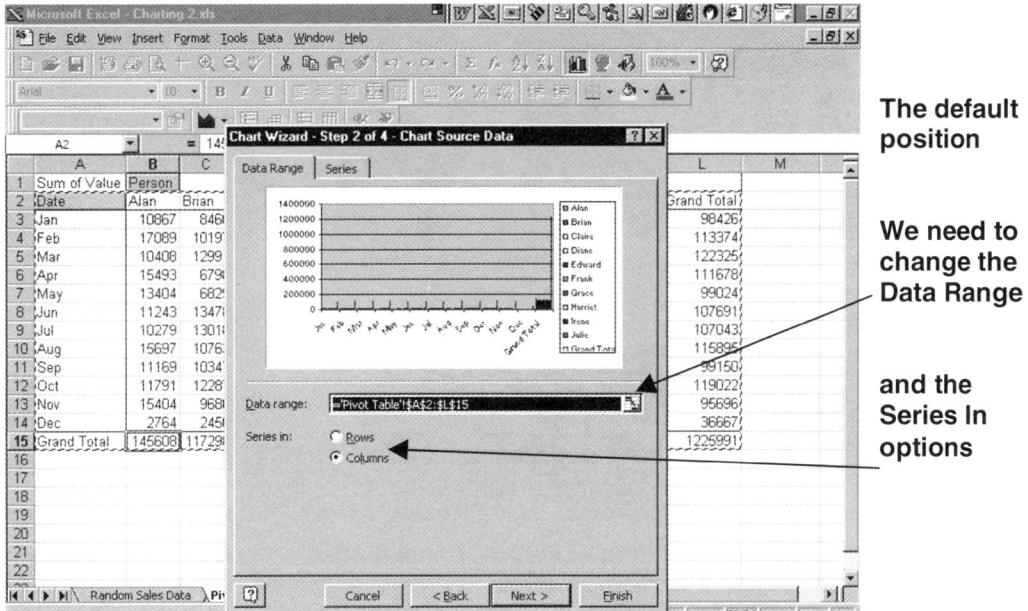

The default
position

We need to
change the
Data Range

and the
Series In
options

Select Rows, instead of Columns, then minimise the dialog box and select the
relevant cells by dragging the mouse.

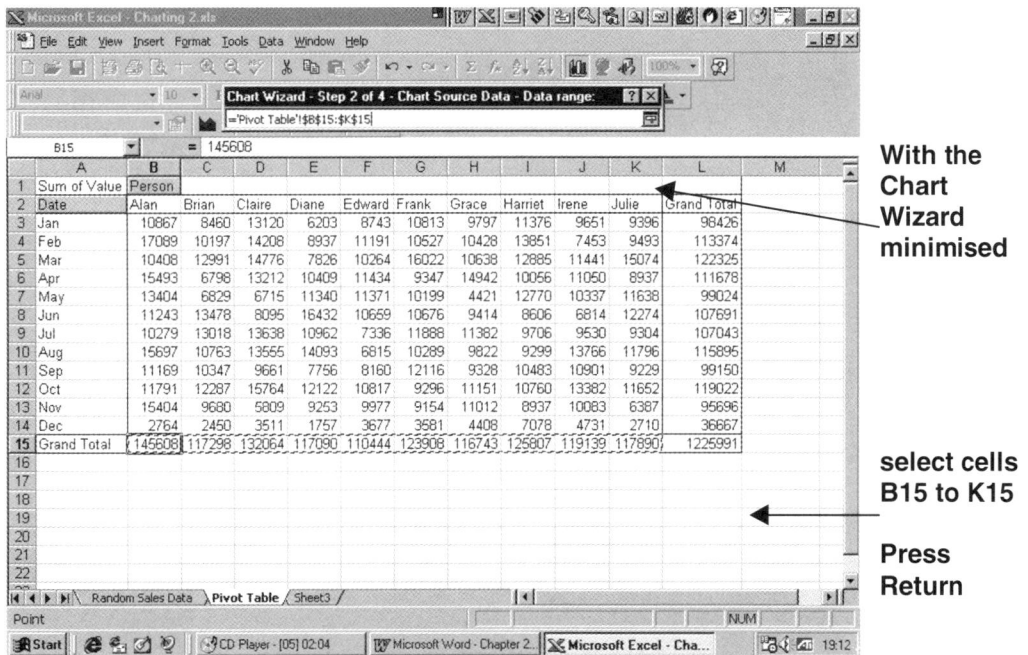

With the
Chart
Wizard
minimised

select cells
B15 to K15

Press
Return

Pressing Return moves us to the next step in the Wizard.

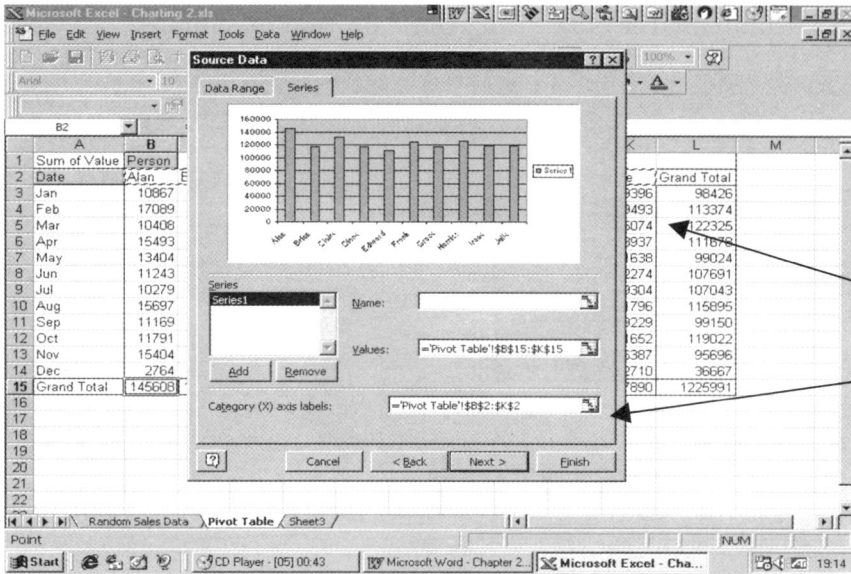

Minimise the box . . .

and drag over the names to fill in the chart x-axis labels

Pressing Return moves us to the next step in the Wizard.

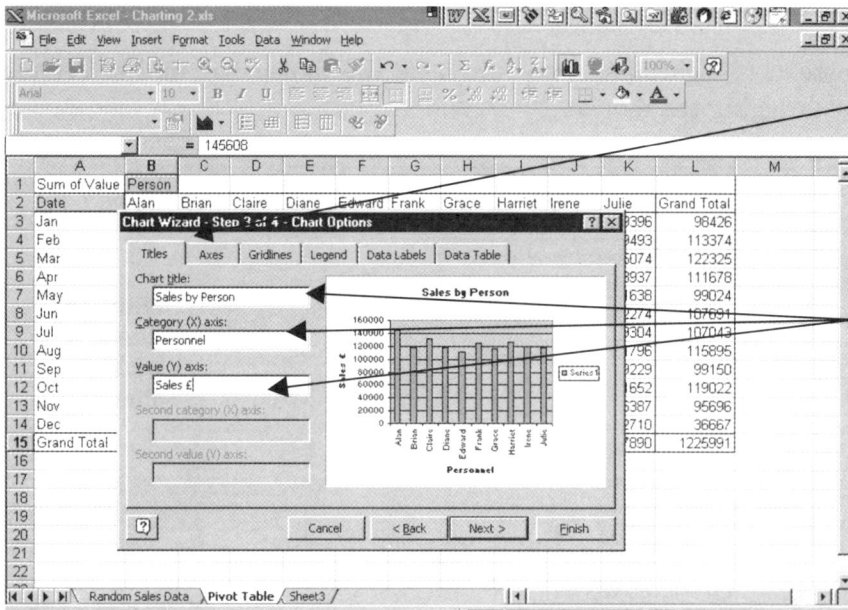

Make the Titles tab active

Fill in the title and category details

Enter the title "Sales by Person", the Category x-axis as "Personnel" and the y-axis category as Sales £.

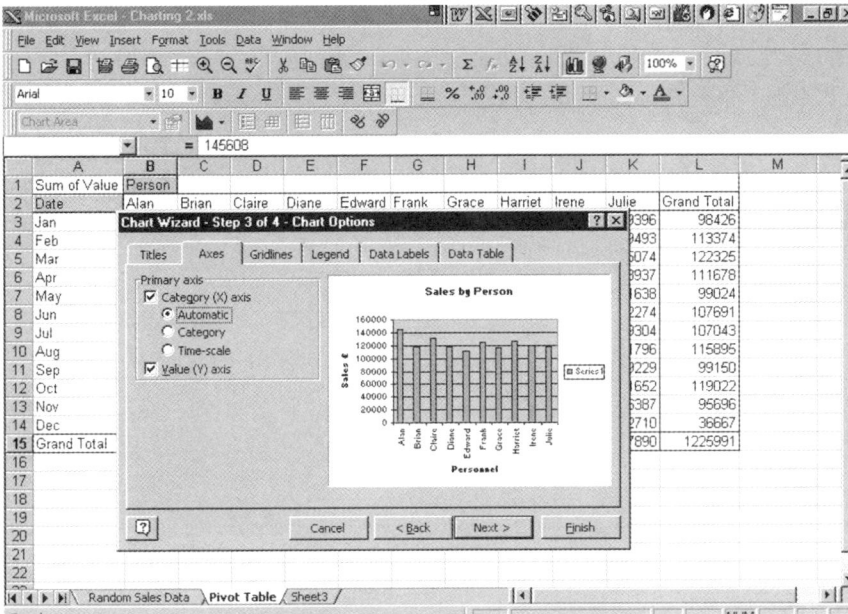

Select the
Axes tab

Click on the Axes tab. Normally these should be left at their default settings.

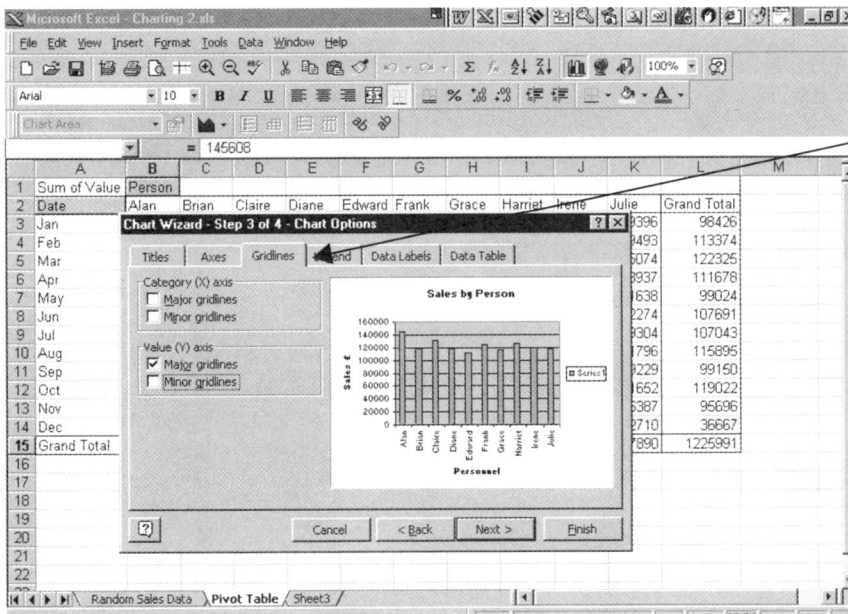

Select the
Gridlines
tab

Click on the gridlines and see the effects in the thumbnail view. They may or may not add to the chart.

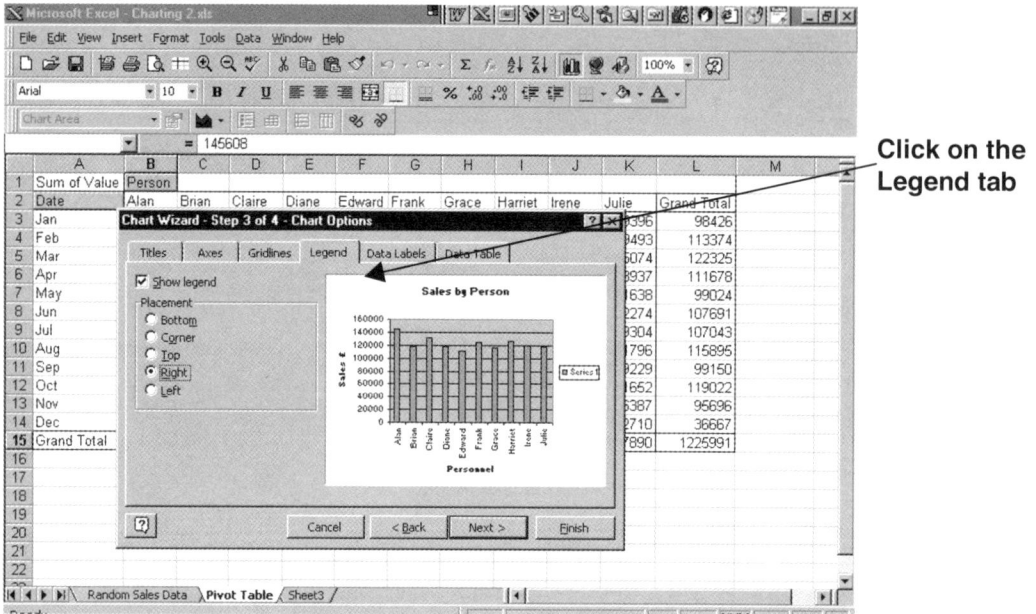

Click on the Legend tab

The Legend tab allows the series legend to be moved to a more convenient area of the chart, or it can be deleted altogether.

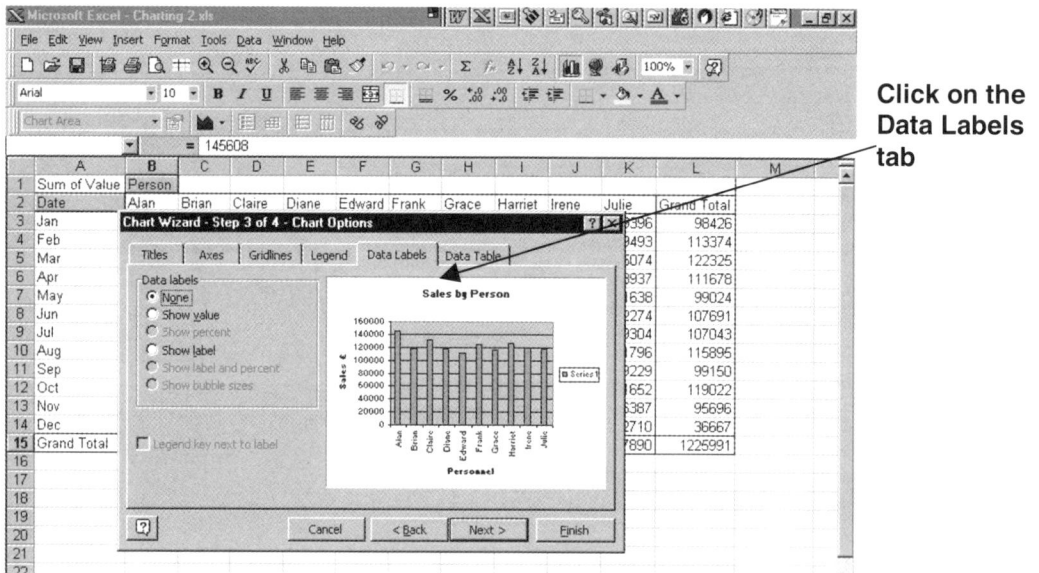

Click on the Data Labels tab

The option to print values or labels or both is only useful if there is not very much detail being represented on the chart.

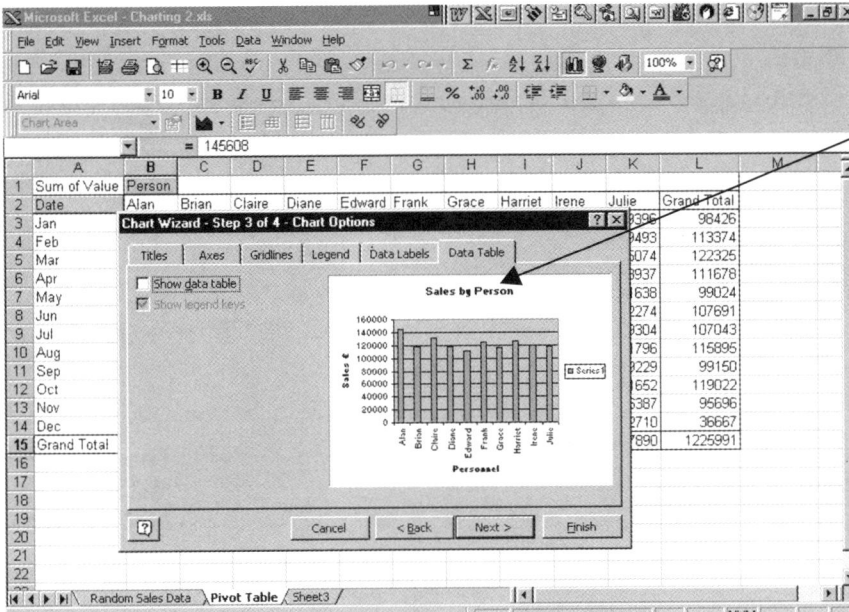

Click on the
Data Table

Generally more useful than printing labels is the option to print a table of values below the chart. This means that the chart and the numbers from which it is derived can be presented together.

Click Next and move to the last step in the Wizard.

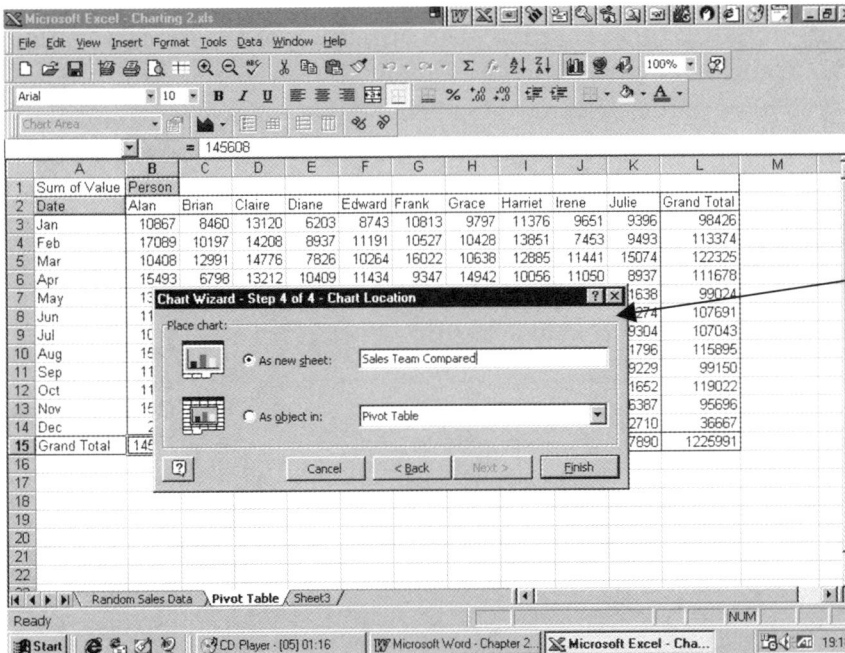

The last step
— choosing
to display in
the current
spreadsheet
or to display
as a new
sheet,
dedicated
solely to the
chart

Generally speaking I prefer placing charts in a new sheet dedicated to the purpose. If the chart is included in an active worksheet it can obscure cells that are being used, and it is not displayed as large as when it is in a separate sheet.

The final chart is shown below.

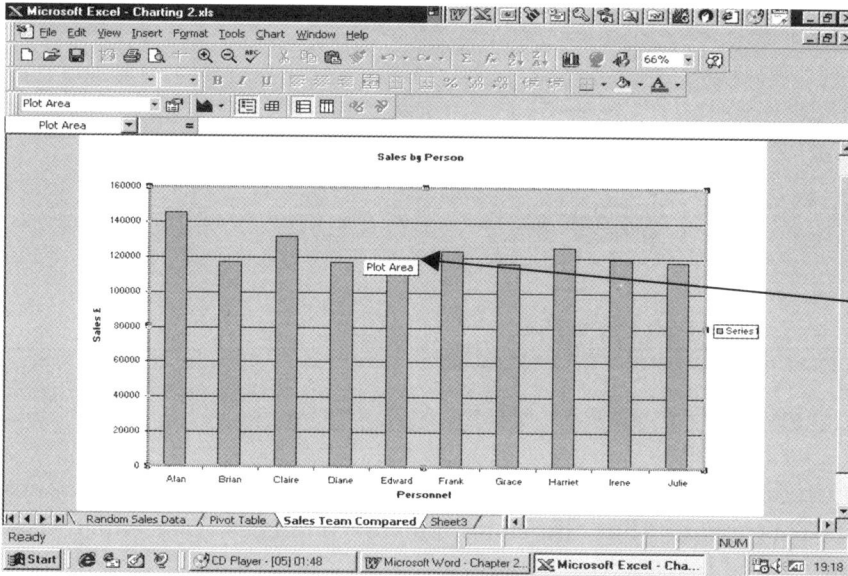

The finished chart

The Plot area is highlighted

REVISIONS

Unlike most things in Excel, this is actually the beginning of the process, rather than the end. The desire is to create a chart as quickly as possible, and then to consider how best to present it once something is available to review.

Therefore there are a substantial number of formatting tools available, the chart type can be changed, the data range can be reselected etc.

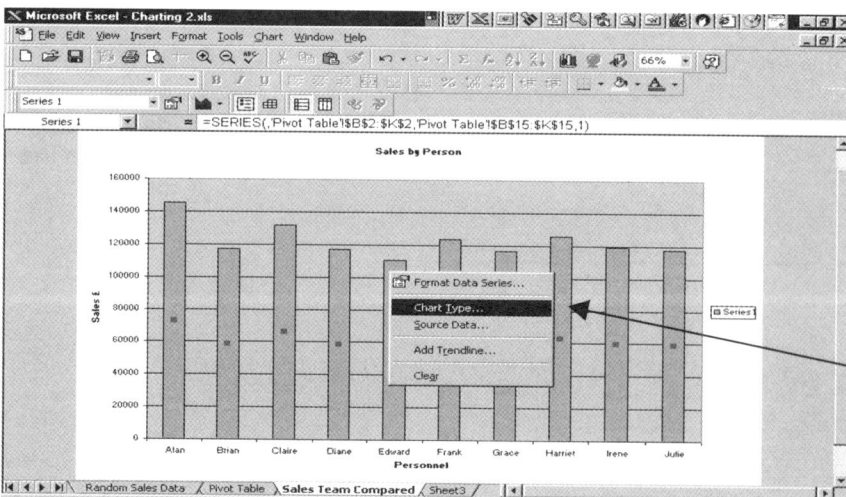

Right click in one of the Chart Bars. A menu appears.

Highlight Chart Type to change. This starts the Wizard again

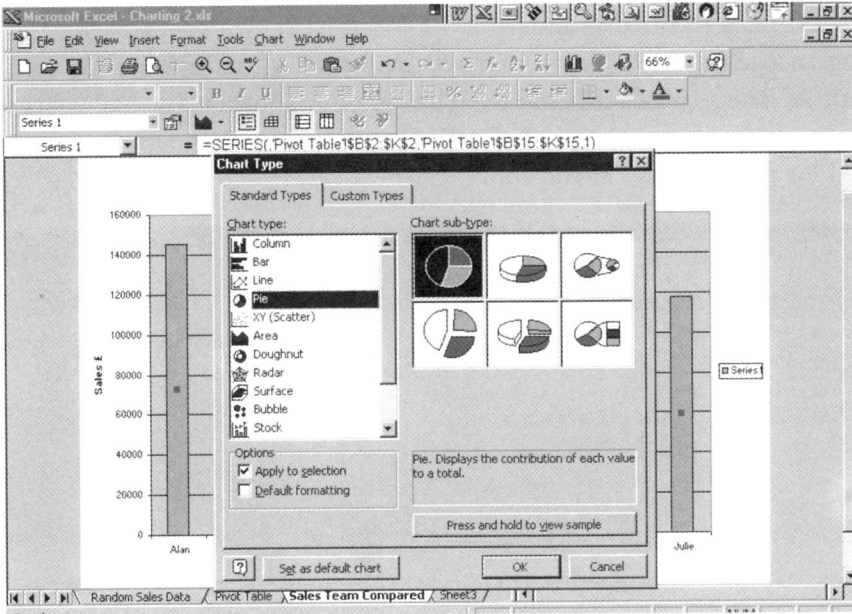

A new chart type can be selected. The other steps of the Wizard do not run, and the chart is updated immediately

The results are not always an improvement.

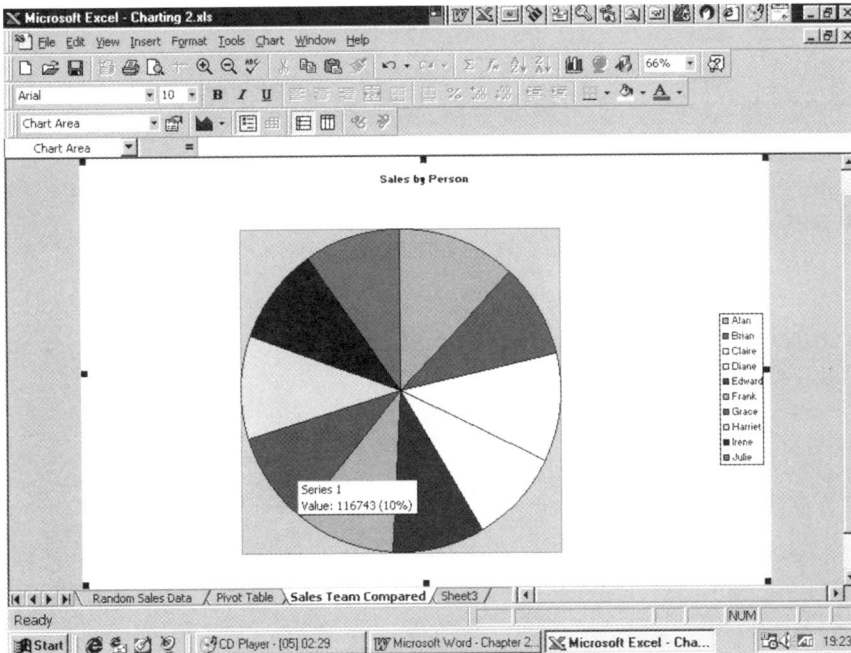

Click Undo to revert back to the original.

Right clicking in each area of the chart will bring up all of the menus and, consequently, all of the choices available. The screen shot below shows the Format Plot Area dialog box, opened by selecting it from the pop up menu activated in the Plot Area section of the chart.

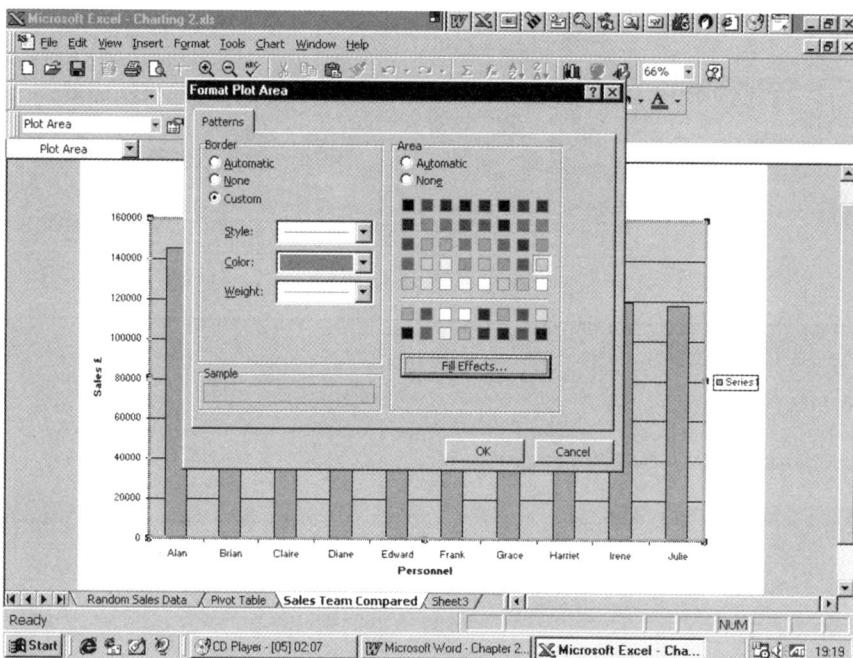

The file is saved as **Charting 3.xls**.

NEXT

That completes the chart basics, and we will finish the chapter there. In the next chapter we will add trend lines, and look at maps.

Chapter Fifteen

CHARTING AND MAPS

Trendy!

One of the potentially more useful options available in charting is Trendlines. This will insert a line, which can be formatted for weight and colour, into the series plotted on the chart. The trendline can be used to plot ahead of the series, and thereby forecast.

Open **Charting 3.xls**. A copy of the PivotTable data has been made in the sheet titled New Data, and a chart has been added, in the same style as before. It is called New Chart.

We will insert a trend line into the chart. However, to make the trend more realistic, change the labels from names to year, starting at 1997, and ending at 2006.

Click on the first bar to activate it then, with the mouse at the top, left click and drag each bar to the following figures:

	£
1997	17,000
1998	19,500
1999	58,000
2000	38,900
2001	32,000
2002	48,000
2003	64,000
2004	73,700
2005	88,000
2006	168,300

The scale of the chart revises when the last figure is input.

The underlying figures in the table are amended accordingly. This is why we could not do this with the PivotTable. The underlying data in the PivotTable cannot be changed, and the chart cannot therefore retain the new figures.

With a bar active, right click and select Add Trendline.

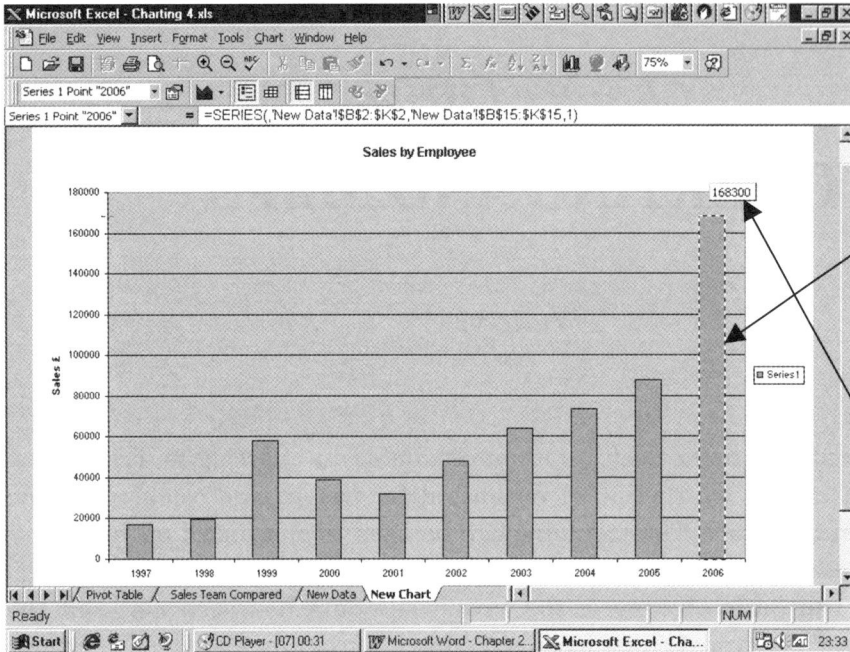

The figures in the table are adjusted accordingly. Note that, in this case, it makes the rest of the table figures a nonsense.

We will now add the trendline. With the mouse pointer in one of the bars right click. Select Add Trendline.

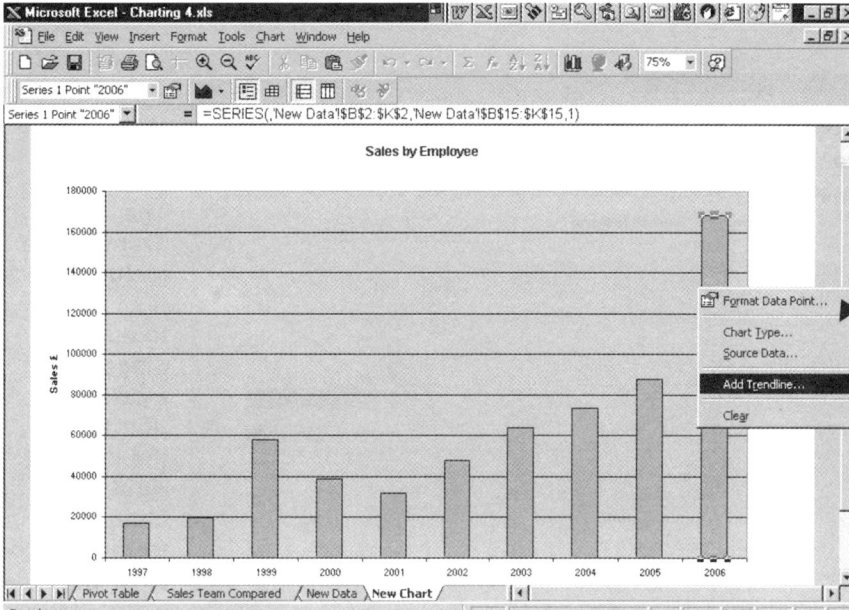

Select Exponential.

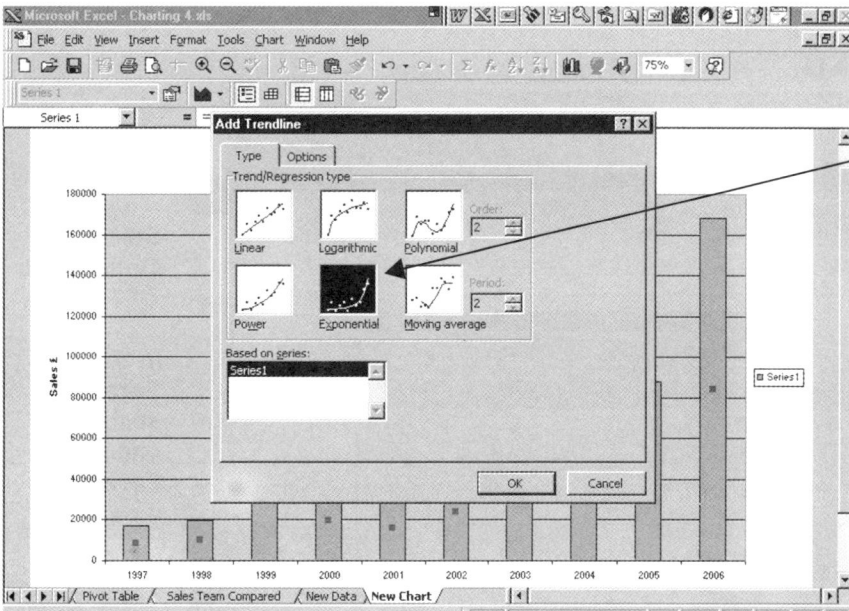

The line is drawn in.

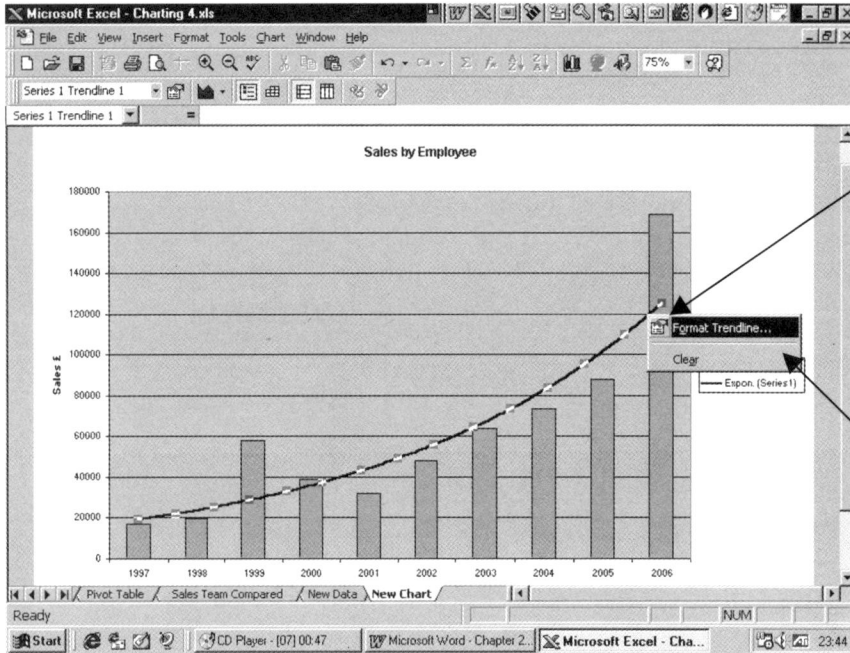

The **Trendline is included**

to edit it place the mouse pointer on the line and right click . . . change formatting, or clear the chart of the line

FORECASTING

Select Format Trendline from the pop up menu.

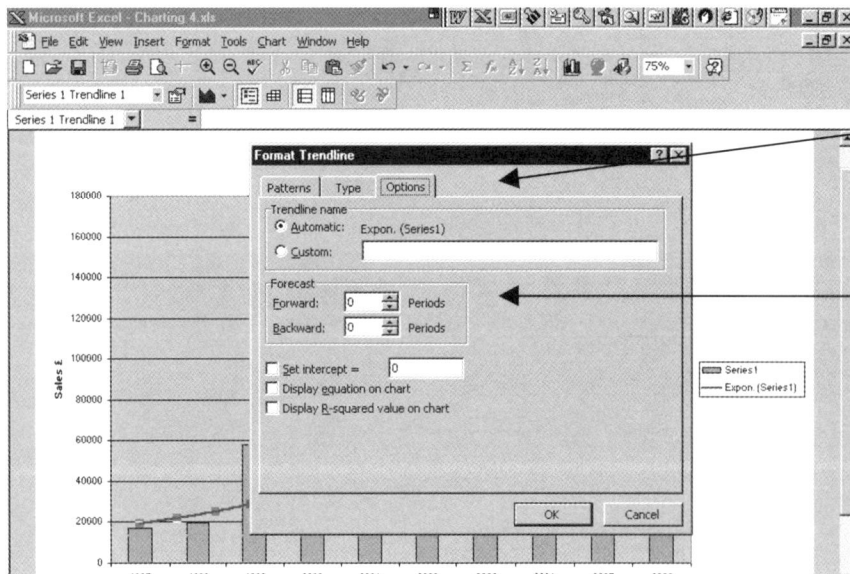

Select the Options tab

In the Forecast section change Forward to 4 periods

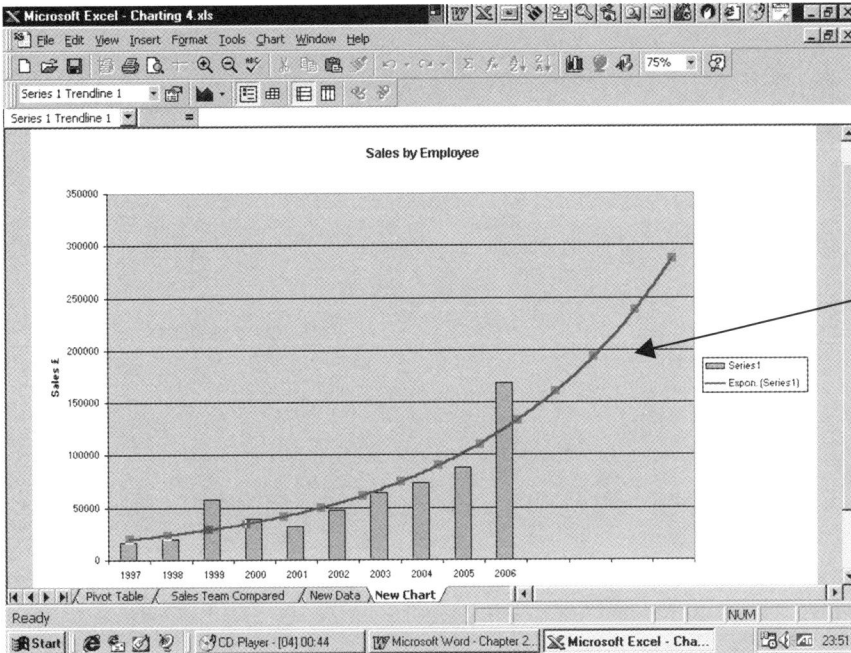

As with all forecasting, use the feature with care. Changing the type of Trendline, or the assumptions made within a specific line type, will adjust the forecast substantially.

Many types of trendlines can be included, and each can be labelled in order to identify it.

The spreadsheet is saved as **Charting 4.xls**.

MAPPING

Finally, in terms of presenting information, we will briefly look at the mapping facility.

Start a blank workbook, and enter the following information into it.

Cell	Enter	Cell	Enter
A1	MAP EXAMPLE		
A3	Country	B3	Sales
A4	UK	B4	500000
A5	Ireland	B5	100000
A6	France	B6	200000
A7	Germany	B7	350000

Move to cell AA1, to provide a clear area on which we can draw the map. Click on the Map icon.

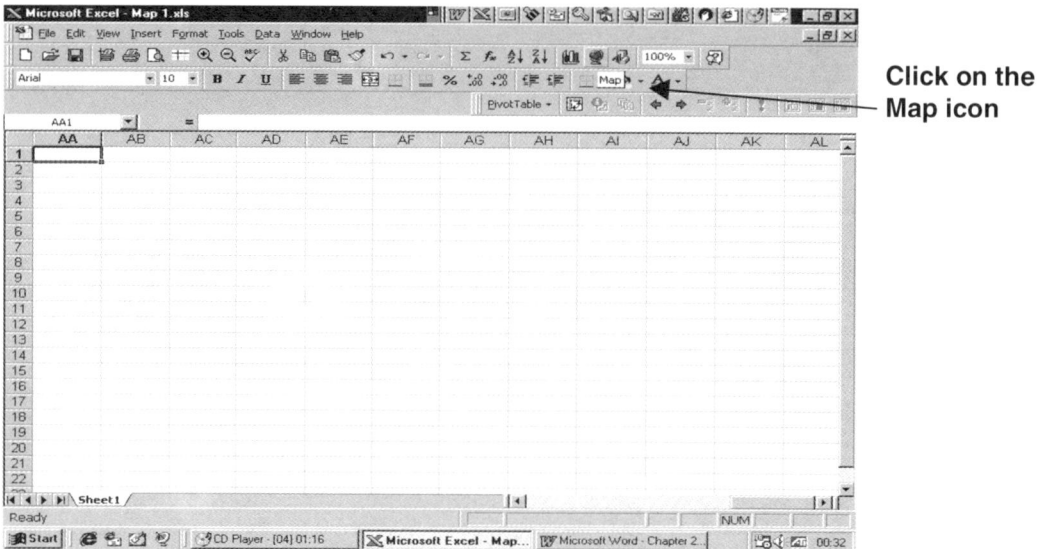

Click on the
Map icon

Drag the mouse across the spreadsheet, and release the mouse button. A choice
of regions is given. Select Europe.

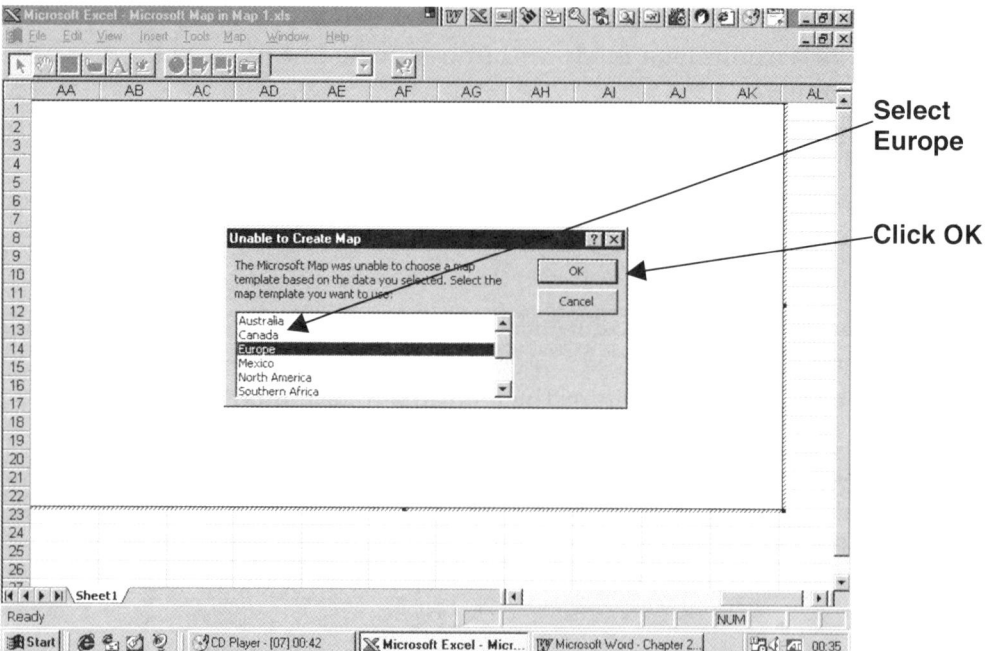

Select
Europe

Click OK

The map is drawn. From the menu select Insert, Data.

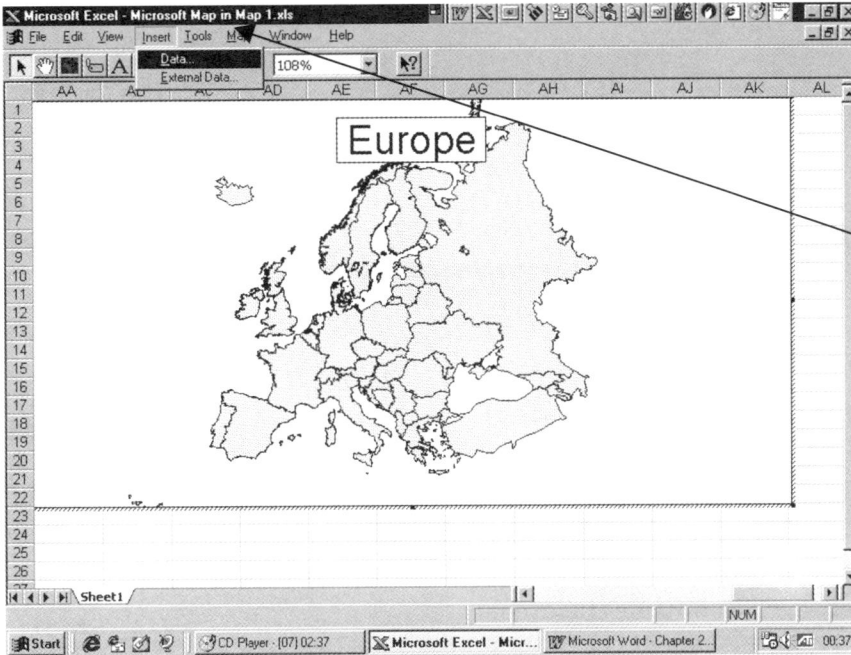

The map is drawn

Select Insert, Data From the menu

Select the data from A3 to B7, to include the headings.

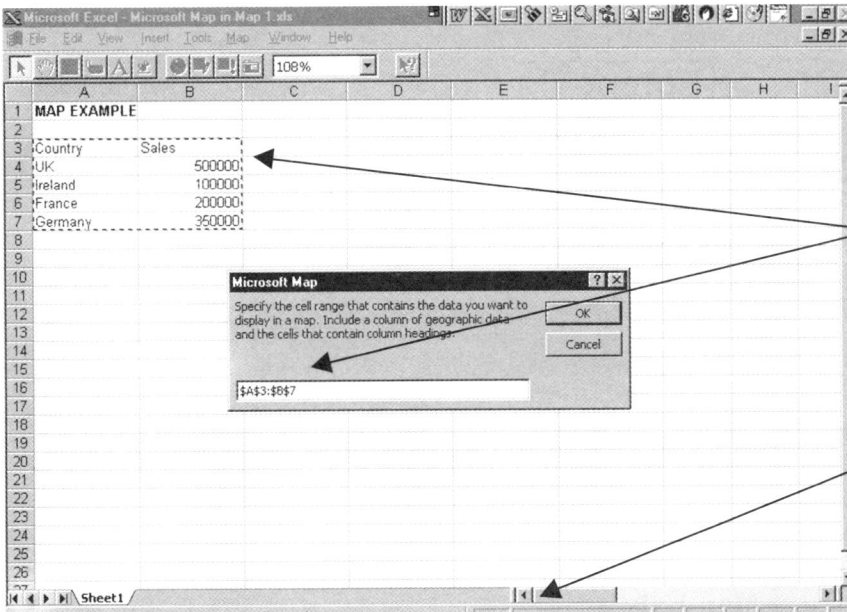

The cells are selected and the references are inserted in the input box

Move to A1 by using the scroll bars

The Map Control is displayed. We will accept the defaults. Turn it on/off from the toolbar.

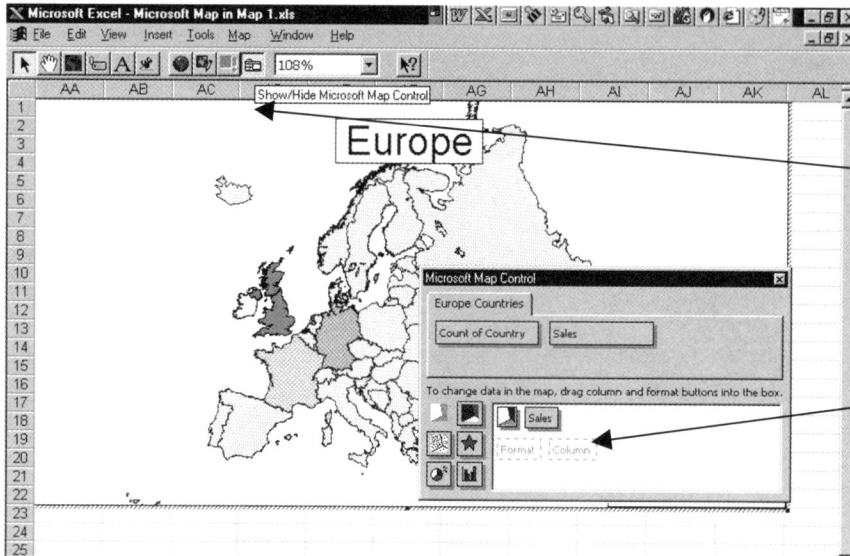

The toolbar is used to show / hide the control centre

Drag the items to change the display. It works the same way as the Pivot Tables

The map is finished. Click outside the area.

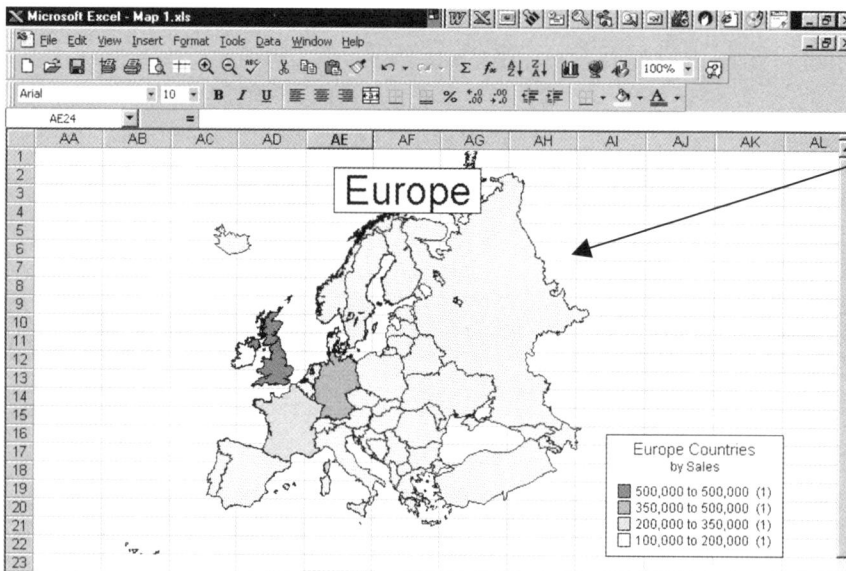

Clicking outside the area cause the map to written onto the spreadsheet

That completes the review of the map feature. It is rather cumbersome and disappointing, but if you want further guidance look at the online documentation.

The file is saved as **Map 1.xls**.

NEXT

In the next chapter we look at the forecasting and analysis tools available.

Chapter Sixteen

FORECASTING AND ANALYSIS

If I could predict the future, I would have won the lottery . . .

When it comes to forecasting, there are many different techniques, many theories, and many arguments about which method is right most often.

At its most extreme, this area should be left to statisticians. However, in order to round out our knowledge base, and to provide a working knowledge of what is possible, we will look at some of the in built functionality available in Excel.

But remember, always use this information with great care. It is not an exact science.

ANALYSIS TOOLS

Excel comes with two analysis ToolPaks. We will start by activating them.

From the menu, select Tools, Add-Ins.

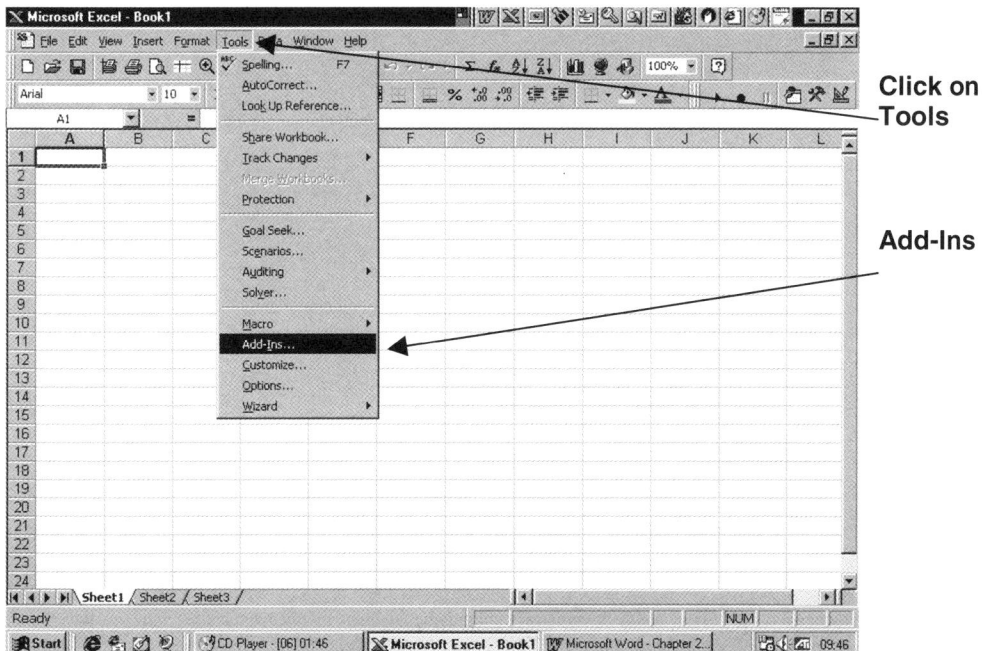

A list of available Add-Ins appears. The first two are Analysis ToolPak and Analysis ToolPak — VBA.

Check both boxes and click on OK.

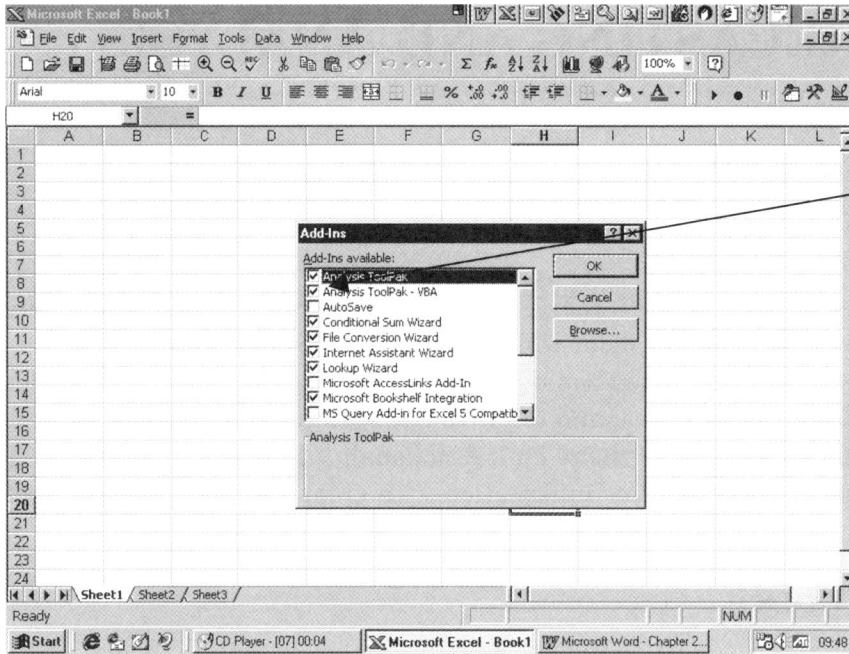

Click on the check box and select the first two items

Excel now has a new line at the bottom of the Tools menu – Data Analysis.

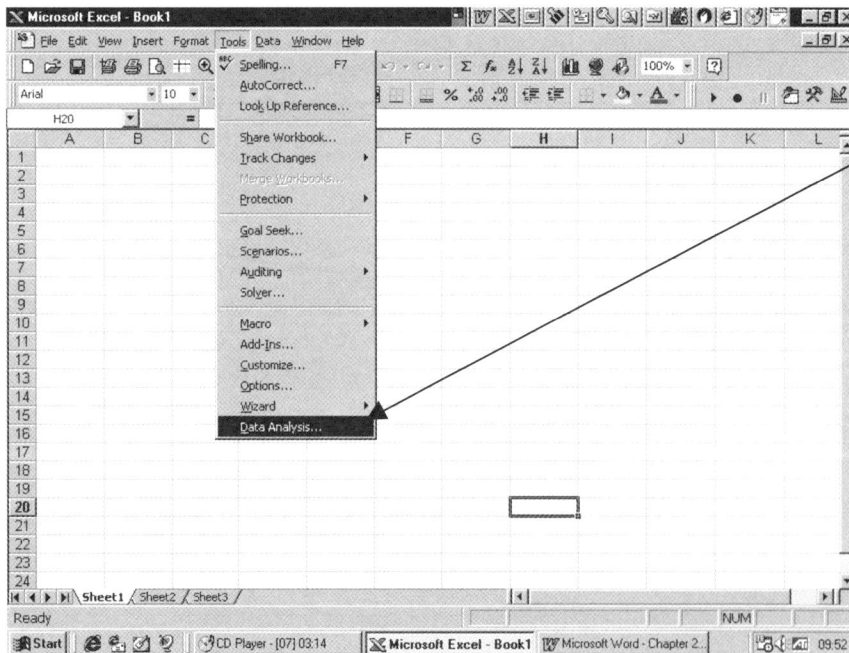

Data Analysis is now shown on the menu

MOVING AVERAGE

We will demonstrate the use of the Data Analysis tool by using it to calculate averages.

The following series of numbers was randomly generated and has been entered into the spreadsheet from A4 to A19:

985, 577, 386, 470, 431, 242, 740, 532, 722, 842, 324, 299, 445, 800, 227, 314

We will calculate a three point moving average. From the menu select Tools, Data Analysis, and scroll down the list to moving average. Click OK.

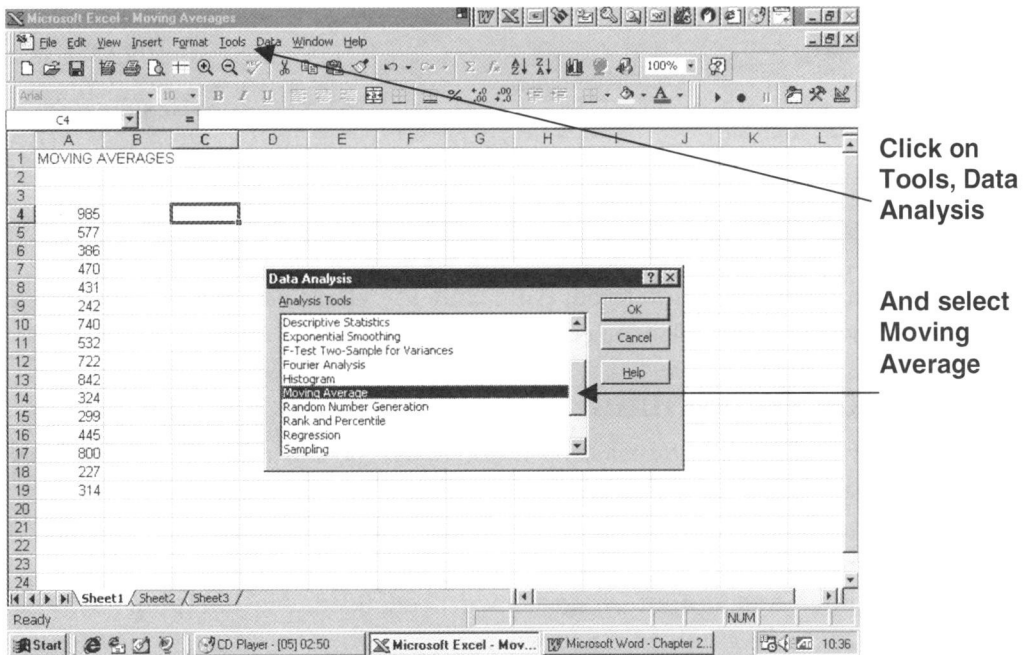

A dialog box appears, and requests the Input Range. Select A4 to A19. For Interval enter 3. For Output range select C4 to C19. Click OK

The figures display to several decimal places. Use cell formatting if desired. The file is saved on the CD as **Moving Averages.xls**.

The results can be charted if desired. Note that the chart associates the average with the last month of the series used to calculate it, not the following month.

EXPONENTIAL SMOOTHING

We have reviewed a simple forecasting method. We now want to look at a more complicated one.

From the menu select Tools, Data Analysis. Scroll down the list and select Exponential Smoothing.

The same input and output ranges have been used. No damping factor is entered, but this can be changed if you wish.

The results are saved on the CD as **Exponential.xls**.

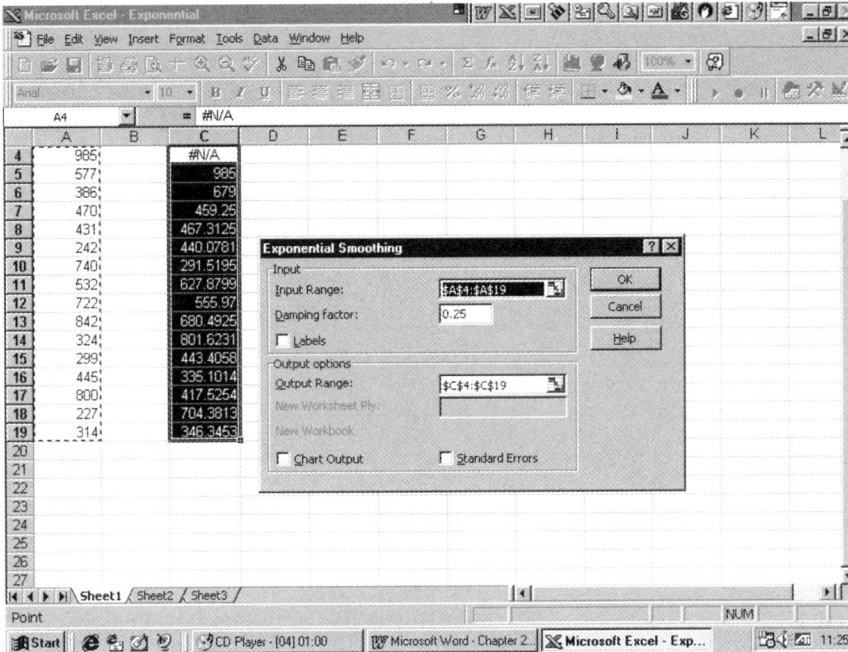

Exponential smoothing is input in a similar manner to Moving Average

We could continue the exercise with other types of analysis function. However, this is selected in order to demonstrate the similarities in method.

In Moving Averages you will note that the formula in cell C19 is =AVERAGE(A17:A19).

In Exponential Smoothing the formula in cell C19 is =0.7*A18+0.3*C18. We could have achieved the same results using Excel's built-in functions. This is discussed below.

FUNCTIONS

Excel contains a substantial number of built-in functions, including Average, which can be used directly.

Paste in the numbers from **Exponential Smoothing.xls** into a blank spreadsheet. Make cell C4 active, and then from the menu select Insert, Function.

The dialog box Paste Function appears. In the left hand box select All. In the right hand box scroll down to Average.

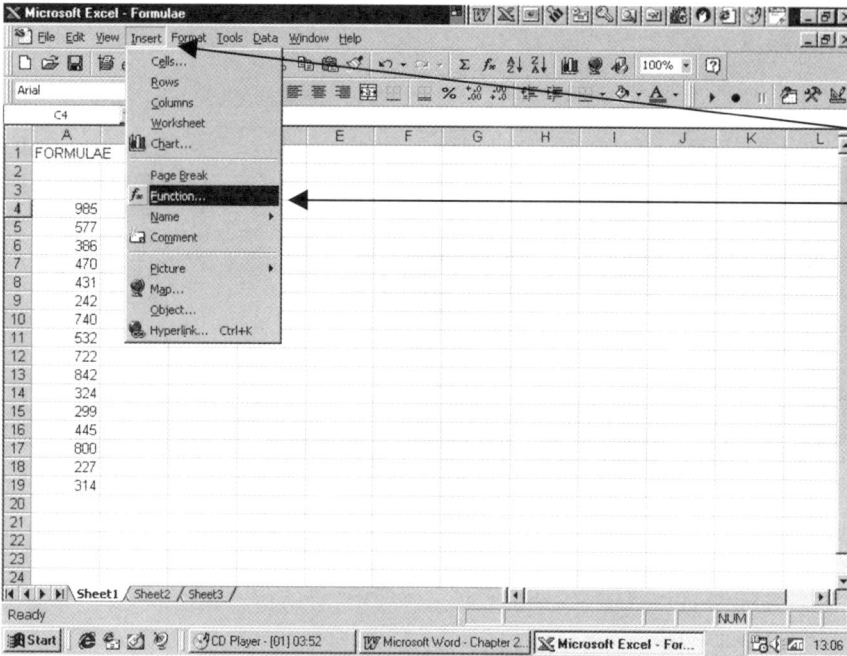

Select Insert

Function

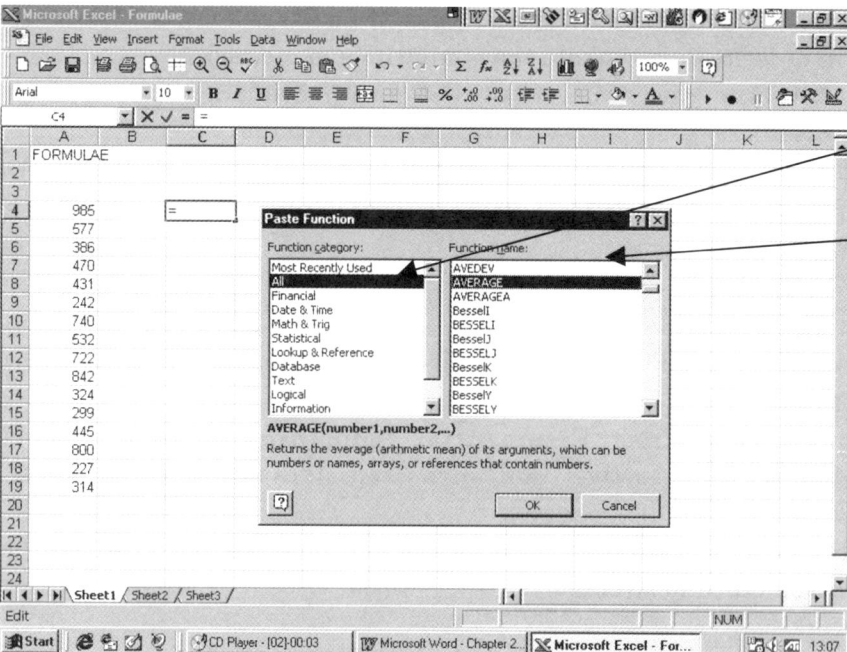

Select All

And scroll down to Average

An explanation of the function and the parameters is given

Click OK, and a dialog box opens, in order to allow the selection of the parameters.

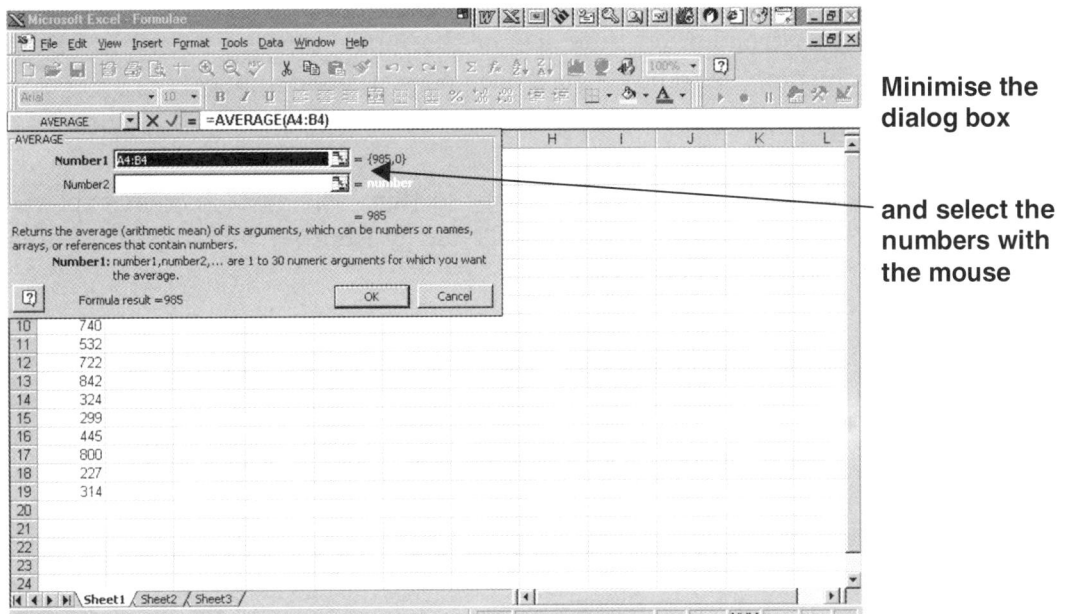

Minimise the dialog box

and select the numbers with the mouse

The formula is entered in cell C4. Drag to AutoFill.

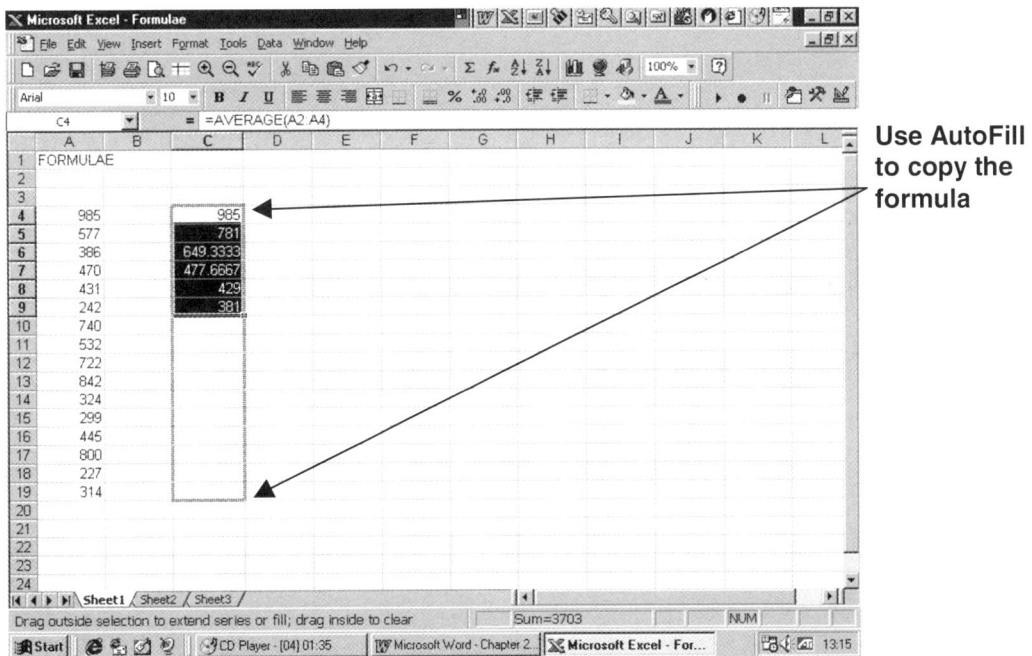

Use AutoFill to copy the formula

STATISTICAL ANALYSIS

The full list of functions available is substantial, and you may or may not want to work with them.

If you require instruction on their use or the input required access the Help files in the first instance, and buy a good book on statistical analysis.

NEXT

That concludes our review of Excel in this section. The next section explores PowerPoint in order to provide the skills for presenting our report in this medium.

Section Three

PRESENTING THE INFORMATION: OVERVIEW

We have learnt how to use Excel to summarise and analyse data, and how to use Excel VBA to improve presentation within spreadsheets.

This section looks at presentation of information in its broadest sense, and therefore we find out how to use PowerPoint to present the information to the management team in a rounded and professional way. PowerPoint will allow us to make our presentation on screen, as well as producing notes and handouts for the attendees.

We will therefore look at:

- Using the PowerPoint program
- Using and amending the templates provided
- Preparing notes as well as slides
- Interacting with Excel.

In **Section Four** we will apply this knowledge to our case study, and draw all of the areas together.

Chapter Seventeen

POWERPOINT PRESENTATIONS

Looking good . . .

PowerPoint is a computer slide show program, and it is part of the Office suite of products. This means it has a similar look and feel to the other Office programs, the commands for Bold etc. are the same, and it fully integrates with the other programs. We should already know a lot of the basics without even having started the program!

In **Section Four** we will build the spreadsheets and prepare the full PowerPoint presentation. Our main concern will be making the program interact with Excel in order to give our report maximum effect.

Here, we want to learn how to use the program, and start to use the features we need in order to be able to complete our task.

Start PowerPoint. This gives the opening screen.

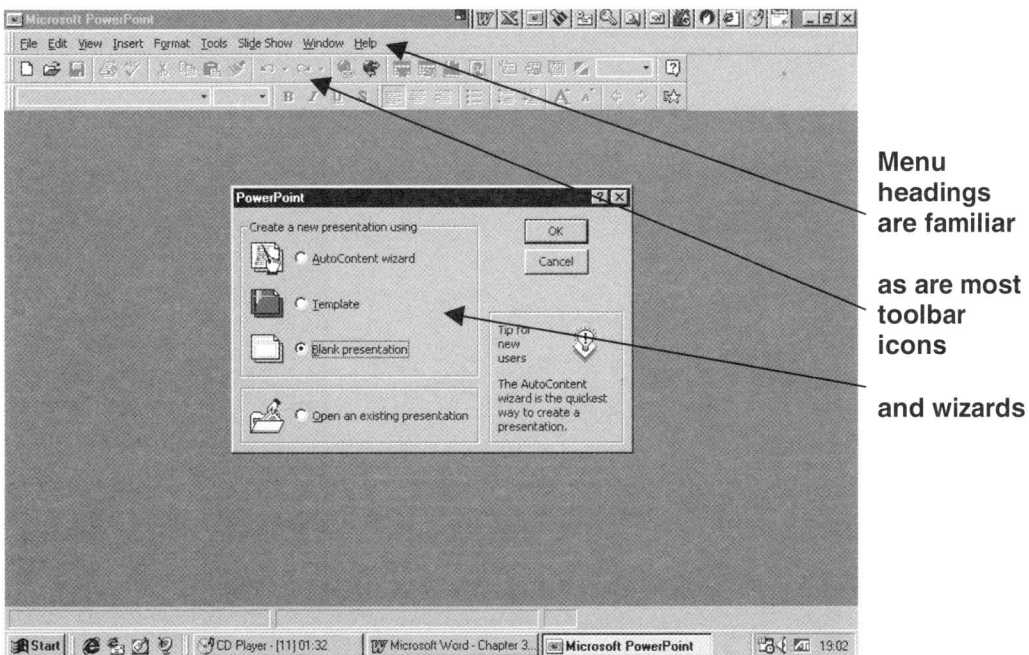

Menu headings are familiar

as are most toolbar icons

and wizards

We will start with a blank presentation. Select the blank presentation option button, and click on OK.

Choose the Title slide and click on OK.

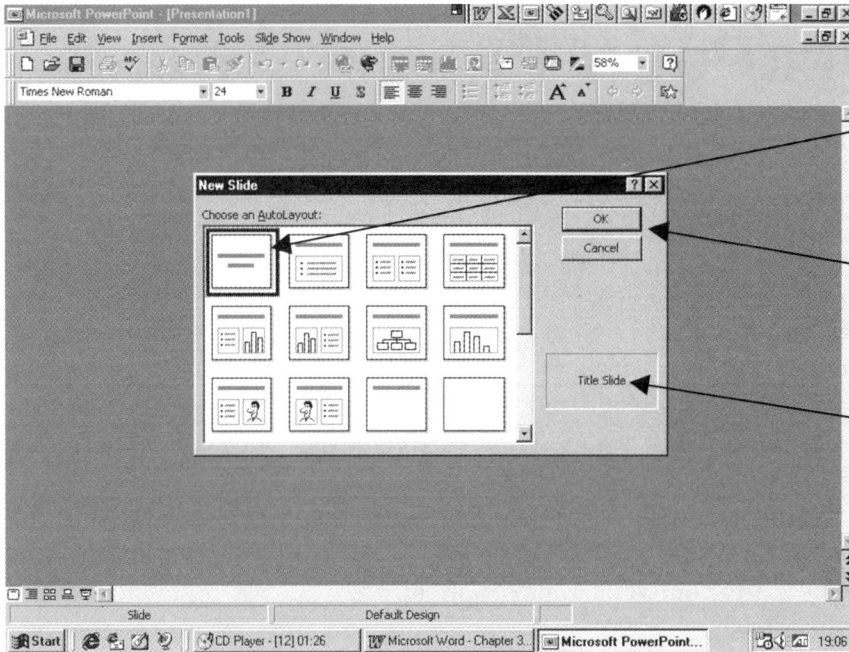

Select the
Title slide

And click OK

The slide
description
is given in
the box

The toolbar is activated, because we now have something to work on.

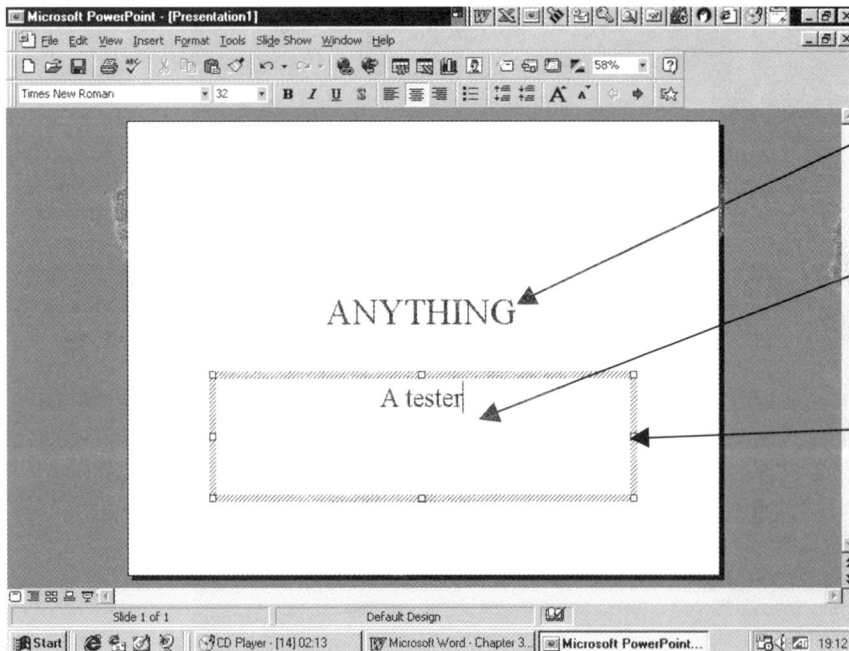

Type in a title

And a sub title

The textbox is
active until
return is
pressed.

We have the first slide completed. The different areas of the screen are labelled below.

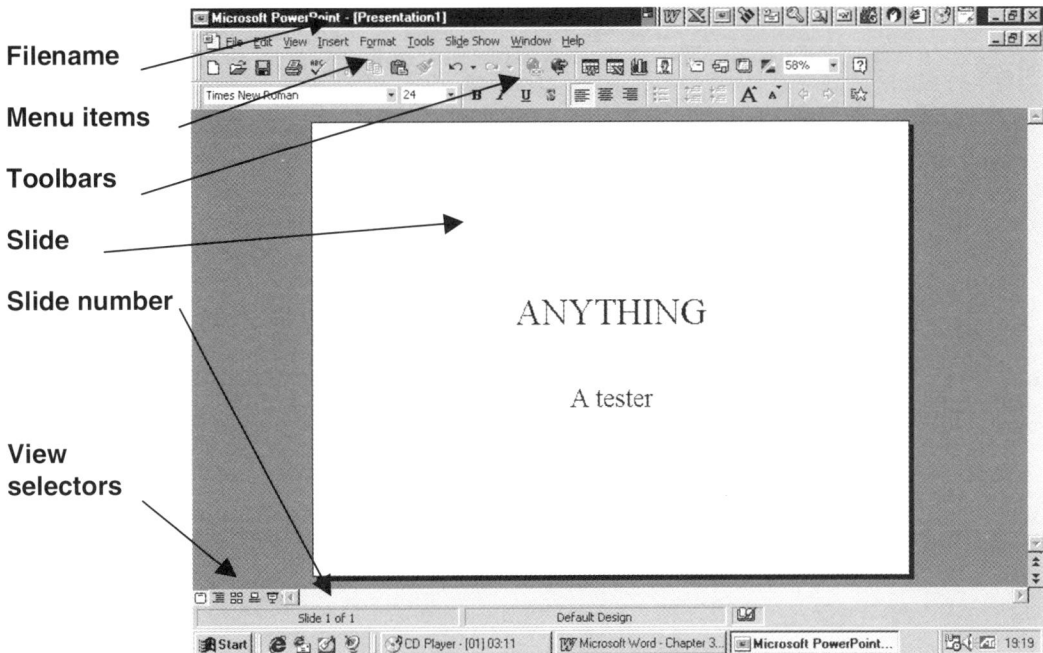

FILENAME

As with Excel, this can be 256 characters long, including spaces. A meaningful name is therefore possible, to facilitate easy location when you come to re-open it. The default name is **Presentation1**.

MENU ITEMS

The menu is discussed in detail in **Chapter Eighteen**.

TOOLBARS

As with Excel, this is equivalent to a macro shortcut area, with the macros being activated by clicking on them with the mouse, or by pressing Alt and the underlined letter.

The toolbars are not discussed as such, but because they are shortcuts to menu items their functionality should be clear.

MESSAGE AREA

This displays, amongst other things, the slide number being worked on, and the total number of slides.

VIEW SELECTORS

This is a mini toolbar for quickly switching between the various views available. The views can also be selected via the menu.

NEXT

That gives us an overview of the screen layout. In the next chapter we look at the menus in detail.

Chapter Eighteen

THE POWERPOINT MENUS

And on the menu we have . . .

We now have a general idea of how the screen is organised, and the important areas of the screen. We want to look at how the menus are organised, to understand the capabilities of the program and how to control the final product — the presentation to senior management.

Open **Presentation1.ppt** from the CD. The screen is shown below.

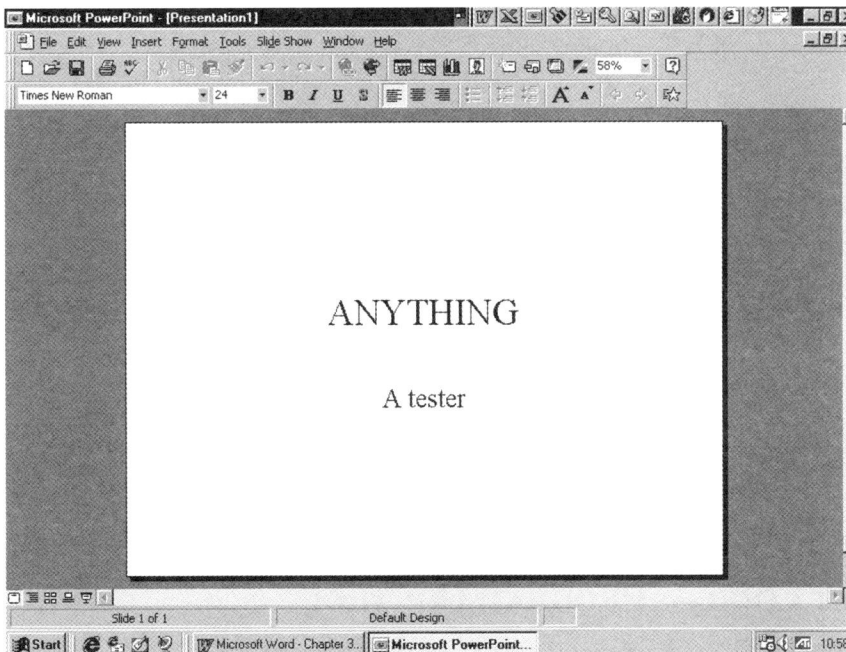

The menu choices are:
PowerPoint Logo; File; Edit; View; Insert; Format; Tools; Slide Show; Window; Help.

In each name one letter is underlined. Pressing the Alt key and the underlined letter together displays the appropriate drop down menu.

We will look at each menu item in turn, but first we will take an overview of the menus.

The menus are listed below, with a brief explanation of each.

Large PowerPoint Icon	Control of the program and how it displays on screen.
Small PowerPoint Icon	Control of the individual presentation within the PowerPoint program, and how it displays on screen.
File	Interaction between files and the Operating System, by using Windows Common Dialogue Boxes as appropriate.
Edit	Word processing type facilities for using the Windows Clipboard.
View	Options for presenting the slide show in word-processing style, draft slide style, slide show style etc.
Insert	Insertion of items into the slide or insertion of a new slide.
Format	Apply formatting to words etc. or slide design.
Tools	This is a catch-all heading for anything that does not fit neatly elsewhere.
Slide Show	Options specifically relating to PowerPoint. There is no equivalent in Excel — and there is no equivalent in PowerPoint to Excel's Data menu.
Window	This is for control of screen presentation of each Window view.
Help	Access on-line Help files.

Now that we have taken an overview of the menu items, we will look at the individual menu options in detail.

POWERPOINT LOGO — PROGRAM CONTROL

The options available are:
Restore; Move; Size; Minimise; Maximise; Close.

These are the same options that exist in Excel, and they have the same functionality. See *The Accountant's Guide to Excel* for more details.

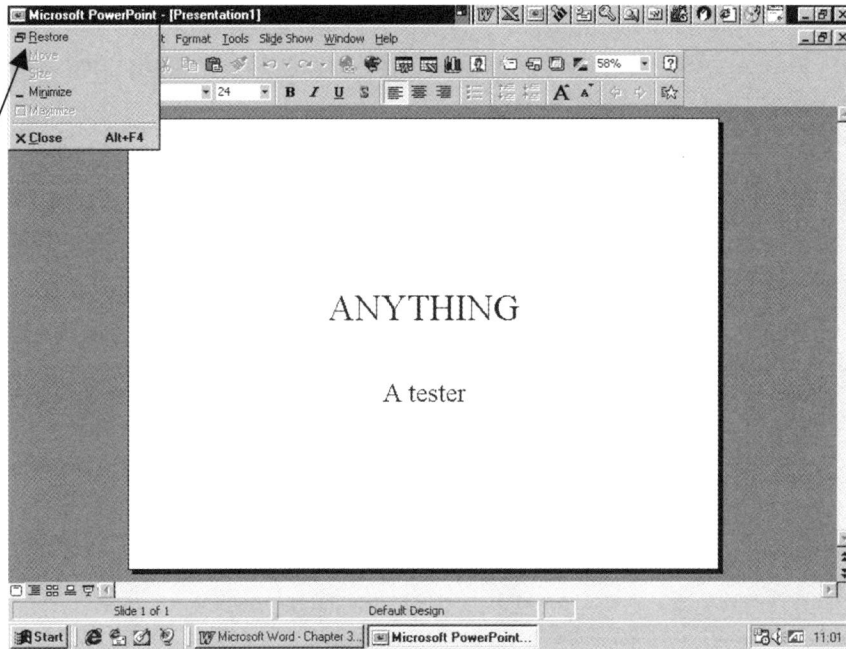

Click on the PowerPoint logo at the top of the screen...

and a drop-down menu appears.

POWERPOINT LOGO — WINDOW CONTROL

There is a second PowerPoint logo, below the one we have just reviewed.

It has the same options that exist in Excel, and they have the same functionality. See *The Accountant's Guide to Excel* for more details.

FILE

Click on **File** to display its contents.

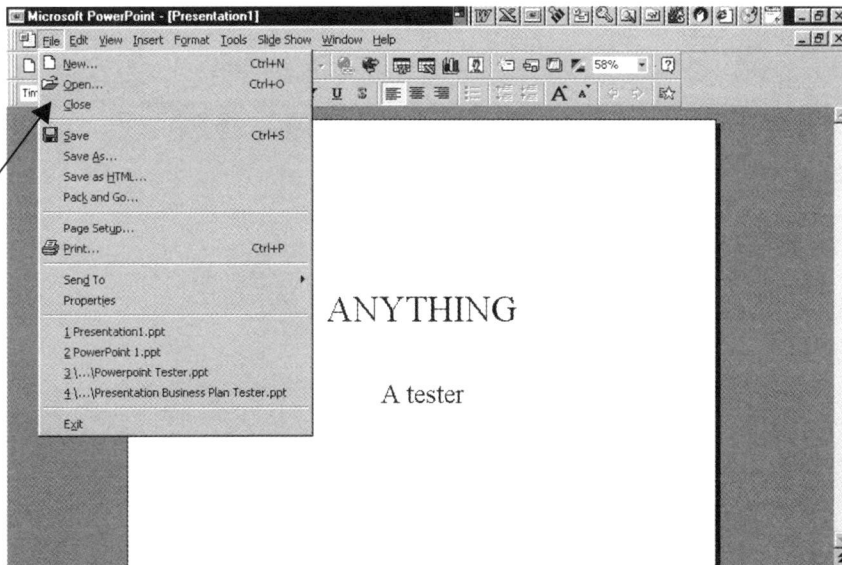

The File drop-down menu is displayed

Each major area is separated by a line, the categorisations being:
- File management (first and second sections) — Open, Close Save etc.
- Printing (third section)
- Transferring and Properties (fourth section) — Send To and Properties
- Recently Used List (fifth section)
- Exit (sixth section).

The sections and most of the functionality are the same as for Excel, and they all relate to interacting with the Operating System. See *The Accountant's Guide To Excel* for more details.

EDIT

Click on **Edit** and look at the drop-down menu.

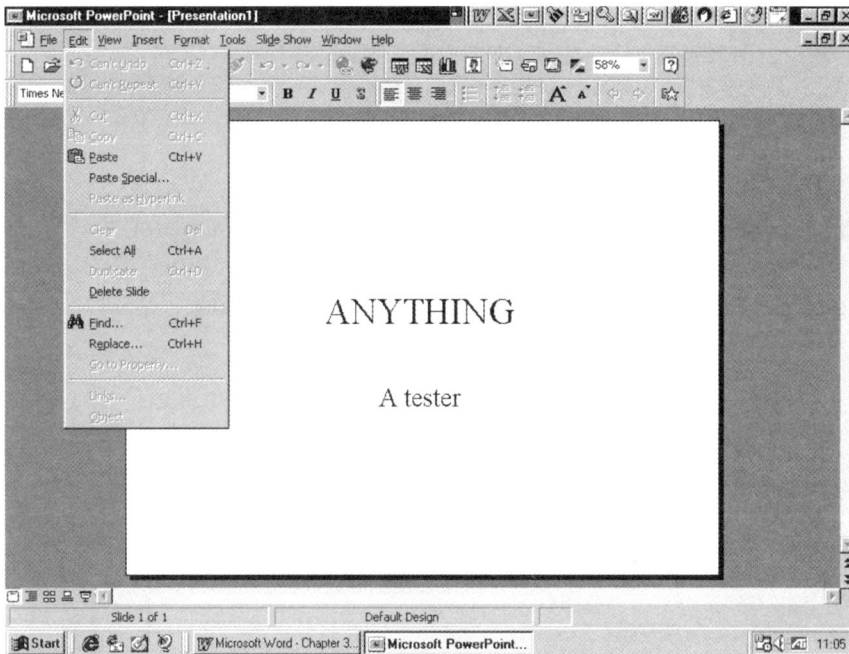

The major categorisations in the menu are:
- Repeating or undoing the last action
- Clipboard controls
- Slide editing and word-processing
- Word-processing edits
- Links and inserts editing.

The sections and most of the functionality are the same as for Excel, and they all relate to word-processing type operations. See *The Accountant's Guide to Excel* for more details.

VIEW

Click on **View** and look at the drop-down menu.

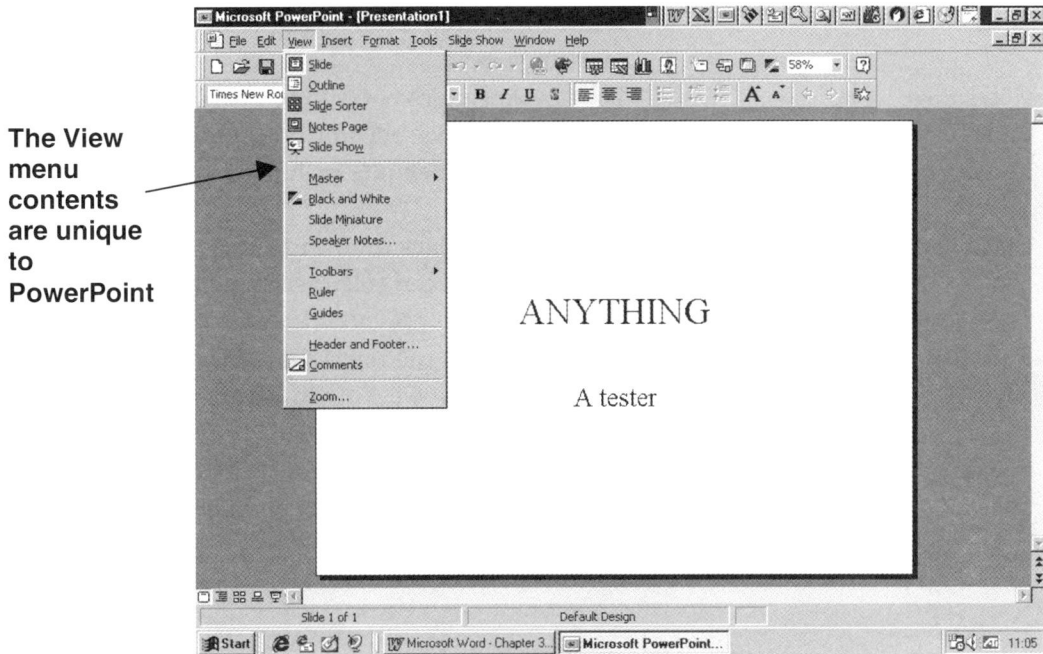

The View menu contents are unique to PowerPoint

The first and second sections of the menu are unique to PowerPoint, because it controls the screen view and manipulation of the style of the slides, which obviously does not apply in Excel. The third, fourth and fifth sections are the same as for Excel.

The major categorisations in the menu are:

- Style of presentation of slides on screen (first section)
- Template and speaker notes (second section)
- Toggle screen display of toolbars, ruler and guides (third section)
- Header and Footer, and Comments (fourth section)
- Zoom (fifth section).

The detailed menu options in the first two sections are:

Slide	The setting shown in the screen shots above.
Outline	Word processing format, to allow drag and drop between slides, promotion and demotion of headings etc.
Slide Sorter	Thumb nail view of all slides, to facilitate rearrangement.
Notes Page	To allow speakers notes to be attached.
Slide Show	This runs the PowerPoint presentation.
Master	Amending the defaults included in the slide layout.
Black and White	If printing in black and white, used to decide if the screen colour scheme is suitable.
Slide Miniature	A thumbnail in the top right corner of the screen. Useful if working in outline view for checking the visual layout.
Speaker Notes	Displays notes on the current slide, but retains the full screen view already chosen.

INSERT

Click on **Insert** and look at the drop-down menu.

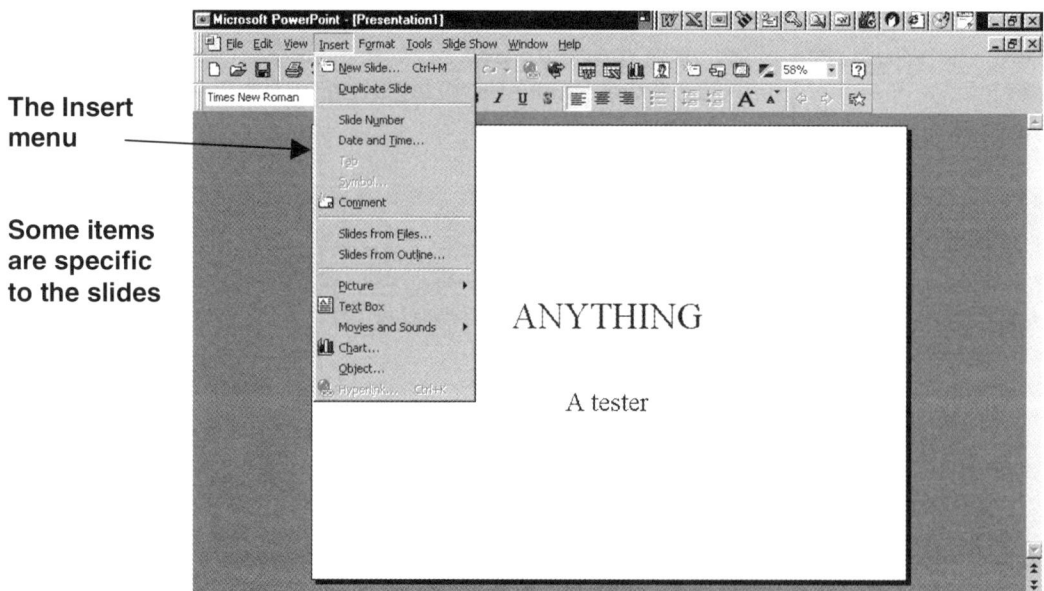

The Insert menu

Some items are specific to the slides

The first, second and third sections of the menu are unique to PowerPoint, because they relate to aspects of dealing with slides, which obviously does not apply in Excel.

The fourth section has similarities to Excel, but is more akin to Word, because PowerPoint is a word-processor based package.

The major categorisations in the menu are:
* Insert a new or duplicate slide (first section)
* Insertions into the current slide (second section)
* Insertion of a slide from Files or from Outlines (third section)
* Insertions on the current slide from outside sources, including pictures and charts.

The detailed menu options are:

New Slide	Select a formatted slide from the template list.
Duplicate Slide	Insert a copy of the present slide.
Slide Number	(Page) Numbering.
Date and Time	Date and Time stamping.
Tab	Tab stop.
Symbol	Special non-keyboard characters.
Comment	Comment slip. Same defaults as Excel.
Slides from Files	Import from another PowerPoint presentation.
Slides from Outline	Import from another package, such as Word.
Picture	Clipart etc, as for Excel.
Text Box	As for Excel drawing toolbar.
Movies and sound	From sound files etc. on the PC.
Chart	Stand alone charting facility, compared to importing an existing Excel chart.
Object	As used in the context of OLE.
Hyperlink	Inserts a hyperlink from PowerPoint to another location.

FORMAT

Click on **Format** and look at the drop-down menu.

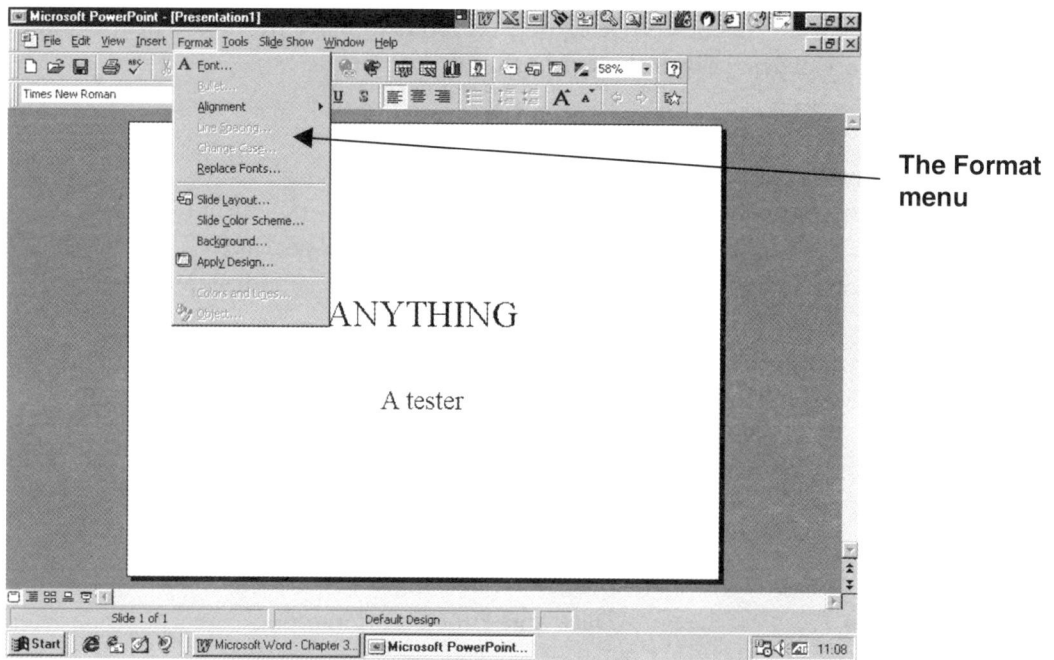

The Format menu

The first section of the menu has similarities to Word, rather than Excel. The formatting toolbar in Excel contains the menu capabilities.

The second section is unique to PowerPoint, because it relates to slide formatting.

The third section of the menu also has similarities to Word, rather than Excel. However, the capabilities in Excel can be accessed from the drawing toolbar.

The major categorisations in the menu are:

- Formatting text etc. (first section)
- Formatting slides (second section)
- Formatting shapes etc. (third section).

The detailed menu options are:

Font	As for Word
Bullet	As for Word
Alignment	As for Word
Line Spacing	As for Word
Change Case	As for Word
Replace Fonts	Global replace of style

Slide Layout	Change slide type
Slide Color Scheme	Change slide content colours
Background	Change slide backdrop colour scheme
Apply Design	Background fill
Colors and Lines	Text box colours etc.
Object	Formatting of objects, including Autoshape.

TOOLS

Click on **Tools** and look at the drop-down menu.

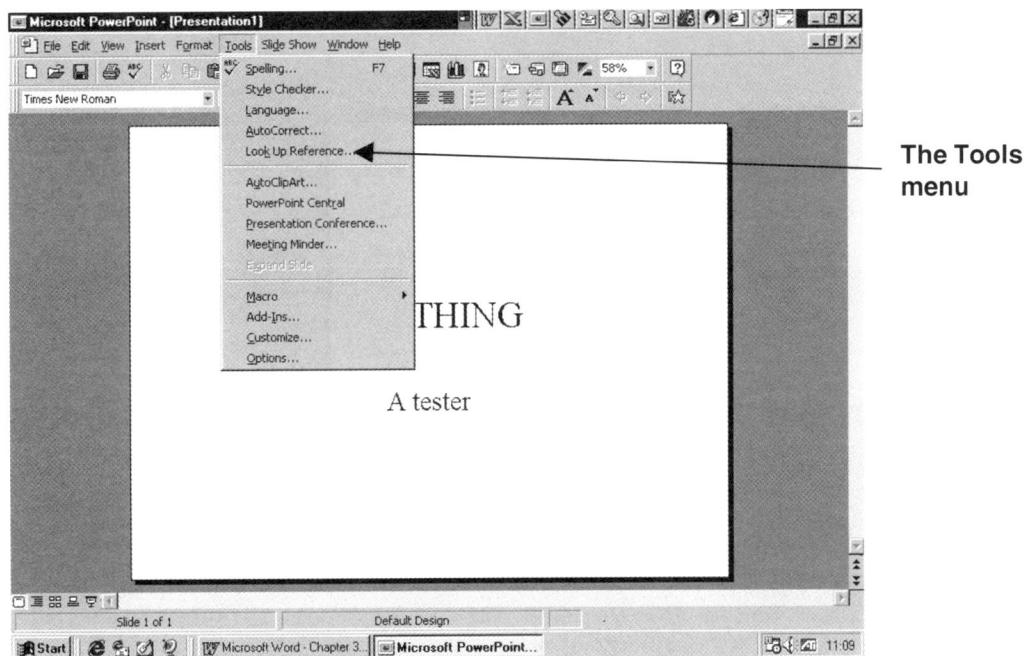

The Tools menu

This is the catch-all menu item. The items are grouped, but they are not really related. The detailed menu options are:

Spelling	Word-processor spell checker
Style Checker	Slide show utility for reviewing slide layout etc.
Language	Select English (UK)
AutoCorrect	Automatic type change for common typing errors
Lookup Reference	Using a CD dictionary etc.
AutoClipArt	Suggested clipart
PowerPoint Central	Web update facility
Presentation Conference	A PC to PC meeting

Meeting Minder	Scheduling
Expand Slide	Spread over one or more slides
Macro	VBA
Add Ins	It works the same as it does in Excel
Customize	It works the same as it does in Excel
Options	It works the same as it does in Excel.

SLIDE SHOW

Click on **Slide Show** and look at the drop-down menu.

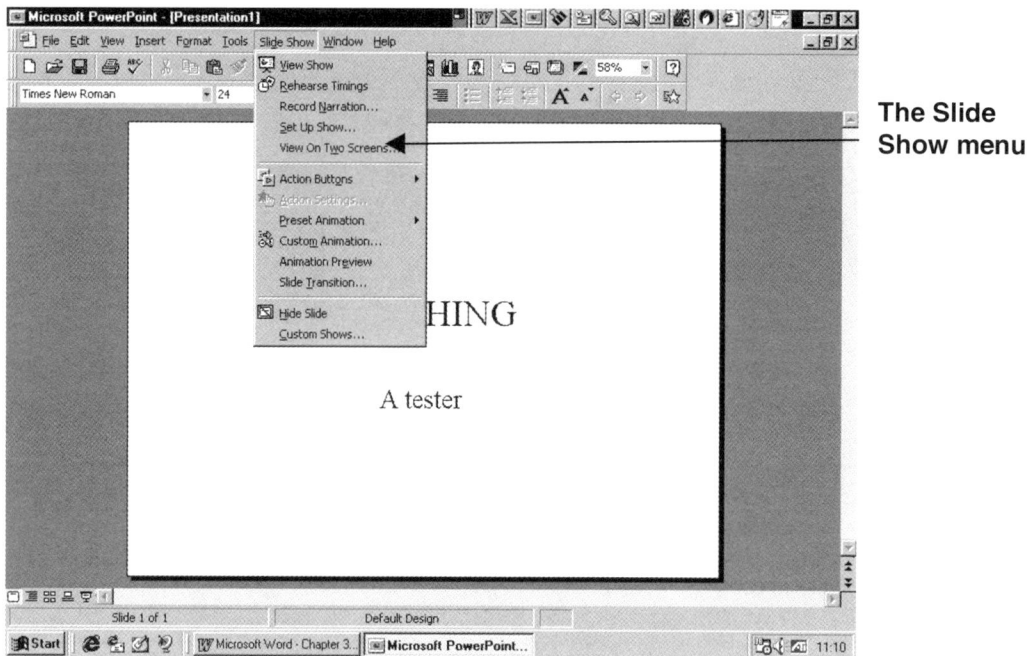

The Slide Show menu

The major categorisations in the menu are:
- Finalising presentation and delivery
- Animating
- Customising.

The detailed menu options are:

View Show	The same as in the View menu
Rehearse Timings	To practice delivery
Record Narration	Verbal recording
Set Up Show	Settings for View Show
View On Two Screens	Two computer screens
Action Buttons	Draw on the slide, and activate

Action Settings	To change settings for action buttons
Preset Animation	Fanciful ideas to liven the show
Custom Animation	If the fanciful just doesn't do
Animation Preview	Thumbnail version
Slide Transition	Different ways to bring in the next slide
Hide Slide	Do not display to the audience
Custom Shows	Customise.

WINDOW

The sections and functionality are the same as for Excel. See *The Accountant's Guide to Excel* for more details.

HELP

The sections and functionality are the same as for Excel. See *The Accountant's Guide to Excel* for more details.

NEXT

This chapter has provided an overview of what is available in PowerPoint, and its functionality.

We are seeking to obtain a working, rather than in-depth, knowledge of PowerPoint. We will not therefore review the toolbars.

In the next chapter we see how to prepare a presentation.

Chapter Nineteen

THE POWERPOINT REPORT STRUCTURE

The pro-forma says . . .

The easiest way to explain how to use the program is to use it for its intended purpose — preparing the presentation for the meeting.

We have not analysed the figures yet, and we have not prepared our spreadsheets etc. either — this is covered in the next section. However, we can set down the parameters here that we are working within, and connect the PowerPoint presentation to the final product in **Section Four**.

The questions we ask, the personnel we need to speak to, the analysis we need to complete is all determined by the report we expect to produce at the end of our work.

Our starting point for the structure of the report must be to review the templates available in PowerPoint, because the bulk of the work — in terms of slide backgrounds, colour etc. has already been completed for us.

START POWERPOINT

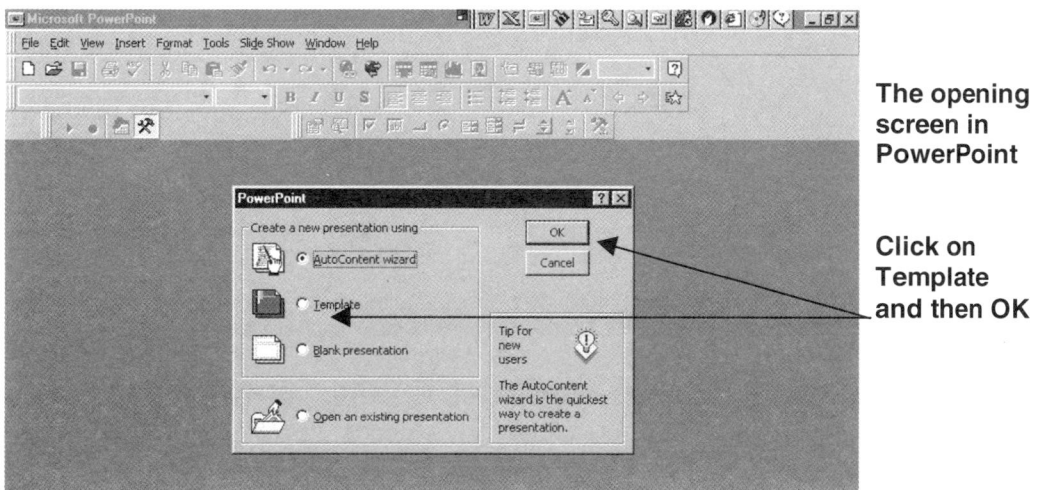

The opening
screen in
PowerPoint

Click on
Template
and then OK

The Templates screen starts. Click on the Presentations Tab and the range of pre-formatted presentations is shown. Select Business Plan (Standard) and click OK.

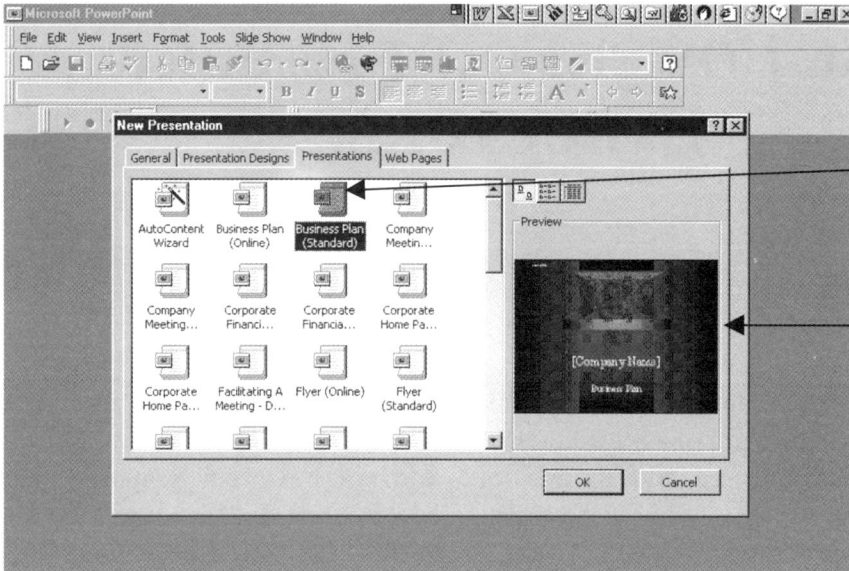

Select Business Plan (Standard)

A preview is displayed

Click on OK to start the presentation

A pro-forma slide show is loaded, ready for amendment.

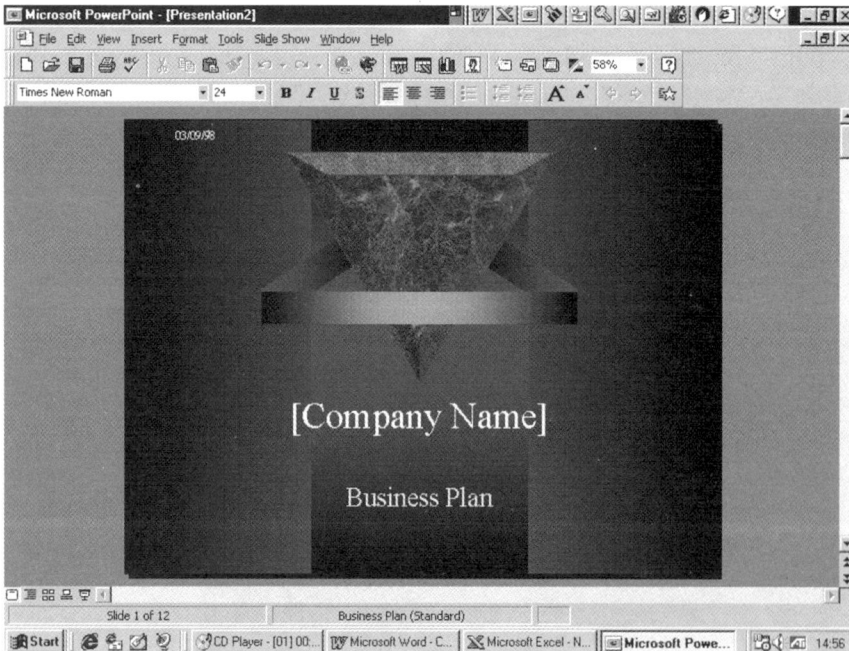

The slide show is shown in draft format

Change to Outline view

See below

Select View from the menu, then Outline. This displays the contents of the slides.

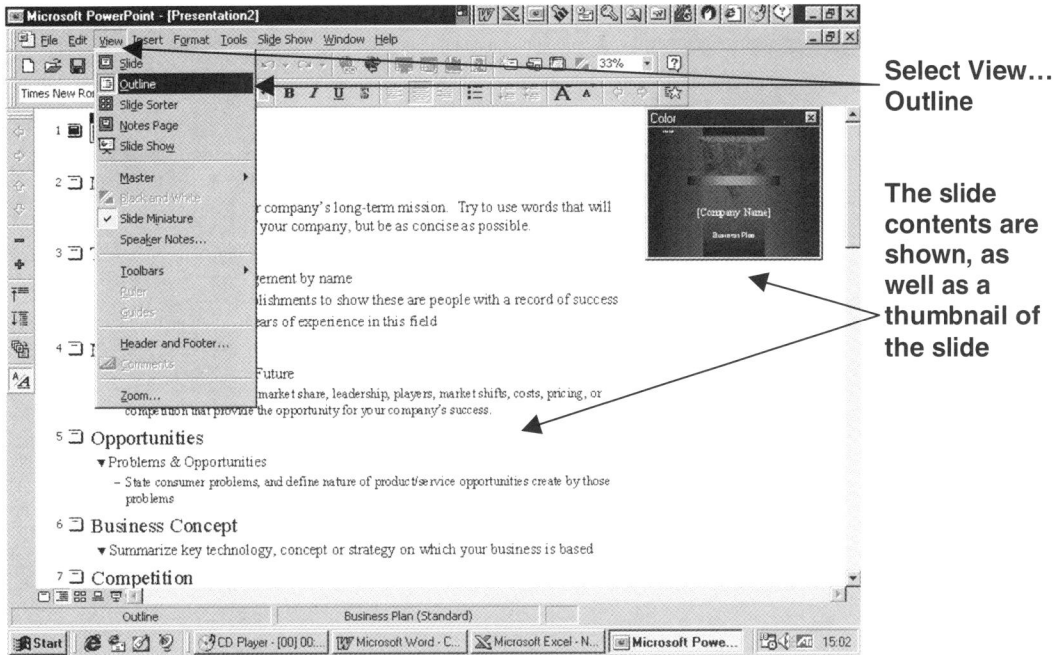

**Select View…
Outline**

**The slide
contents are
shown, as
well as a
thumbnail of
the slide**

We want to import the pro-forma into Word, so that we can review it and amend
it to suit our needs. We will also want to look at two other templates. However,
first of all select all of the text by choosing Edit from the menu, then Select All.
Press Ctrl+C to copy the text to the Clipboard.

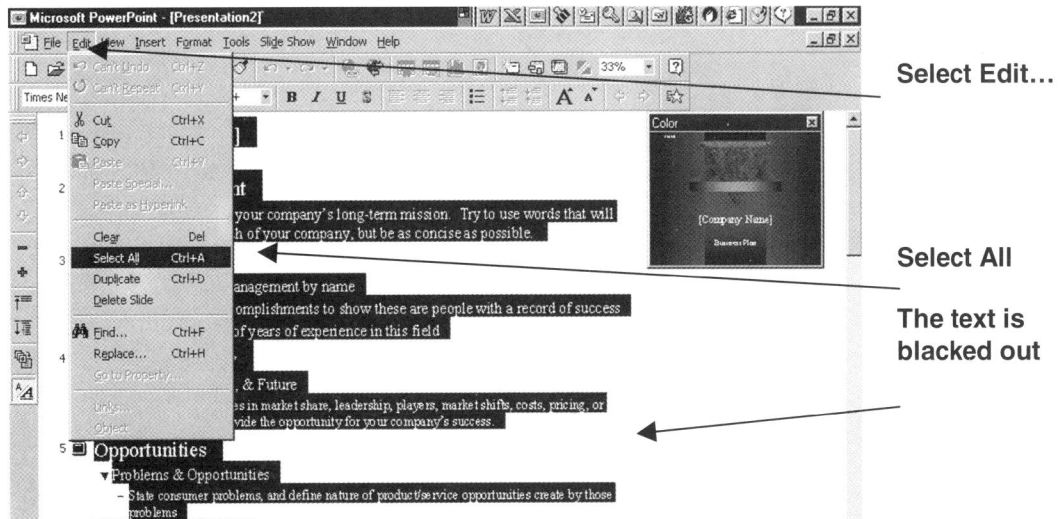

Select Edit…

Select All

**The text is
blacked out**

With the text copied to the Clipboard, start Word, and select Edit from the menu, then Paste Special.

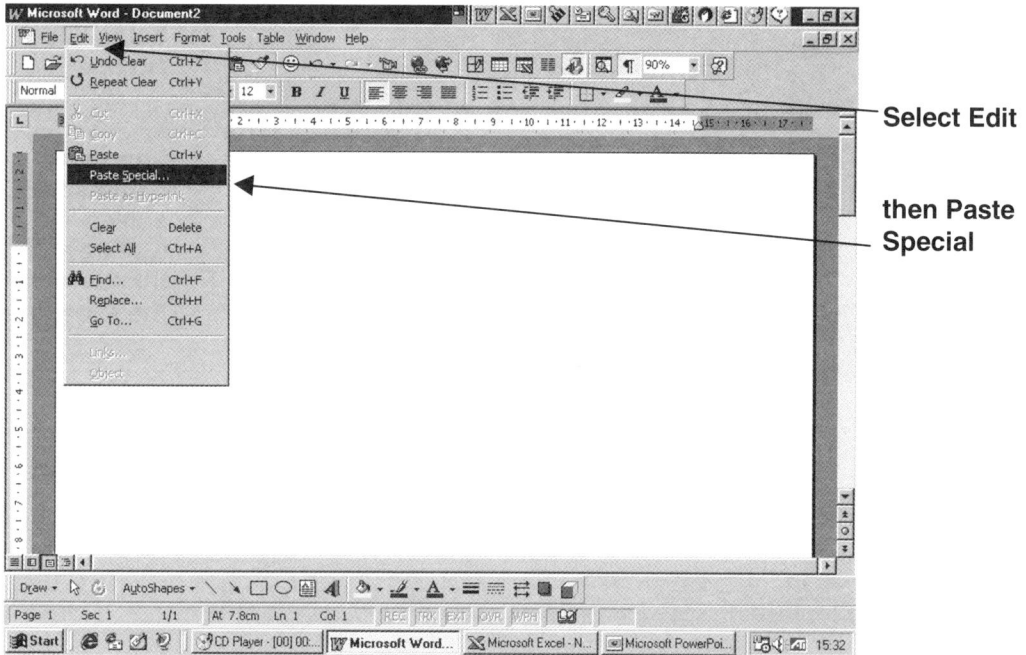

Select Edit

then Paste Special

The Paste Special dialog box appears. This gives a choice of methods for pasting the information. We want to deal with the text of the slides, not the slides themselves, so we will choose Unformatted Text.

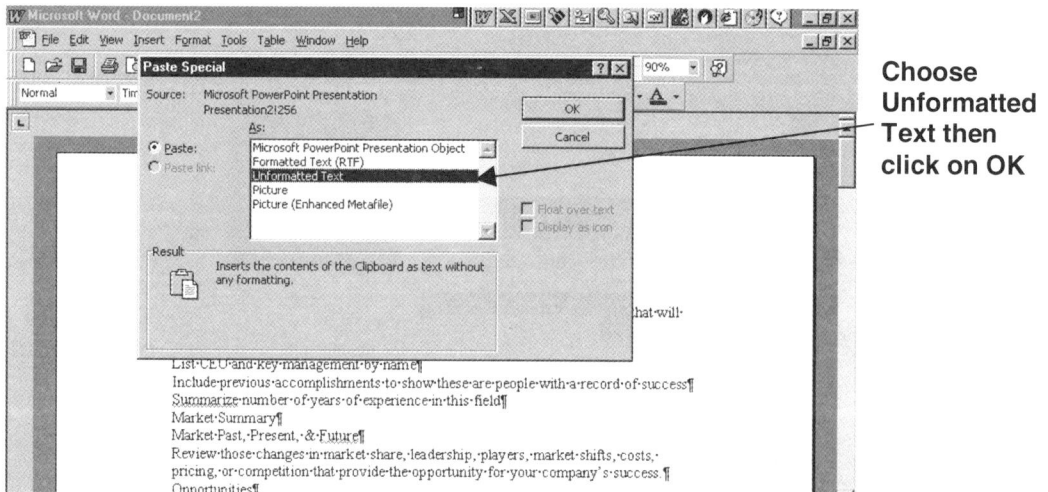

Choose Unformatted Text then click on OK

The pro-forma can now be printed in Word, or amended as desired.

There are two other pro-formas we are interested in — Marketing Plan (Standard) and Recommending a Strategy (Standard). Copying these into Word and printing them out allows the three suggested presentations to be blended into the presentation we want to achieve.

The three pro-formas, amended for bolding of headings etc., are reproduced in **Appendix 2**.

The three pro-formas each have a different slide background. We will choose one of these later, but for the moment we want to prepare our questions for the interviews that we will have to have in order to gather the information for our meeting.

THE POWERPOINT REPORT FORMAT

The reason we have taken three different reports — business plan, marketing and strategy, is because our problem is a potential one, and it has aspects that appear in each type of report. Thingies are not yet on sale, and we are anticipating defending our market, so the marketing plan is relevant. We need to formulate a strategic plan in order to anticipate what our competitor might try to achieve, so the strategic plan is relevant. The business plan includes financial and resource planning, as well as an analysis of our existing business and the threats and opportunities arising, so the business plan is definitely relevant.

After excluding the aspects of each plan that are not relevant to our specific circumstances we are left with the following content for the presentation:

Thingies Presentation

[Company Name]
Business Plan

Mission Statement / Vision Statement

A clear statement of your company's long-term mission. Try to use words that will help direct the growth of your company, but be as concise as possible. State the vision and long term direction.

Market Summary

Market Past, Present, & Future
Review those changes in market share, leadership, players, market shifts, costs, pricing, or competition that provide the opportunity for your company's success.

Competition

The competitive landscape
Provide an overview of product competitors, their strengths and weaknesses.
Position each competitor's product against new product.
Summarize competition.
Outline your company's competitive advantage.

Positioning

Positioning of product or service
Statement that distinctly defines the product in its market and against its competition over time.
Consumer promise.
Statement summarizing the benefit of the product or service to the consumer.

Opportunities / Threats

Problems & Opportunities
State consumer problems, and define nature of product/service opportunities create by those problems.

Goals & Objectives

5-Year Goals.
State specific measurable objectives.
State Market share objectives.
State revenue/profitability objectives.

Available Options

State the alternative strategies.
List advantages & disadvantages of each.
State cost of each option.

Launch Strategies / Public Relations / Advertising / Other

Launch plan
if product is being announced.
Promotion budget.
Supply back up material with detailed budget information for review.
Strategy & execution.
Overview of strategy.
Overview of media & timing.
Overview of ad spending.

Pricing

Pricing
Summarize specific pricing or pricing strategies.
Compare to similar products.
Policies
Summarize policy relevant to understanding key pricing issues.

Financial Plan

High-level financial plan that defines financial model, pricing assumptions
and reviews yearly expected sales and profits for the next three years.
Use several slides to cover this material appropriately.

Success Metrics

First year goals.
Additional year goals.
Measures of success/failure.
Requirements for success.

Schedule

18-month schedule highlights.
Timing.
Isolate timing dependencies critical to success.

Resource Requirements

Technology Requirements.
Personnel Requirements.
Resource Requirements.
financial, distribution, promotion, etc.
External Requirements.
products/services/technology required to be purchased outside company.

Risks & Rewards

Risks
Summarize risks of proposed project.
Addressing Risk
Summarize how risks will be addressed.
Rewards
Estimate expected pay-off, particularly if seeking funding.

Key Issues

Near Term
Isolate key decisions and issues that need immediate or near-term resolution.
Long Term
Isolate issues needing long-term resolution.
State consequences of decision postponement.
If you are seeking funding, state specifics.

Recommendation

Recommend one or more of the strategies.
Summarize the results if things go as proposed.
What to do next.
Identify Action Items.

NEXT

Now that we have the skeleton for our plan we can arrange to meet the relevant personnel and gather the information together for our presentation. This is done in **Section Four**.

However, first we also need to polish off our slide show as much as possible. We look at this in the next chapter.

Chapter Twenty

WORKING WITH THE POWERPOINT REPORT

The pro-forma says. . . . But ours is different.

We have revised the content of our report from the templates available. Now we want to amend the slides in our presentation, and choose backgrounds etc. This will also tell us where the spreadsheets, charts etc. will fit in, and what type of information we should present, and in which format.

Start PowerPoint, select Template and choose Business Plan (Standard). We will use this as our starting point. It is saved on the CD as **PowerPoint 1.ppt**. Right click on the green background, and select Apply Design from the pop up menu.

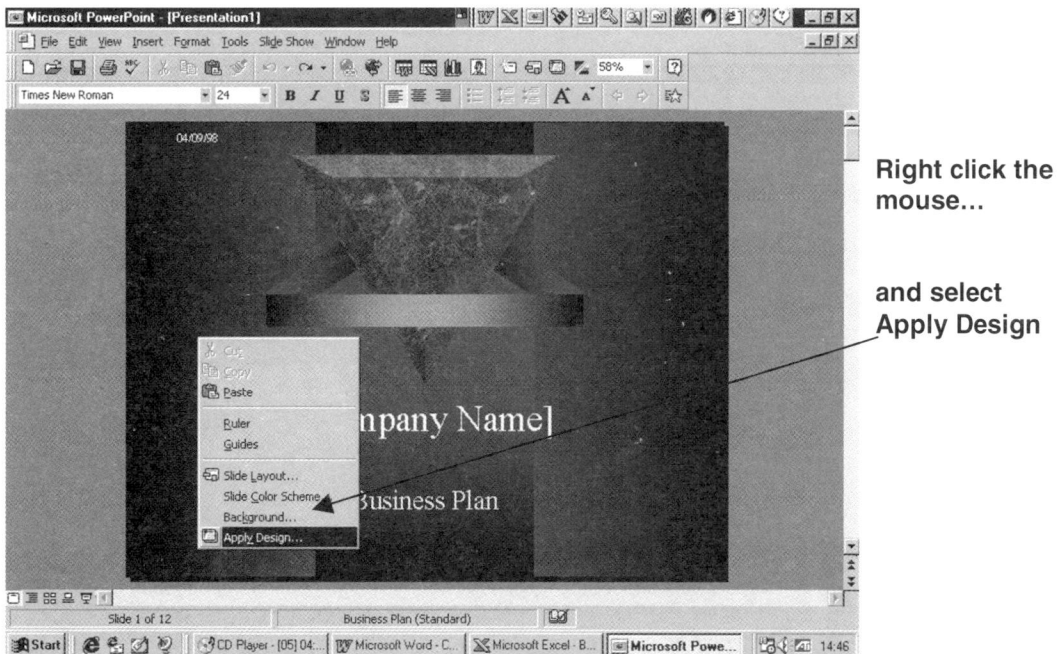

Right click the mouse...

and select Apply Design

A list of alternative designs is shown. Select Professional and click Apply.

The slide background changes to grey slate, and this is automatically applied to all of the slides. The slideshow is saved on the CD as **PowerPoint 2.ppt**.

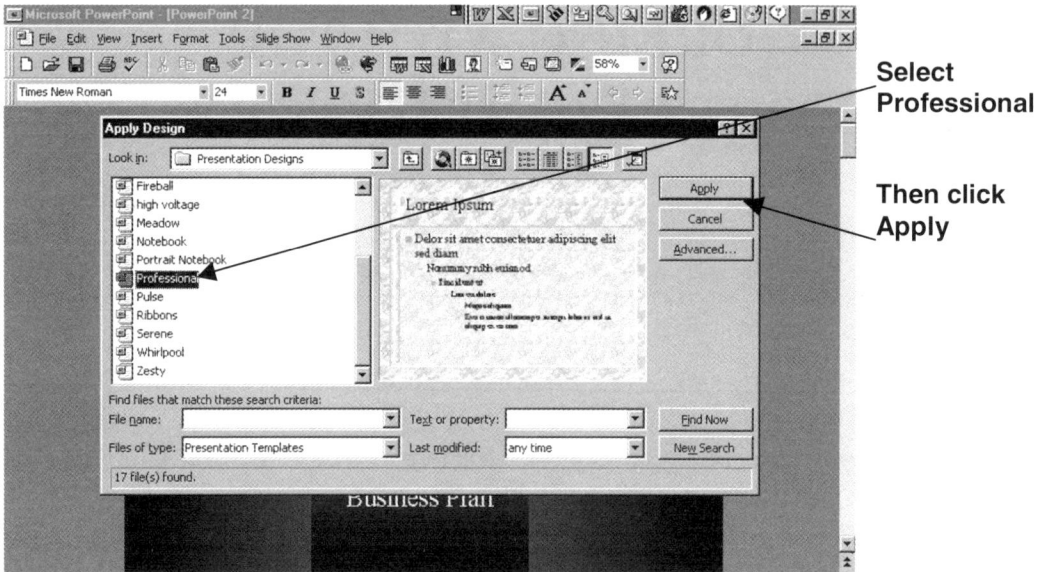

We will amend the slide contents first, and format all of the slides later. Change to outline view (select View from the menu, and then Outline). The screen layout is explained below.

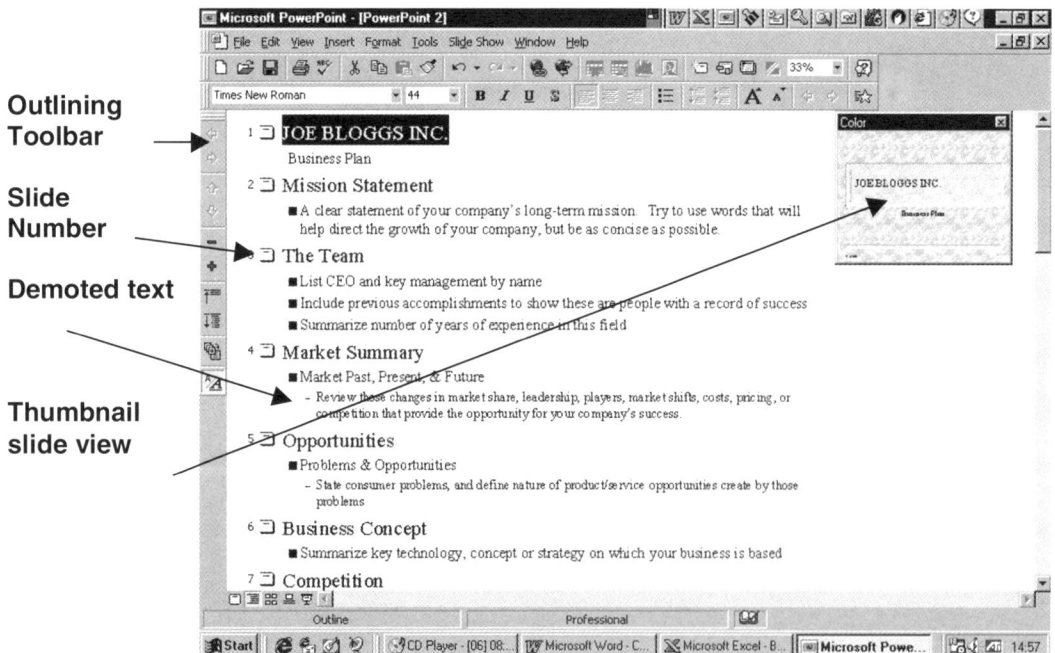

Outlining Toolbar

This allows a selected paragraph to be promoted to a slide heading, or demoted to (smaller) sub text by clicking the left and right arrows. The up and down arrows switch the line around with the line above. Formatting can be turned off and on in order to make it easier to review the text.

Slide Number

The entire slide can be moved to a new position by drag and drop.

Demoted Text

Use the Outline Toolbar to promote

Thumbnail

When the text of the slides is changed the Thumbnail Slide updates at the same time, so that you can check that it looks as you intended.

AMENDING THE PRO-FORMA

We will amend the contents of the slide show to agree with the revised contents as per the previous chapter.

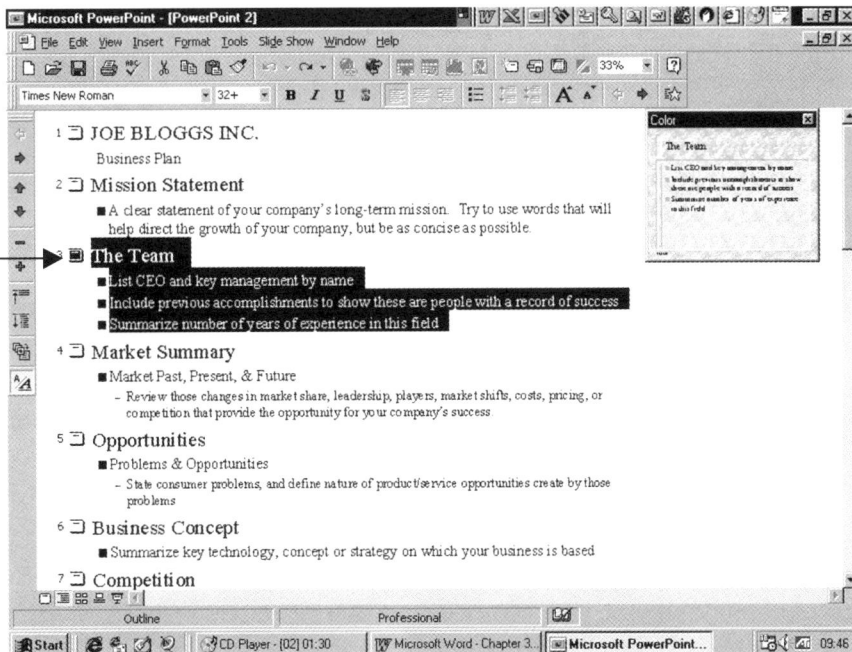

We want to delete slide three

Click on the slide — all of the text is highlighted

Press delete

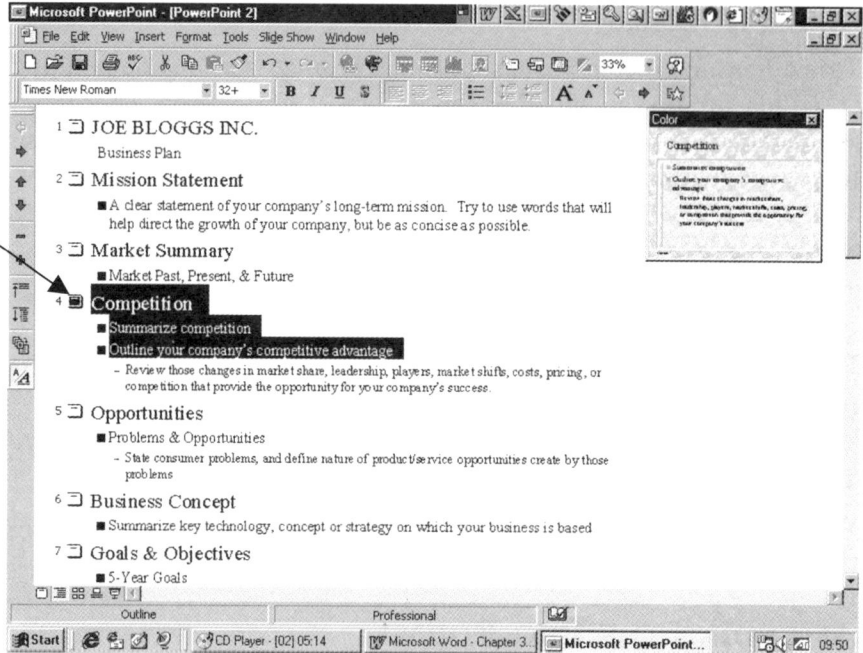

Use Drag and Drop to rearrange the order of slides

Type in the new text as appropriate

A new slide can be inserted by entering a new line and then promoting it.

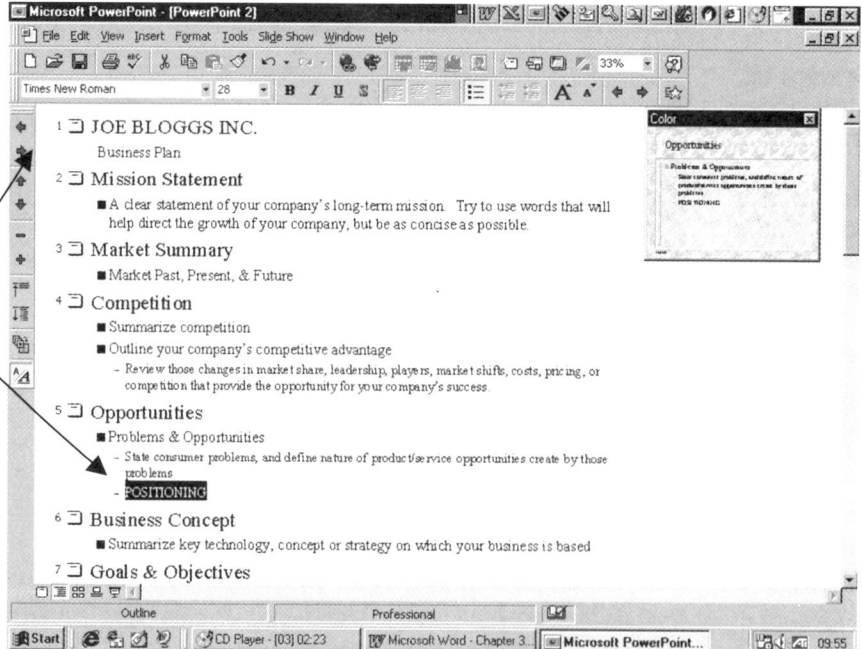

Promote the text to create a new slide

The file is saved on the CD as **PowerPoint 3.ppt**.

FINALISING THE FORMATTING

You will notice that in Outline View the Centre Text, Left Justify, Right Justify are greyed out and are not available.

To centre text etc. change to Slide View, select the appropriate text and format as required.

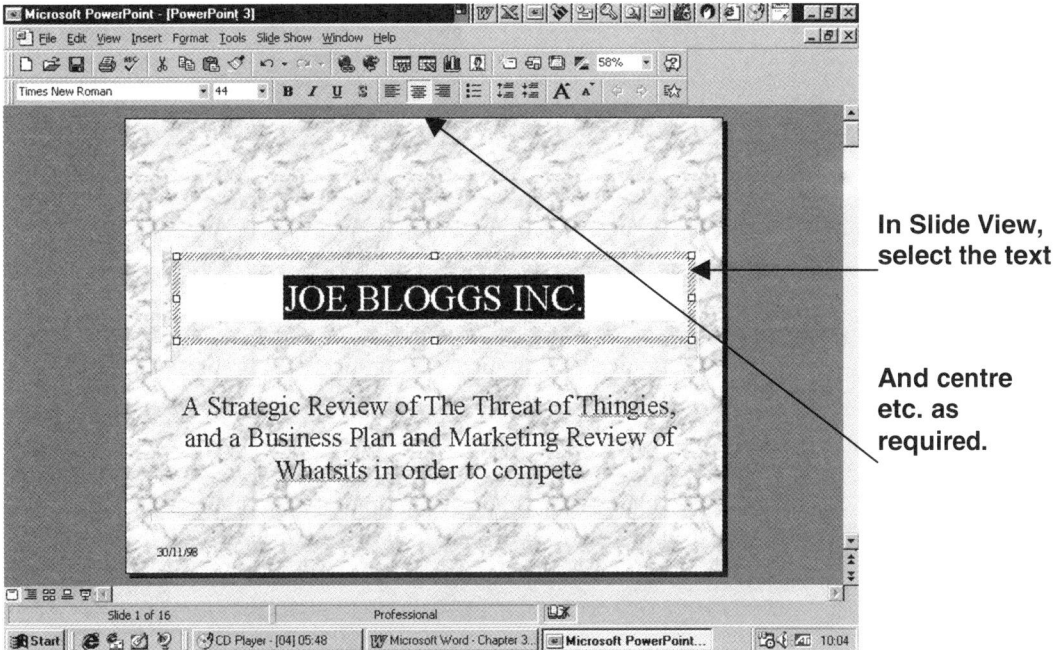

In Slide View, select the text

And centre etc. as required.

NOTES

Notes can be added to the slides in order to aid the discussion surrounding each slide, and to provide notes to the attendees.

Select View, Notes Page.

The screen displays the slide at the top, and a text box below for notes. Type notes in the text box to explain and expand on the slides.

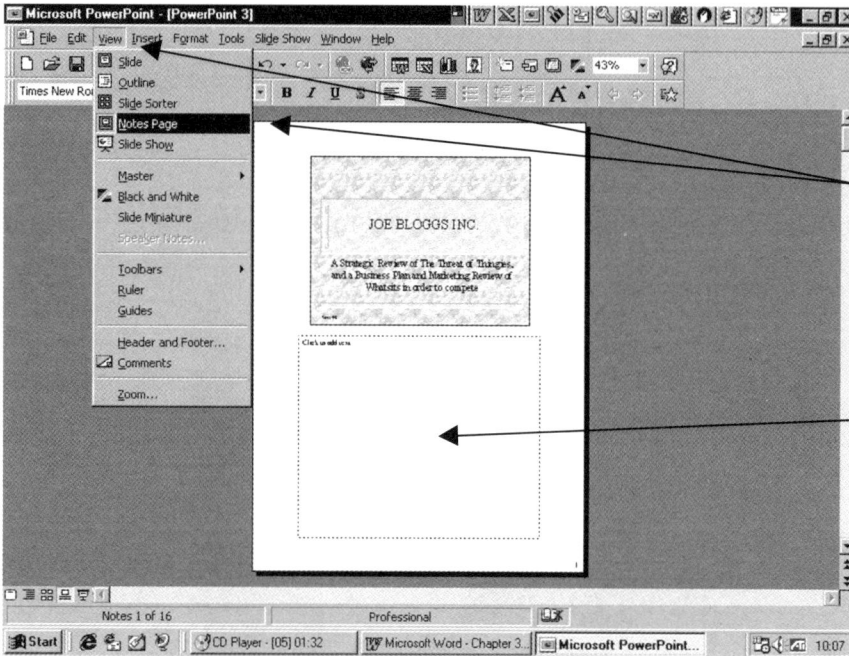

The notes pages are printed by selecting File, Print, and then choosing Notes Pages from the Print What drop down box.

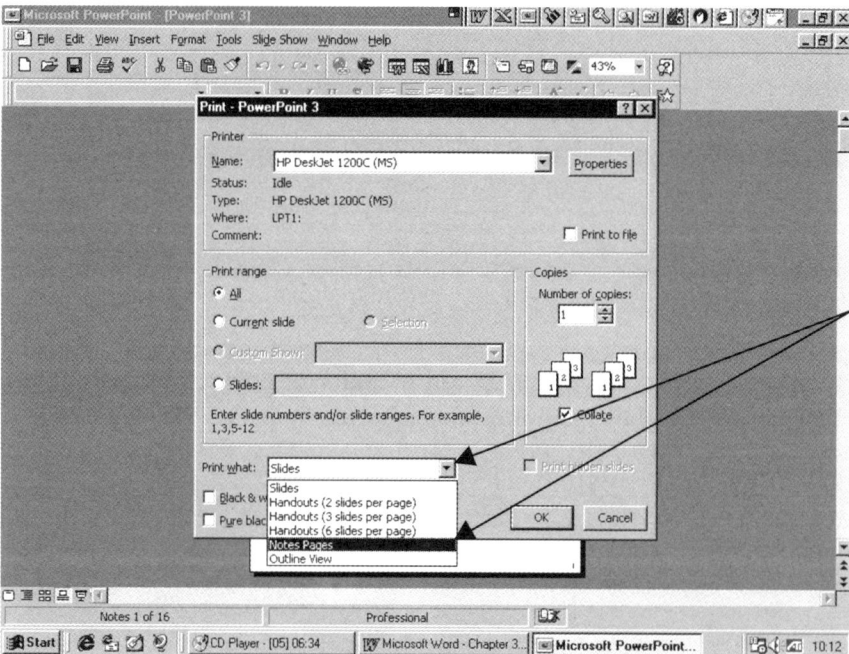

CHARTS AND SPREADSHEETS

These can be created directly in PowerPoint. However, we will link from PowerPoint to spreadsheets prepared in Excel, which we will build in the next section.

We will look at linking at that stage.

THE SLIDE SHOW

That only leaves the live slide show.

**Right click
for options.**

**Left click for
next slide**

**Backspace
for previous
slide**

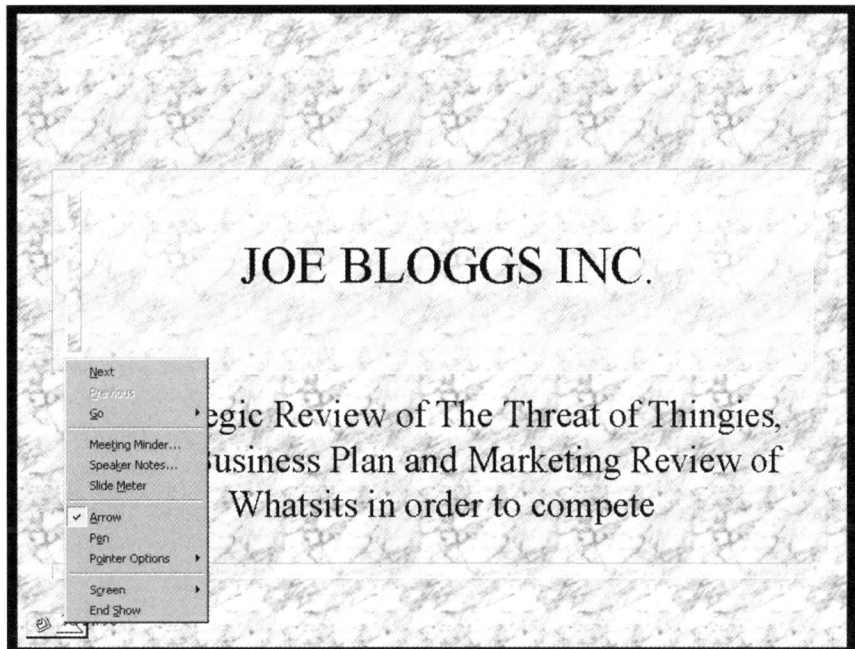

NEXT

That concludes our review of PowerPoint. We have enough knowledge to make a fully completed, professional presentation at our meeting. Now we want to review the Whatsits information, prepare our spreadsheet and finalise everything.

Section Four

WHATSITS ANALYSIS: OVERVIEW

We are now ready to begin our analysis of the Whatsits trading figures in Excel, and prepare the groundwork for our meeting with the senior management team.

This section therefore involves:

- Gathering information from the various departments — Sales, Production, and Finance
- Analysing and summarising this information
- Projecting as necessary
- Preparing "What If" analysis
- Charting, using VBA, setting up spreadsheets . . . whatever is necessary to properly and professionally convey our message to the audience.

It is the groundwork rather than the final, finished product. We will incorporate the end results in the final part of the section.

Chapter Twenty-one

INITIAL MEETINGS

We think the problem is . . .

We are ready to speak to the personnel, and glean the information we need for our review. Let's talk.

HISTORICAL DATA

First of all I will introduce you to Nigel. He is the Network Administrator for the group.

"Hello Nigel."

"Hello James. And this is your colleague . . . yes. How do you do?"

"Nigel. We were just wondering about getting historical data in order to prepare for a meeting on Thursday. We need to import data into Excel then set up some PivotTables to summarise the information."

"Okay. I will need to authorise the access to the database, because it contains all of the sensitive stuff about sales to customers and the like, but that shouldn't be a problem. I presume you will password protect your spreadsheet?"

"Yes."

"Right." Nigel looked over my shoulder. *"I don't know if you are aware of the security procedures here, but I have to generate all of the passwords for sensitive information. It keeps everything in order."*

"That's okay Nigel," I said. *"I think he was given the low-down when he joined."*

Next, the sales people.

SALES DATA

The sales people were having a discussion.

"Do you want us to come back later?" I was speaking to Alan, the head of the Sales team.

"No, that's all right. We were just having a discussion about Blue Co and the fact that they will be distributing Thingies. The sooner we nip it in the bud the better."

"Yes. We have the meeting on Thursday, and we need to get some information together. I was wanting to pick your brains for a while if that's alright."

"Yep. Fire away."

He gave us a lengthy review of the problems he foresaw with the sale of Thingies into what has traditionally been our market.

What he subsequently told us would be allocated under the draft headings from the PowerPoint presentation but, for the purposes of the tutorial, we are going to analyse the historical data provided by Nigel and prepare charts and PivotTables for the final PowerPoint presentation, and then use VBA to improve its impact.

Chapter Twenty-two

SPREADSHEET OUTLINE

Art in the making

We will need to build several different spreadsheets in order to consider each area of the report. Some of the spreadsheet work will be drawn forward into tables and summaries, and it is these single screen summaries that we will want to present at our meeting.

The range of topics we want to analyse on the spreadsheet, and some of the parameters for our design, are noted below. Each spreadsheet is then built in the chapters that follow in the rest of this section.

Historical Data	Use PivotTables to analyse and summarise the data.
	Chart the results.
Production	Summarise the machine time required compared to present capacity.
	Use VBA to switch between each scenario.
	Chart the results.
Sales Review	Prepare Sales Tables to look at forecast growth in the entire market.
	Chart the results.
Sales Units Forecasts	Prepare forecasts for the number of units expected to be sold, reflecting forecast change in market size and competition.
Sales Pricing	Impact on profitability of changing prices, including a price war with competitors.

NEXT

We start building our spreadsheets in the next chapter, where we look at the analysis of the historical results.

Chapter Twenty-three

HISTORICAL DATA

We were there!

We have been given a copy of the actual sales achieved from 1 January 1998 to 7 February 2002. The spreadsheet is saved on the CD as **Imported Sales Data.xls**.

We will analyse the results with PivotTables, and then prepare charts of the data. If, when you are opening the files and creating the PivotTables etc. your machine runs very slowly, because of the size of the spreadsheet files, open the file **Whatsits Random Data Generator.xls** and generate a smaller number of records. The program is explained in **Appendix 1**.

Note that, for convenience and speed, password protection has been removed from the file **Imported Sales Data 1.xls** forward. Compare the speed of opening this file and the file **Imported Sales Data.xls**, which is encrypted in order to avoid importing the data into Access, Excel etc. The password is ENTER.

The only difference between **Imported Sales Data.xls** and **Imported Sales Data 1.xls** is that protection is activated in the first, and not the second.

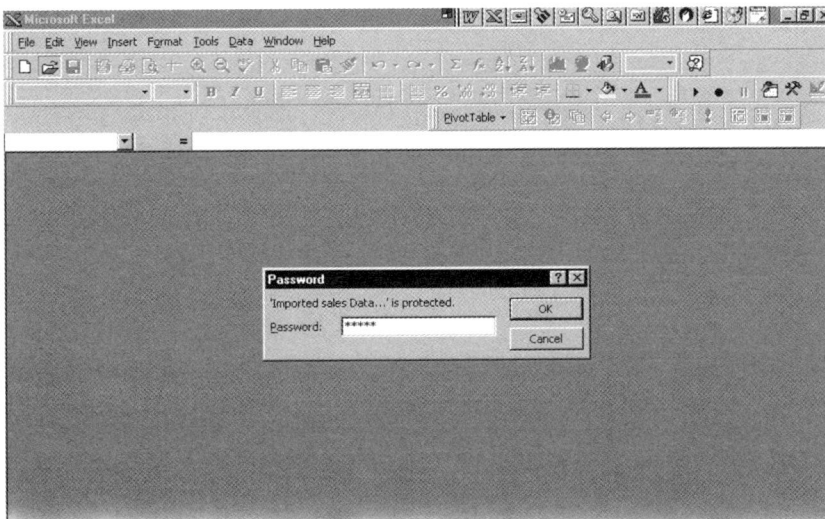

The password is ENTER . . .

however, opening and closing is VERY slow

SUMMARISE SALES VALUES BY MONTH

We will prepare a PivotTable to summarise the sales by value, monthly. The table will be shown in Sheet 2, and the sheet will be relabelled Sales Values.

Firstly, turn on the PivotTable toolbar. With the mouse pointer in the toolbar section, right click and select the PivotTable Toolbar. Drag it into the toolbar area if necessary.

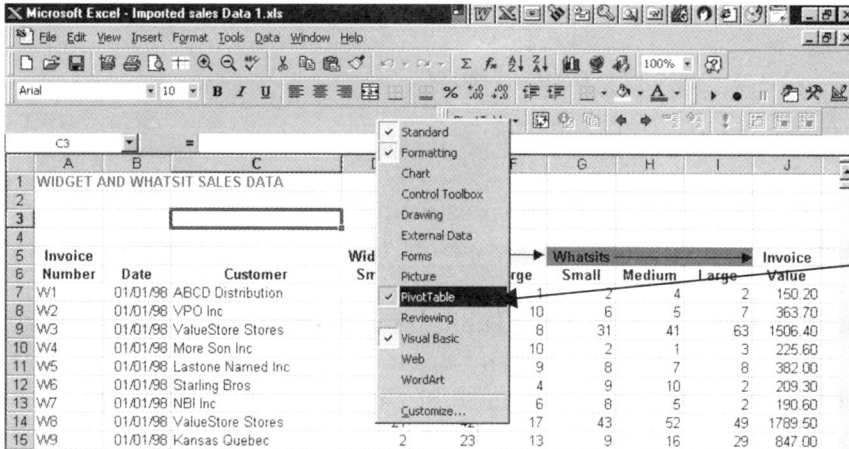

Right click with the mouse, and select the PivotTable Toolbar

Activate Sheet 2, then click on the down arrow in the PivotTable toolbar menu item, and select Wizard.

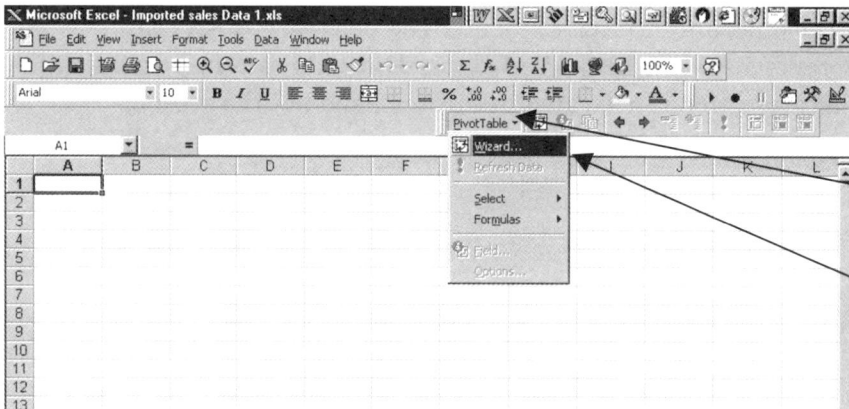

With Sheet 2 active . . .

Click on PivotTable . . .

and select Wizard

When the Wizard starts, select the range of cells from Sheet 1, i.e., from A6 to J60006 (including the headings).

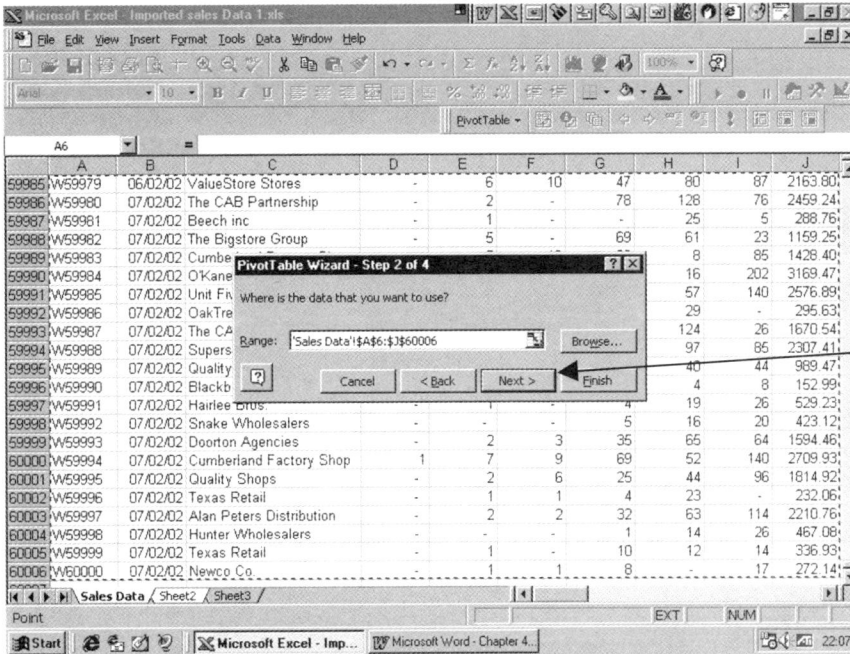

The range has been selected by using F8 to anchor the cell at A6, and then using Ctrl+ arrow keys to quickly move to J60006

Click Next

Drag Date to the Row section, and Value to the Data section. The description changes to Sum of Value.

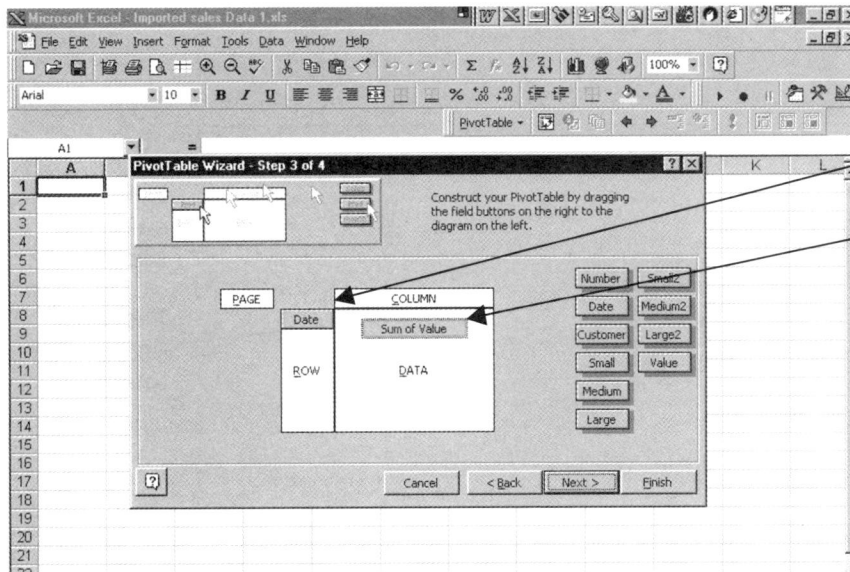

Drag Date

and Value

to the grid

Click Next

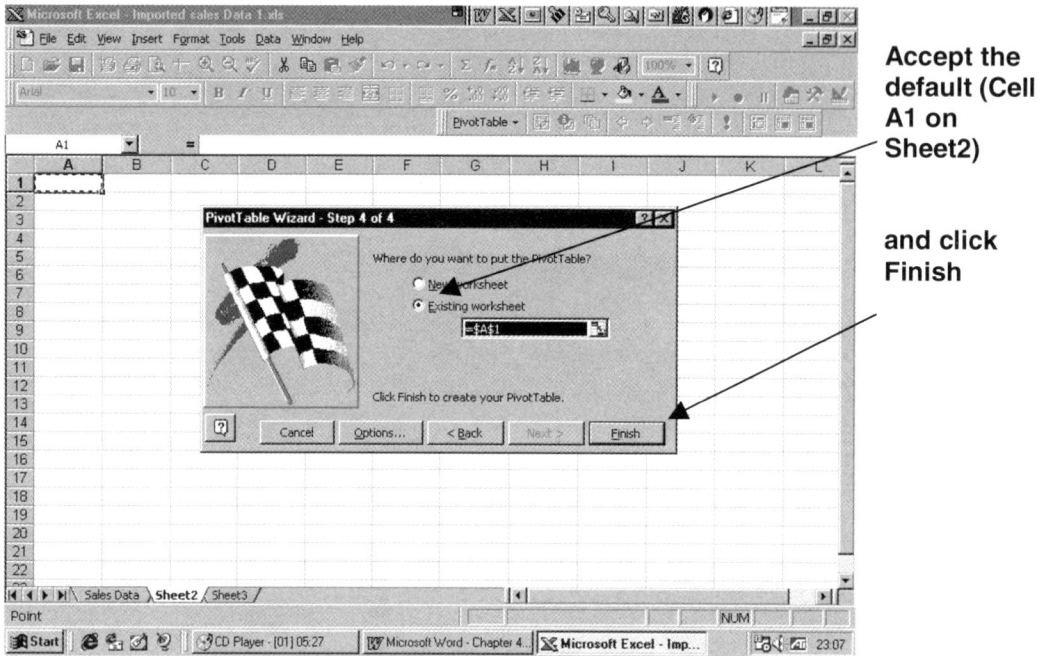

Accept the default (Cell A1 on Sheet2)

and click Finish

The sales are summarised daily.

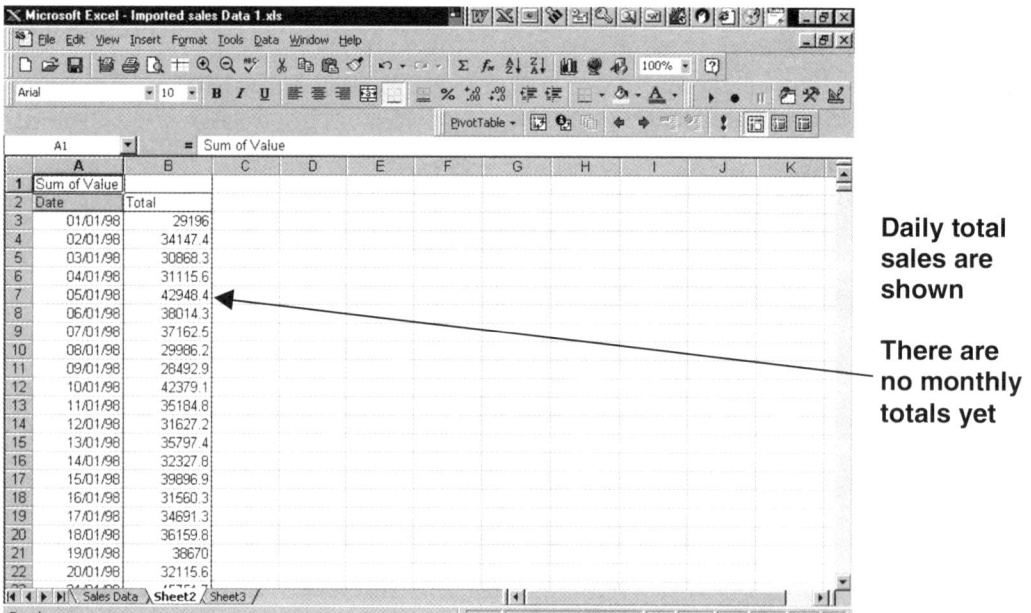

Daily total sales are shown

There are no monthly totals yet

The spreadsheet is saved as **Imported Sales Data 2.xls**. With the mouse cursor over the Date column, right click and select Group and Outline, then Group.

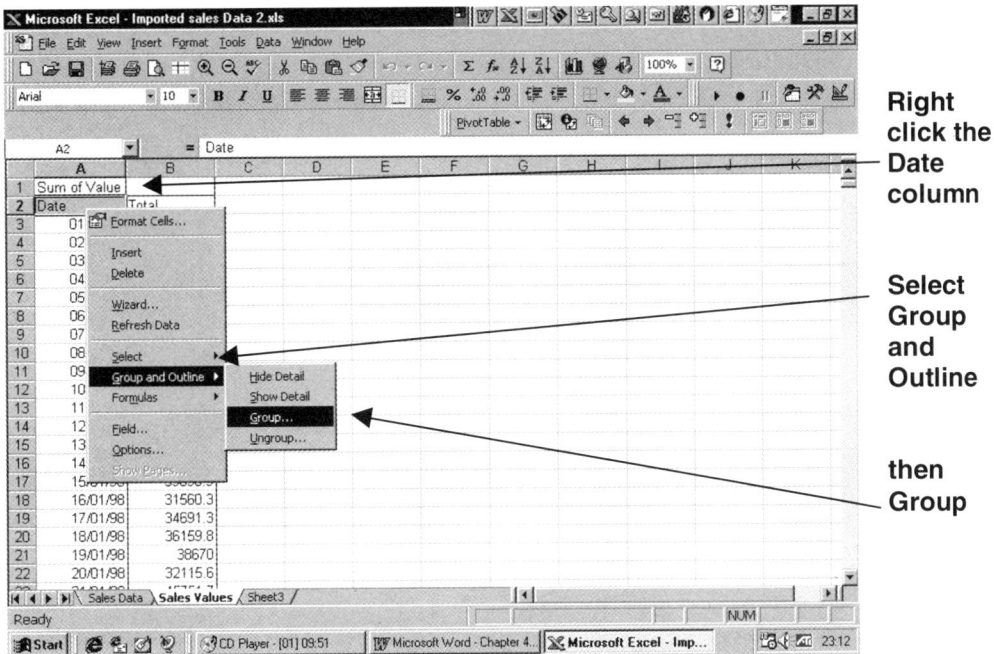

Right click the Date column

Select Group and Outline

then Group

Enter the month end (31/1/98) in the second box, AND CLICK THE BOX TO TICK IT. If it is not ticked only one month will be shown.

In the By list box select month and year. Both are then highlighted. This is one of the few occasions when you do not have to hold down Ctrl when making the second selection. To deselect, click the item again.

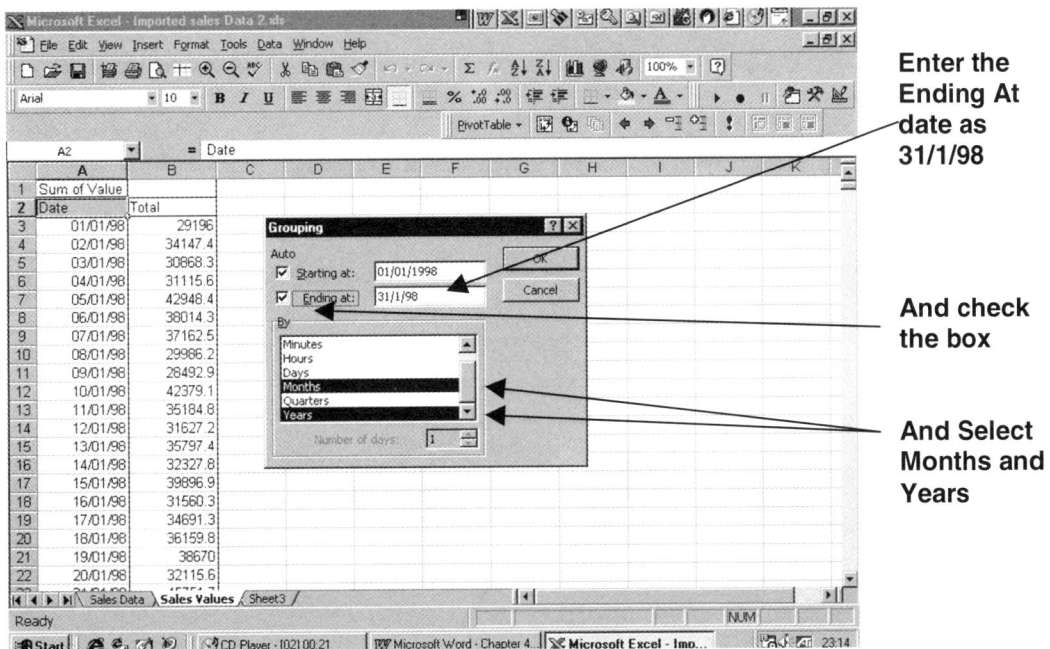

Enter the Ending At date as 31/1/98

And check the box

And Select Months and Years

The file is saved as **Imported Sales Data 3.xls**. The sales are now totalled by month and year, as shown below.

However, this is not the best way to view the information, because there are no annual totals, and it is difficult to compare each month with the same month in a different year.

Drag Year to cell C1, and the table is revised to show this detail.

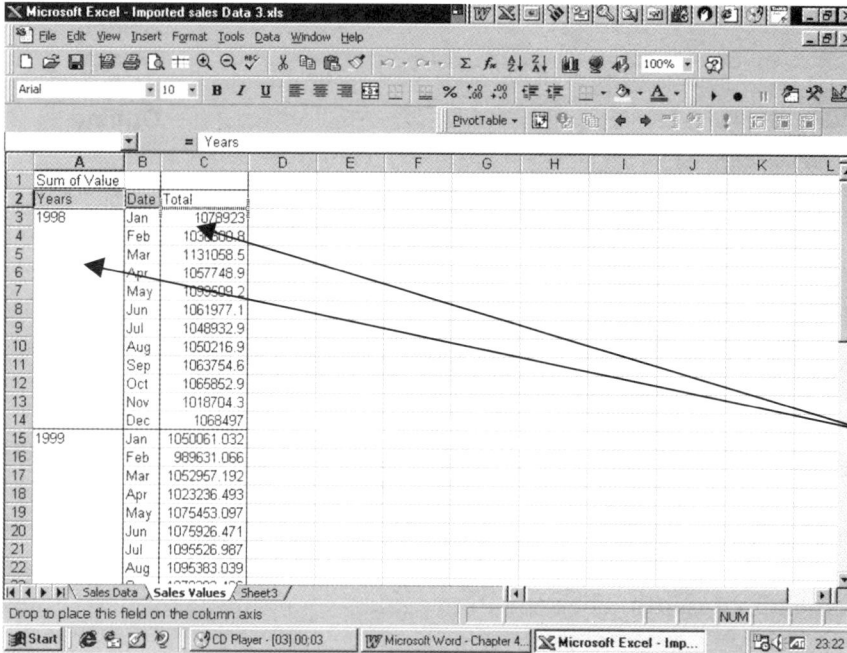

Sales by month and year

But it can be improved

Drag Years to C1

The same data in another view. The file is saved on the CD as **Imported Sales Data 4.xls**.

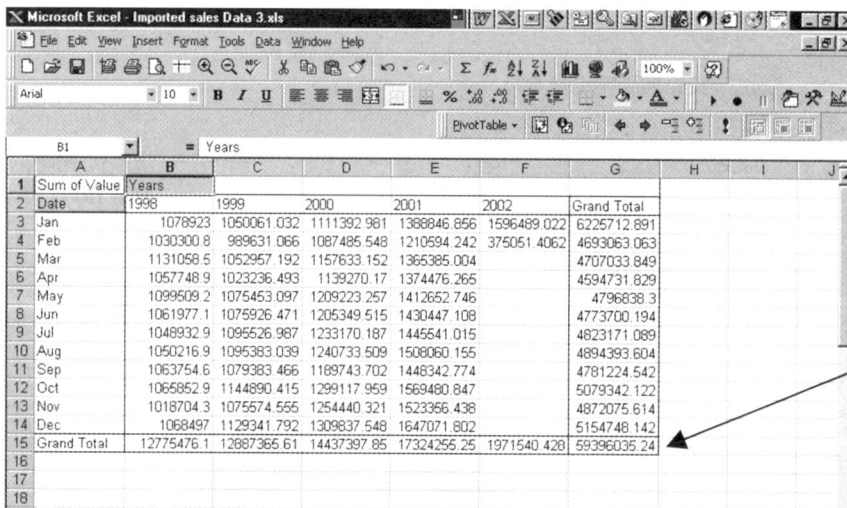

The revised PivotTable

The overall total is the same as before

UNITS SOLD

We want to summarise the number of units sold for each type of goods. Make cell AA1 active, and start the PivotTable Wizard. This time in Step 1 select Another PivotTable.

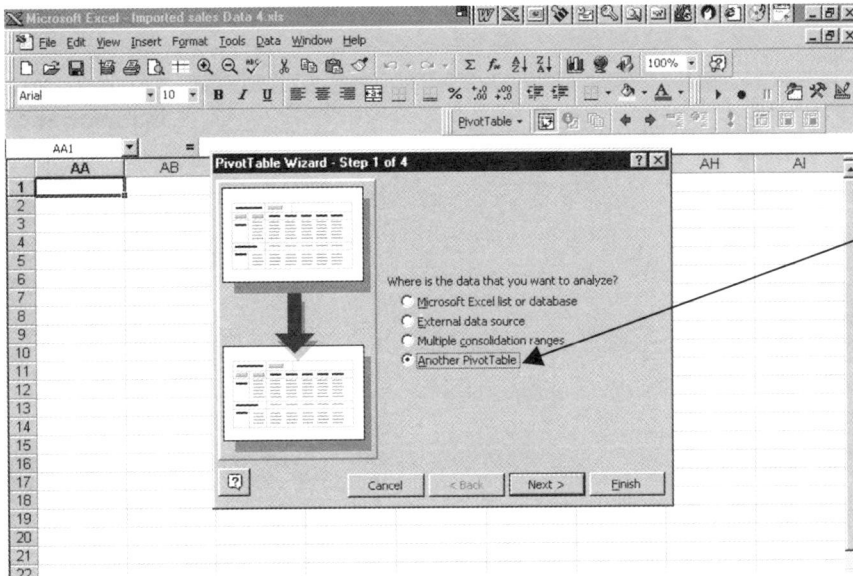

Select
Another
PivotTable

Click on Next

In Step 2 there is only one PivotTable listed. Click Next. Select the unit headings.

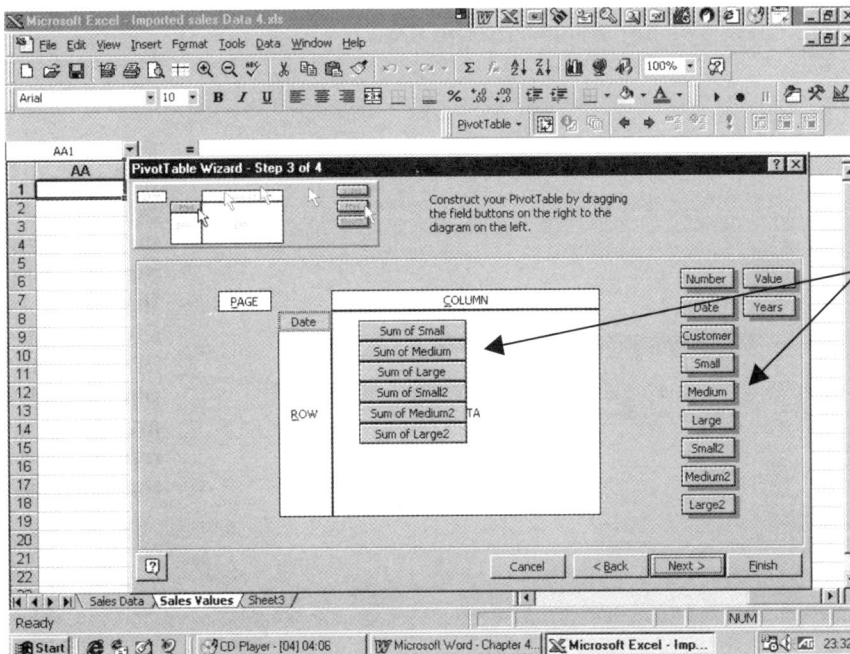

Drag the
Widget
headings
(Small,
Medium
and Large)
and the
Whatsits
headings
(Small2,
Medium2
and Large2)
to the data
area

Click Next, accept the default of placing the PivotTable at AA1, and then click Finish.

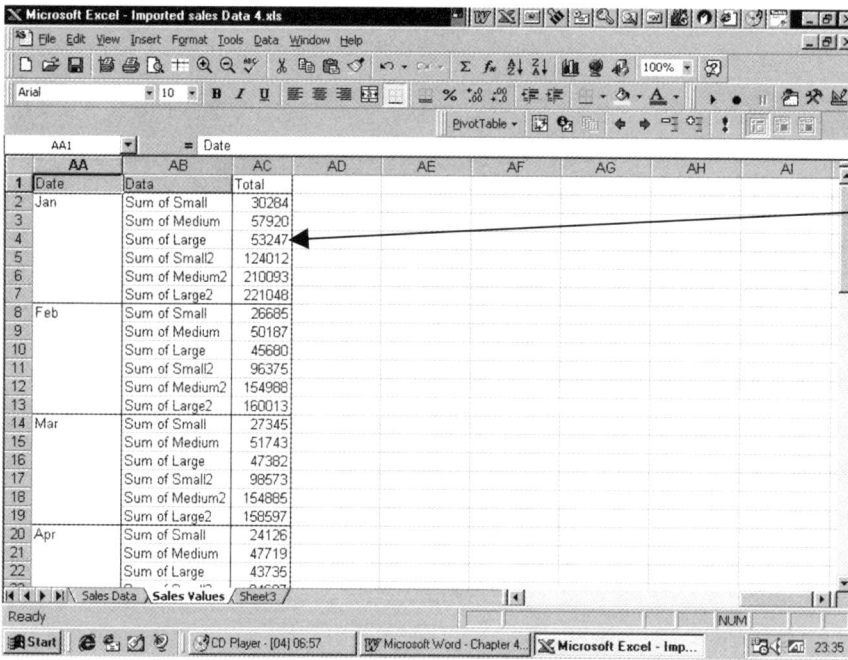

The data is summarised

Once again, it is difficult to interpret

The spreadsheet is saved on the CD as **Imported Sales Data 5.xls**. Right click on Date and group by month and year. A warning appears that the present data will be overwritten. Click Yes and overwrite the data.

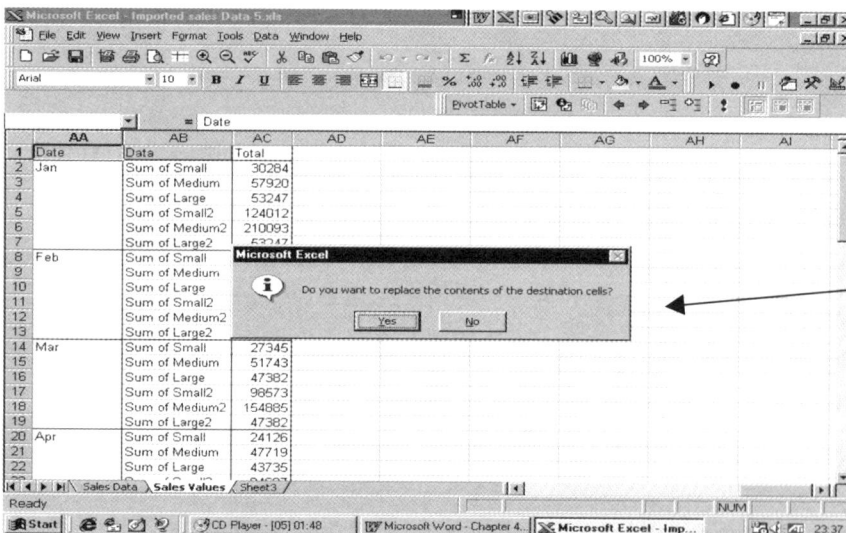

The warning message appears, because we are rewriting the PivotTable in the same place, and are overwriting the original

Drag Years across to AD1.

The data looks better, but it is still not perfect

Drag Data to AC1

The change in unit sales is dramatically highlighted

The decline in sales of Widgets is now seen with great clarity. The spreadsheet is saved on the CD as **Imported Sales Data 6.xls**.

The sheet tab has been revised to **Sales Values and Quantities**.

CUSTOMERS BY VALUE

We have information on the turnover in the last four years, and the sales volumes in the period. We now want to know who our most important customers are, both in terms of value and quantity.

With **Imported Sales Data 6.xls** open, rename Sheet 3 to Customer Value and Quantity. Make cell A1 active, start the PivotTable Wizard, and select Another PivotTable. Choose the PivotTable, described as **[Imported Sales Data.xls]Sales Values and Quantities!PivotTable4**. It should be the first one listed.

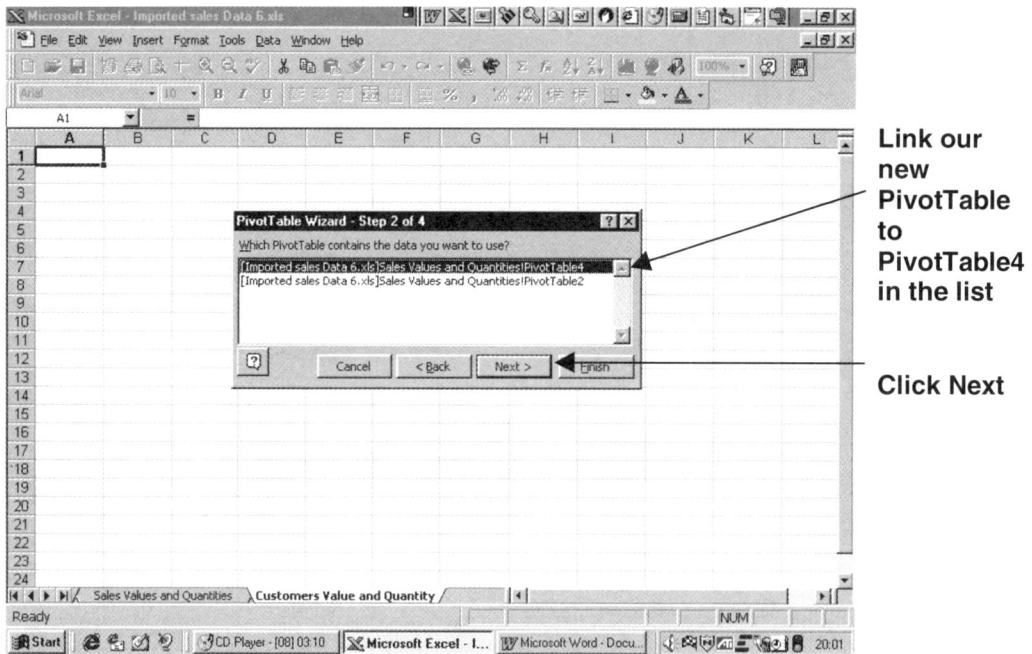

The PivotTable Wizard moves to Step 3. This time, the available headings now include Years, because we are working from an existing PivotTable with this level of grouping in place. Drag Customer to Row, Years to Column, Date to Column, and Value to Data. Click Next, then Finish. This then summarises the data as shown below.

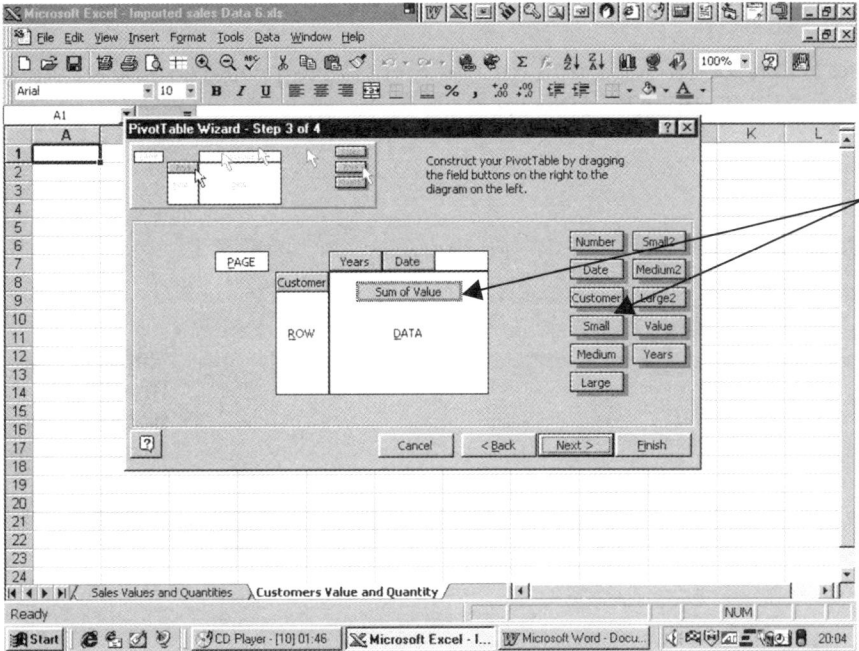

Drag Customer to Row, Year to Column, Date to Column, and Value to Data

The PivotTable is inserted. HOWEVER, there is an error! The spreadsheet is saved as **Imported Sales Data 7.xls**.

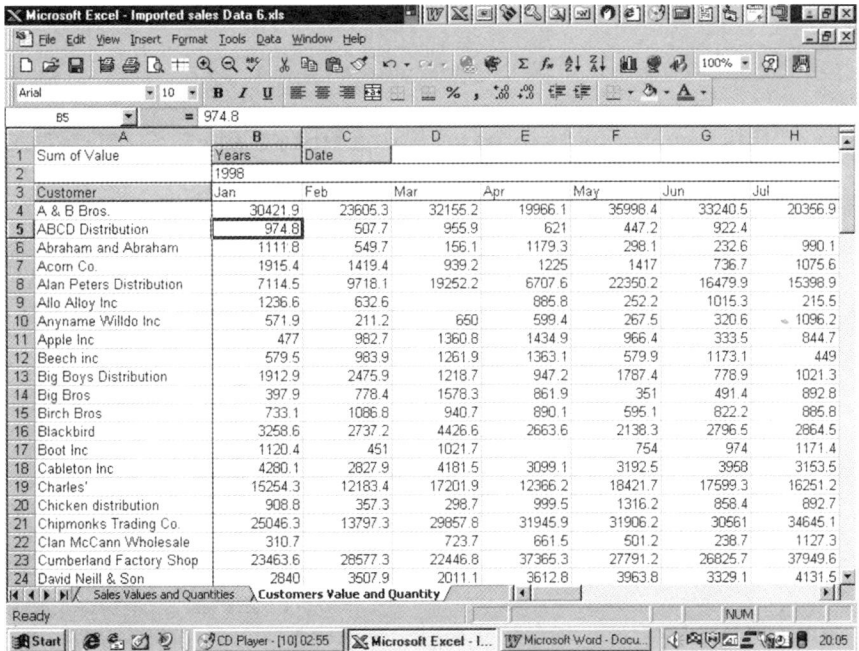

The PivotTable is completed

However, see over for an error!

PIVOTTABLE ERROR

Open **Imported Sales Data 7.xls** and, in the PivotTable prepared above, move to the last customer. It is (blank). However, we know that all customers have a name.

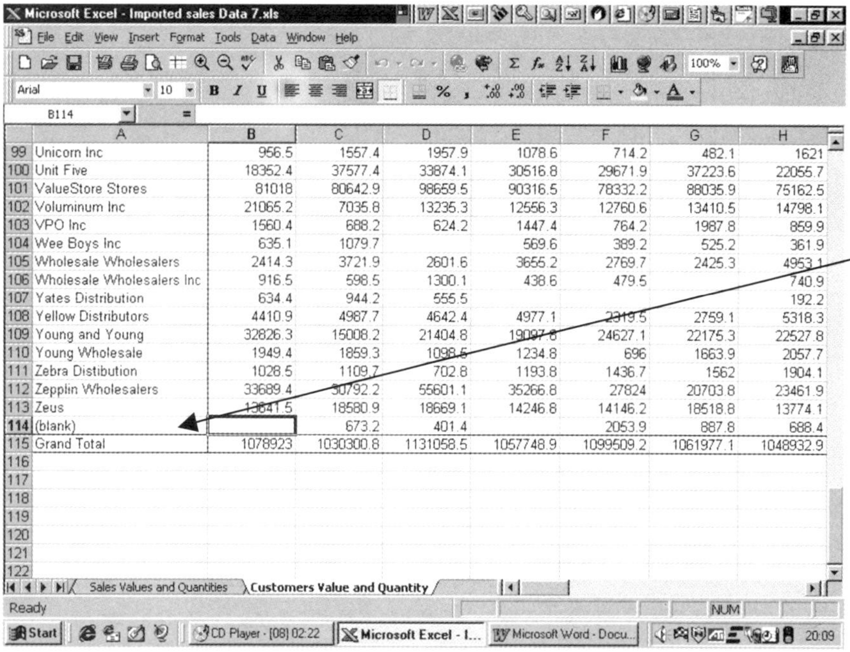

Refresh the PivotTable.

	A	B	C	D	E	F	G	H
99	Unicorn Inc	956.5	1557.4	1957.9	1078.6	714.2	482.1	1621
100	Unit Five	18352.4	37577.4	33874.1	30516.8	29671.9	37223.6	22055.7
101	ValueStore Stores	81018	80642.9	98659.5	90316.5	78332.2	88035.9	75162.5
102	Voluminum Inc	21065.2	7035.8	13235.3	12556.3	12760.6	13410.5	14798.1
103	VPO Inc	1560.4	688.2	624.2	1447.4	764.2	1987.8	859.9
104	Wee Boys Inc	635.1	1079.7		569.6	389.2	525.2	361.9
105	Wholesale Wholesalers	2414.3	3721.9	2601.6	3655.2	2769.7	2425.3	4953.1
106	Wholesale Wholesalers Inc	916.5	598.5	1300.1	438.6	479.5		740.9
107	Yates Distribution	634.4	944.2	555.5				192.2
108	Yellow Distributors	4410.9	4987.7	4642.4	4977.1	2319.5	2759.1	5318.3
109	Young and Young	32826.3	15008.2	21404.8	19097.8	24627.1	22175.3	22527.8
110	Young Wholesale	1949.4	1859.3	1098.5	1234.8	696	1663.9	2057.7
111	Zebra Distibution	1028.5	1109.7	702.8	1193.8	1436.7	1562	1904.1
112	Zepplin Wholesalers	33689.4	30792.2	55601.1	35266.8	27824	20703.8	23461.9
113	Zeus	13641.5	18580.9	18669.1	14246.8	14146.2	18518.8	13774.1
114	(blank)		673.2	401.4		2053.9	887.8	688.4
115	Grand Total	1078923	1030300.8	1131058.5	1057748.9	1099509.2	1061977.1	1048932.9

Refresh the PivotTable because there is an error in the data summarisation

The refreshed PivotTable is saved as **Imported Sales Data 8.xls**.

	A	B	C	D	E	F	G	H
99	Unicorn Inc	956.5	1557.4	1957.9	1078.6	714.2	482.1	1621
100	Unit Five	18352.4	37577.4	33874.1	30516.8	29671.9	37223.6	22055.7
101	ValueStore Stores	81018	80642.9	98659.5	90316.5	78332.2	88035.9	75162.5
102	Voluminum Inc	21065.2	7035.8	13235.3	12556.3	12760.6	13410.5	14798.1
103	VPO Inc	1560.4	688.2	624.2	1447.4	764.2	1987.8	859.9
104	Wee Boys Inc	635.1	1079.7		569.6	389.2	525.2	361.9
105	Wholesale Wholesalers	2414.3	3721.9	2601.6	3655.2	2769.7	2425.3	4953.1
106	Wholesale Wholesalers Inc	916.5	598.5	1300.1	438.6	479.5		740.9
107	Yates Distribution	634.4	944.2	555.5				192.2
108	Yellow Distributors	4410.9	4987.7	4642.4	4977.1	2319.5	2759.1	5318.3
109	Young and Young	32826.3	15008.2	21404.8	19097.8	24627.1	22175.3	22527.8
110	Young Wholesale	1949.4	1859.3	1098.5	1234.8	696	1663.9	2057.7
111	Zebra Distibution	1028.5	1109.7	702.8	1193.8	1436.7	1562	1904.1
112	Zepplin Wholesalers	33689.4	30792.2	55601.1	35266.8	27824	20703.8	23461.9
113	Zeus	13641.5	18580.9	18669.1	14246.8	14146.2	18518.8	13774.1
114	Grand Total	1078923	1030300.8	1131058.5	1057748.9	1099509.2	1061977.1	1048932.9

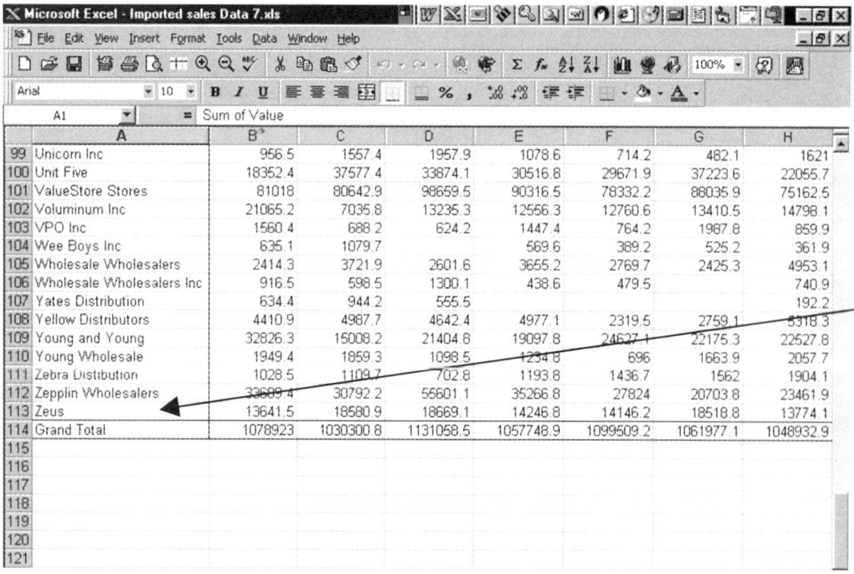

The blank customers are reallocated after Refresh

As with everything in accountancy, DO NOT assume that the computer generated information is correct. Try, as far as possible, to build in self-checking. In this case, confirming that only valid customer names are used, and that the Grand Total agrees with the total in the ORIGINAL data list.

This is discussed in the next chapter.

You will recall from Section Two that we could view the individual items marked as errors by double clicking on the item in the PivotTable to activate the Drill Down process.

To view the customers in order of size, freeze the panes and move to the last column, Grand Total. Make a cell in the column active, and click on Sort Descending. This reorganises the list by value, largest sales first.

With the Grand Total column active, click on Sort Descending

The spreadsheet is saved on the CD as **Imported Sales Data 9.xls**.

CUSTOMERS BY VOLUME

We will now prepare our final PivotTable; a summary of the sales volumes to the various customers.

The first PivotTable spans across to column AZ. In order to leave a reasonable amount of space between them, we will place the new PivotTable at cell CA1.

Make cell CA1 active and start the PivotTable Wizard. Drag Customer to Row, Year to Column and Small, Medium, Large, Small2, Medium2 and Large2 to Data.

We are not interested in monthly quantities per customer, only annual totals, so we are not dragging Date into the grid.

The table is shown below.

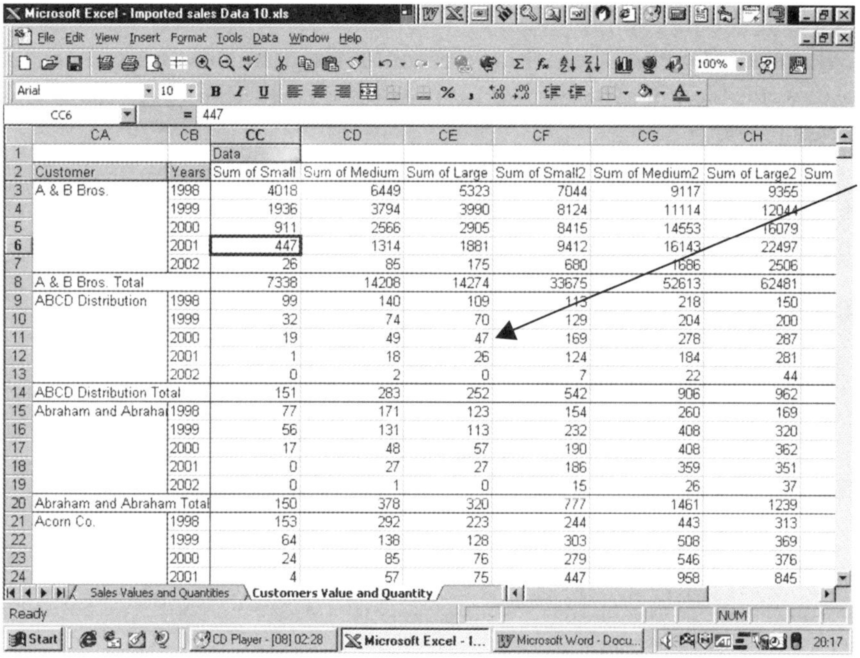

The sales volume for each customer is shown

We want to sort the list in descending order, as we did with the Customers by Value list. However, how will we sort them? We could:

- Sort on the basis of one column, such as sales of Large Whatsits
- Enter a value column, and sort on it
- Sort on the basis of total units sold, irrespective of the individual categories.

It depends on what we are seeking to achieve with the analysis. For our purposes we already know the customers sorted by value, so we will sort on the basis of the total quantity of goods sold.

To this end we want to insert a total quantity sold field. The steps are shown on the next page.

HIDE THE DETAIL

We want to deal with the names of customers only, and it would be useful to hide the detail of the individual years.

Click on Hide Detail.

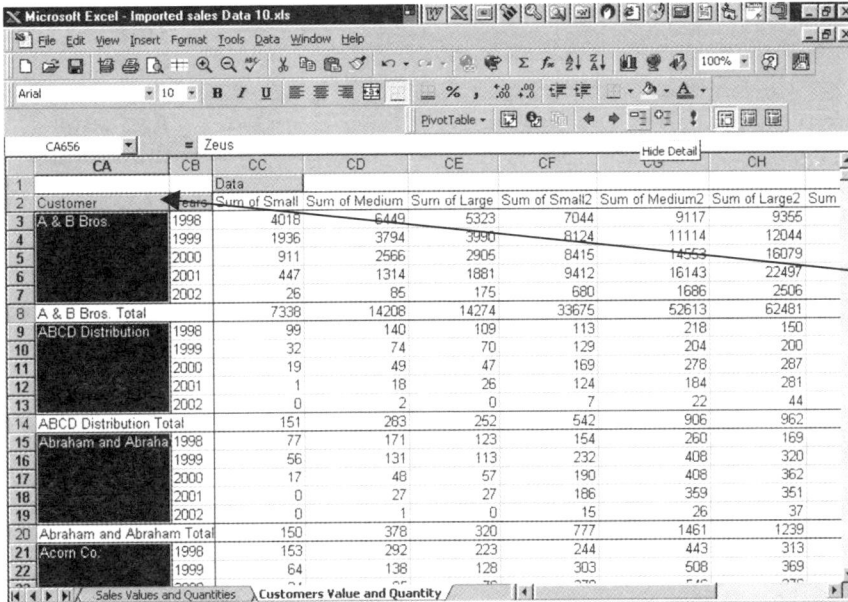

Click on the
Customer
heading to
select all
customers

Then click
Hide Detail
in the
toolbar

SELECT THE PIVOTTABLE AND INSERT A NEW FIELD

Click in cell CA1 to select the entire table, then right click the mouse and Formulas, Calculated Field.

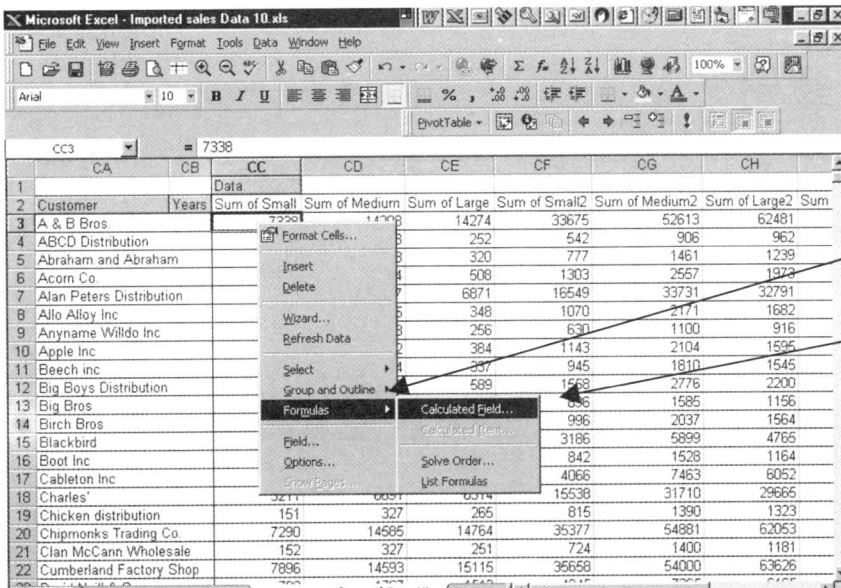

Right click
to display
the menu

Select
Formulas

Calculated
Field

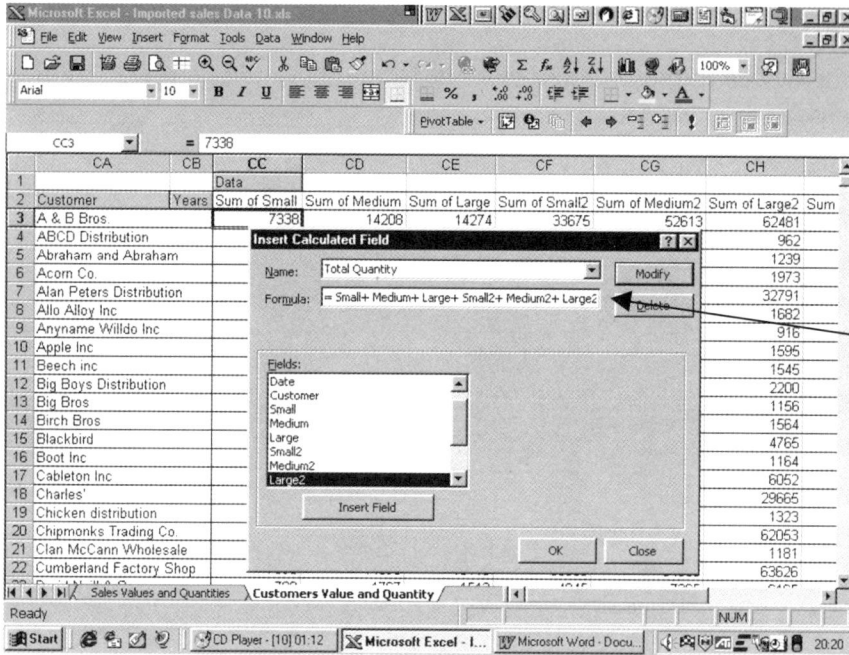

Name the field name Total Quantity

And enter the formula by selecting from the list

The new column is entered into the PivotTable.

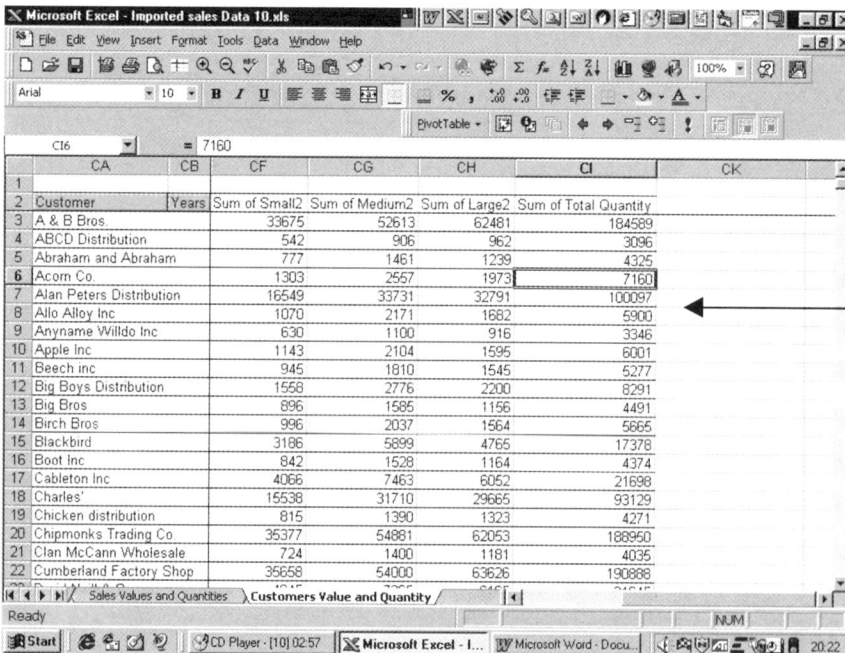

The new column is displayed

ALTERNATIVE FORMULAE

The formula for the total quantity is =Small + Medium + Large + Small2 + Medium2 + Large2.

We could calculate a figure weighted in favour of those customers who are buying the Whatsits, compared to the Widgets, which will be phased out.

We could also weight in favour of sales of large units, compared to medium, and compared to small.

A second column has been added to the spreadsheet, with a formula =Small*0.5 + Medium*0.75 + Large *1.0 + Small2*1.5 + Medium2*1.75 + Large2*2.0.

The customers have been sorted in descending order by using the Weighted Total column.

The spreadsheet is saved on the CD as **Imported Sales Data 10.xls**.

SHOW DETAIL

If the Show Detail button is clicked in the toolbar the individual years are listed, with separate totals each year as per the above formulae.

Click on Show Detail

The years are displayed

Totals are inserted for each line

POWERPOINT

We will be hyperlinking from our PowerPoint presentation to Excel. At present the spreadsheets are too slow to open, because of their size, and their format is not professional enough.

However, we are dealing with historic data, and the analysis in the PivotTables will not be changing. We will therefore prepare a new spreadsheet, one that contains only the results of the PivotTables, not the data itself, and we will apply proper professional formatting to the tables in the new spreadsheet.

In our PowerPoint presentation we will also display the information in charts. We will, therefore, finalise our PivotTables in a new spreadsheet, and then prepare the charts in the new spreadsheet directly.

NEXT

We will end the chapter there, in order to keep it reasonably short. In the next chapter we will build the spreadsheet we are going to hyperlink to.

Chapter Twenty-four

PRESENTING THE HISTORICAL DATA (I)

Speeding it up

We have prepared the groundwork — we have the information provided by the PivotTables; now we want to put these summaries into single screen shots, in order to maximise the impact of our presentation, and minimise the amount of distraction caused by our audience "waiting for it to happen".

We will look at each table in turn. Open **Imported Sales Data 10.xls**, which contains all of the PivotTables we prepared earlier. Also open a new workbook, so that we can transfer the information to it. Save the new workbook as **Historical Presentation.xls**.

HISTORICAL TURNOVER

The table at cell A1 on the tab Sales Values and Quantities contains the historical turnover figures.

There are two problems with the data:
1. The figures are exact, and are not rounded
2. The figures for the last month are not for a complete month

Presentation-wise, we are near enough to our financial year-end that we can run our sales summary to 31 December 2002. So, let's design our front screen.

SCREEN LAYOUT

A rough sketch is shown on the next page.

```
+-----------------------------------------------------+
|   +-------------------------------+                 |
|   |            Title              |                 |
|   +-------------------------------+                 |
|   +-------------------------------+                 |
|   | Table of figures, rounded off |                 |
|   | and set out for high impact   |                 |
|   |                               |                 |
|   |                               |  +------------+ |
|   |                               |  | VBA button | |
|   +-------------------------------+  | to chart   | |
|                                      +------------+ |
+-----------------------------------------------------+
```

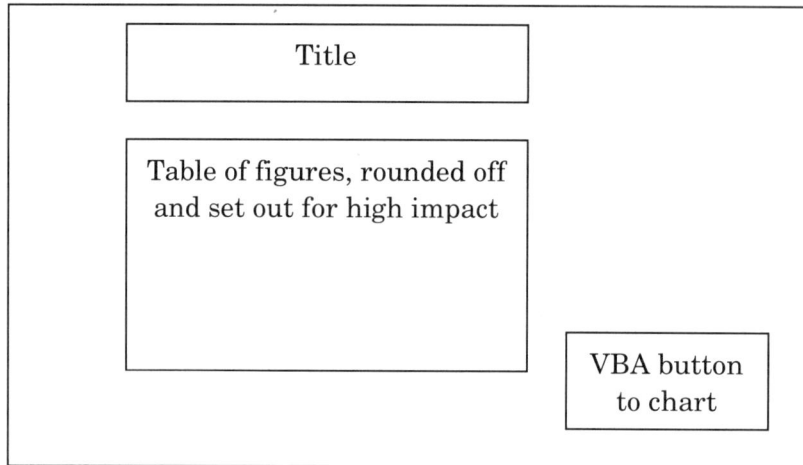

The easiest way to display the table will be to AutoFormat it using Excel. The information needs to be displayed on an Excel chart, so we will use a command button to switch to it.

The layout of the chart will be:

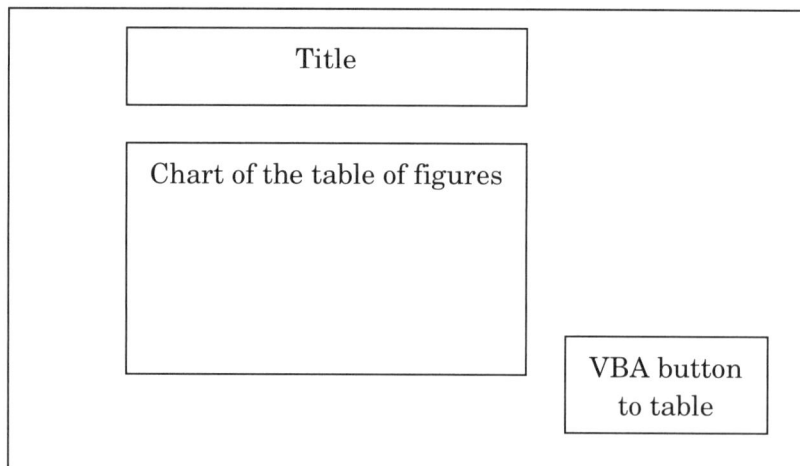

```
+-----------------------------------------------------+
|      +-------------------------------+              |
|      |            Title              |              |
|      +-------------------------------+              |
|      +-------------------------------+              |
|      | Chart of the table of figures |              |
|      |                               |              |
|      |                               |  +----------+|
|      |                               |  |VBA button||
|      +-------------------------------+  |to table  ||
|                                         +----------+|
+-----------------------------------------------------+
```

The command button to move back to the table of figures is in case someone wants to see the table again, after we have moved forward. This should be unlikely, but it is better to cover the possibility instead of the embarrassment of being thrown during the presentation.

PREPARE THE NEW SPREADSHEET TABLE

If we select all of the PivotTable and copy it into the new spreadsheet, it will copy the underlying data as well. There would then be no speed advantage.

We will set up the headings in Sheet1.

Type in the heading "Historical Turnover" in cell C3, and then merge the heading across cells C3 to G3. The Merge and Centre button should be on the formatting toolbar. Change the text colour to blue, and put a border around the merged cells.

Create headings in a table for months and years. Type Jan in cell C8, and use drag to AutoFill. Type Total in cell C21. Enter 1998 into cell D6, 1999 into cell E6, and then AutoFill. Finally, enter headings of £'000 below the years.

We are ready to put the figures in the table. Select the figures from the table in **Imported Sales Data 10.xls**. You will note that the PivotTable has entered them as numbers, not formulae. This is why the table needs to be refreshed if the underlying data has changed. However, as regards our historical data this does not apply.

Drag to select the table

Ctrl+C to copy

Paste the figures into the table in **Historical Presentation.xls**.

	A	B	C	D	E	F	G	H	I	J	K	L
1												
2												
3				HISTORICAL TURNOVER								
4												
5												
6				1998	1999	2000	2001					
7				£'000	£'000	£'000	£'000					
8			Jan	1078923	1050061	1111393	1388847					
9			Feb	1030301	989631.1	1087486	1210594					
10			Mar	1131059	1052957	1157633	1365385					
11			Apr	1057749	1023236	1139270	1374476					
12			May	1099509	1075453	1209223	1412653					
13			Jun	1061977	1075926	1205350	1430447					
14			Jul	1048933	1095527	1233170	1445541					
15			Aug	1050217	1095383	1240734	1508060					
16			Sep	1063755	1079383	1189744	1448343					
17			Oct	1065853	1144890	1299118	1569481					
18			Nov	1018704	1075575	1254440	1523356					
19			Dec	1068497	1129342	1309838	1647072					
20												
21			Total									
22												
23												

The headings are set up

Ctrl+V to paste the table figures in

ROUNDING OFF

In order to maximise the impact of the figures, they need to be rounded off to the nearest thousand, and we want to insert commas to separate millions.

The easiest way to do this is to copy the entire table to an unseen part of the spreadsheet and then link the table at C to the full figures. We will put the copy of the table at AC.

We could have copied the figures to AA directly. We copied it here first because we want to select the entire table, including headings. Without headings at AC it makes reviewing the spreadsheet for errors very difficult.

Select the entire table, Ctrl+C to copy and move to cell AA6. Ctrl+V to paste. Enter the heading "Original table data, unrounded" at cell AA1.

The entry at cell AA1 is to allow us to move to the area quickly by starting at cell A1 and pressing Ctrl+ right arrow key. This will help to ensure the table does not get "lost".

We can now use AutoSum to complete the totals at cells D21 to G21. The spreadsheet is saved as **Historical Presentation.xls**.

Before we round off we will format the table. From the menu select Format, AutoFormat. Choose 3D Effects1.

Select Format, AutoFormat

Choose 3D Effects1

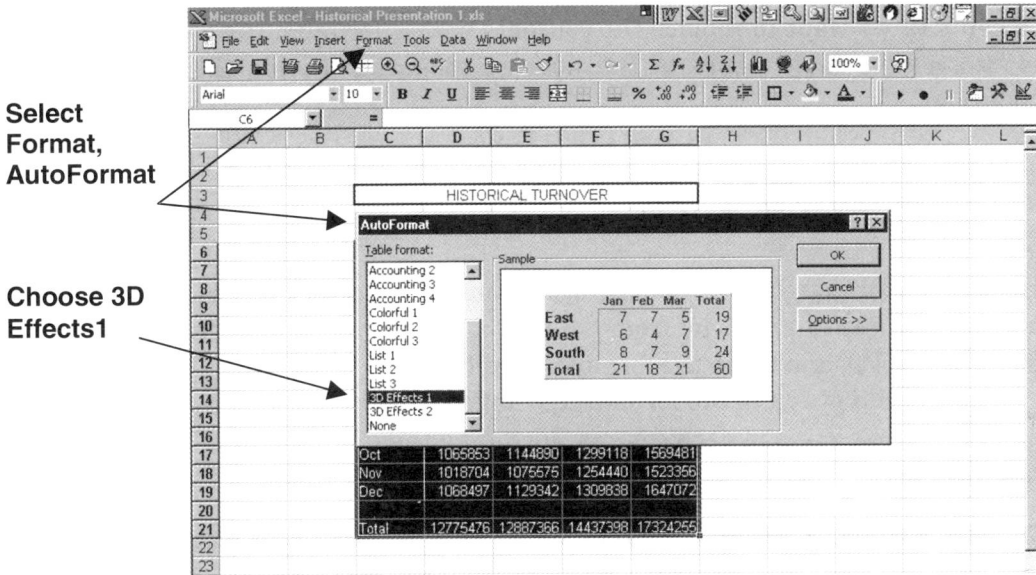

The reason we used AutoFormat first, before rounding the numbers off, is to avoid the program from automatically adjusting the column widths.

We need to widen column C again.

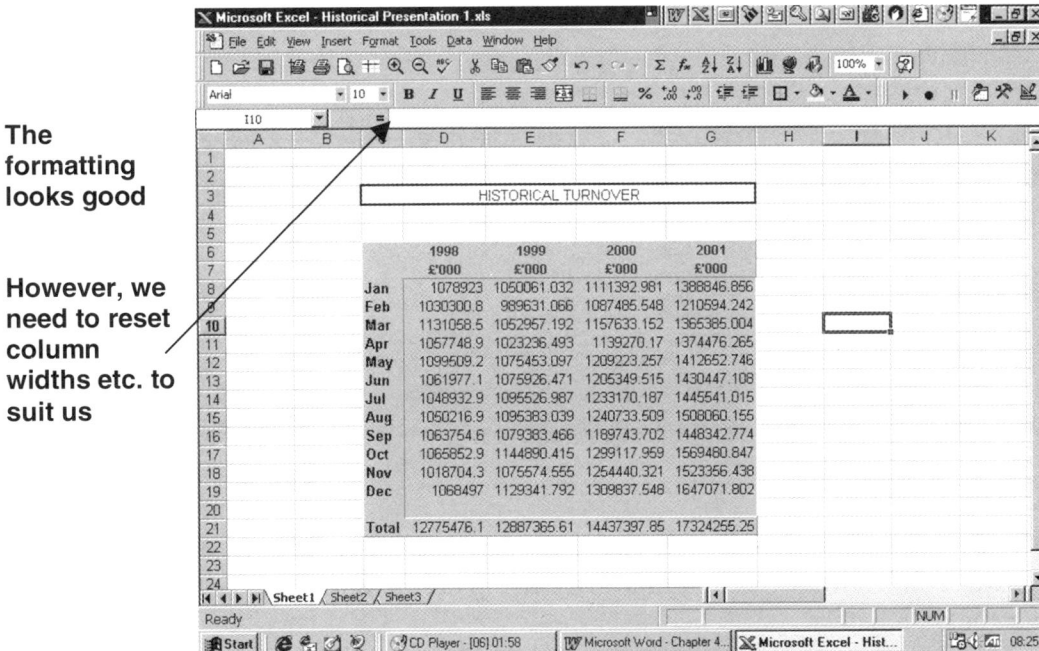

The formatting looks good

However, we need to reset column widths etc. to suit us

The file is saved as Historical Presentation 1.xls. We will now round off the figures.

In cell E19 we want to replace the contents with a formula, the English of which is "Round the table figure to the nearest thousand. Divide the result by one thousand".

The formula to enter is therefore:
=ROUND(AC19,-3)/1000

Keep the address relative, then drag to copy for all cells from E19 to G9. Enter the formula in G8 and copy from G8 to E8, enter the formula in D19 and copy from D19 to D9, and enter the formula in cell D8.

That should preserve the formatting that already exists.

Centre the figures in each column, including the totals column, and format the numbers to display commas to separate thousands.

The figures are rounded, centred and formatted

CHECK TOTALS

Finally, before we accept that the table is finalised and move on to chart the results, confirm that the figures we are using are in agreement with the totals as per the data list.

Use AutoSum to obtain the total of the sales value in **Imported Sales Data 10.xls** from 1/1/98 to 31/12/01 then copy the total to the Clipboard (Ctrl+C). Use Paste Special, Value to copy the figure (instead of the formula) to **Historical Presentation 2.xls**. The two figures should agree.

CHARTING

We are now ready to chart the figures.

To chart the results we need a continuous stream of data, rather than a table. We must therefore set up an area on the spreadsheet to record the results in a format more suitable for charting. We will use the same sheet, starting at cell BA1

At cell BA1 place the heading Charting Setup. This allows us to reach this area of the spreadsheet quickly using Ctrl + right arrow key.

Enter the month Jan 98 at BA5, and drag down to AutoFill to Dec 2001. Pick up the rounded figures from the table (=D8 etc.), and total the column. Pick up the totals per the table and ensure the two agree.

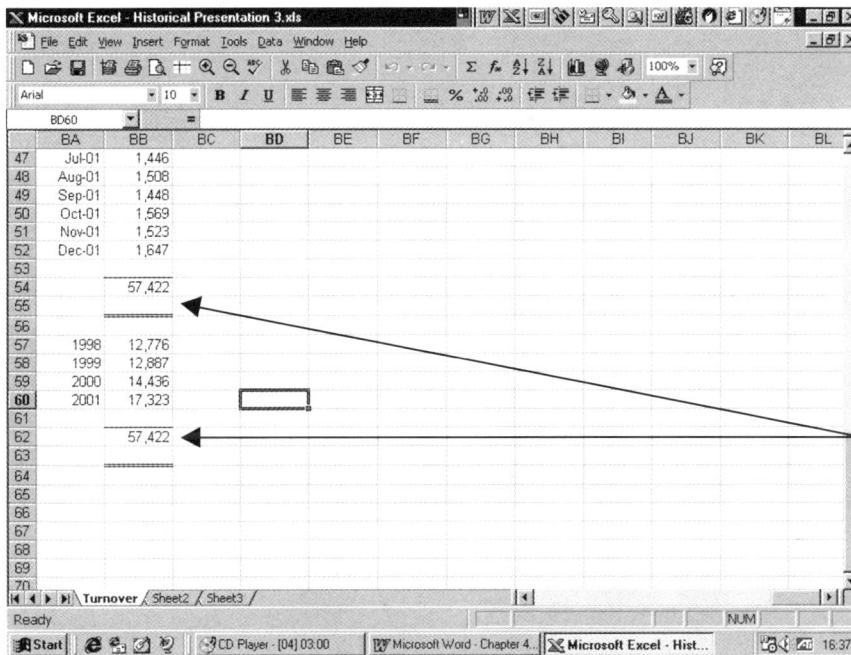

Link figures to the table

As a cross check, ensure the total agrees to the table total

Enter the month Jan 98 at BD5, and drag down to AutoFill to Dec 2001. In BE5 enter the formula =BB5 - $BB$5, and drag it to the end of the time series.

In English, this formula states "Calculate the value of the current month's sales minus the sales at January 1998".

In effect, this makes January a base month, and the growth in sales in the period is compared to this starting position.

The spreadsheet is saved as **Historical Presentation 3.xls**.

Select cells BD5 to BE52, and click on the Chart Wizard.

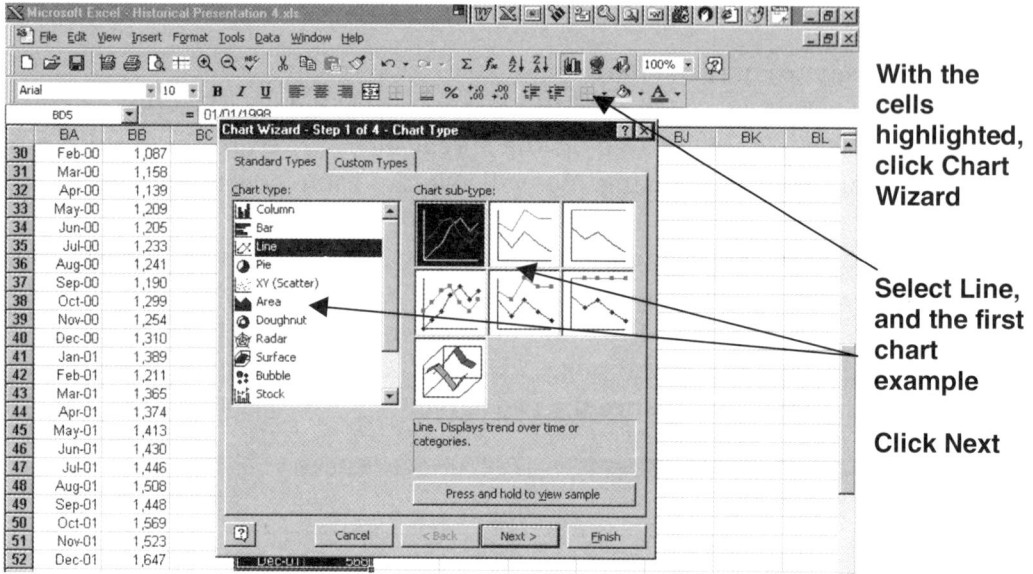

On Step 2 click next. On Step 3 complete Chart Title (Turnover), Category (X) axis (Month), and Category (Y) Axis (£'000). Click Next.

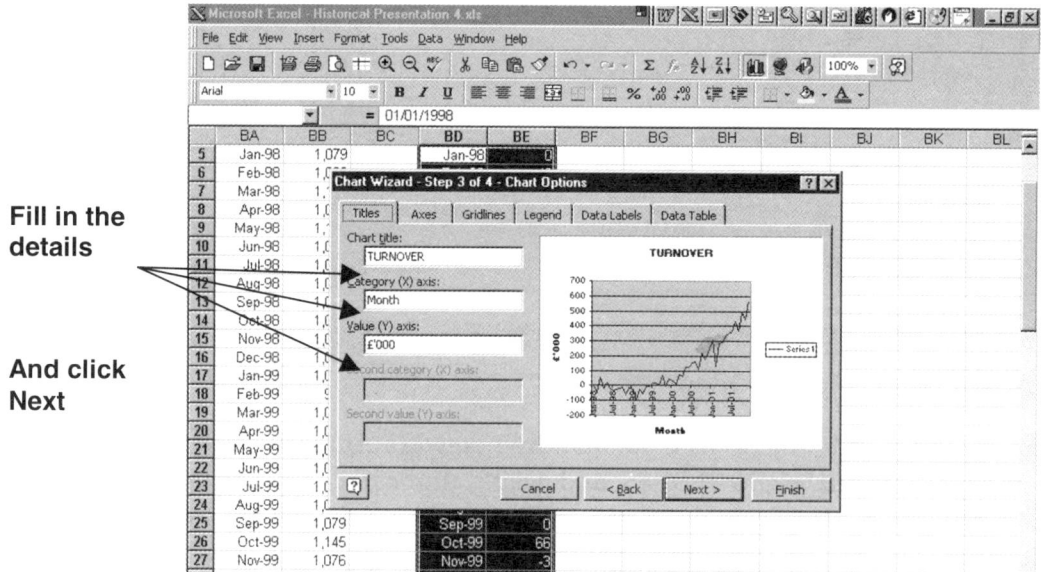

Enter it as a new Sheet, named Turnover Chart.

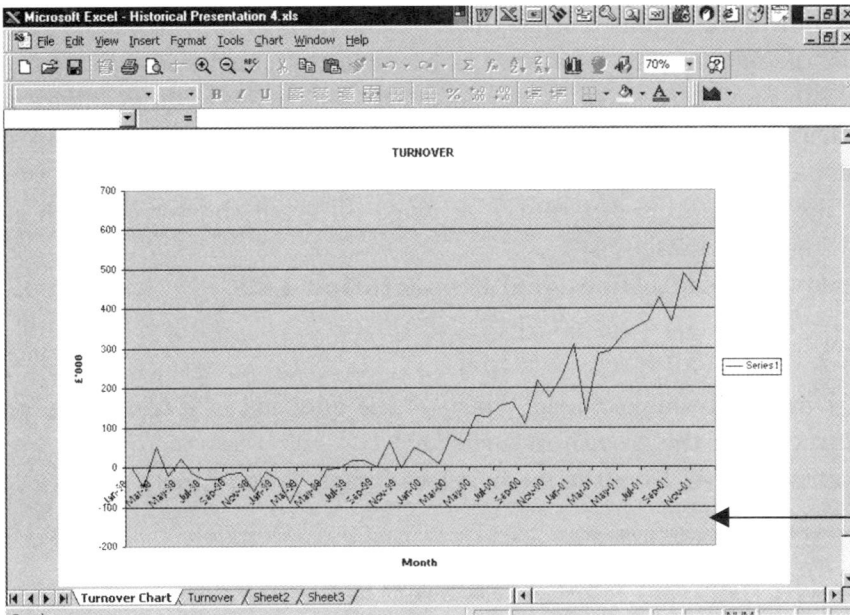

The months
are not very
legible...
Change
their
alignment
to 90°

Double click on the Chart Axis, select the Alignment tab, and drag the line to 90°.

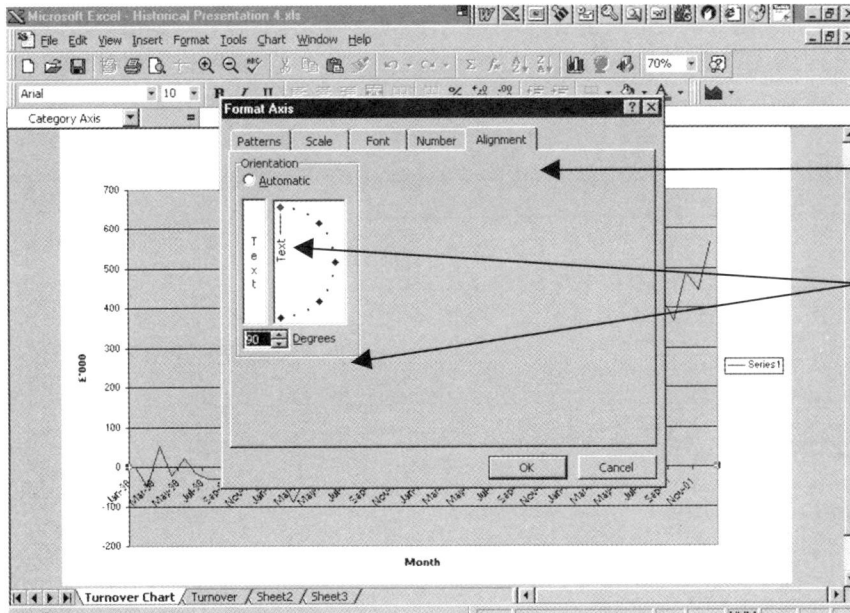

Select the
Alignment
tab

And drag the
line to 90°

The chart now displays the X-axis more legibly.

The reason for using January as a base is because the chart shows, to more dramatic effect, the growth in sales in the period under review. The gradient of the line is much greater than that achieved by charting the absolute figures. However, decisions on how to present graphically are largely personal. If you wish to present the information differently, or use a different chart type, such as a bar chart, feel free to do so.

The spreadsheet is saved as **Historical Presentation 4.xls**.

AND FINALLY . . .

There is one last update to make to the chart — the addition of a trend line, to emphasise the direction of the growth in turnover.

With the chart tab active, from the menu select Chart, Trend Line.

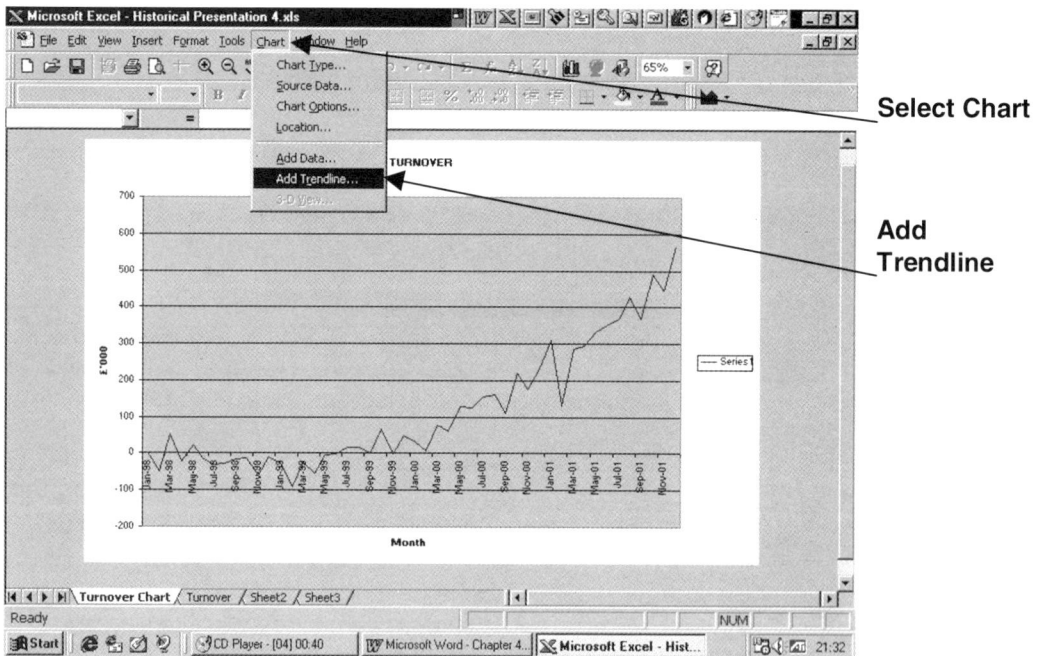

Select Linear, and choose OK.

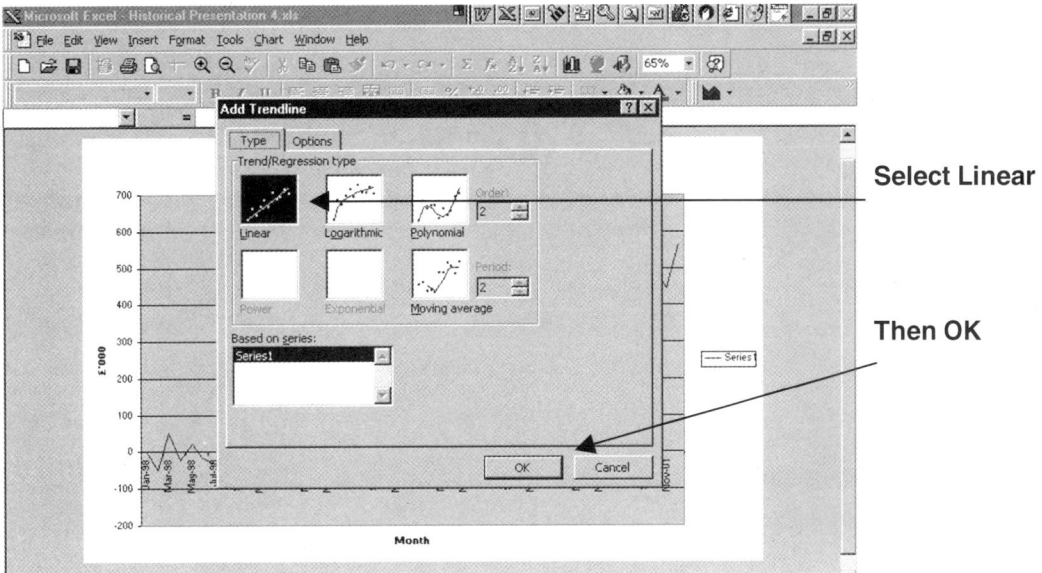

The line is entered on the chart. Double click the line, and the Format Trendline dialog box opens. Under the Patterns tab select Custom, increase the weight of the line and change the colour the red.

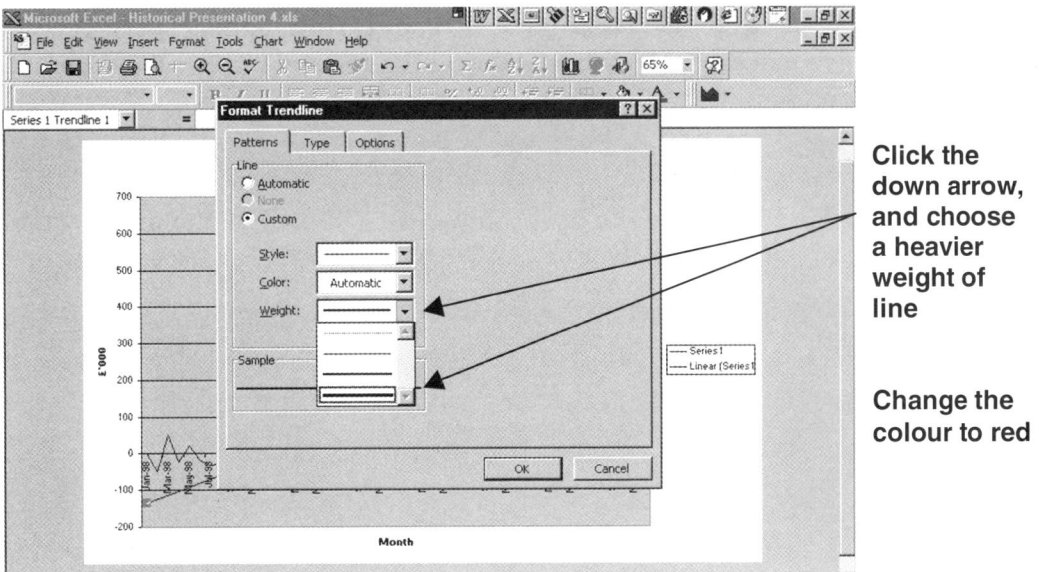

Finally, select the Type tab and see the effect of the different line styles.

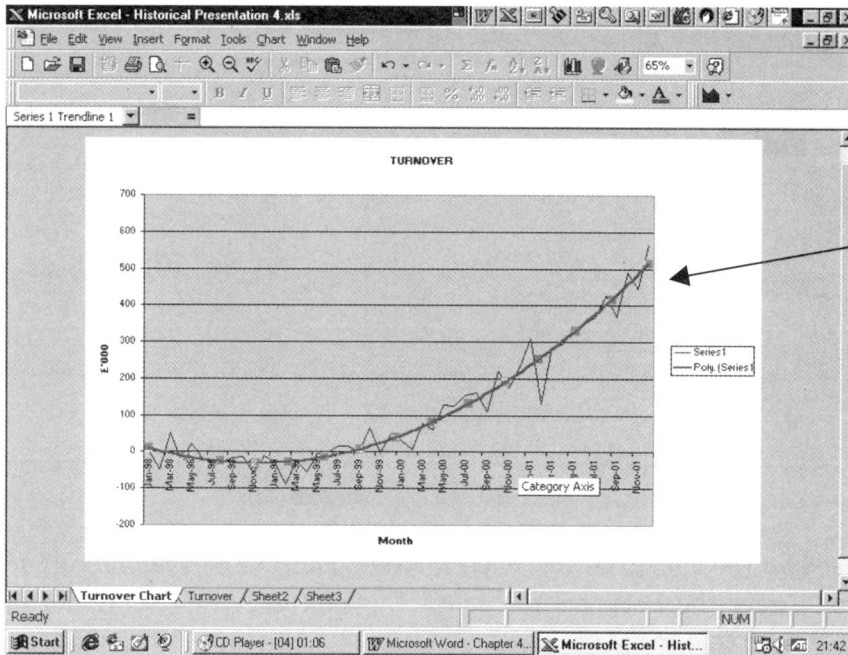

A Polynomial trend line in red, with a heavier weight line.

The spreadsheet is saved as **Historical Presentation 5.xls**. There are no further changes to make, and the above table of figures and chart will be used in the PowerPoint presentation.

NEXT

That concludes this chapter. In the next chapter we will finalise the presentation of the information in the other pivot tables. We will look at VBA towards the end of this section.

Chapter Twenty-five

PRESENTING THE
HISTORICAL DATA (II)

The numbers game!

The next PivotTable in the spreadsheet is the one that looks at the volume of units sold, rather than the turnover. The principles are the same as those covered already, so we will prepare the table without showing all of the detailed steps.

THE UNITS TABLE

Open **Imported Sales Data 10.xls**. The second PivotTable on the **Sales Values and Quantities tab** at AA1 contains our figures.

However, it is too large to fit into one screen. We will change its presentation slightly. We need the monthly detail in order to project forward, but for the PowerPoint presentation we will only present the annual totals — the trend in the figures will still be demonstrable to our audience.

Drag the years heading to cell AA1, and then drag Date heading outside the table. It will be removed. Total the number of units in the original data list, then paste special the values (not the formulae), below the table and confirm that they agree.

We are now ready to transfer the information to our fast spreadsheet.

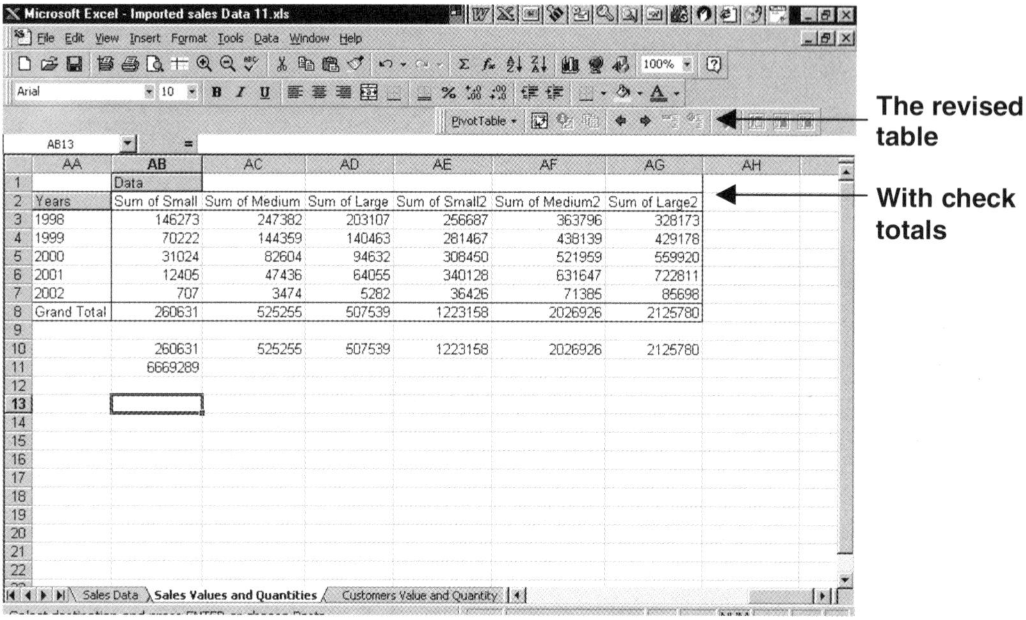

The revised table

With check totals

Open **Historical Presentation 5.xls**. Change Sheet2 to Sales Volume, and make cell A1 active.

Place the heading "Sales Volume" in cell B4, format it and centre it across cells B4 to J4. Set up the years from 1998 to 2001. As previously, we will ignore the first five weeks of the current year.

Set up headings for the type of goods, but place Small Widgets beside Small Whatsits etc. The completed table is saved as **Historical Presentation 6.xls**.

Copy the table to AA7, and put a heading "Original table data, unrounded" at AA1. Format the table at A1 as Colourful2, in order to distinguish it from the previous one, then round off the numbers to the nearest thousand and put in number headings.

Centre the figures in the columns. The spreadsheet is saved as **Historical Presentation 7.xls**.

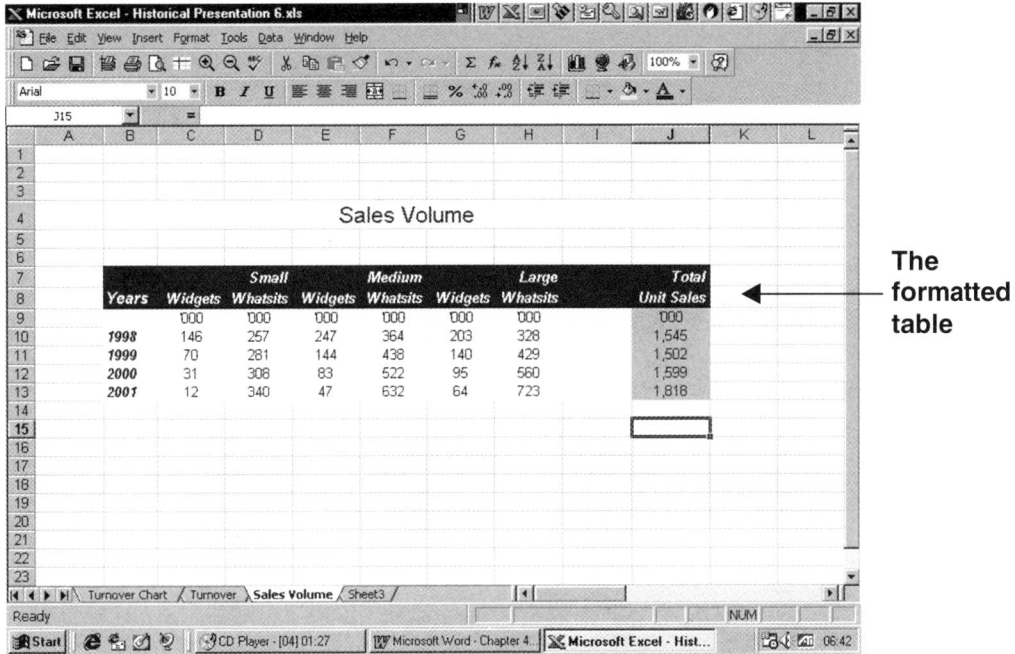

The formatted table

Years	Small		Medium		Large		Total Unit Sales
	Widgets	Whatsits	Widgets	Whatsits	Widgets	Whatsits	
	'000	'000	'000	'000	'000	'000	'000
1998	146	257	247	364	203	328	1,545
1999	70	281	144	438	140	429	1,502
2000	31	308	83	522	95	560	1,599
2001	12	340	47	632	64	723	1,818

The replacement of sales of Widgets by Whatsits is clearly seen. In our PowerPoint presentation this will lead to the question, "At what point will we stop producing Widgets, either in individual lines or completely?"

However, to finish this particular part of the presentation we need to chart the table results.

CHARTING

The figures are so stark that there is nothing to be gained in presenting them "as is." However, we can use the chart to clearly demonstrate the decline in importance in Widgets to the company over the four year period.

We will chart the total volume of sales in a bar chart, split between the different categories of goods.

Open **Historical Presentation 7.xls**, and highlight the table from C7 to H13. Start the Chart Wizard from the toolbar. Select the Stacked Column item, and click Next.

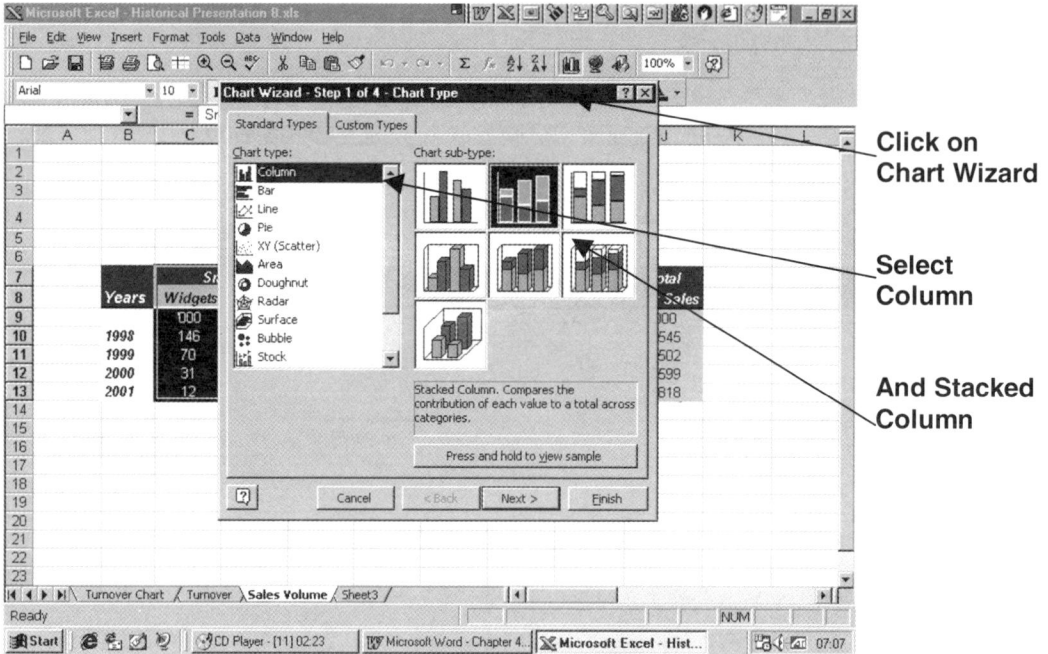

The chart defaults to Rows, and the chart shown is the wrong one. Select Columns, and it displays correctly.

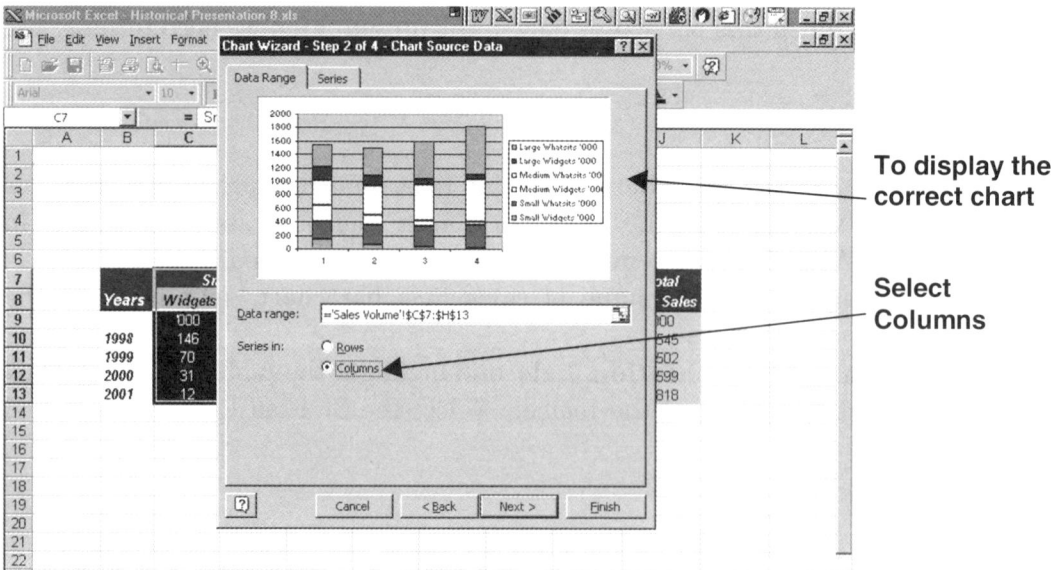

In Step 3 type in the heading (UNIT SALES), the x-axis (Year) and the y-axis (Number of Units). In Step 4 place the chart in a new sheet, called Units Chart.

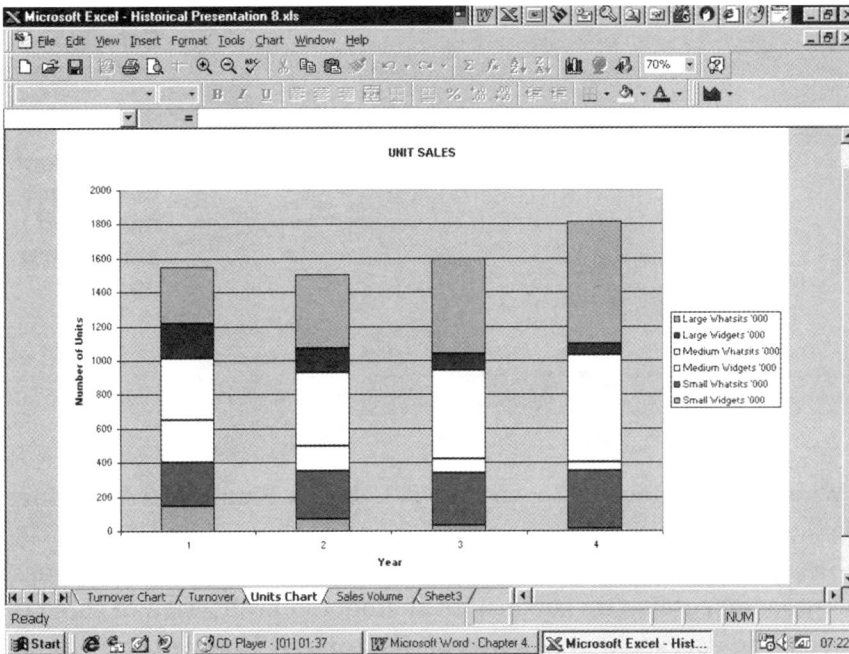

The chart so far

There are still some revisions required

The spreadsheet is saved as **Historical Presentation 8.xls**.

The format of the chart is now correct. However, the table is being used to demonstrate within each category of goods how Whatsits have replaced their Widget counterpart.

In this chart we are showing how Whatsits as a grouping have replaced Widgets. We therefore want to group all of the Whatsits at the top part of the bar chart, and all of the Widgets at the bottom. Click on the Series tab

Double click one of the columns in the Units chart, and select the Series tab.

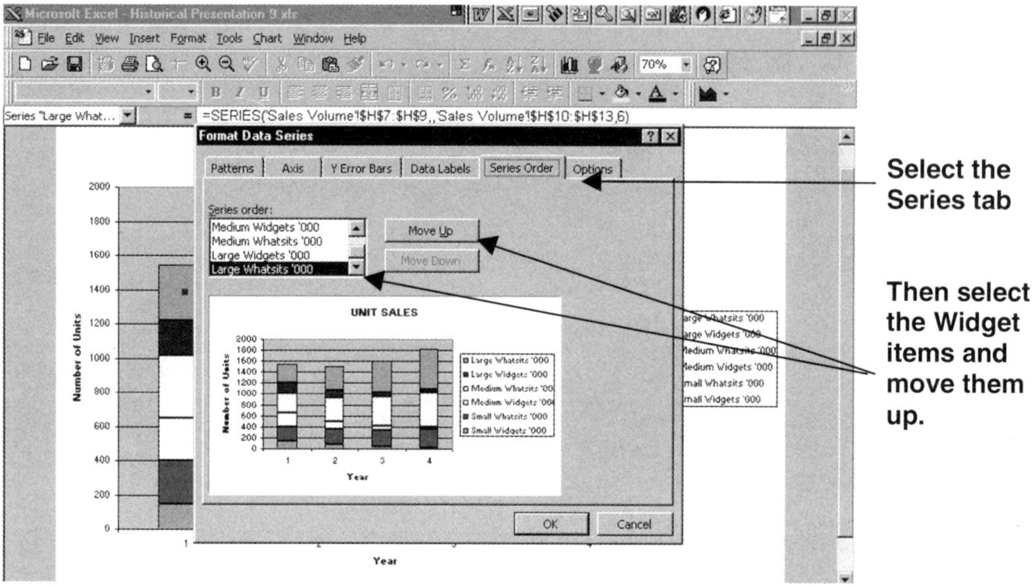

Select the
Series tab

Then select
the Widget
items and
move them
up.

Select Medium Widgets and move it up, so that it is below Small Widgets. Move Large Widgets below Medium Widgets. Click OK, and the chart is updated.

The chart shows how the importance of Widgets has declined over the years, and leads nicely into a discussion on the merits of stopping production of some or all types of Widgets. The spreadsheet is saved as **Historical Presentation 9.xls** completing our second PivotTable and Chart.

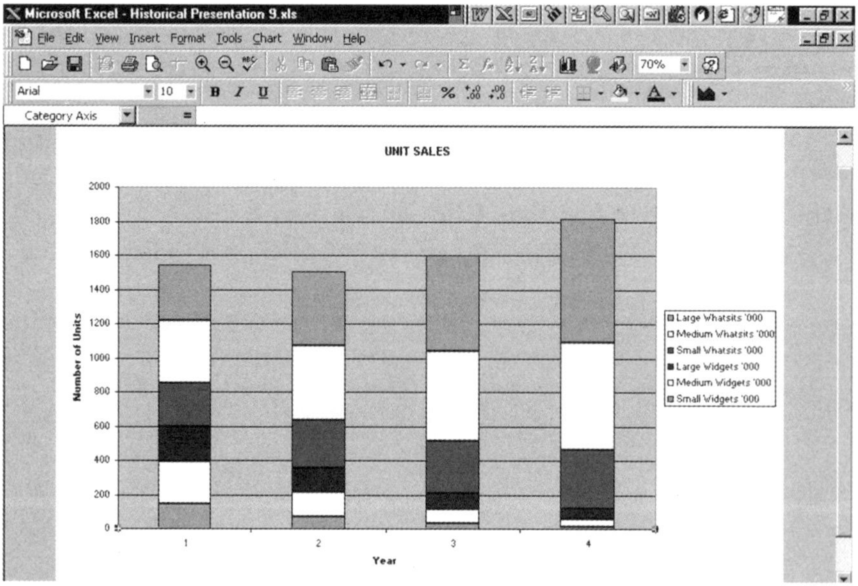

The finished chart, grouping the Widgets at the bottom of each column

NEXT

In the next chapter we move the Customer PivotTables to the fast spreadsheet.

Chapter Twenty-six

PRESENTING THE HISTORICAL DATA (III)

The customer is King, but which customer?

The database is an excellent source for the sales team to review how sales are proceeding against target, when a particular customer last ordered etc.

The purpose of our pivot table is to assess the risks to our company if one or more customers switch to Thingies, either completely or partially. We therefore want to analyse the percentage of sales achieved with each customer.

At present the pivot table has summarised the size of customer by turnover. However, it lists everyone, and it gives the value of turnover, rather than the percentage. We need to calculate the percentages, and at the same time reduce some of the detail in order to see the broader picture.

Open Imported Sales data 10.xls and Historical Presentation 9.xls.

Rename Sheet3 in **Historical Presentation 9.xls** as Customers, and copy the sorted list of customers names and the grand total column from the PivotTable at A1 (Customers by value) on the Customers Value and Quantity sheet in **Imported Sales data 10.xls** to AA1. Confirm that the total agrees to the total per the original data list.

The new columns to be inserted at AC and AD are:

Column AC	% of Total	=AB4/$AB$114
Column AD	Cumulative %	Cell AD4 is =AC4
		Cell AD5 onward is =AD4+AC5

Note that the total (at cell AB114) is given an absolute address so that the formula can be dragged to AutoFill.

The spreadsheet is saved as **Historical Presentation 10.xls**.

We want to chart the results in order to emphasise that a small number of customers are responsible for a substantial percentage of turnover. Start the Chart Wizard, and select Line for type, and Stacked Line for the sub-type.

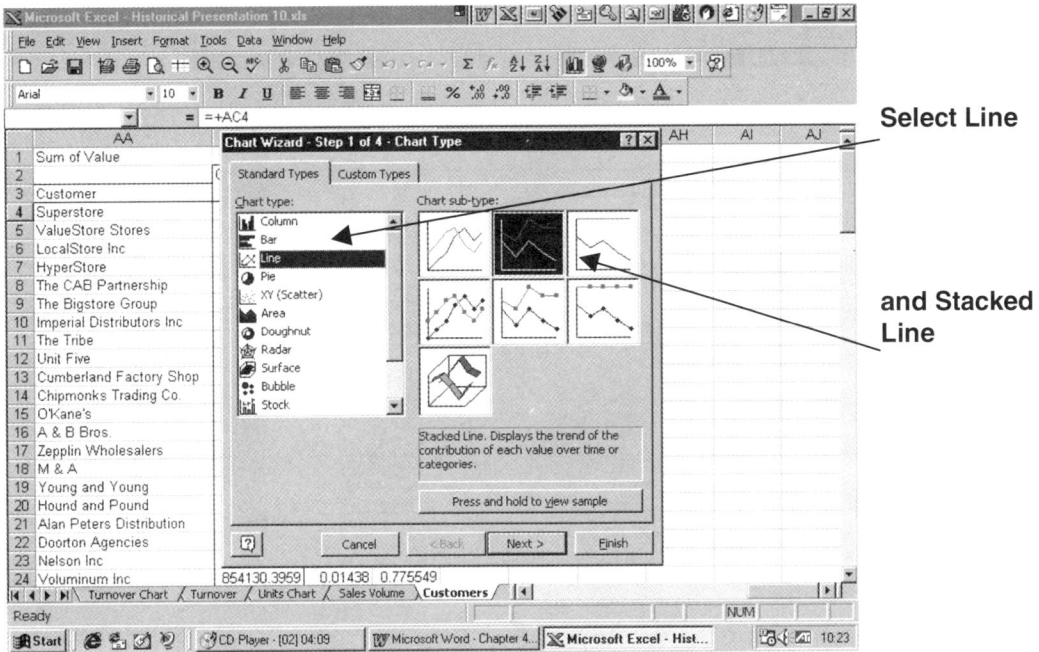

Click Next. The selected data series defaults to the entire area, and the displayed example looks most unsatisfactory.

Delete the Data Range, minimise the box and select the range from AD4 to AD113.

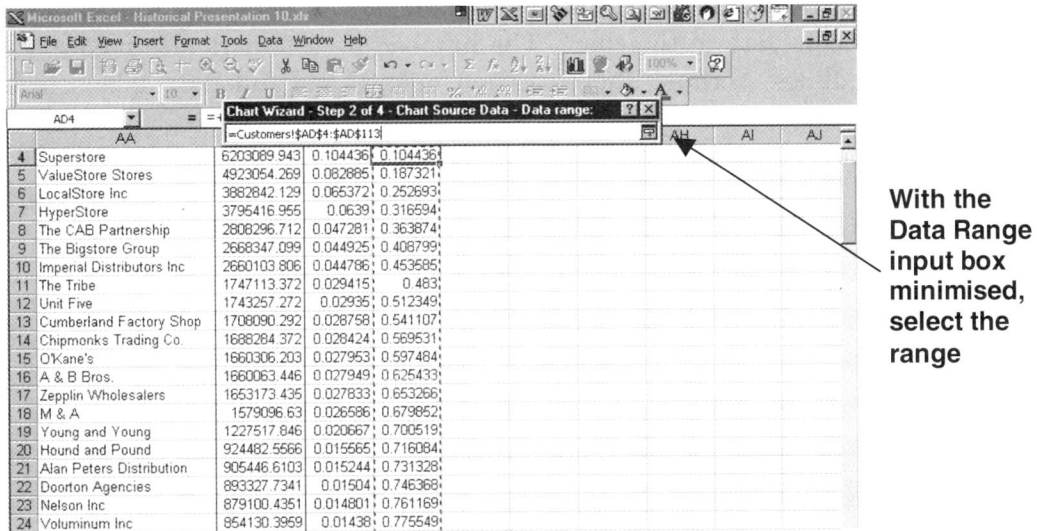

Enter the title as "% Of Turnover By Customer", the x-axis as "No. Of Customers" and the y-axis as "Percentage". Enter the chart as a new sheet called **Customers Chart**.

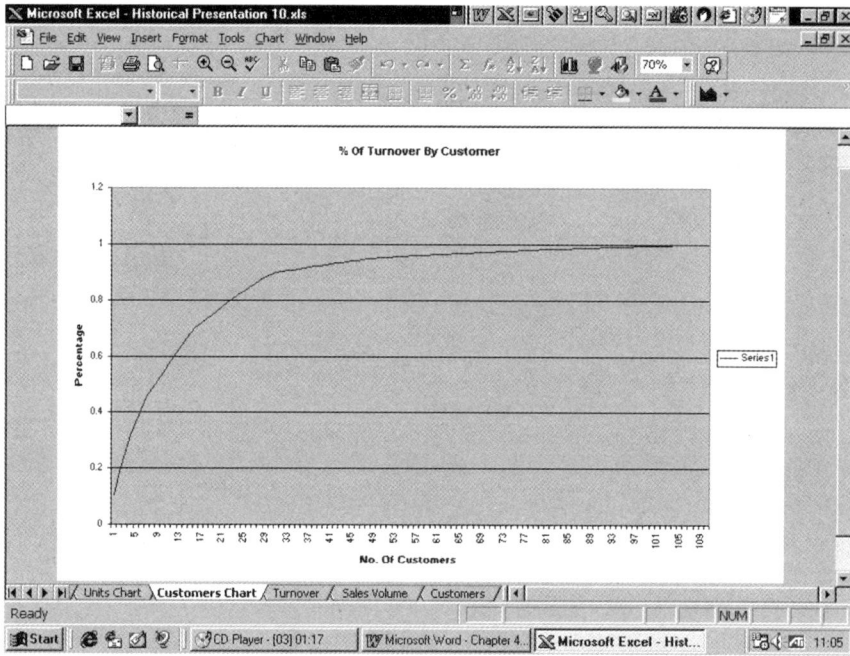

The finished chart, but, more formatting is required

The spreadsheet is saved as **Historical Presentation 10.xls**.

FORMATTING THE CHART

The chart shows the trend but, because of the numbers of customers, it is difficult to read any specific data in the chart. The number of customers also means we cannot add gridlines (because there are too many), and full data labels look messy.

In order to help emphasise this detail we will add individual data labels.

Click on the line Data Line in the chart, then hold the mouse over one of the data points on the chart, and the number and value are displayed.

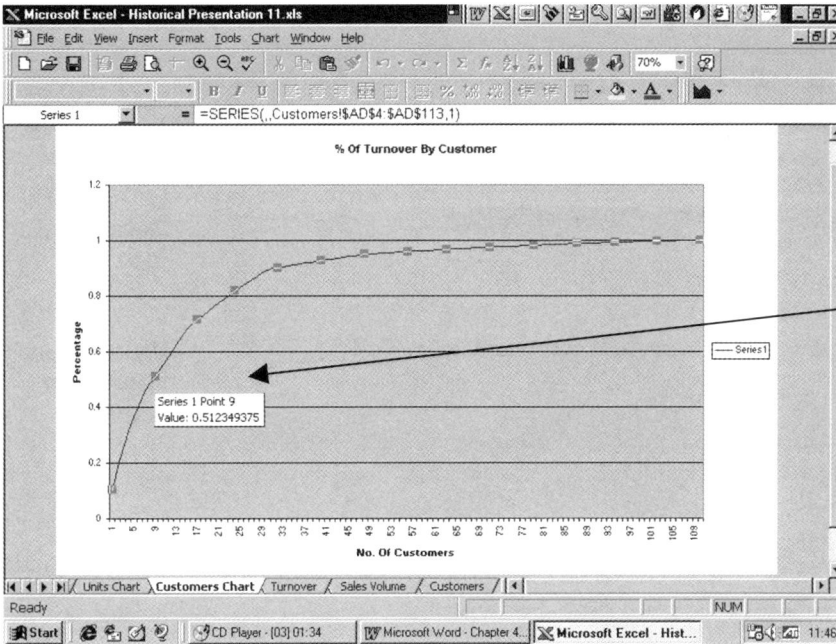

The mouse activates a label to display point number and value

The value shown at point nine in the above chart is 0.512349375.

Format column AD in the Customers tab as Percentage, with two decimal points of accuracy. The value shown at point nine in the chart is now 51.23%.

What we want to do is to display a few highlights in the data series permanently, rather than using the mouse to activate the display.

Highlight point one in the data line, then right click. Select Format Data Point. Note that if the full data line is highlighted the menu option is Format Data Series, which is what we do not want.

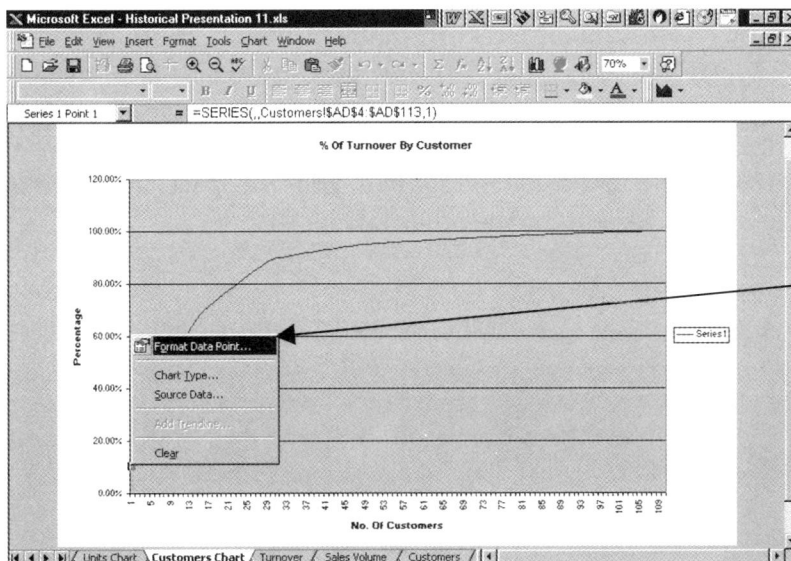

With one data point highlighted, right click

Select Format Data Point

If the menu Format Data Series, restart

The Format Data Point dialog box opens.

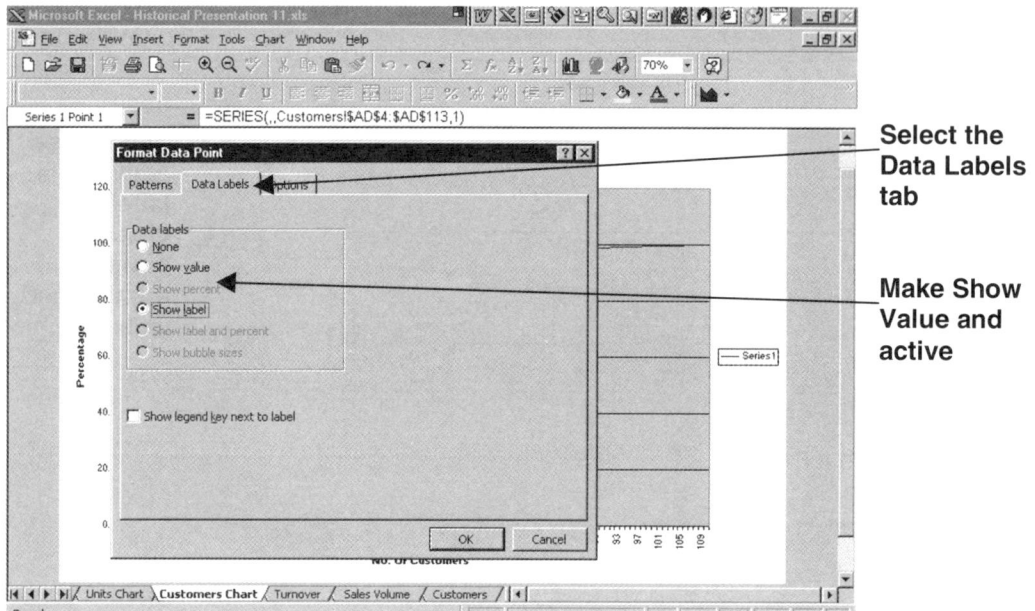

Select the
Data Labels
tab

Make Show
Value and
active

Add labels to the data line at the following points:

Point 1	10.44%
Point 3	25.27%
Point 9	51.23%
Point 19	74.64%
Point 30	89.24%

The spreadsheet is saved as **Historical Presentation 11.xls**.

The Format Data Labels tab uses radio buttons, and the choice is to display either the number, or the value, but not both.

However, we can easily get round this problem. Left click on the label at Point1. A normal textbox with handles is highlighted. Enter a space, and type in the number 1 after the figure. Repeat for the other labels.

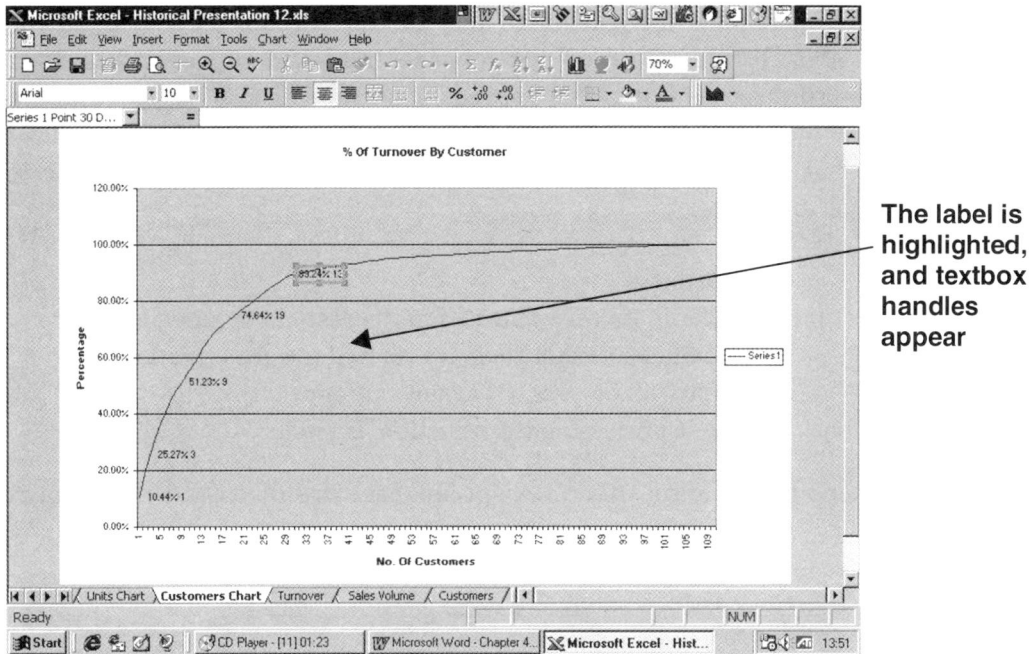

The spreadsheet is saved as **Historical Presentation 12.xls**.

ALTERNATIVE CHART FORMATS

We could have prepared the chart using values, and selecting the third Chart sub-type (i.e. 100% stacked). This automatically calculates percentages when charting. However, this was not chosen for our presentation, because we did not want the data Labels to display the turnover values.

Note that, if turnover values are being used, only the last twelve months figures should be used — not the figures for the full period in the data series.

TABLES OF FIGURES

We can prepare a formatted table of figures at A1 on the Customer sheet if required. In this presentation we will use the chart to aid our discussion, and will not include a table.

VBA CONTROL CENTRE

Finally, we want to finalise navigation between the various spreadsheets. It could be managed with the mouse, and the fact that all of the final data is in section A1 of each spreadsheet makes this easier.

However, we can also include a structured way to progress from sheet to sheet in a prearranged order by including VBA buttons for Forward>> and <<Back.

A central control panel for navigating to any of the spreadsheets will be the opening screen shot. It will round off the presentation, and will provide a focal point for the co-ordination of all of the spreadsheets. It will also set the tone, in terms of professionalism, of the presentation.

The screen shot below is shown in order to show you what we are trying to create. The major areas are:

Heading	Label.
Option Buttons	Set in an area apart from the rest of the spreadsheet, to emphasise that they are related to each other i.e., only one can be selected at any one time.
Command buttons	For processing the selection as made.

The detailed steps for building this VBA spreadsheet are discussed in the next chapter.

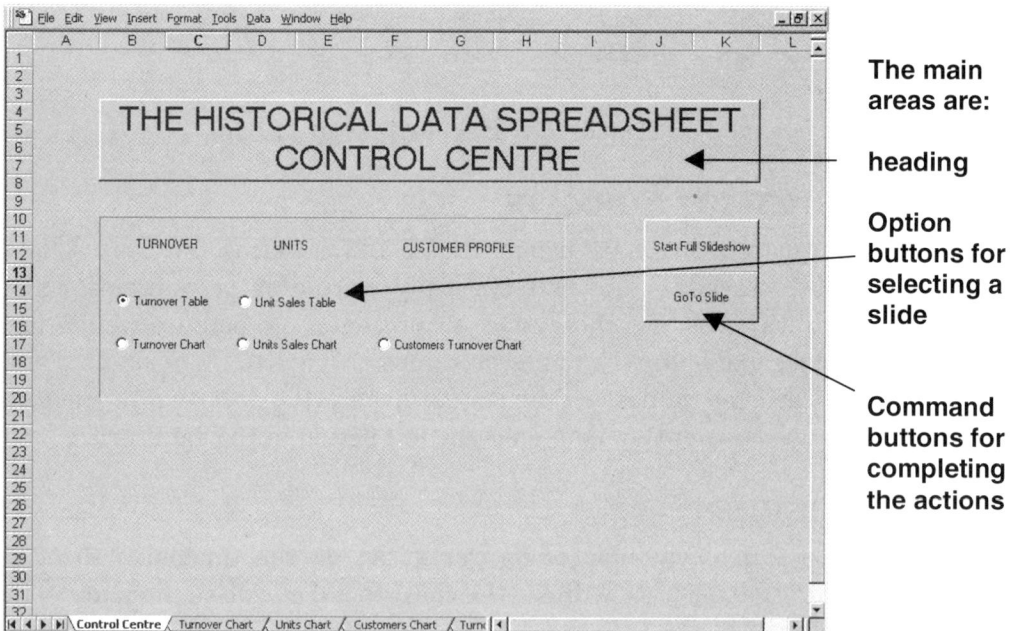

Note that the above screen is in its final form, ready for the PowerPoint presentation. The menu option Full Screen (in the View item) has been activated.

NEXT

In order to keep the chapter short we will stop here. The next chapter explains the detailed steps in building the VBA control centre.

Chapter Twenty-seven

THE VBA CONTROL CENTRE

VBA — the ultimate control!

As a starting point, open **Historical Presentation 17.xls** and select the Control Centre tab. Run the program to get a feel for how the program works. Notice that the gridlines have been turned off in the spreadsheets with tables, in order to improve the visual presentation. This will put in context the steps that are highlighted below.

TO BEGIN

Open **Historical Presentation 12.xls** and insert a blank sheet at the front of the other sheets. Rename it Control Centre.

Activate the VB toolbar and the Toolbox if they are not already displayed on the toolbar.

First of all, make the cell background of the entire sheet grey.

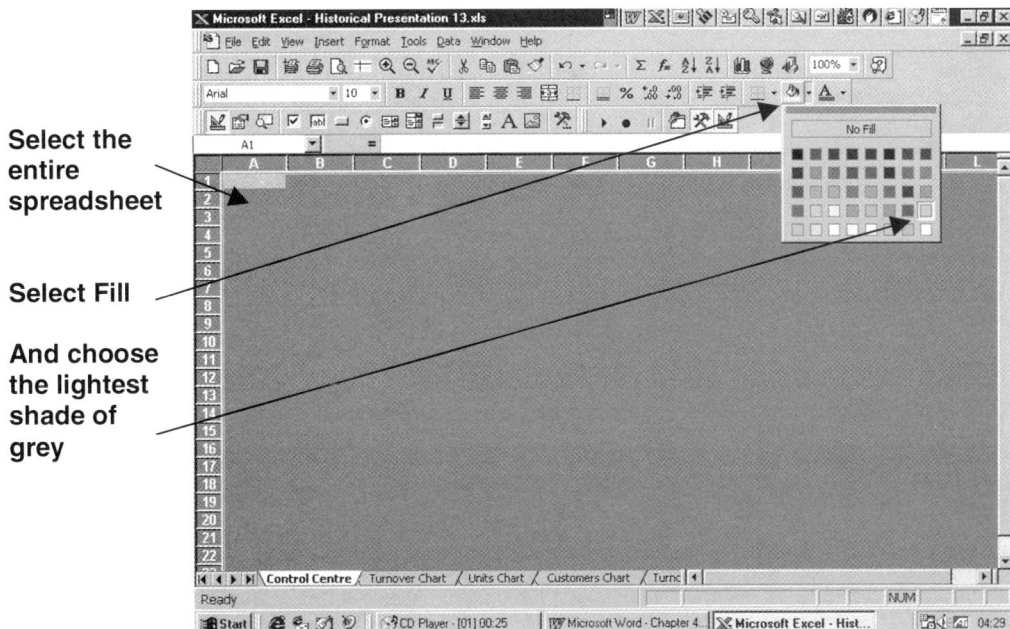

Select the entire spreadsheet

Select Fill

And choose the lightest shade of grey

Next, from the Toolbox toolbar select Label and draw a label from B4 to K7 (approximately). Add three command buttons from J/K 10 to J/K 18. Finally, activate the Drawing toolbar, and draw a rectangle from B10 to H20.

The controls and the rectangle "float" above the cells of the spreadsheet, so the placing is not restricted to the cell references. All of the above placings are therefore approximate.

Format as follows:

Item	Format	Detail
Label	Caption	"THE HISTORICAL DATA SPREADSHEET CONTROL CENTRE"
	ForeColor	Blue
	Font	24
	SpecialEffect	1 – fmSpecialEffectRaised
	TextAlign	2 – fmTextAlignCenter
	WordWrap	True
Command Button 1	Caption	Start Full Slideshow
Command Button 3	Caption	Go To Slide

The above items are adjusted from the Properties icon on the toolbar.

Item	Format	Detail
Rectangle	Colour	Grey
	Sunken	Shadow Style 18

The above items are adjusted from the Drawing toolbar.

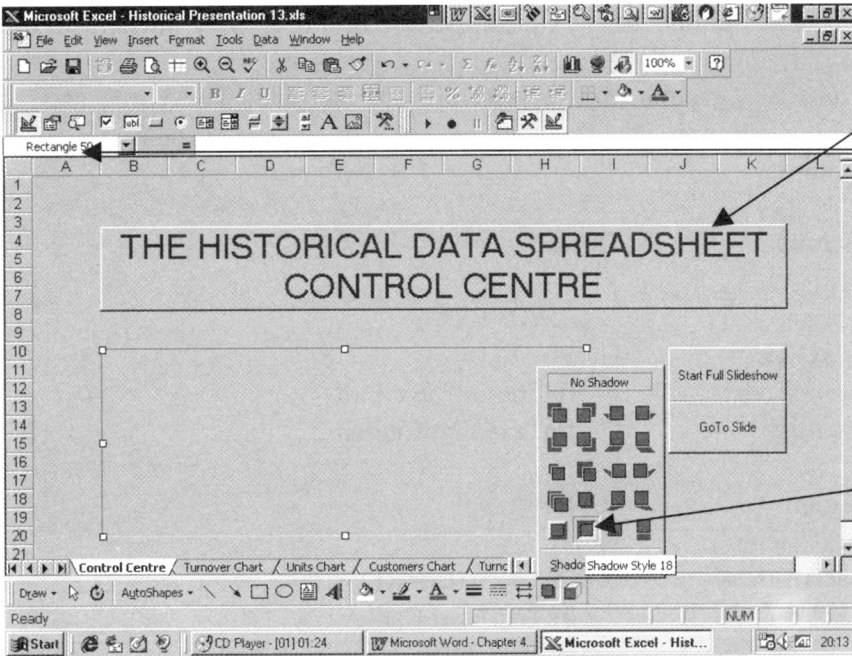

The Label is formatted via the Properties icon

The box is adjusted from the drawing toolbar

Select the Shadow icon for creating the Sunken effect

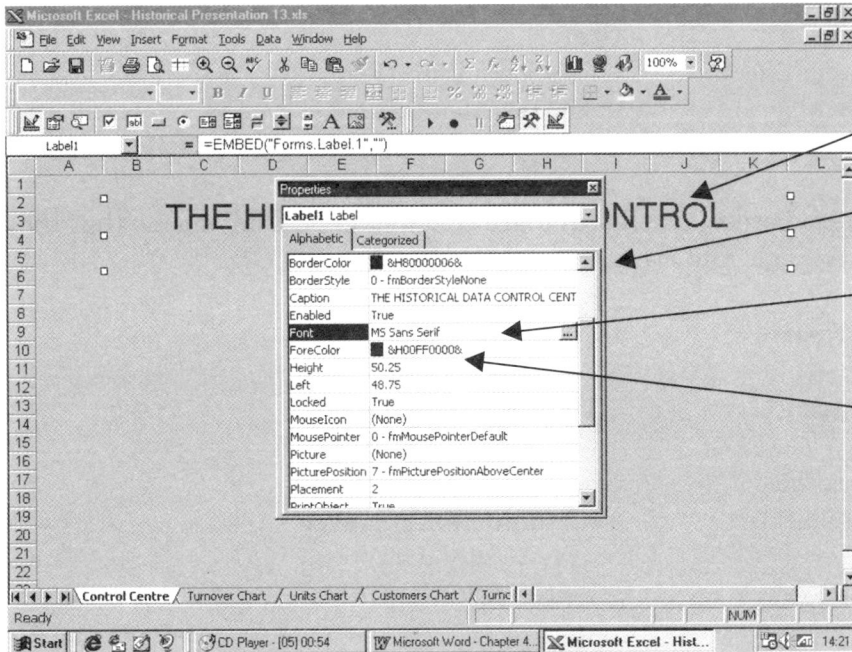

Highlight the label, then activate Properties

Change Font

and ForeColor

The formatted spreadsheet is saved as **Historical Presentation 13.xls**.

Next, from the Toolbox toolbar select Option Button and draw five buttons on top of the rectangle.

Split them into two groups of two, and one on its own. The three sets of buttons are then headed by labels. Draw three labels at the top of the rectangle.

Format as follows:

Item	Format	Detail
Label 1	Caption	"TURNOVER"
	BackColor	Grey
	SpecialEffect	0 – fmSpecialEffectFlat
	TextAlign	2 – fmTextAlignCenter
Label 2	Caption	"UNITS"
	BackColor	Grey
	SpecialEffect	0 – fmSpecialEffectFlat
	TextAlign	2 – fmTextAlignCenter
Label 3	Caption	"CUSTOMER PROFILE"
	BackColor	Grey
	SpecialEffect	0 – fmSpecialEffectFlat
	TextAlign	2 – fmTextAlignCenter

The labels have no border, are flat and are coloured grey. This means that they blend into the rectangle and are not separately highlighted.

Item	Format	Detail
Option Button 1	Caption	"TURNOVER TABLE"
	BackColor	Grey
	SpecialEffect	0 – fmButtonEffectSunken
Option Button 2	Caption	"TURNOVER CHART"
	BackColor	Grey
	SpecialEffect	0 – fmButtonEffectSunken

Option Button 3	Caption	"UNIT SALES TABLE"
	BackColor	Grey
	SpecialEffect	0 – fmButtonEffectSunken
Option Button 4	Caption	"UNIT SALES CHART"
	BackColor	Grey
	SpecialEffect	0 – fmButtonEffectSunken
Option Button 5	Caption	"CUSTOMERS TURNOVER CHART"
	BackColor	Grey
	SpecialEffect	0 – fmButtonEffectSunken

The spreadsheet is saved as **Historical Presentation 14.xls**.

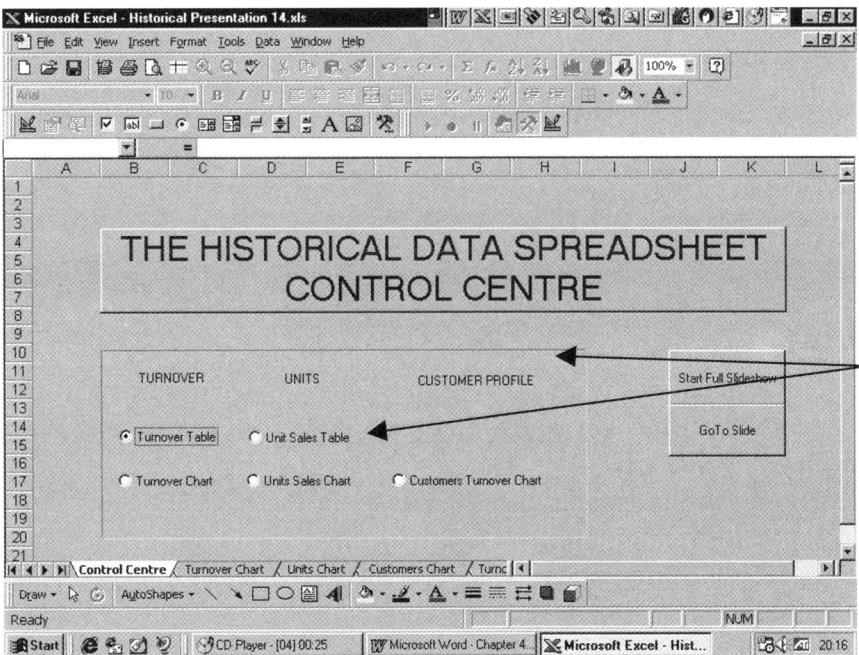

The Option Buttons and labels have been added

LINING UP

All of the elements we need have now been drawn onto the spreadsheet. Before we lock everything in place, we need to check that everything is lined up to our satisfaction.

Open the Drawing Toolbar, and select the line icon. Draw a vertical line from above the edge of the label, and down beyond the edge of the rectangle. Use the line to ensure that they are lined up. Repeat across the other items on the spreadsheet, and either drag or resize as appropriate.

When everything is to your satisfaction, select the lines and press the delete key to remove them.

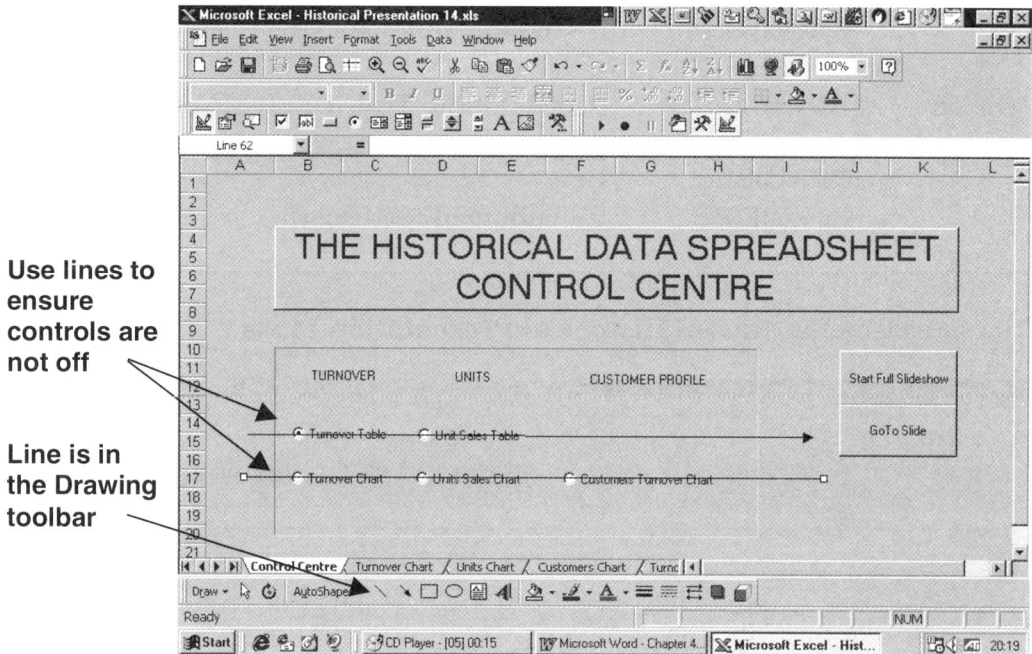

LOCKING DOWN

When we are satisfied that everything is exactly where it should be, and the correct size, hold down the Shift key and select each item with the mouse. Each item selected displays a white grid

When all of the items are selected, with the mouse in the relevant area, right click.

Select Grouping, Group from the pop up menu. The white grids disappear, and are replaced by a single set.

Now, if you move one of the items, they will all move.

The spreadsheet is saved as **Historical Presentation 15.xls**.

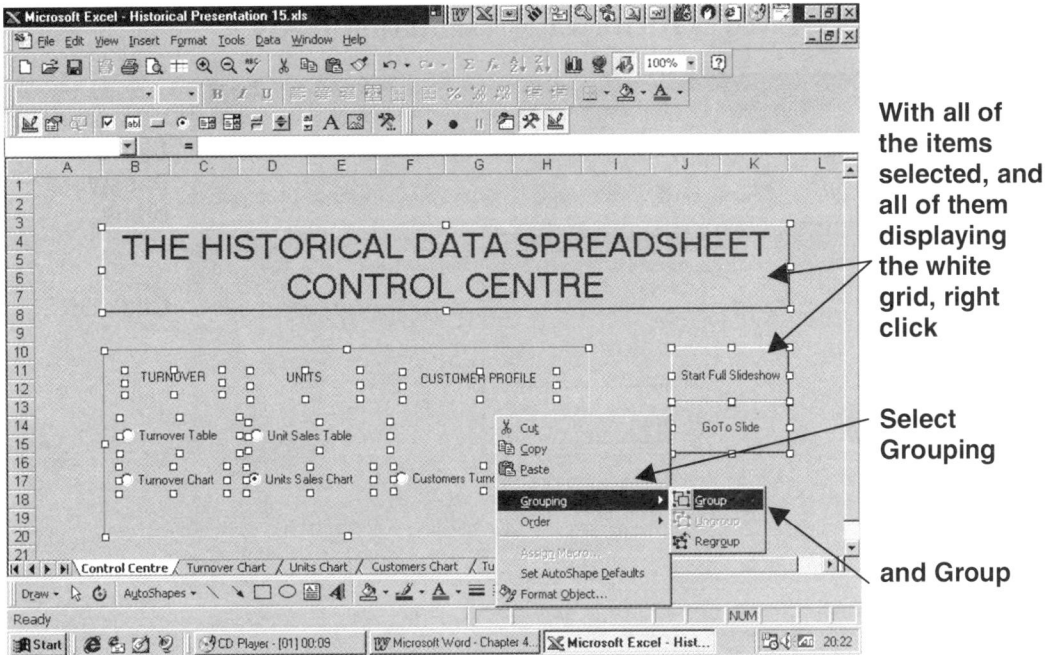

With all of the items selected, and all of them displaying the white grid, right click

Select Grouping

and Group

PROTECTION

There is one more change that must be done before the design stage is completed. Open **Historical Presentation 15.xls** and click on the command buttons and option buttons.

Everything appears to work properly. However, click in an area of the rectangle that does not have any buttons or labels. The white grid appears. In order to stop this happening, on the menu select Tools, Protection then select Protect Sheet. Click OK without entering a password. The problem does not now arise.

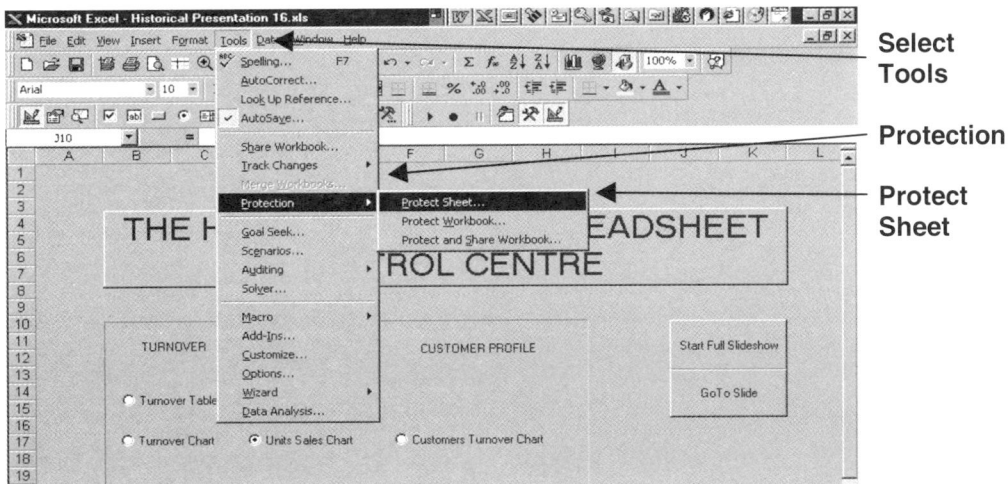

Select Tools

Protection

Protect Sheet

The spreadsheet is saved as **Historical Presentation 16.xls**.

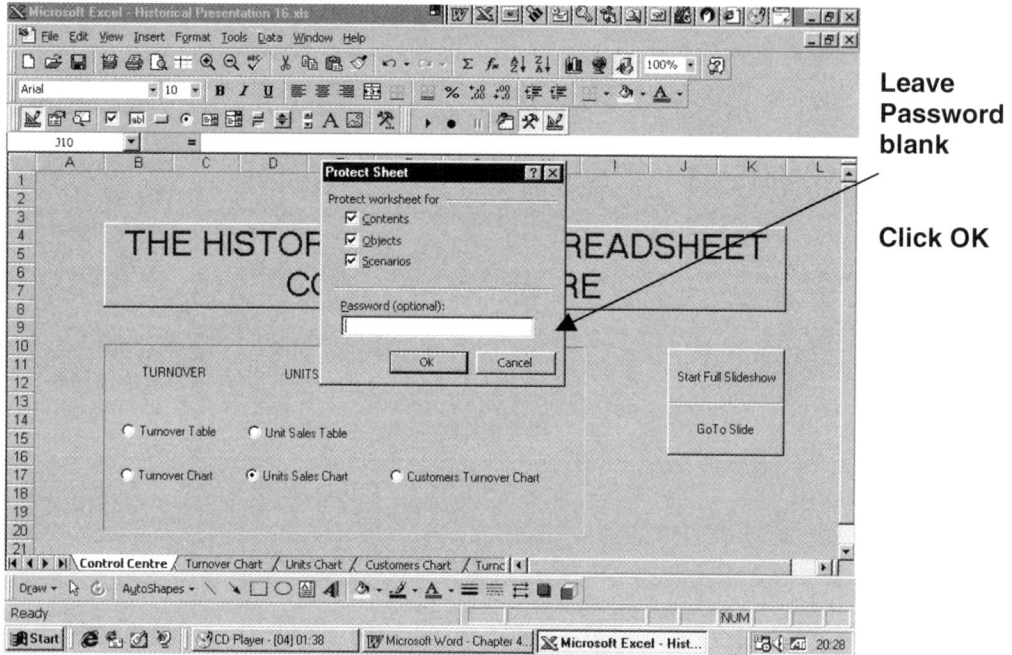

NEXT

The only thing that remains is to code the Command Buttons. We will complete this in the next chapter.

Chapter Twenty-eight

CODING THE VBA CONTROL CENTRE

Not just looking pretty . . .

In this chapter we are going to code the Control Centre. The idea is straightforward enough:

- If we click on the Start Full Slideshow we want to move from slide to slide in a pre-defined order;
- We want to be able to move to the previous slide, should the discussion at the meeting necessitate;
- We want to be able to navigate back to the Control Centre;
- We want to be able to go to a specific slide selected in the Control Centre, if the discussion at our meeting necessitates it.

Irrespective of which method we use to navigate around the various spreadsheets, we want the view to be full screen. This must therefore be set on loading the spreadsheet.

We will look at each area of coding in the above order.

CODING OVERVIEW

The code will apply at different levels:

Global workbook code	Always open the workbook in Full Screen view on loading. Always make the Control Centre spreadsheet the active spreadsheet on loading.
Spreadsheet level code	Coding specific to the page involved, in order to move forward, backward and navigate back to the Control Centre.

We will look at the global workbook code first.

Open **Historical Presentation 16.xls**. Click on the View Code icon in the toolbar. The VB program starts. Select the Workbook spreadsheet in the left pane, and Workbook from the drop-down list on the right.

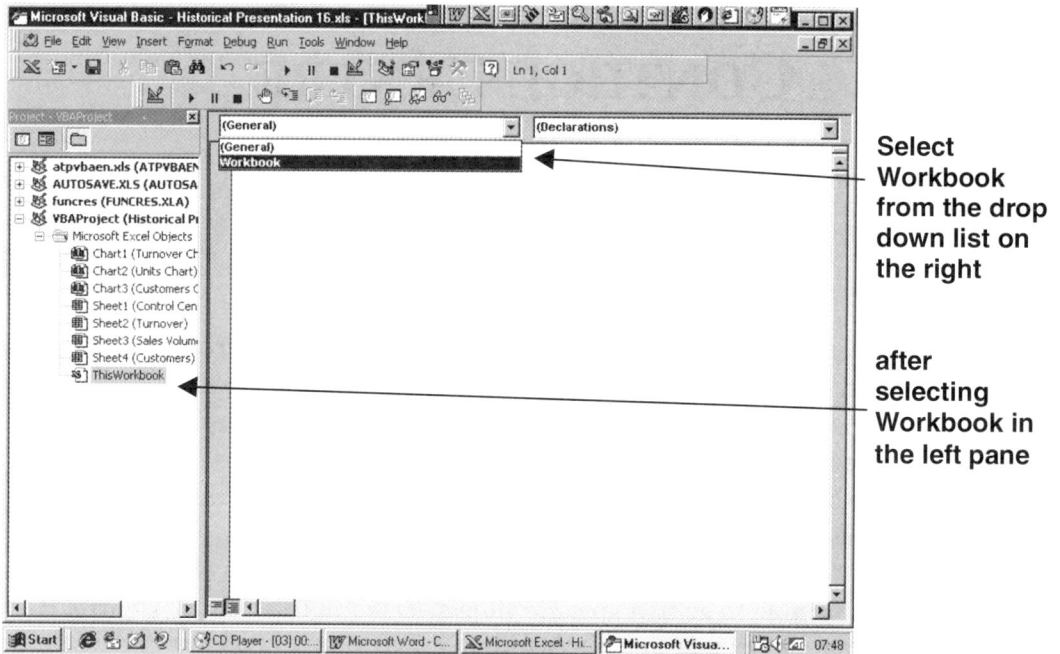

Select Workbook from the drop down list on the right

after selecting Workbook in the left pane

The following line appears in the right hand pane.

    Private Sub Workbook_Open( )
    End Sub

This is the sub routine that will run every time the workbook opens.

THE GLOBAL WORKBOOK CODE

In **Section One** we discussed recording a macro, so that the program actually codes in VB for us. If you run a macro to record making the screen full view it gives the following code:

    Application.DisplayFullScreen = True

The code to move to the Control Centre spreadsheet is:

    sheets("Control Centre").Activate

Combining the two will open the workbook in Full Screen view, with the Control Centre active.

You will have noticed that the active cell in the Control Centre spreadsheet is a darker grey than the background. This is a distraction, and we want to hide the active cell. The easiest way to achieve this is to make a cell below one of our objects active.

We will place it under the box, for convenience.

To move the cell pointer, the code is:

Range("A1").Select

However, this applies if the code is entered in the spreadsheet that is active. We will enter the code in the workbook code. The full address must therefore be given:

sheets("Control Centre").Range("C13").Select

Finally, we always want the option buttons to default to the first item – the Turnover Table. Note that this code cannot be determined by running a macro, and this is where direct VB coding becomes necessary.

We therefore set it to a value of True, which is minus one. The code is

sheets("Control Centre").OptTurnTable.Value = True

The full code is shown below.

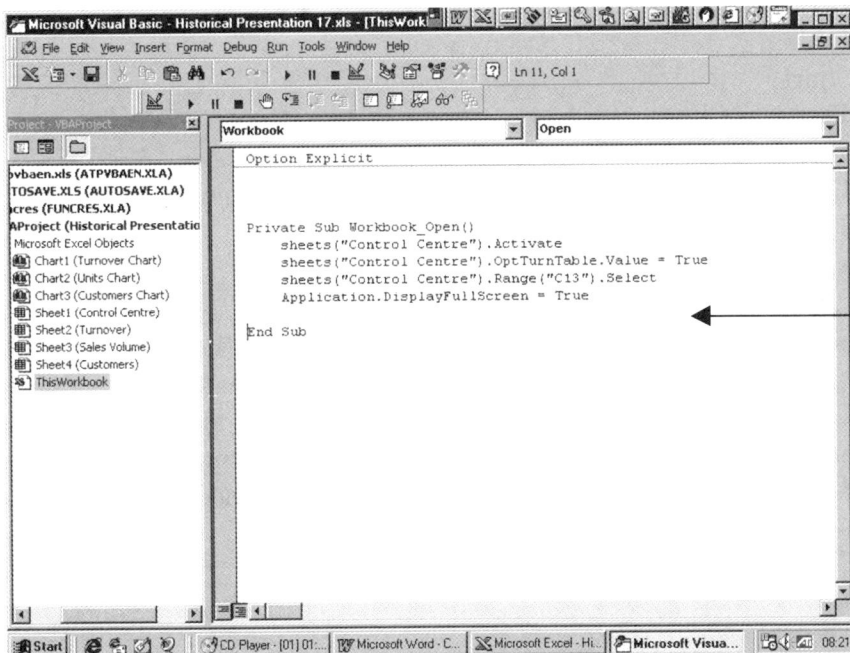

The code to open the workbook at the correct sheet, in the correct view, with the active cell hidden and the first option button selected

The complete code is:

```
Private Sub Workbook_Open()
    sheets("Control Centre").Activate
    sheets("Control Centre").OptTurnTable.Value = True
    sheets("Control Centre").Range("C13").Select
    Application.DisplayFullScreen = True

End Sub.
```

THE CONTROL CENTRE CODE

That gives us a spreadsheet that opens with the correct sheet active, and the correct option button highlighted. We now want to code the two command buttons, Start Full Slideshow and Go To Slide.

Start Full Slideshow

This code is straightforward. All we need to do is to go to the first sheet when the button is clicked.

The order we will be discussing the spreadsheets is the same order as appears in Control Centre:

- Turnover Table
- Turnover Chart
- Unit Sales Table
- Unit Sales Chart
- Customers Turnover Chart.

To move to the first sheet we code the Command Button click event with:

```
sheets("Turnover").Activate
```

Go To Slide

The code in this button must check which slide was selected (i.e. which option button is active). The result will then determine which spreadsheet to make active.

The Command Button click event therefore has to review each possible option. We have used If...ElseIf statements, although other coding methods can be used.

The code is:

```
If OptTurnTable.Value = True Then
        sheets("Turnover").Activate
ElseIf OptTurnChart.Value = True Then
        Charts("Turnover chart").Activate
ElseIf OptUnitTable.Value = True Then
        sheets("Sales volume").Activate
ElseIf OptUnitChart.Value = True Then
        Charts("units chart").Activate
ElseIf OptCustChart.Value = True Then
        Charts("customers chart").Activate


End If
```

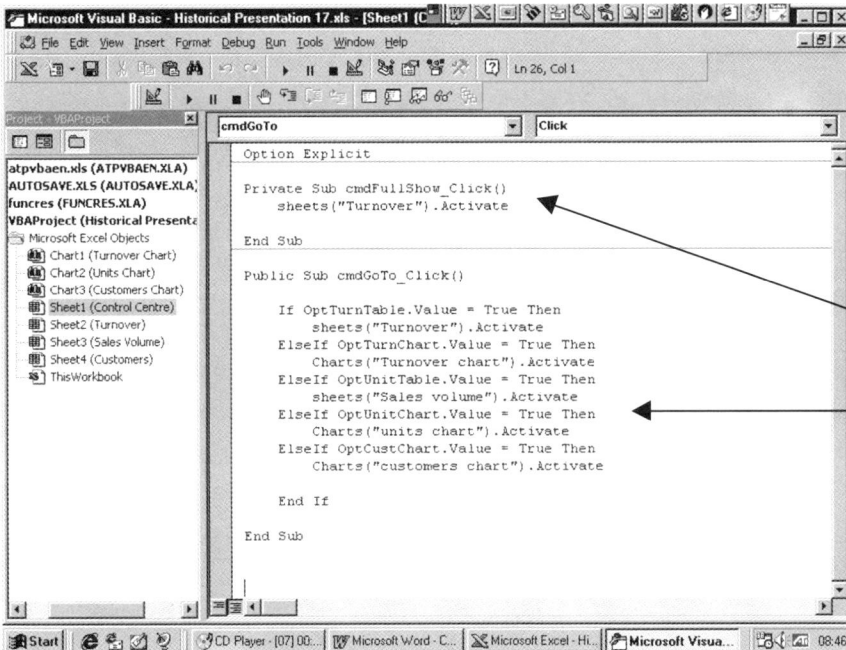

The code window, showing the code for both command buttons

Full Show

and Go To

THE SLIDE SHOW

The above coding will take us to the correct individual spreadsheet. How do we navigate from there? We are going to use two solutions:

• We will use Command Buttons on the spreadsheets
• We will use click events with the mouse for the charts.

This will illustrate the two main choices.

The code for each button is straightforward:
- Next   Charts("Turnover chart").Activate
- Back   sheets("control centre").Activate
- Control Centre   sheets("control centre").Activate

Note that the buttons are not seen when the spreadsheet is in Normal view. They have been placed to enhance the spreadsheet screen in Full Screen view.

To code the Back button, select the relevant sheet in the left hand pane, then select cmdBack from the drop down list in the right pane. The click command should be activated. If not select it from the drop down list on the extreme right.

All of the spreadsheets are coded in the same way.

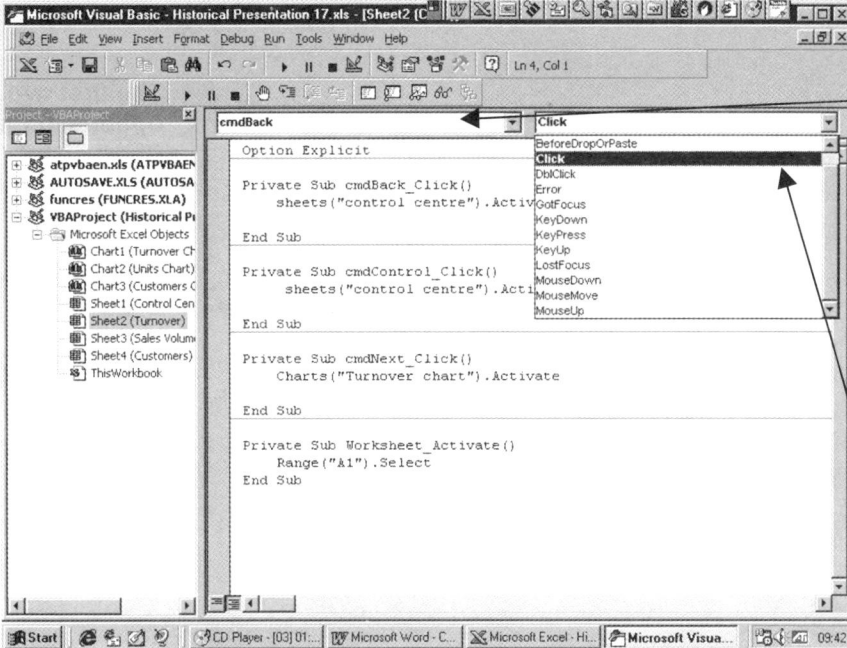

CODING THE CHARTS

If the charts are placed into a separate sheet the VB buttons are deactivated when the sheet is activated. Therefore the VB buttons cannot be used.

There are two choices — either place the charts within a current spreadsheet, or use the mouse to navigate from one chart to another. We will use the second option.

Specifically, we will make a right click move forward to the next sheet, and a double click move back to the previous sheet.

They are titled BeforeDoubleClick and BeforeRightClick. They intercept the mouse clicks, and apply the revised code instead of the default code of Edit and Pop Up Menu respectively.

The actual code is the same as for the Command Buttons: Sheets("Sales Volume").Activate etc. Note that there is no "return to Control Centre" option. You must navigate to a spreadsheet to be able to select the Command Button, or move past the last chart, which automatically activates the Control Centre.

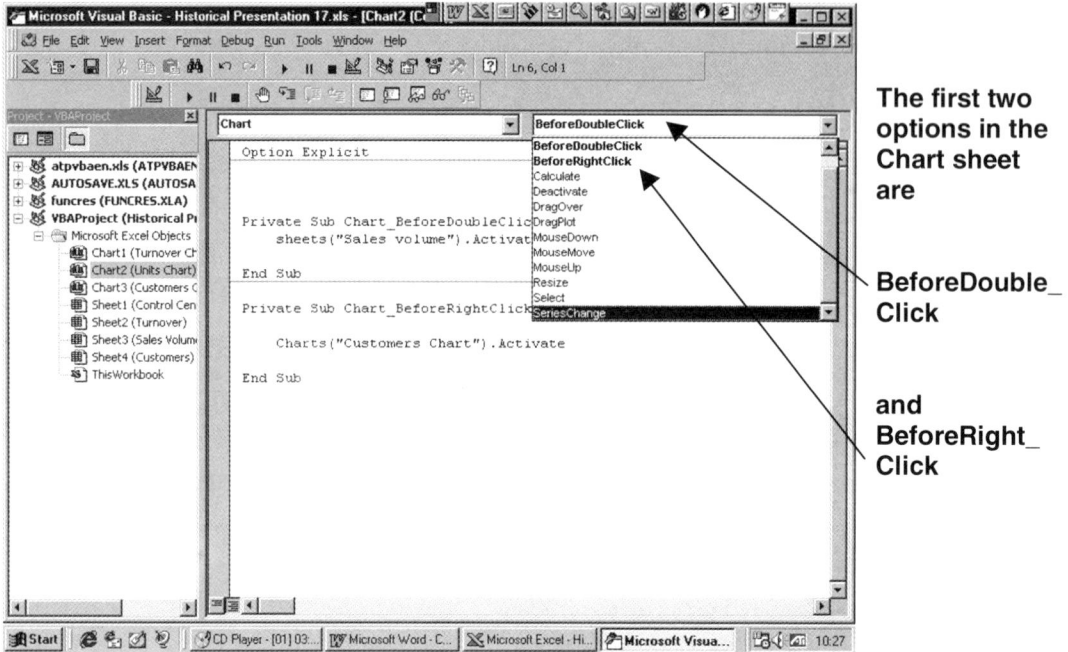

The first two options in the Chart sheet are

BeforeDouble_Click

and **BeforeRight_Click**

The spreadsheet, fully coded, is saved as **Historical Presentation 17.xls**.

The spreadsheet is now ready for inclusion in the PowerPoint presentation. We will do this at the end of the section.

NEXT

That completes the preparation of the spreadsheets based on historical results. We did not use the data on the number and types of units sold to customers in the period. We will use this information in the Sales spreadsheets in the next chapter.

Chapter Twenty-nine

SALES AND PRODUCTION FORECASTING

Can we sell it? And, if we can, can we make it?

Historical data is easy. Deciding on the level of future sales, and having an adequate production capacity, especially in a growth market with a new competitor trying to break into it, is very difficult.

We will meet the Sales and Marketing team to gain their insight into the market, and the perceived threat posed by Thingies. In order to conduct a more meaningful meeting we will prepare information. So, we will prepare tables of figures from the historic figures, to answer the following questions:

- What were the sales volumes, split between each product? Prepare a chart, and project forward by six months.
- What were the prices for each product in the period?

We want the Sales team to tell us their views on:

- Future pricing
- Market Growth
- Thingies, and their market share.

From the above we must calculate:

- Projected turnover, based on the projected sales volume and price
- Projected profit, based on the contribution per unit.

Open **Imported Sales Data 10.xls**, and also start a new blank workbook.

Revise the PivotTable for unit sales, so that it shows years down the column, instead of across the page. Start the Wizard, and move the columns so that both types of small product appear beside each other. Likewise with medium and large.

Copy the table (Ctrl + C) and then Paste Special the values and the formats into the blank workbook.

In order to produce the correct labels in the charts, change the first month to 1/98, and then AutoFill.

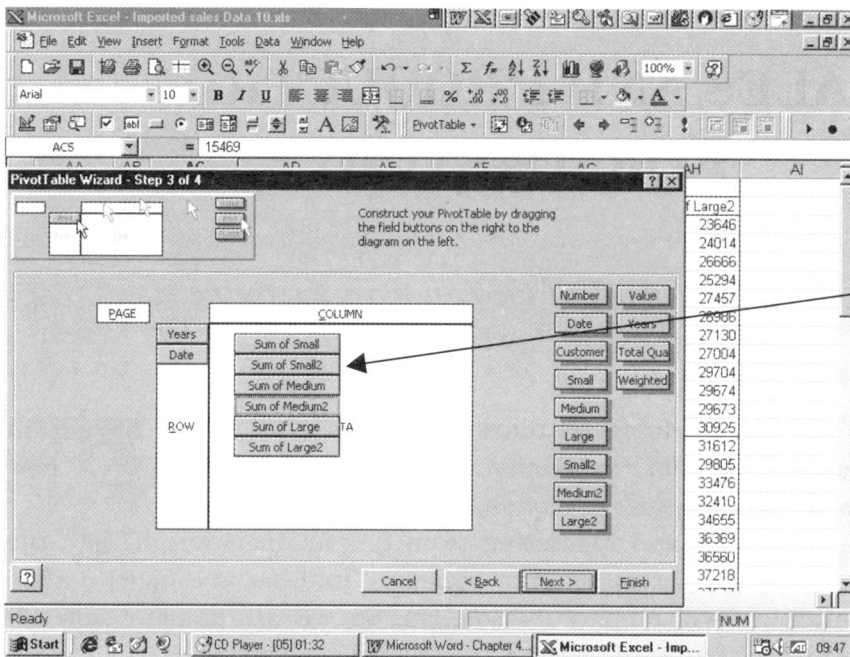

Drag the columns to the new position

Click Next, then Finish

After pasting, confirm the totals are correct compared to the original data, then delete Feb 2002. It is not a full month's data.

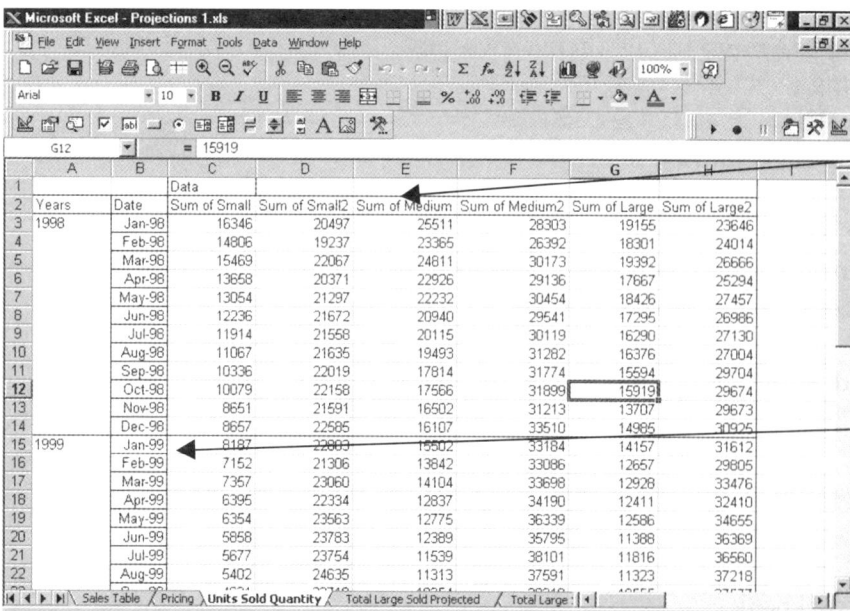

The revised table, with re-ordered headings, has been pasted into a new spreadsheet

The Date has been manually changed to 1/98 and AutoFilled

This gives us our starting point for charting. Start the Chart Wizard, and prepare three charts, one for each size of product. The chart for Small Units is shown below.

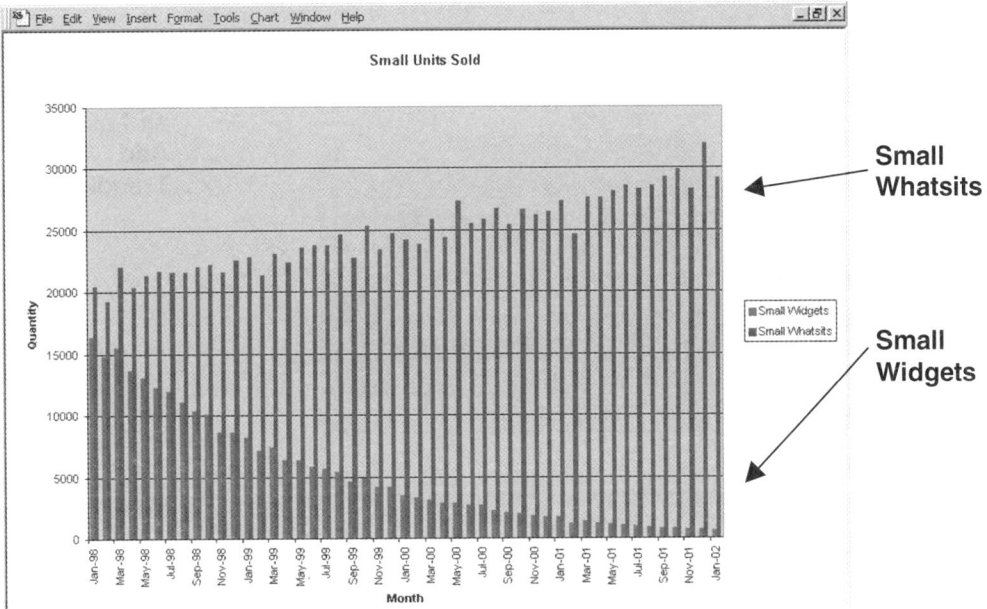

FORECASTING

Next we will add a trendline to the chart, and forecast it forward by six months.

To add a trendline, click on one of the bars that we want to add a trendline to. The bars now display a data handle in the centre of all of the bars.

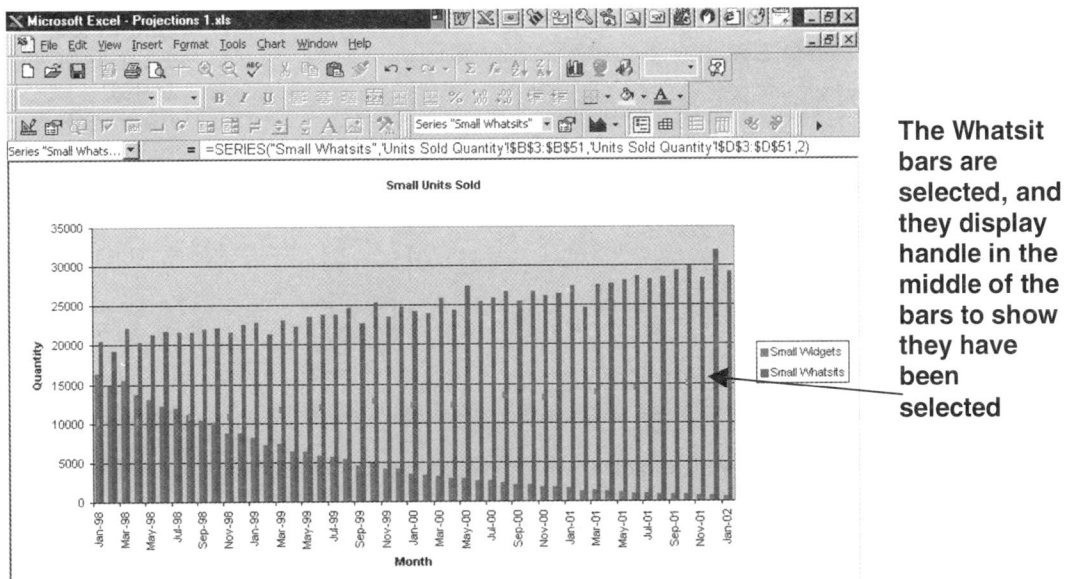

The Whatsit bars are selected, and they display handle in the middle of the bars to show they have been selected

With the mouse over one of the bars, right click and select Add Trendline.

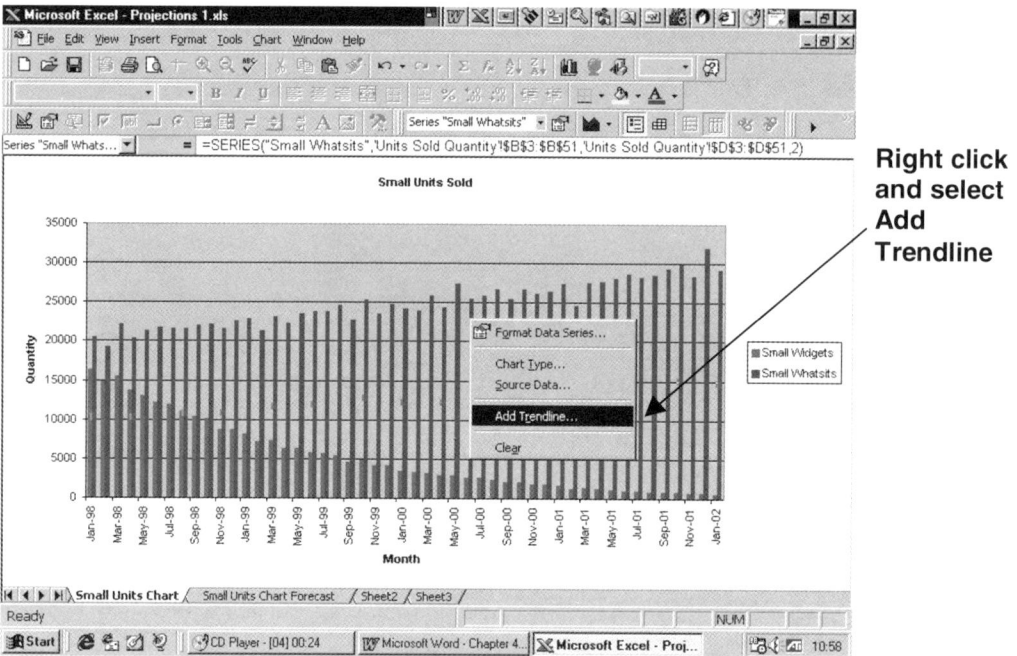

Select Exponential, then select the Options tab.

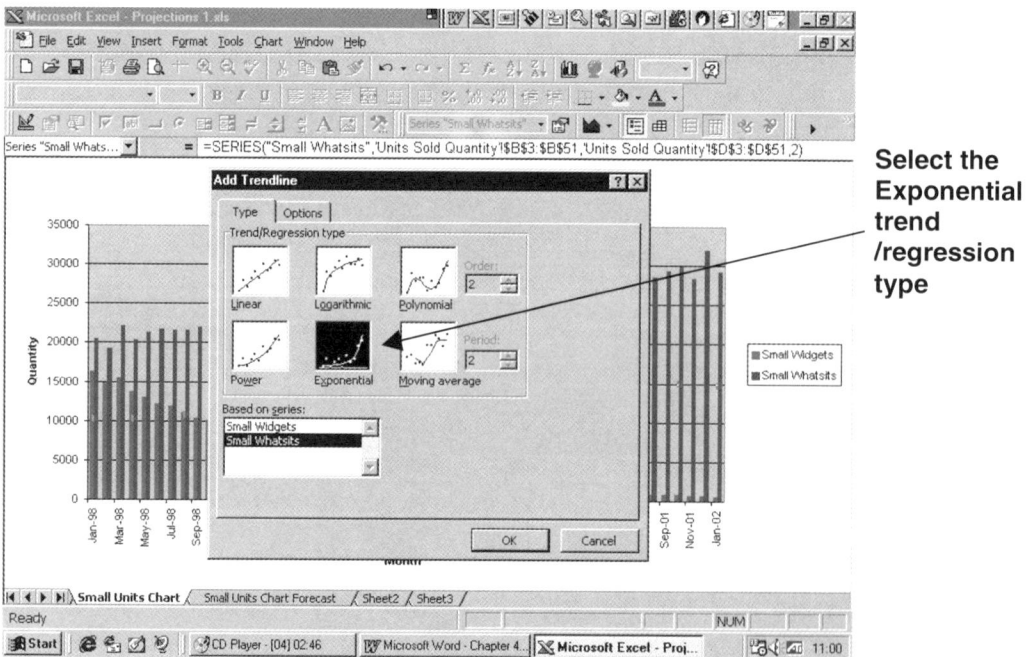

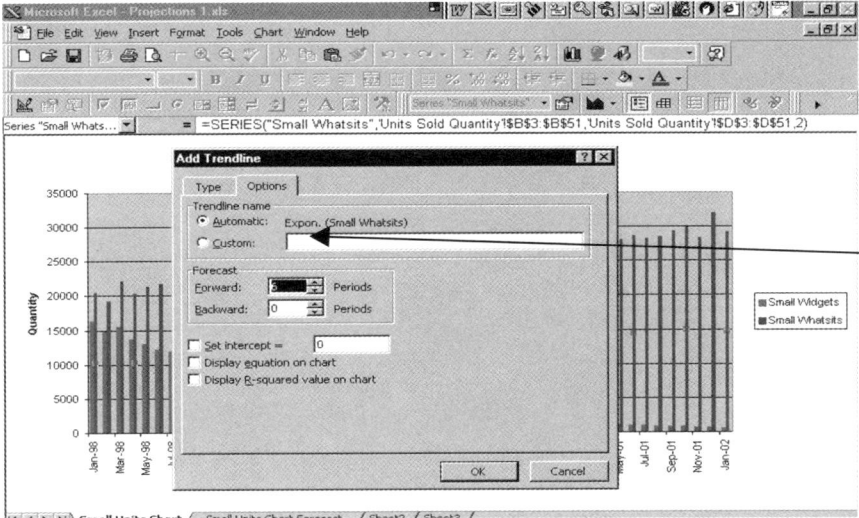

In the Trendline dialog box, click on the Options button and enter 6 in the Forecast Forward input box

Click OK, and the line is entered in black. We will reformat it.

The trendline handle should be displayed. If not, left click on the trendline. With the mouse pointer on the trendline, right click and select Format Trendline. Note that this is also the menu used to delete the trendline.

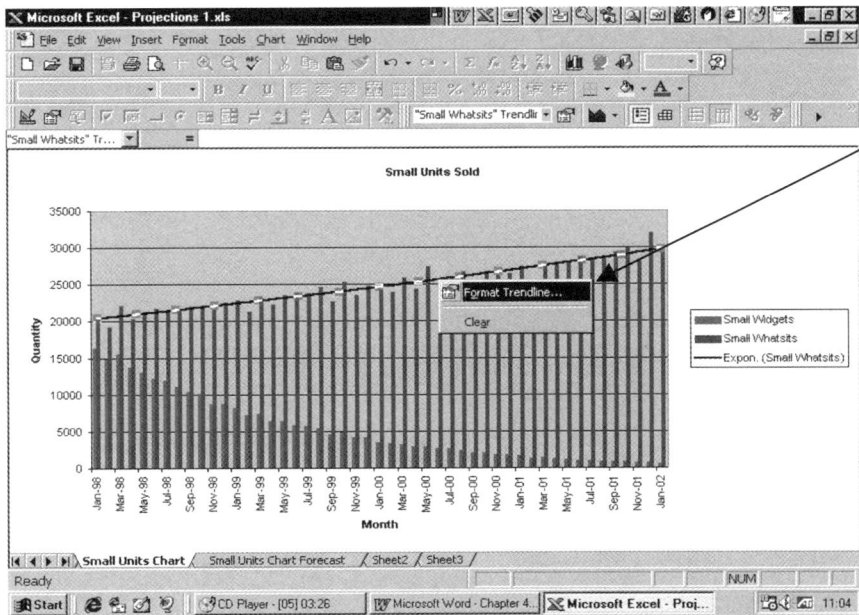

Right click and select Format Trendline

The Format Trendline appears.

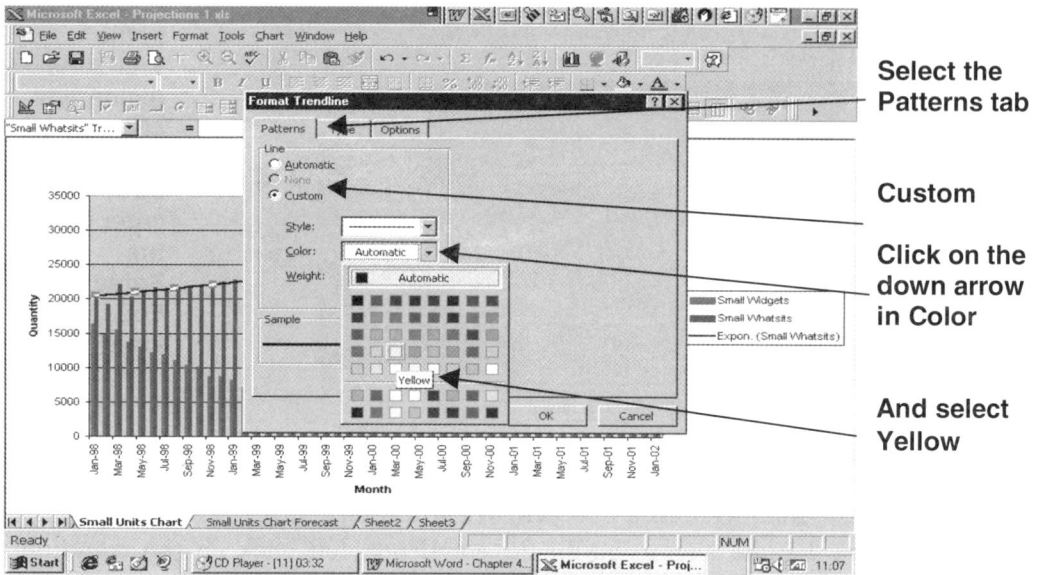

The chart is finished, and the trendline is shown.

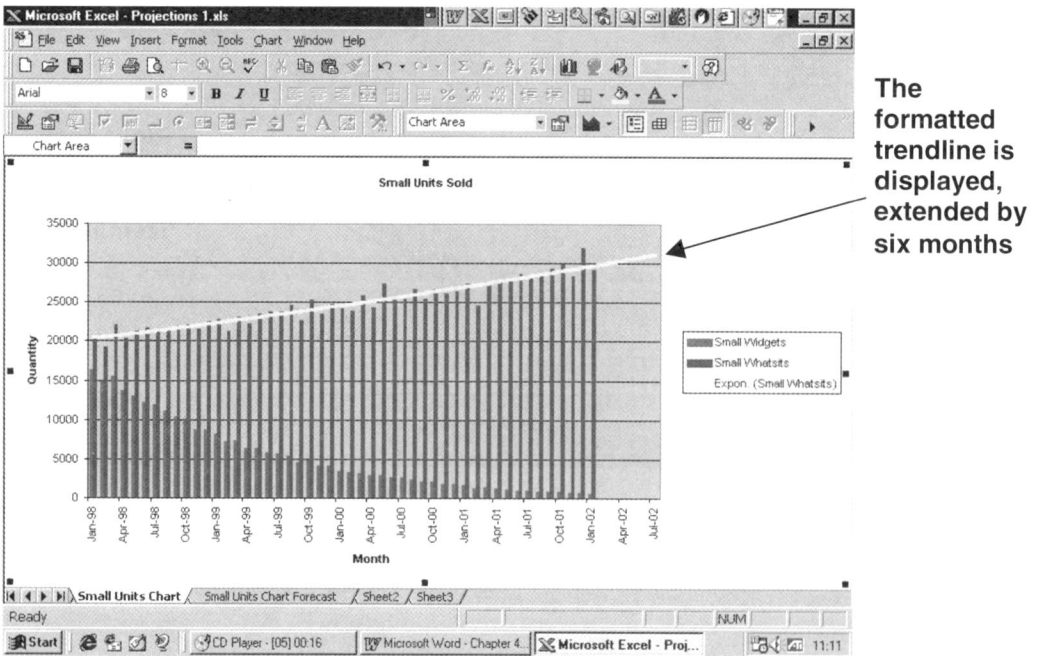

Add a trendline to the Widgets data, and format it in green.

Prepare charts for Medium and Large units, and add trendlines to these as well. All of the charts, and charts with trendlines, are saved as separate sheets on **Projections 1.xls**.

TOTAL SOLD

The charts, and the trends shown, are interesting. Another way of summarising the information is to prepare a table of total units sold, irrespective of whether they are Widgets or Whatsits.

The Whatsits are replacing the Widgets, and it would show trends as regards small versus medium versus large.

Make a new table of figures at cell AA1, and add the small units etc. from A1.

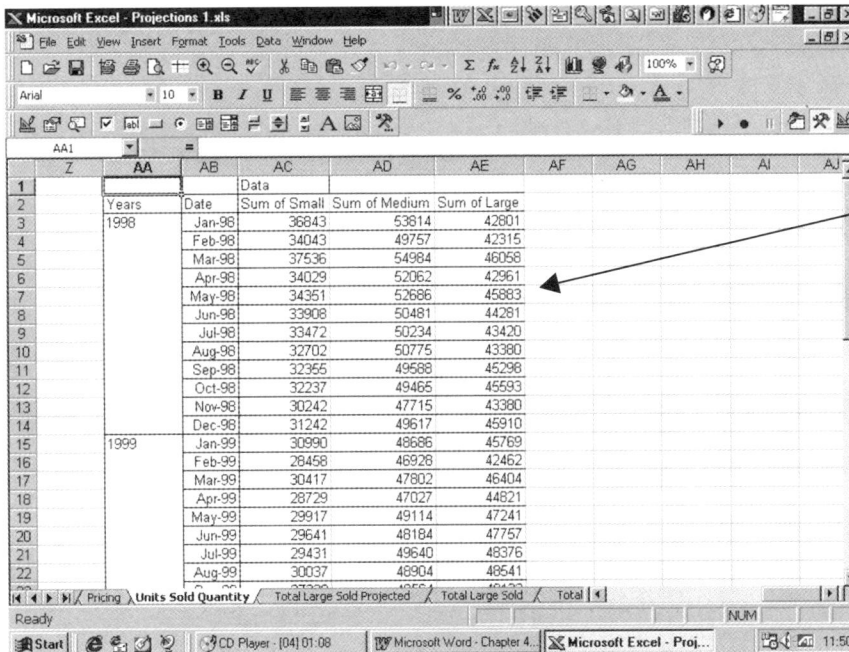

The units table at AA1, showing the total number of units of each size sold

As before, chart the results and enter the trendline for the next six months.

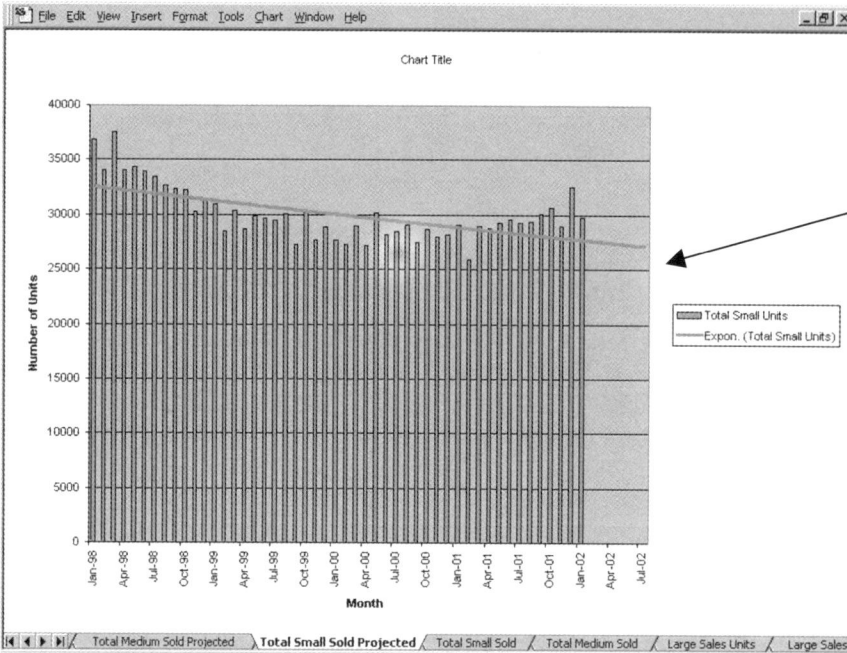

Sales of medium-sized units is increasing.

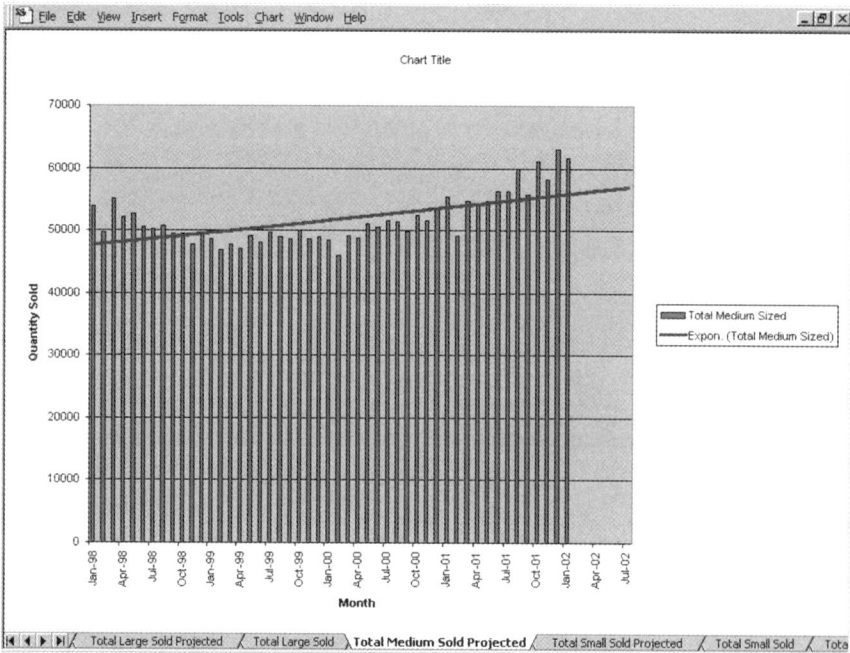

Large unit sales are increasing fastest of all.

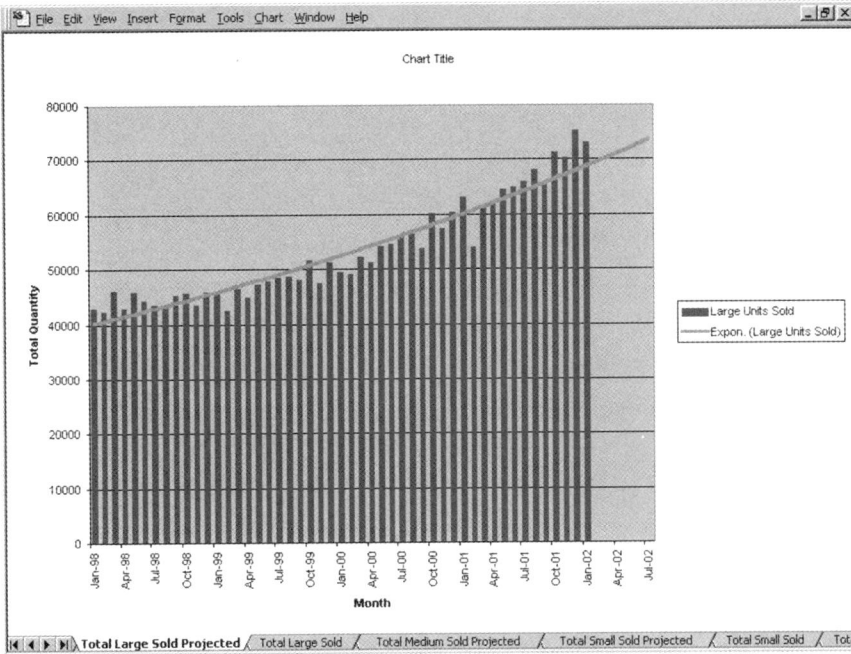

PRICING

The final piece of information we need is the historic pricing of the products. The pricing for each product in the period was:

Year	Widgets			Whatsits		
	Small	*Medium*	*Large*	*Small*	*Medium*	*Large*
	£	£	£	£	£	£
1998	4.00	7.50	11.50	4.20	8.20	12.00
1999	3.60	6.83	10.58	4.24	8.36	12.36
2000	3.24	6.21	9.73	4.28	8.53	12.73
2001	2.92	5.65	8.95	4.33	8.70	13.11

The file is saved as **Projections 1.xls**, and it includes charts as set out above, and forecasting charts, which give the trendlines.

NEXT

We have all of the information, and are ready to meet the Sales and Marketing team.

Chapter Thirty

SALES AND PRODUCTION MEETINGS

Machine time is the key.
That's what H.G. Wells thought anyway. . .

We have an appointment to see Simon, the Sales Director, to show him our charts and analysis, and to ask his opinion on future growth, pricing and market share now that Thingies are starting to be sold. The Production Director was there as well . . .

"Hello James. And you brought your colleague, good. I thought we may as well have Peter here to hear everything first-hand."

Peter, the Production Director, smiled and we all shook hands. They both reviewed our PivotTables and charts with interest.

"Right. The market research we have been conducting fits in with what you have, in terms of the phasing out of Widgets and the move towards the larger Whatsits. We think the market is moving like this . . ."

He showed us a report that estimated the total market for the coming year. With the economic growth forecasts and the change in disposable income the total sales volume was projected at:

Size	Number	Price
Small	360,000	4.50
Medium	725,000	9.00
Large	875,000	14.00

"This assumes we drop Widgets altogether, which I was just discussing with Peter. If we continue with Widgets I reckon the prices will drop to £2.20 for the small, £5.50 for the medium and they should stabilise at £9.00 for the large. My gut reaction is to keep Widgets going, in order to keep our spread as wide as possible to counter these Thingies. The sales of Widgets will probably fall 20%.

"Could you do me a table to see what the numbers are like if the market is at this level, plus and minus, and our market share is anywhere from, say, 75% to 100%?"

"Can I mention machine time?" asked Peter. *"We are working overtime at the moment, and if we switch completely to Whatsits I don't think we can cope. I think we would need to buy another machine in order to increase capacity."*

We agreed to look into it. The machine time required for each product is:

Type	Size	Machine time
Widgets	Small	3.50
	Medium	7.00
	Large	10.50
Whatsits	Small	4.50
	Medium	9.00
	Large	13.50

"And one more thing. If Thingies get too large a foothold, we will start a price war. I think that if we cut prices by 10% we should bring back 5% of the turnover. However, I'm not sure at what point it is worth doing.

"Can you prepare a program for me so that I can work through some numbers. Then we can co-ordinate for your presentation."

So, there we are. Now we have the basic information to write up some of the presentation. But first, we need to do some ground work on the figures and prepare a program for Simon.

Chapter Thirty-one

THE "WHAT IF" MODEL (I)

Another building block . . .

We have been given various parameters by the Sales Director; the Production Director has expressed concerns about being able to meet demand; and we have to produce an easy-to-use spreadsheet for them to kick the figures around before we finalise the ideas in our presentation.

Let's start.

DATA TABLES

We know what the expected growth in the market will be, and we want to consider what impact the market share of Thingies will have.

This is ideal for Data Tables. We will prepare tables for each size of unit, ignoring the split between Widgets and Whatsits in the meantime.

Open **Projections 1.xls** and insert a new sheet.

Place a heading of Sales Table in cell A1, and a heading of Large at cell A5. The details we were given are an expected market size of 875,000 units, and we have to calculate from 75% to 100% market share. We will therefore calculate from 800,000 to 975,000 units, with an interval of 25,000. The percentages will run from 75% to 100% in intervals of 5%.

Enter the figures from 800,000 to 975,000 from A7 to A14, and 100% to 75% from B6 to G6. Cell A6 contains the calculation cell, and we will use cells I6 to I8 to calculate.

Place a heading Calculator in cell I4, the value 800,000 in I6, the value 100% in I7 and =I6*I7 in cell I8.

We are ready to calculate the table. Select cells A6 to G14 and, from the menu, select Data, Table and select the cells for the input box. The table is inserted.

Complete for Medium and Small. The unit ranges are 650,000 to 825,000 for medium, with intervals of 25,000, and 335,000 to 380,000 for small, with intervals of 5,000.

The medium unit table is placed at A18 to G26 and the small unit table is placed at A31 to A41.

The file is saved as **Projections 2.xls**.

WIDGETS OR NOT?

The above tables are for the full market, and do not split turnover between Widgets and Whatsits.

Widget sales are expected to be 20% down from last year, across the board. The annual sales of units for last year is shown on the Units Sold Quantity tab in **Projections 2.xls**.

The figures for widgets are therefore expected to be:

Type	Sales Volume	80% of Volume
Small	12,405	10,000
Medium	47,436	38,000
Large	64,055	51,000

The expected total market is set out below. The widgets are given as a percentage.

Type	Total Market Size	Widgets as a %
Small	360,000	2.78%
Medium	725,000	5.24%
Large	875,000	5.83%

The table is a two-dimensional structure, and we are trying to see a three-dimensional view.

Instead, what we will do is set up tables that are linked to the originals, and which expand on the analysis contained in the tables.

At cell AA1 enter the heading "Sales Tables, Including Widgets". Tile two windows so that we can pick up the cell references more easily.

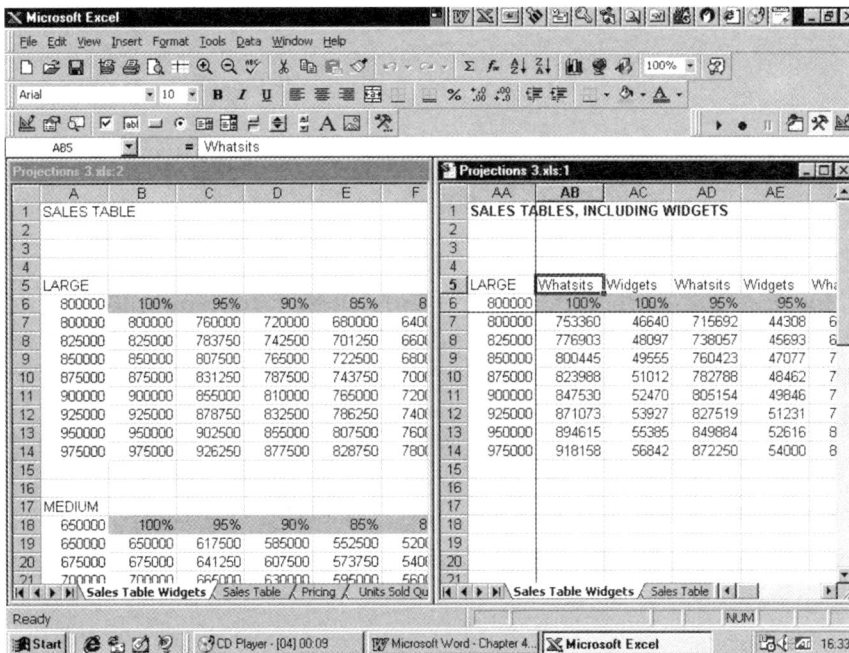

Tile two windows

set up a new table

and enter the formula, picking up the cell references required.

Pick up the column headings, and in the row headings enter two headings for each percentage. Label the first Whatsits, and the second Widgets.

LARGE	Whatsits	Widgets	Whatsits	Widgets	Whatsits	Widgets	Whatsits	Widgets	Whatsits	Widgets	Whatsits
800000	100%	100%	95%	95%	90%	90%	85%	85%	80%	80%	75
800000	753360	46640	715692	44308	678024	41976	640356	39644	602688	37312	56502
825000	776903	48097	738057	45693	699212	43288	660367	40883	621522	38478	58267
850000	800445	49555	760423	47077	720401	44599	680378	42122	640356	39644	60033
875000	823988	51012	782788	48462	741589	45911	700389	43361	659190	40810	61799
900000	847530	52470	805154	49846	762777	47223	720401	44599	678024	41976	63564
925000	871073	53927	827519	51231	783965	48535	740412	45838	696858	43142	65330
950000	894615	55385	849884	52616	805154	49846	760423	47077	715692	44308	67096
975000	918158	56842	872250	54000	826342	51158	780434	48316	734526	45474	68861

SALES TABLES, INCLUDING WIDGETS

The headings are repeated twice.

In English, the formula we need to insert is "Whatsits are the value in column AA, multiplied by the percentage in row 6, multiplied by one minus the percentage of Widgets sold. The answer is rounded off to the nearest thousand".

In Excel the formula is:

=ROUND($AA7*AB$6*(1-$AP$7),-3)

The cell references are:

$AA7 – always column AA, not necessarily row 7

AB$6 – always row 6, not necessarily column AB

$AP$7 – always cell AP7

Complete the other tables.

The spreadsheet is saved as **Projections 3.xls**.

MODEL BUILDING

The table is still comprehensible, but it is becoming unwieldy for further amendment, such as the effects of a reduction in price.

We will therefore provide a hard copy of the table as it stands, for reference material, and we will build a VBA-controlled model for "what if" questions and answers

ADDITIONAL PARAMETERS

The additional parameters we need to build into the model, as well as the price war scenario, are:

- Machine time for production
- Stocking policy, for machine time
- Profitability.

NEXT

We will finish the chapter here, and start to build the VBA model in the next chapter.

Chapter Thirty-two

THE "WHAT IF" MODEL (II)

More choice . . .

In **Section One** we produced a VBA model that allowed us to flex items using
spin buttons, and linked these to spreadsheet cells. It uses spin buttons in order
to switch options on and off, and it uses option buttons to select one of a range of
pre-set options, in this case gross profit margin. The spreadsheet is saved on the
CD as **Excel VBA 5.xls** if you want to refresh your memory about how it looks
and how it works.

	A	B	C	D	E	F	G	H	I	J	K	L
1				Sales	Cost							
2												
3												
4	Television Advertising			60%	40%	Sales			77500			
5	Postal Advertising			30%	20%							
6	Telephone Sales			25%	40%	Purchases			31000			
7												
8						Gross Profit			46500	GP%	60%	
9	Base Sales in units		◄ ►	31000								
10	Selling Price per unit			2		Expenses						
11						Television Advertising		0				
12	Additional Sales in units					Postal Advertising		0				
13	Television Advertising	FALSE		0		Telephone Sales		6200				
14	Postal Advertising	FALSE		0					6200			
15	Telephone Sales	TRUE		7750								
16						Net Profit			40300			
17												
18												
19			☐ TV Advertising									
20			☐ Postal Advertising			○ GP Markup 40%		○ GP Markup 50%		● GP Markup 60%		
21			☑ Telephone Sales									
22												
23												
24												
25												
26												
27												
28												
29												
30												
31												
32												

Sheet1 / Sheet2 / Sheet3

In this section we built a VBA model for navigating through spreadsheets and charts. It uses option buttons to determine which slide has been chosen, and command buttons to implement the actions, based on the selection made.

Code runs in the background, to control how the spreadsheet displays on opening, which sheet is active and, within the specific sheet, which option button is selected by default.

It is saved on the CD as **Historical Presentation 17.xls** and it is shown below.

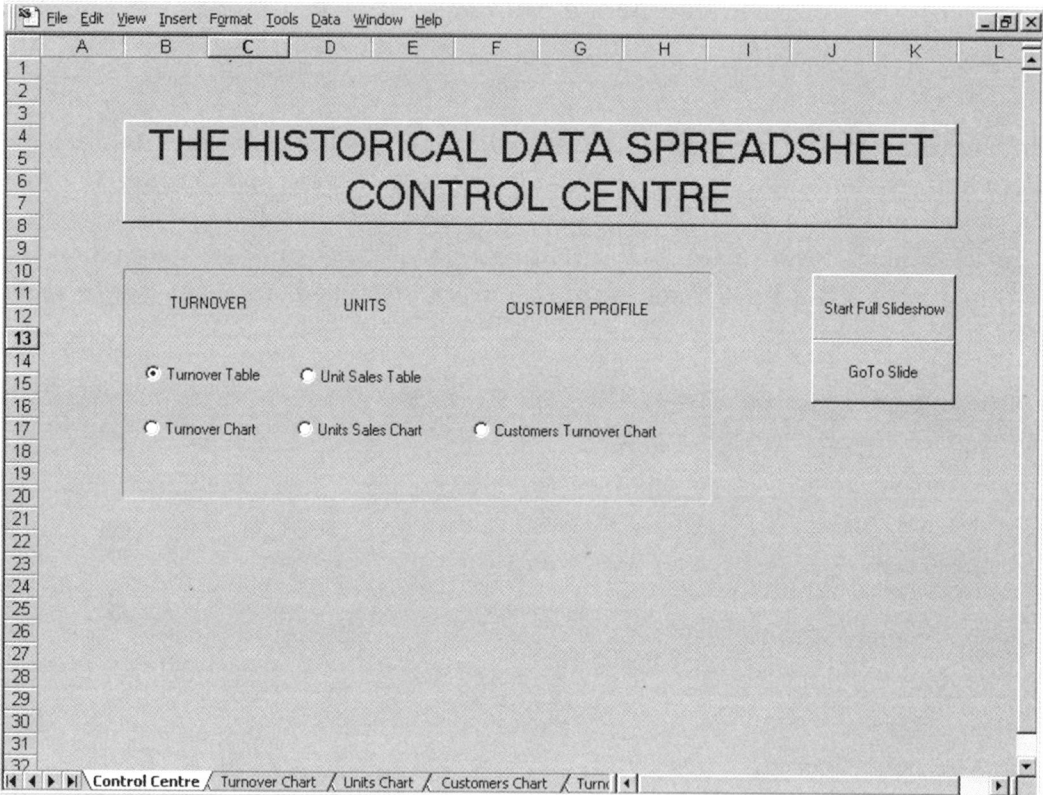

We will build the "What If" model by using the full power of VBA, and combine aspects of both spreadsheets.

STARTING

First of all, we want control in the screen shot area to be completely controlled by VBA. We do not want any of the spreadsheet cells to be available.

Instead of working directly in the spreadsheet area and masking cells with a rectangle over the relevant area, as we did on the spreadsheet above, we will use VBA forms.

Open a blank workbook, and click on View Code in the VB toolbar. The VB program starts.

On the menu, select Insert, User Form.

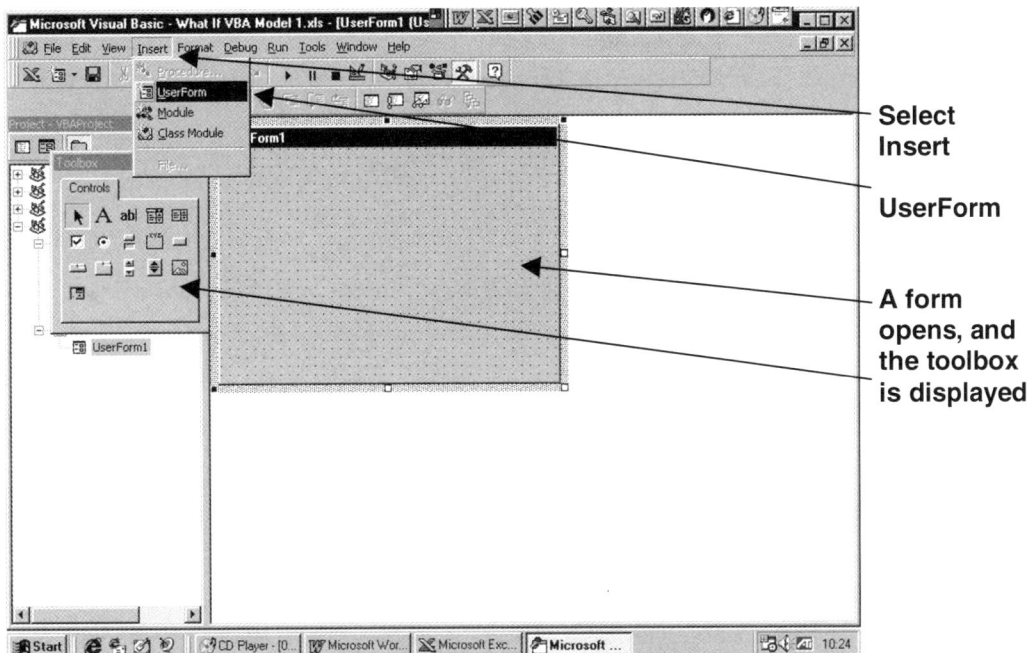

We can draw labels, textboxes etc. on the form as we did on the Excel spreadsheet. The difference is that the form is operating at a layer above the spreadsheet, and we do not have the problem of activating cells in error.

Control is exercised totally from the form, and it is only after the form is completed and control is passed to the spreadsheet that the user can work with the cells.

Close the Project Window on the left, and the form screen is resized. Increase the size of the form to cover the area, and drag the toolbox to a convenient area of the form. It is switched on and off from the View menu, but it will not add to the toolbar area.

This will be our opening screenshot, and we will pre-set the spreadsheet to open with this form.

We therefore need to give it a suitable title, add a label, and include a picture to liven it up.

CHANGE PROPERTIES

Right click in the form and select Properties from the pop up menu. The properties can be set, as we did in Excel earlier. Change the properties as follows:

(Name)	frmOpening
Caption	The What If Model Builder

Close the Properties window. Draw a label at the top of the form, and change its properties as follows:

(Name)	lblHeading
Caption	The What If Model Builder
Font	Size – 36
ForeColor	Blue
SpecialEffect	2 – fmSpecialEffectSunken
TextAlign	2 – fmTextAlignCentre

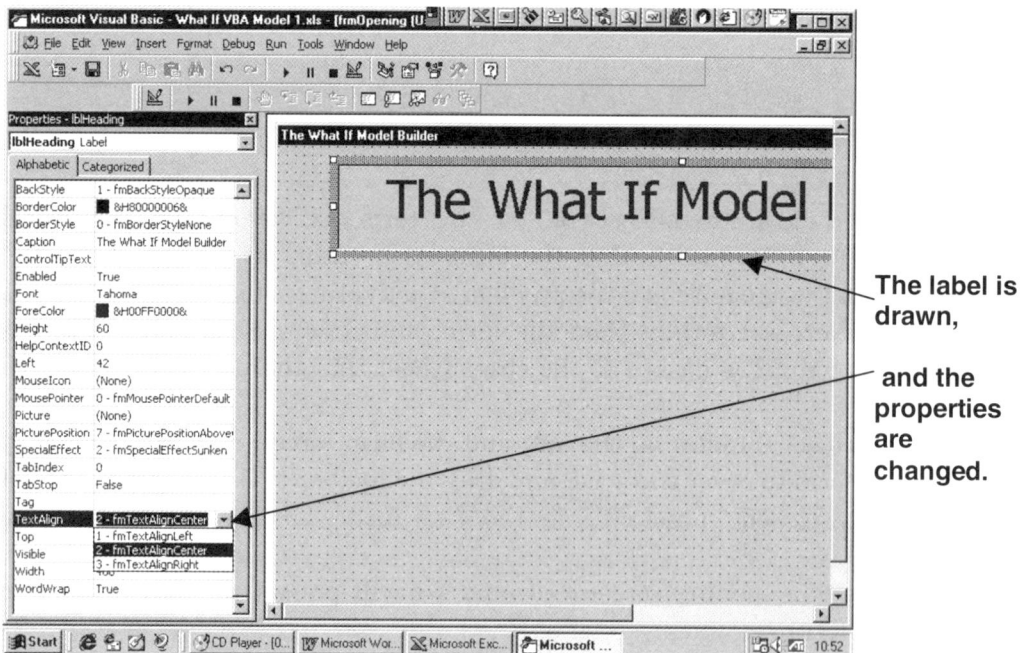

The label is drawn,

and the properties are changed.

Close the Properties window and make sure the form looks as you wish. At any stage you can click Run Sub/UserForm to see how it will look live.

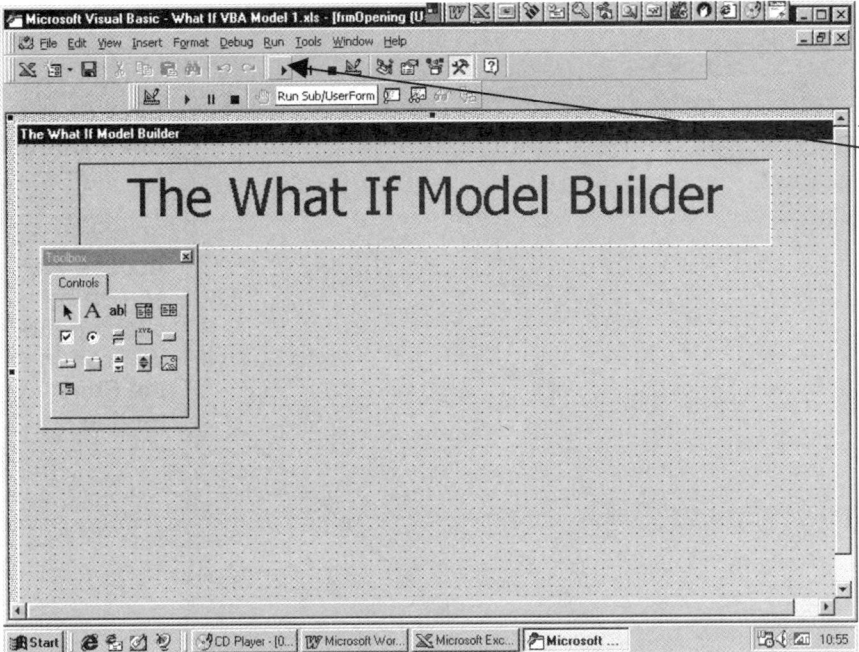

Clicking the Run button activates the form

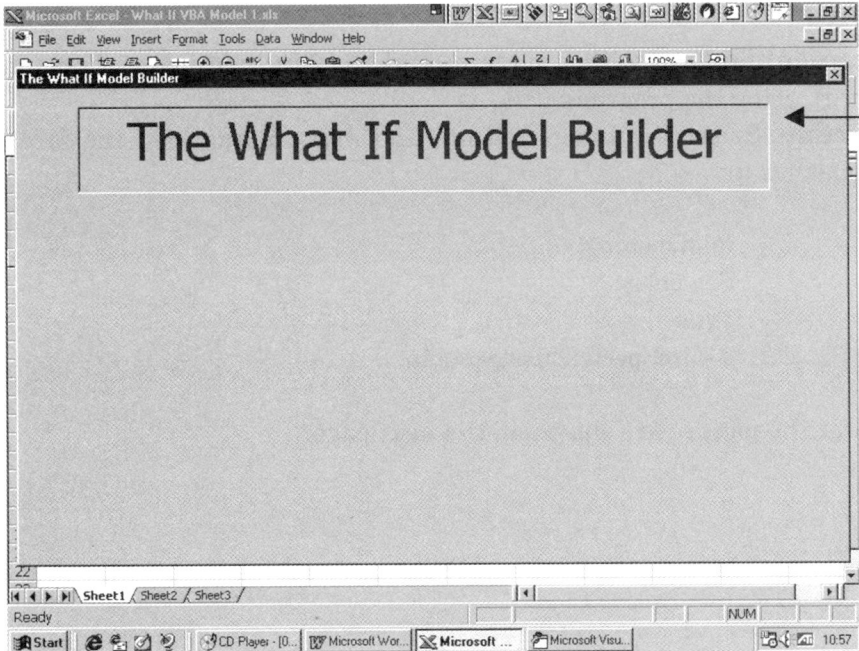

You then see it as it will appear in the final program

To return to the form click on the VB icon in the Start toolbar, and then click on the Reset button.

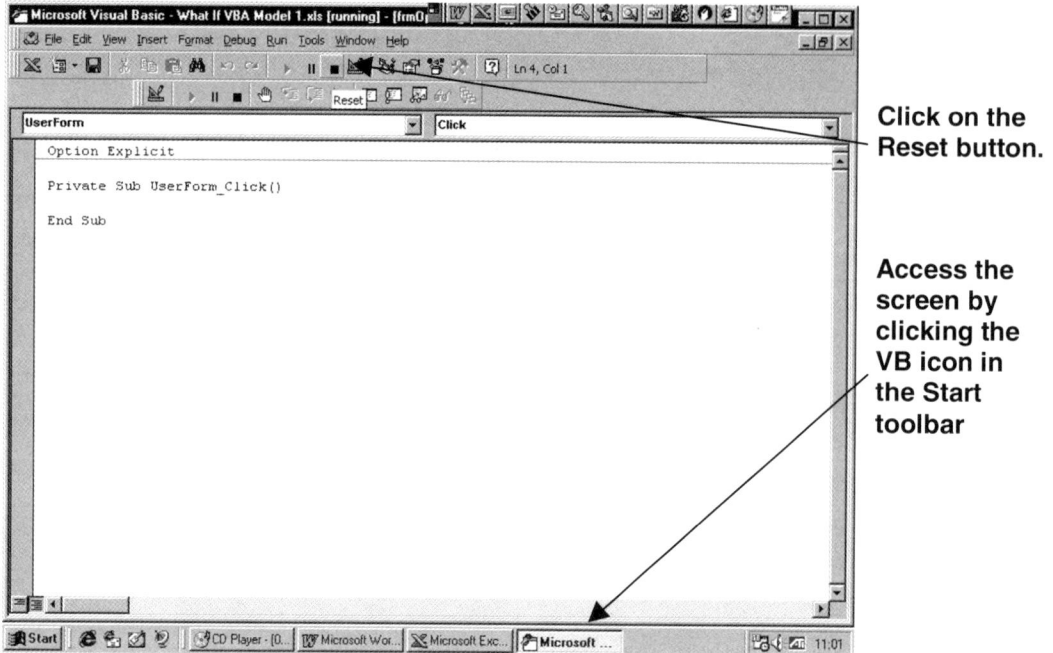

Click on the Reset button.

Access the screen by clicking the VB icon in the Start toolbar

ADD AN IMAGE

We will brighten up the form with a picture, and then include instructions on what to do to start using the program.

First, the picture. Select the Image button, and draw a frame on the form. Change the properties to:

(Name)	imgOpening
Picture	See below
Picture Tiling	True
SpecialEffect	2 – fmSpecialEffectSunken

The steps to enter the picture are shown on the next page.

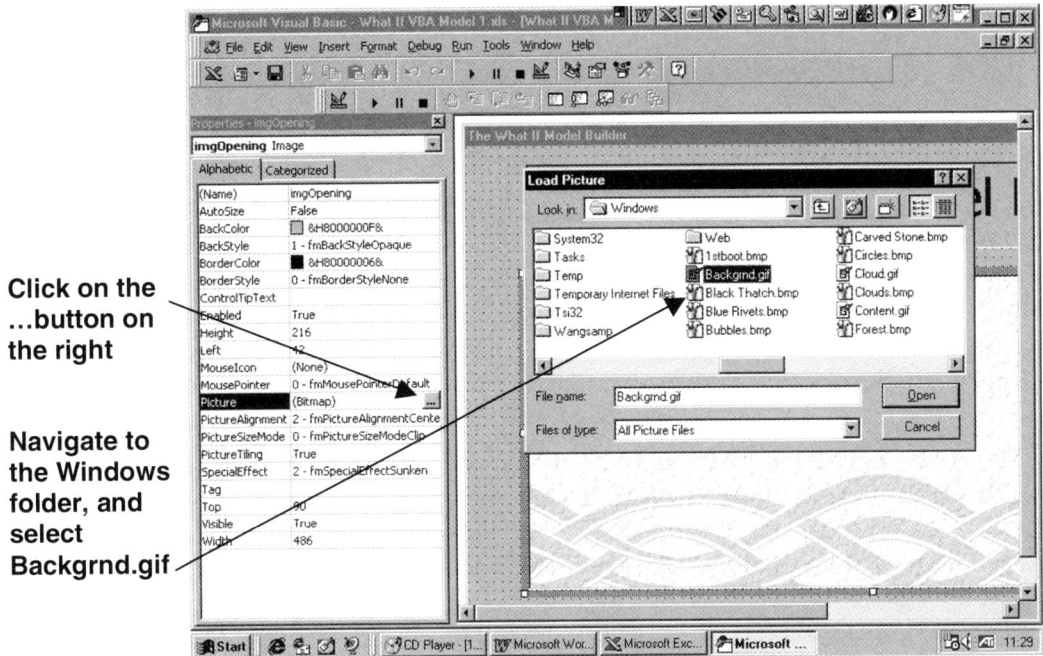

Click on the
...button on
the right

Navigate to
the Windows
folder, and
select
Backgrnd.gif

The picture does not fit the full size of the image control. However, the Picture Tiling property is set to true, so it is extended to fill the available area.

COMMAND BUTTON

The only thing we need now is a command button to run the program. Draw a command button near the top of the image. Set the properties as follows:

(Name)	cmdStart
Caption	Start
Default	True
Locked	True

We will code the command button later.

The spreadsheet is saved as **What If VBA Model 1.xls**.

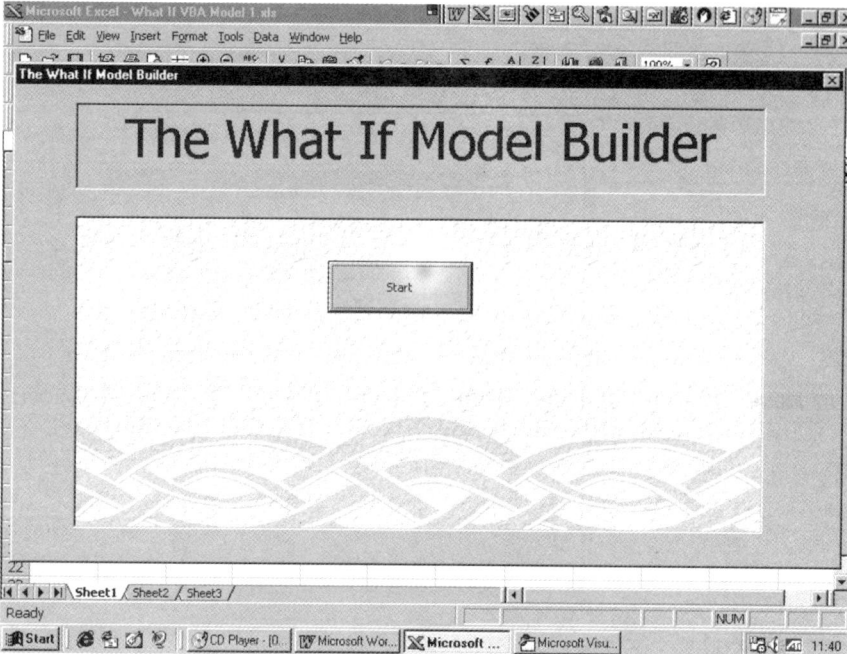

What If VBA Model 1.xls

It certainly looks more impressive than a plain spreadsheet

THE INPUT FORM — INPUT STEP 1

We will prepare a second form, which will accept the figures to actually prepare the What If model.

From the menu select Insert, UserForm.

| (Name) | FrmInputStep1 |
| Caption | The What If Model Builder – Input Section Step 1 |

As before, close the Properties window and resize the form.

THE INPUT FORM DESIGN

From a review of the parameters given to us by Simon, the Sales Director, we need the following:
* Boxes to accept the input of the total market
* Boxes for the level of market share
* Check boxes to include/exclude sale of some or all types of Widgets.
* Price changes, for a price war.

Everything else is calculated, based on this input. This includes:
* Required machine time, compared to available capacity
* Turnover
* Contribution.

We will place all the labels etc. on the form now.

IMAGE

We will use the image that we included on the first form as a theme to run through the rest of the forms.

Draw an image control over the entire area of the form, and set its properties as follows:

(Name)	imgBackground
Picture	As above
Picture Tiling	True
SpecialEffect	0 - fmSpecialEffectFlat

INSTRUCTION LABEL

We will place a set of instructions at the bottom of the screen. Draw a label, and set its properties as follows:

(Name)	LblInstructions1
Caption	Input the volume of sales expected for the market in total. Do NOT enter market share yet.
SpecialEffect	2 – fmSpecialEffectSunken
TextAlign	1 – fmTextLeftAlign

HEADING LABELS

Labels are added for a generic heading, and then labels are placed on the form for Small Medium and Large headings. Properties are similar to the above, except that font size is increased and changed to Bold for the heading Total Market Size.

TEXT BOXES

Text boxes are added below each unit size label, ready to receive the input of the figures. Set the properties of the three text boxes as follows:

(Name)	txtSmallSize
	txtMediumSize
	txtLargeSize
MaxLength	6
SpecialEffect	2 – fmSpecialEffectSunken

The tab order should be pre-set by the program, so that pressing tab automatically moves from one text box to another.

COMMAND BUTTONS

Finally, place two command buttons on the form. Set the properties to:

(Name)	cmdNext
	cmdClose
Caption	Next
	Close

The spreadsheet is saved as **What If VBA Model 2.xls**. The form frmInput1 is shown below.

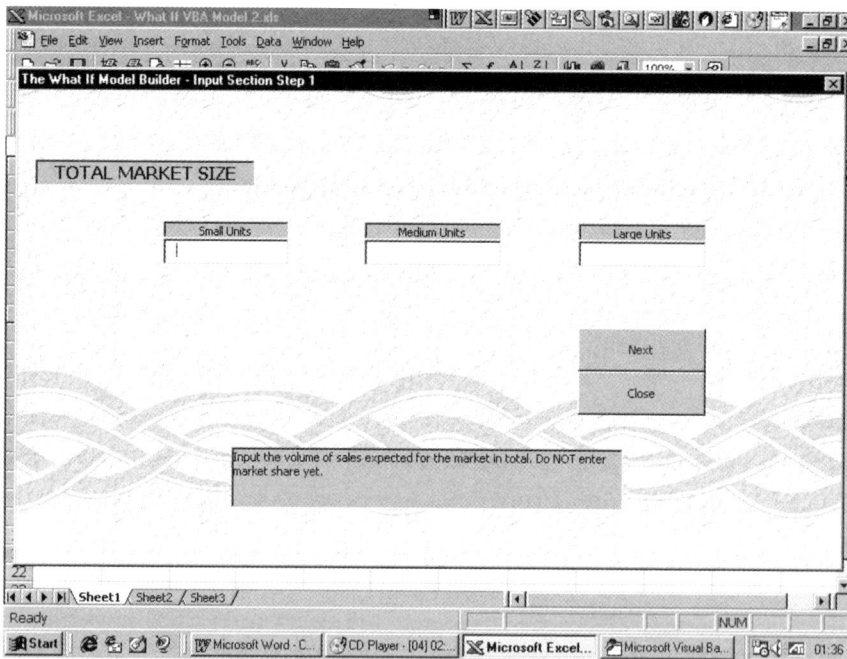

That completes the input form for Market Size. We will now create a screen for market share

THE INPUT FORM — INPUT STEP 2

Prepare the form in the same style as the previous one, and add labels for market share for each size of unit.

We will use list boxes for selection of percentages of market share.

Change the properties of the form to:

(Name)	FrmInputStep2
Caption	The What If Model Builder — Input Section Step 2

INSTRUCTION LABEL

We will place a set of instructions at the bottom of the screen. Draw a label, and set its properties as follows:

(Name)	LblInstructions2
Caption	Select the market share for each size of unit, then click on Next.

The type of products sold is then displayed.

SpecialEffect	2 – fmSpecialEffectSunken
TextAlign	1 – fmTextLeftAlign

HEADING LABELS

Labels are added for a generic heading, and then labels are placed on the form for Small Medium and Large headings. Properties are the same as for the previous form.

LIST BOXES

Draw a list box under each unit name. The properties to amend are:

(Name)	lstSmallPercent
	lstMediumPercent
	lstLargePercent
SpecialEffect	2 – fmSpecialEffectSunken

We will complete the list contents later.

COMMAND BUTTONS

Draw a command button to the right of the three list boxes.

(Name)	cmdNextPercent
Caption	Next

Add two command buttons the same as the ones appearing on the previous form.
The screen looks like this.

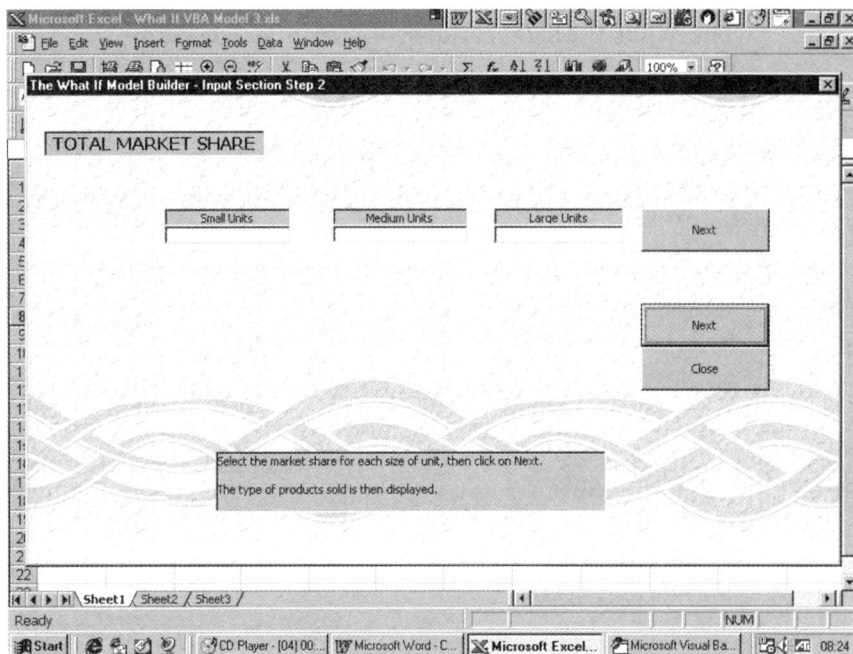

The list boxes, labels and command buttons are added

The spreadsheet is saved as **What If VBA Model 3.xls**.

SELLING WIDGETS?

We will also include a set of check boxes for confirming that we are still selling each size of Widgets, and then we will include text boxes for input of the expected level of sales.

Draw a header label at the left of the form, and add three check boxes below it.
The properties are:

Header Label

Caption	ARE WIDGETS INCLUDED?
Font	Size 12
SpecialEffect	2 – fmSpecialEffectSunken
TextAlign	2 – fmTextAlignCenter

CHECK BOXES

The properties for the check boxes are:

(Name)	chkSmall
	chkMedium
	chkLarge
Caption	Sale of Small Widgets? Tick for yes.
	Sale of Medium Widgets? Tick for yes.
	Sale of Large Widgets? Tick for yes.
BackStyle	0 – fmBackStyleTransparent

LABELS AND TEXT BOXES

Once the check boxes are ticked we want the user to input the figures into a text box, as they did in the previous form.

Draw labels to the right of each checkbox, and then draw a text box to the right of each label.

The properties are:

Labels

Caption	Number of Small Widgets
	Sale of Medium Widgets? Tick for yes.
	Sale of Large Widgets? Tick for yes.
SpecialEffect	2 – fmSpecialEffectSunken

Text Boxes

(Name)	txtSmallWidgNo
	txtMediumWidgNo
	txtLargeWidgNo
MaxLength	6
SpecialEffect	2 – fmSpecialEffectSunken

The spreadsheet is saved as **What If VBA Model 4.xls**. The form is shown in the screenshot on the next page.

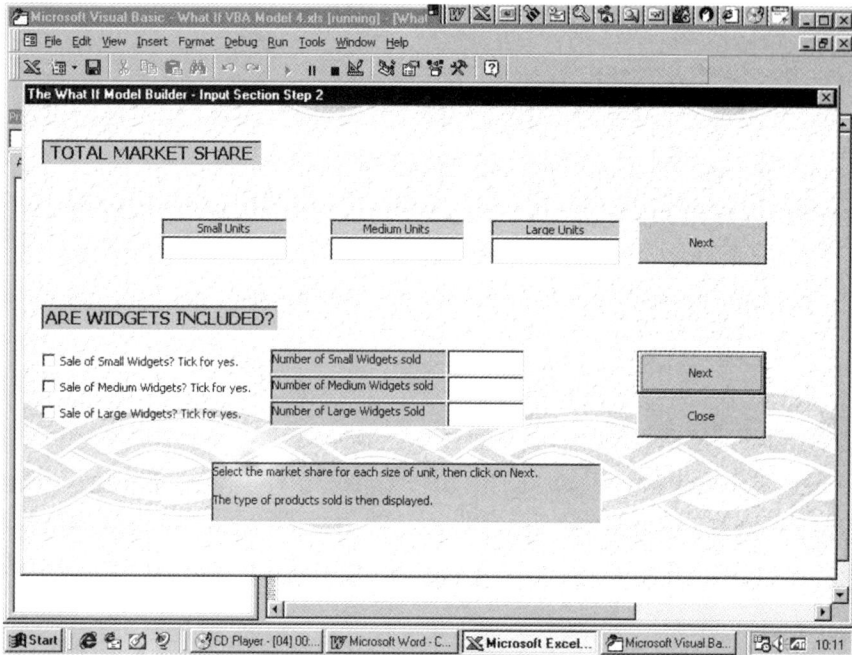

NEXT

The chapter is longer than usual, and we will finish here. In the next chapter we finalise the forms, and start to code them.

Chapter Thirty-three
THE "WHAT IF" MODEL (III)

Why did they call Visual Basic *basic?*

In this chapter we complete the last of the forms in our "What If" Wizard, and then code the forms and link them to the spreadsheet.

Add a new form and change the properties:

(Name)	frmInputStep3
Caption	The What If Model Builder - Input Section Step 3

Add an image as before.

PRICE CHANGES

We want to offer the user a choice of price reductions, ranging from 0% (no change) to a 50% reduction.

Each 10% drop in price will increase market share by 5%, and we want a label to display the original percentage and the revised percentage market share.

We will use option buttons this time, rather than spin buttons, list boxes or combo boxes. Each set of option buttons must work independently of each other, and to achieve this we include each set in a frame.

Place labels on the form for each size of unit, to act as headings, and then draw a frame below each label.

The properties are:

Frame

(Name)	fraSmallPrice
	fraMediumPrice
	fraLargePrice
BackColor	White
Caption	Price change

Option Buttons

(Name)	optNoChangeSmall	
	opt10PercentSmall	etc.
	fraLargePrice	
BackColor	White	
Caption	No change	
	10% Decrease	etc.

INFORMATION LABELS

As with the previous forms, place an instruction label at the bottom to clarify the instructions on how to use this part of the program.

The properties are:

(Name)	lblInstructions1
Caption	If prices will be reduced in order to increase market share, enter the details in this section. Select the appropriate percentage. The effect is noted below each set of option buttons.
SpecialEffect	2 - fmSpecialEffectSunken

Below each frame we will have an information label, to show how the price change has affected the market share.

Draw three labels on the form. The properties are:

(Name)	lblSmallPrice
	lblMediumPrice
	lblLargePrice
Caption	This should increase market share from x% to y%
SpecialEffect	2 - fmSpecialEffectSunken

COMMAND BUTTONS

Finally, add two command buttons. The properties are:

(Name)	cmdFinish
	cmdClose
Caption	Finish
	Cancel
SpecialEffect	2 - fmSpecialEffectSunken

The form is shown below, and is saved as **What If VBA Model 5.xls**.

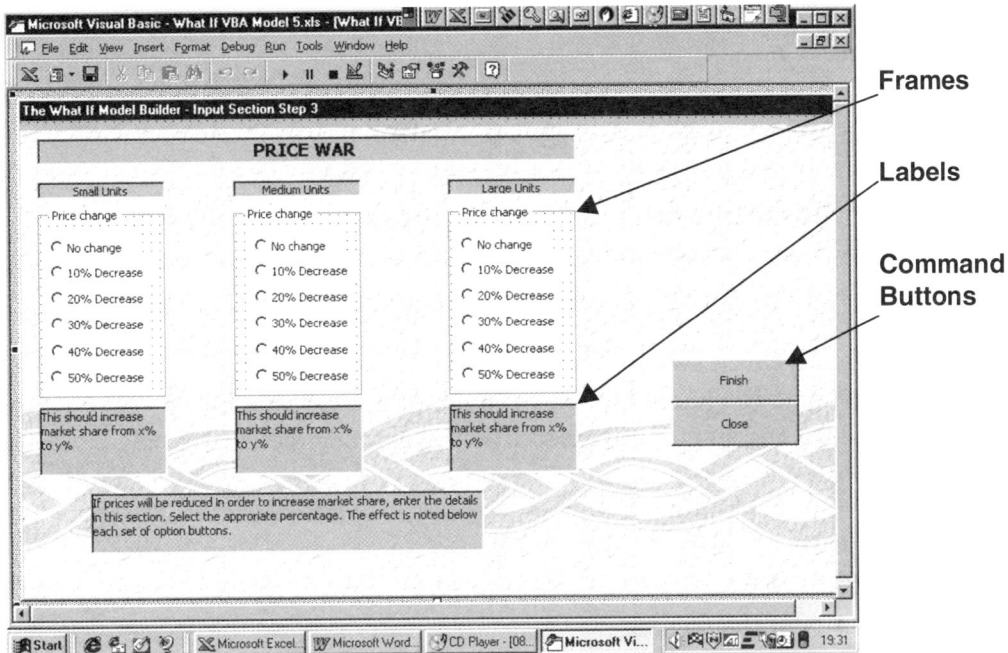

CODING

The forms are complete and they are now ready to be coded.

Coding involves two things:

- Linking from the forms to the spreadsheet, in order to allow the spreadsheet to calculate, using the figures the user has generated
- Coding the forms so that, within each form, the user's actions are controlled and feedback (message boxes etc.) is provided in order to guide his actions.

We will code in English, and then convert the concepts into VBA language.

THE CODING CONCEPTS

Starting
- The spreadsheet will open in Full Screen view.
- The program will run automatically.

Spreadsheet User Input
- The spreadsheet will be locked in order to stop direct input from the user.
- The output area will be A1. Linked cells, updated by the program, will be at AA1.

- A command button on the spreadsheet will be used to run the program a second and subsequent times.

Opening Form

- Clicking on the Start Button will load the second form.
- The form should be hidden when the second form loads.

Market Size Form

The characteristics of the form are:
- The maximum length allowed to be input in the text boxes is 6 digits. The maximum figure is therefore 999,999
- The code should check that only digits are being entered
- An error message box should display if a non-digit key is pressed
- The figures entered should be copied into the spreadsheet
- The Next button should hide the current form and open the next form
- The Cancel button should return the user to the spreadsheet.

Market Share Form

The characteristics of the form are:
- The spin buttons should default to the previously set value
- The checkboxes etc. at the bottom part of the form should be hidden until after Next button is clicked
- A message box should display when the Next box is clicked, to give the user the option of retaining the previous Widget sales details, or cancelling them
- If the checkbox is ticked, the text box should be displayed in order to allow the user to input the information
- If the checkbox is not ticked the text box value should be changed to zero, and the text box should be hidden
- The Widget labels should be hidden or display in unison with the text boxes;
- The Widget text boxes should restrict the maximum length allowed to be input to 6 digits. The maximum figure is therefore 999,999
- An error message should be displayed if the number of Widgets is greater than the total market share. The message should advise the user of the maximum permissible number
- Next and Close buttons should work as for other forms
- The spreadsheet should update with figures for market share percentage and the number of Widgets of each type sold.

Price War Form

The characteristics of the form are:
- The No Change option buttons should be selected by default

- The label below each frame should indicate the change in market share from that originally set in the previous form because of the particular option button that has been selected
- An error message should be displayed if the price change takes market share above 100%. The market share should then be adjusted to 100%, but the redundancy of the price change should be flagged up
- The Finish command button should hide the form, and return the user to the spreadsheet. The spreadsheet will default to the A1 area
- The Close button should work as for other forms.

SPREADSHEET FORMATTING

Before we finalise the VBA coding we should format the spreadsheet, ready to receive the information.

Just because we are generating a lot of information in code is no reason to ignore preparing a proper trail on the spreadsheet to explain the figures.

The screen shot below shows the linked cells we are using in our program, as well as other, calculated, cells in order to be able to read the trail properly.

Open **What If VBA Model 6.xls** and look at AA1. The cells are a mixture of linked, coded and calculated.

The calculated cells are:

- Increase in market share — price reduction divided by two.
- Revised % Market share - =IF(AC12/100+AC14>1,1,AC12/100+AC14)
  In English this reads "If the market share percentage plus the increase in market share are greater than 100%, the figure is 100%, otherwise it is the market share percentage plus the increase in market share.
- Total Sales - =ROUND(+AC9*AC15,0)
  The figure is rounded to the nearest whole number.
- Whatsits — Total Sales minus Widgets.

LINKING

The objects on the form are linked to the cells in the spreadsheet by putting their address in the properties section of each item.

Select ControlSource in Properties, and enter the cell reference

AC9 in this case

Now that you know which cell addresses you want to link to, the Properties section can be completed for all of the forms.

SPREADSHEET FRONT END

With the details entered on the spreadsheet at AA1 we can prepare the summary position at A1. This is the area that the user use to review the results.

Open **What If VBA Model 6.xls** and look at A1. The spreadsheet is shown below.

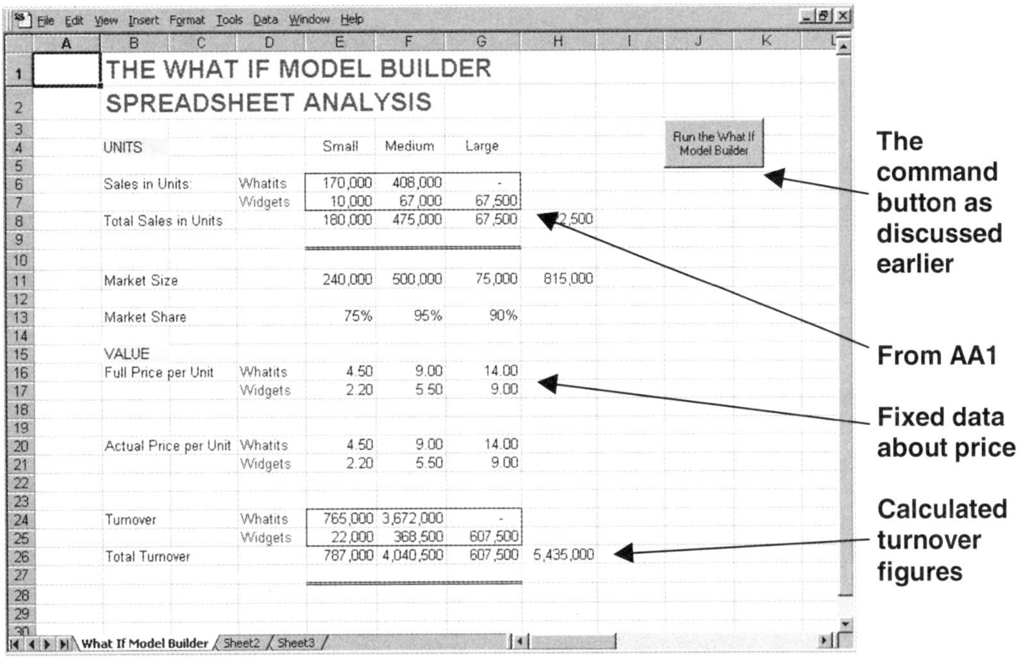

Figures are picked up from AA1 using =Cell Reference.

Prices are entered at E16. They are static data that did not need to be captured on the forms, so it has been left on the spreadsheet only.

In order to stop the user from inadvertently changing items such as price, the spreadsheet has been protected. The cells that are linked to the forms, and are therefore updated by them, have been unlocked before protection was turned on. This is accessed through Formatting, Protection tab. Uncheck the Locked check box.

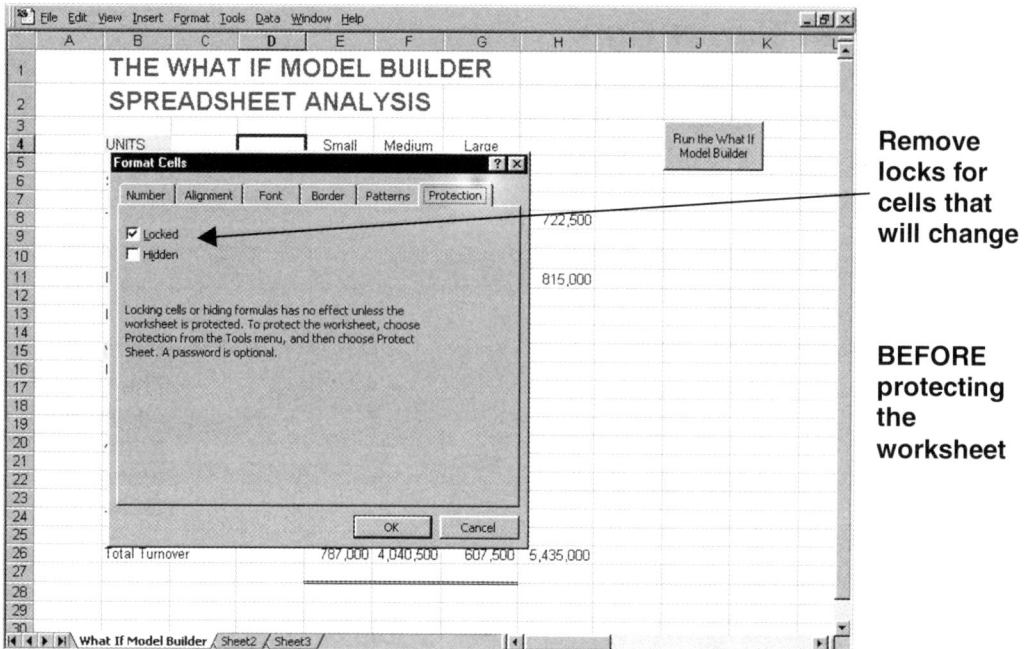

Remove locks for cells that will change

BEFORE protecting the worksheet

CODING THE FORMS

The main areas of coding are covered below. All of the code can be accessed and reviewed in **What If VBA Model 6.xls**.

Starting

- The spreadsheet will open in Full Screen view.
- The program will run automatically.

The code must be attached to the Worksheet. Select the Workbook, Open event and code it as follows:

```
Private Sub Workbook_Open()
    Application.DisplayFullScreen = True
    frmOpening.Show

End Sub
```

You will notice that the screen is set to return to Normal View on closing the workbook. The code is Application.DisplayFullScreen = False and is attached to the Workbook, BeforeClose event.

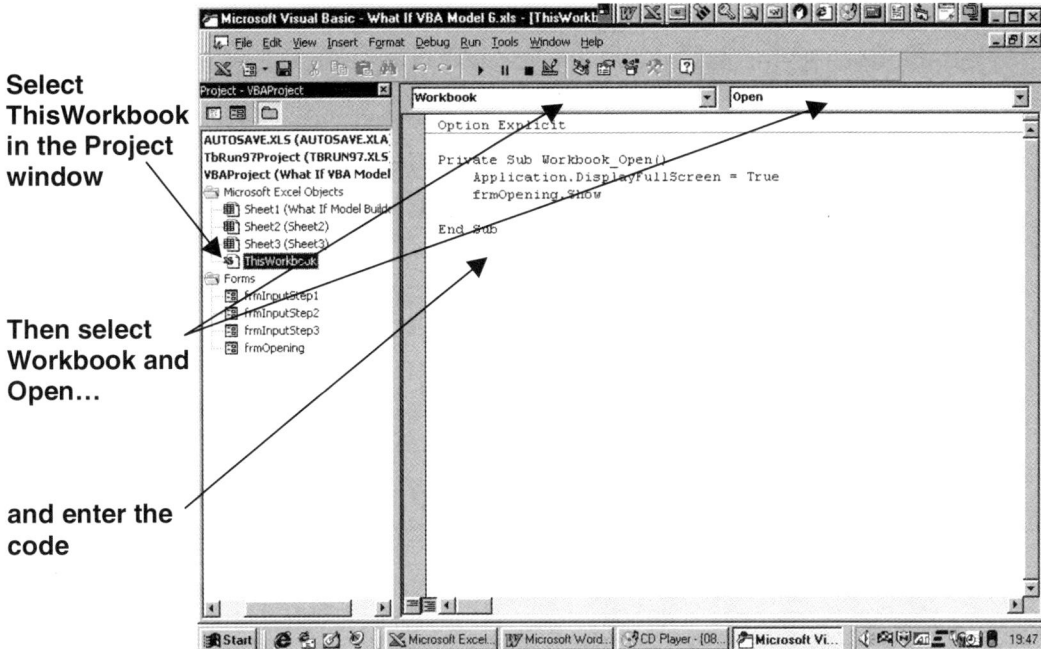

Select ThisWorkbook in the Project window

Then select Workbook and Open...

and enter the code

Opening Form

- Clicking on the Start Button will load the second form.
- The form should be hidden when the second form loads.

Select fmOpening and code it as follows

```
Private Sub cmdStart_Click()
    frmInputStep1.Show
    frmOpening.Hide

End Sub
```

Market Size Form

The characteristics of the form are:
- The maximum length allowed to be input in the text boxes is 6 digits. The maximum figure is therefore 999,999
- The code should check that only digits are being entered
- An error message box should display if a non-digit key is pressed
- The figures entered should be copied into the spreadsheet
- The Next button should hide the current form and open the next form
- The Cancel button should return the user to the spreadsheet.

Maximum length is set in the Properties window.

The code for checking only digits are pressed is set in the KeyPress event. The code is:

```
Private Sub txtLargeSize_KeyPress(ByVal KeyAscii As MSForms.ReturnInteger)
    'Check that number keys are pressed. Beep if anything
    'else is pressed

    'If the key is not a digit from 0 to 9 then
    If KeyAscii < Asc("0") Or KeyAscii _
    > Asc("9") Then
     'Beep
     Beep
     'Cancel the key input
     KeyAscii = 0
     'Display an error message
     MsgBox ("Enter whole numbers only. No decimals or letters thank you."),
        vbOKOnly, "Number Input Box"
    'Close the if statement
    End If

End Sub
```

It is the same code for each textbox.

The line — MsgBox ("Enter whole numbers only. No decimals or letters thank you."), vbOKOnly, "Number Input Box" — in the above code displays the message if the wrong keyboard keys are pressed.

The code for the Next button is similar to that shown previously. The code for the Close button is:

```
Private Sub cmdClose_Click()

    frmInputStep1.Hide
    Range("A1").Select
    ActiveCell.Select

End Sub
```

The line Range("A1").Select is used to ensure that the spreadsheet screen defaults to the A1 part of the screen.

Market Share Form

The characteristics of the form are:
- The spin buttons should default to the previously set value
- The checkboxes etc. at the bottom part of the form should be hidden until after Next button is clicked
- A message box should display when the Next box is clicked, to give the user the option of retaining the previous Widget sales details, or cancelling them
- If the checkbox is ticked, the text box should be displayed in order to allow the user to input the information
- If the checkbox is not ticked the text box value should be changed to zero, and the text box should be hidden
- The Widget labels should be hidden or display in unison with the text boxes
- The Widget text boxes should restrict the maximum length allowed to be input to 6 digits. The maximum figure is therefore 999,999
- An error message should be displayed if the number of Widgets is greater than the total market share. The message should advise the user of the maximum permissible number
- Next and Close buttons should work as for other forms
- The spreadsheet should update with figures for market share percentage and the number of Widgets of each type sold.

The default value for the spin buttons is set through the Properties window.

The code for the Next button, which displays the other objects on the form and then hides itself, is:

```
Private Sub cmdNextPercent_Click()
    'Set a message question. Do you want to zeroise widgets?
    Dim Response
    Response = MsgBox("Do you want to keep the existing Widget sales data?",
        vbYesNo, "Widget Sales")
    If Response = vbYes Then    ' User chose Yes.
      chkSmall.Visible = True
      chkSmall.Value = True
      chkMedium.Visible = True
      chkMedium.Value = True
      chkLarge.Visible = True
      chkLarge.Value = True
      cmdClose.Visible = True
```

```
        cmdNext.Visible = True
        Label5.Visible = True
        cmdNextPercent.Visible = False
        cmdNext.SetFocus
        txtSmallWidgNo.Visible = True
        txtMediumWidgNo.Visible = True
        txtLargeWidgNo.Visible = True
        Label6.Visible = True
        Label7.Visible = True
        Label8.Visible = True


    Else    'User chose No.
     'Set the widget sales values to zero
     Sheets("What if model builder").Cells.Range("ac18").Select
     ActiveCell.Select
     ""''Second part of the working message set
     ActiveCell.Value = 0
     Cells.Range("ad18").Select
     ActiveCell.Select
     ActiveCell.Value = 0
     Cells.Range("ae18").Select
     ActiveCell.Select
     ActiveCell.Value = 0


     'Display the checkboxes to give the user the option to input
     chkSmall.Visible = True
     chkMedium.Visible = True
     chkLarge.Visible = True
     cmdClose.Visible = True
     cmdNext.Visible = True
     Label5.Visible = True
     cmdNextPercent.Visible = False
     cmdNext.SetFocus


    End If


End Sub
```

The lines:

```
Dim Response
    Response = MsgBox("Do you want to keep the existing Widget sales data?",
    vbYesNo, "Widget Sales")
        If Response = vbYes Then    'User chose Yes.
        Else    'User chose No
```

define the message that is displayed, and activate one part of the code if the user selects the "Yes" button, and a different part of the code if the user selects "No".

The code for the checkbox is

```
Private Sub chkSmall_Click()
    "If the check box is ticked, display the input box
    If chkSmall.Value = True Then
        Label6.Visible = True
        txtSmallWidgNo.Visible = True
        txtSmallWidgNo.SetFocus
    "otherwise blank out the input box value and make invisible"
    Else
        Label6.Visible = False
        txtSmallWidgNo.Value = 0
        txtSmallWidgNo.Visible = False
    End If

End Sub
```

If the checkbox is ticked (value = true) the visible properties of the label and textbox are set to true, and they are displayed.

If the checkbox is unticked (value = false) the visible properties of the label and textbox are set to false, and they are not displayed. In addition, the value of the textbox is set to zero, and the spreadsheet is updated because of the linked cell attribute that was set via the Properties window.

Error Checking

The error checking is attached to the Next button. When it is clicked the program calculates the total number of units that can be sold, and compares it to the number of small Widgets.

If the number is too great an error message is generated, and the focus is set back to the small Widget textbox. If the number of small items is correct, a calculation is made for medium numbers etc.

```
Private Sub cmdNext_Click()
    'Define the parameters
    'Small
    Dim Market_Size_Small As Long
    Dim Market_Share_Small As Long
    Dim Market_Percentage_Small As Long
    'Medium
    Dim Market_Size_Medium As Long
    Dim Market_Share_Medium As Long
    Dim Market_Percentage_Medium As Long
    'Large
    Dim Market_Size_Large As Long
    Dim Market_Share_Large As Long
    Dim Market_Percentage_Large As Long

    'Calculate Small, Medium and Large units sold
    Market_Size_Small = frmInputStep1.txtSmallSize.Value
    Market_Percentage_Small = spnSmallTotal
    Market_Share_Small = Market_Size_Small * Market_Percentage_Small / 100

    Market_Size_Medium = frmInputStep1.txtMediumSize.Value
    Market_Percentage_Medium = spnMediumTotal
    Market_Share_Medium = Market_Size_Medium * Market_Percentage_Medium / 100

    Market_Size_Large = frmInputStep1.txtLargeSize.Value
    Market_Percentage_Large = spnLargeTotal
    Market_Share_Large = Market_Size_Large * Market_Percentage_Large / 100

If txtSmallWidgNo.Value > Market_Share_Small Then
    MsgBox ("The number of small Widgets is greater than the total market
        share." & Chr$(10) & _
    "It should be "& Market_Share_Small &" or less"), vbOKOnly, "Small Widget
        Check"
    txtSmallWidgNo.SetFocus
    Exit Sub

ElseIf txtMediumWidgNo.Value > Market_Share_Medium Then
    MsgBox ("The number of medium Widgets is greater than the total market
        share." & Chr$(10) & _
    "It should be "& Market_Share_Medium &" or less"), vbOKOnly, "Medium
        Widget Check"
```

```
        txtMediumWidgNo.SetFocus
        Exit Sub

    ElseIf txtLargeWidgNo.Value > Market_Share_Large Then
        MsgBox ("The number of large Widgets is greater than the total market share."
            & Chr$(10) & _
        "It should be "& Market_Share_Large &" or less"), vbOKOnly, "Large Widget
            Check"
        txtLargeWidgNo.SetFocus
        Exit Sub

    End If

    frmInputStep3.Show
    frmInputStep2.Hide
End Sub
```

Note that the spin button deals in whole numbers. To convert to percentages the figure per the spin button is divided by 100.

At each stage, if the program finds that the number of units is incorrect, Exit Sub exits from the procedure. It is only if none of the Exit Subs is invoked that the final part of the code (**frmInputStep3.Show** and **frmInputStep2.Hide**) runs.

As part of the calculation the maximum permissible number of units is calculated. The message merely displays this number, and it uses the format "Text of message" & Number & "more text." This is similar to Excel formulae.

Price-war Form

The characteristics of the form are:
- The No Change option buttons should be selected by default.
- The label below each frame should indicate the change in market share from that originally set in the previous form because of the particular option button that has been selected.
- An error message should be displayed if the price change takes market share above 100%. The market share should then be adjusted to 100%, but the redundancy of the price change should be flagged up.
- The Finish command button should hide the form, and return the user to the spreadsheet. The spreadsheet will default to the A1 area.
- The Close button should work as for other forms.

To set the defaults when a form opens the code is attached to the Activate event. The code is:

```
Private Sub UserForm_Activate()
    optNoChangeSmall.Value = True
    optNoChangeMedium.Value = True
    optNoChangeLarge.Value = True
    Call optNoChangeSmall_Click
    Call optNoChangeMedium_Click
    Call optNoChangeLarge_Click

End Sub
```

This achieves two things. Firstly, it sets the default option button as No change. It then calls the code attached to the No Change click event, in order to ensure that the text in the box below each frame is correct.

Calling the code from another procedure eliminates the need to reproduce it in several places.

Code is attached to each option button, and a different message is set, specific to each button. This is not particularly onerous, because once one is set for the 10% button, copy and paste are used for the other buttons. Changes to the message box etc. are then easily made.

The code is shown on the next page.

```
Private Sub opt10PercentSmall_Click()
""""""""""""""""""This is the pro forma for the other option buttons.
    'Define the message as a string, and the values as whole numbers
    Dim Text As String
    Dim Market_Share As Integer

    'The text message is the spin button value from the previous form
    Text = frmInputStep2.spnSmallTotal
    The value is the value of the text
    Market_Share = Val(Text)

    Dim Value_Change As Integer
    'Check that the figure is not more than 100%.
    Value_Change = Market_Share + 5
```

```
If Value_Change > 100 Then
  'If it is, make the figure 100%, and display an error message.
  Value_Change = 100
  MsgBox "Reducing prices by 10% has had no effect on market share.", _
      vbOKOnly, "Ten Percent Price Change"

End If
If opt10PercentSmall.Value = True Then
  lblSmallPrice.Caption = _
  "A 10% price reduction is assumed to increase market share from " & _
  Text & "% to " & Value_Change & "%"

'Select the cell and insert the value per the option button.
Range("AC13").Select
ActiveCell.Select
ActiveCell.Value = 10 / 100

End If

End Sub
```

Note that the message format is the same as the previous section as regards entering a variable number into the body of set text.

Instead of updating the spreadsheet from the Properties window, and having six option buttons all pointing to the same cell, the code enters the figure to the the spreadsheet cell directly.

The code is:

```
'Select the cell and insert the value per the option button.
Range("AC13").Select
ActiveCell.Select
ActiveCell.Value = 10 / 100
```

This follows the same format that we used in our earlier VBA models.

REVIEW THE PROGRAM

Although the code is reproduced here, it would be beneficial to review the code in situ. The code includes comments to explain the code and, although they have been included above, in the program they are highlighted in green — compared to blue and black for the actual program code.

MORE SOPHISTICATION

The program is complicated, not because of the calculations that we are producing — these are very straightforward — but because of the control we are exercising over the user.

The program could be expanded to consider the effect on production capacity, as requested by Peter, the Production Director. It could also be changed to reflect a longer time period, time lag for production, and therefore stock-holding considerations etc.

However, the principles, as regards what can be done and the procedure to achieve it, have been well explored.

WAS IT WORTH IT?

That concludes our look in depth at a full VBA program. The advantages of coding in VBA are substantial, especially as regards giving feedback to the user, and controlling the input to make sure it is within pre-set parameters.

However, to program at this level requires a detailed understanding of programming concepts, as well as the commands available. There is certainly a much greater professionalism in building a VBA solution, and it would enhance the view that others have about your computer skills if you use it.

However, the amount of time taken to develop a VBA solution is substantially longer than a simple spreadsheet solution would be. Ideally, balance the two.

NEXT

In the next chapter we finalise the integration of our spreadsheets and the PowerPoint presentation.

Chapter Thirty-four

LOADING FROM POWERPOINT

The art of co-ordination

The PivotTables and Charts have been prepared. The PowerPoint presentation has been started, with slides and slide headings. A "What If" model has been built to assist the Sales Director when he is reviewing his marketing information. . .

When the Sales team produce the five year plan for inclusion in the analysis, a spreadsheet will have to be prepared to confirm the production capacity required, timing of expansion of production facilities, review of stock-holdings projected etc.

This is a variation on what we have done previously, and it can either be built in Excel, in VB or in a combination of the two.

We will not therefore repeat the process of building a spreadsheet for reviewing production here. What we want to look at now is how to access the spreadsheets from within the PowerPoint presentation.

We will link from PowerPoint to the spreadsheet collection of charts and tables we prepared earlier, and saved as **Historical Presentation 17.xls**.

HYPERLINKING BETWEEN POWERPOINT AND EXCEL

Start PowerPoint, and open **PowerPoint 4.ppt**.

Slide 3, Market Summary, has been noted as "charts required". Select the slide and change to Slide View. We will hyperlink to the spreadsheet.

From the menu, choose Slide Show, Action Buttons. Select the tenth button: Action Button, Document, and draw the button on the slide.

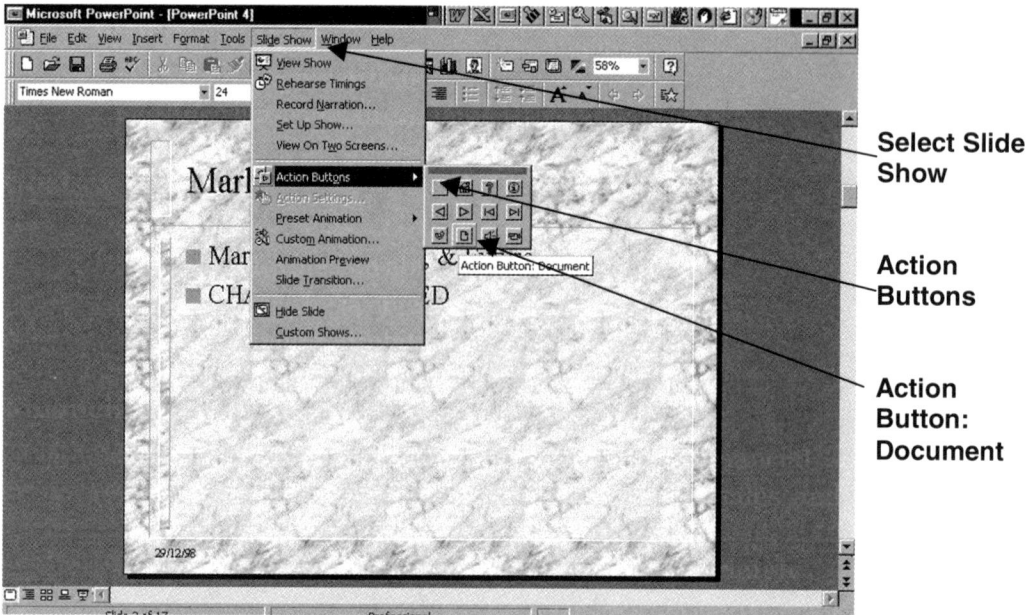

Draw the button onto the slide.

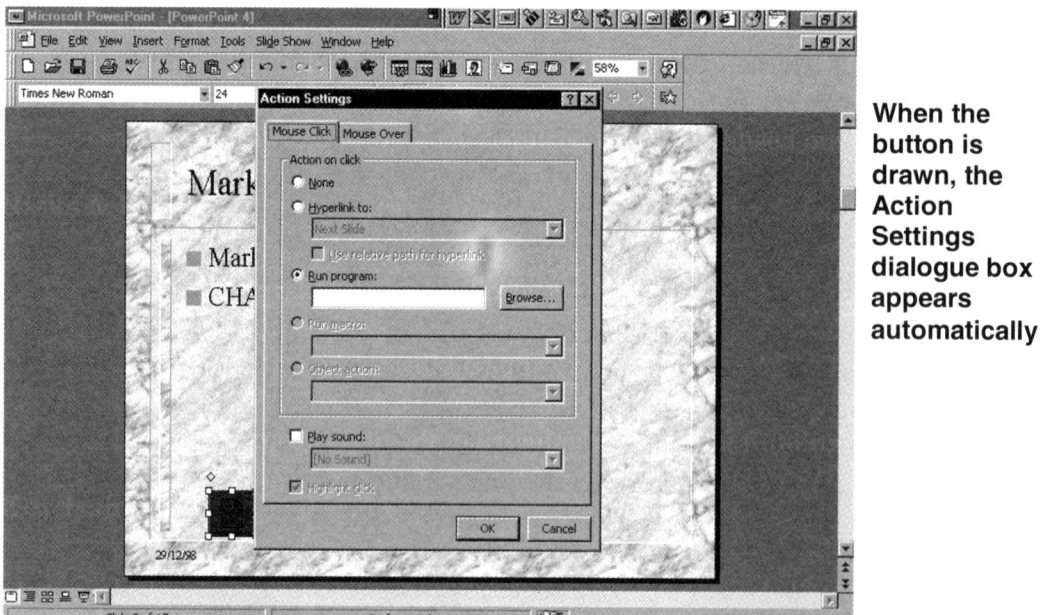

Select the Hyperlink To option button, and from the drop down list select the last item — Other File.

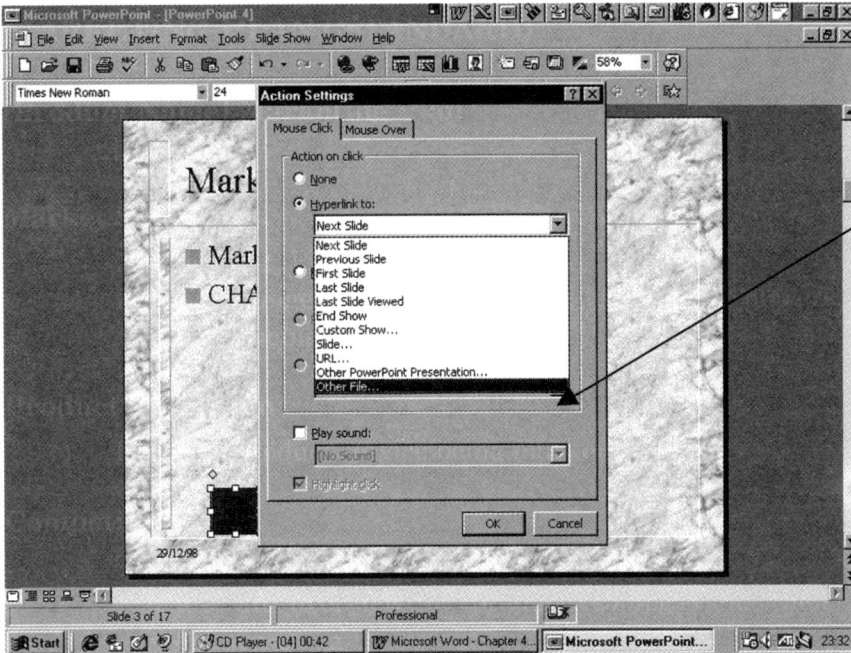

From the drop down list choose Other Files

Browse and select the file **Historical Presentation 17.xls**.

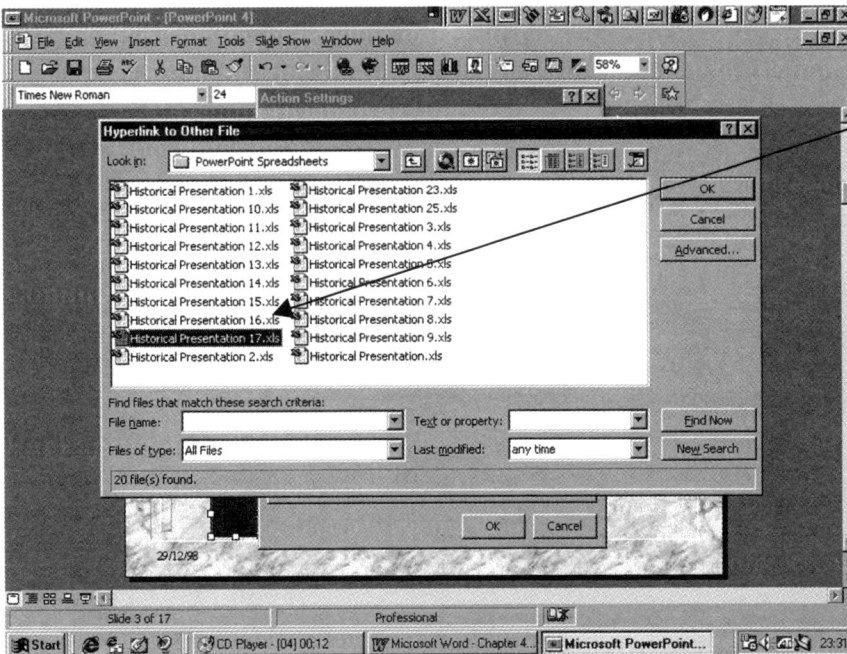

Select the file and click OK

Click OK in the dialogue box to close it.

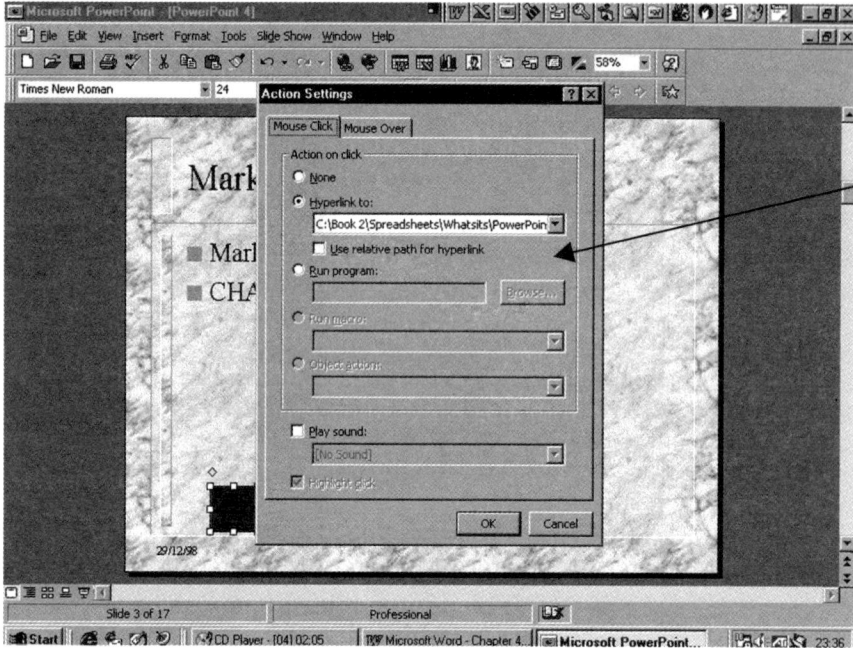

The path to
the file is
stored

Click OK to
close the
dialogue box

EFFICIENT HYPERLINKING

If you start the slide show and click on the icon an error message is generated. In
order to run the hyperlink efficiently macro protection should be turned off. It
can be reset after the presentation is completed.

To turn off macro protection in Excel, uncheck the box in the dialogue box.
Otherwise, toggle the feature from the menu.

Select Tools, Options, General Tab. The Macro Protection checkbox is listed.
Check to switch it on, uncheck to turn it off.

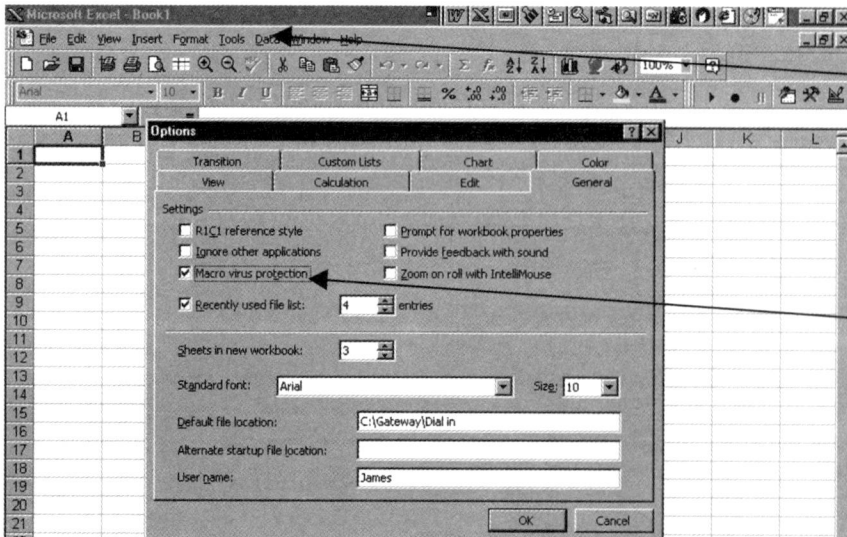

Select Tools

Options

General tab

Uncheck the
Macro virus
protection
setting

The features of PowerPoint, and therefore the style of dialogue box, are different from Excel. However, it is found in the same place – Tools, Options, General tab, Macro checkbox.

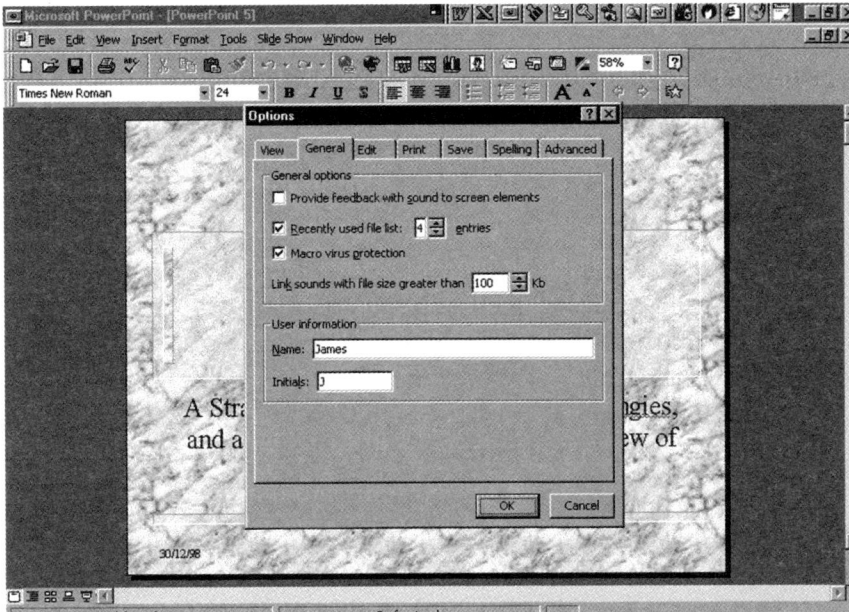

The macro feature is accessed from the same menu headings in PowerPoint

Start Excel, but leave the spreadsheet unloaded. Start the PowerPoint presentation and move to the relevant slide. Click on the icon. The spreadsheet should load, and operate as normal.

The Web toolbar is automatically activated. To navigate back to the PowerPoint presentation click on the Back arrow. Alternatively, hold down Alt and press the Tab key. Pressing Tab cycles through the open programs. Releasing Tab brings the highlighted program to the front screen.

Select Back

Or press Alt and Tab to cycle through the programs running.

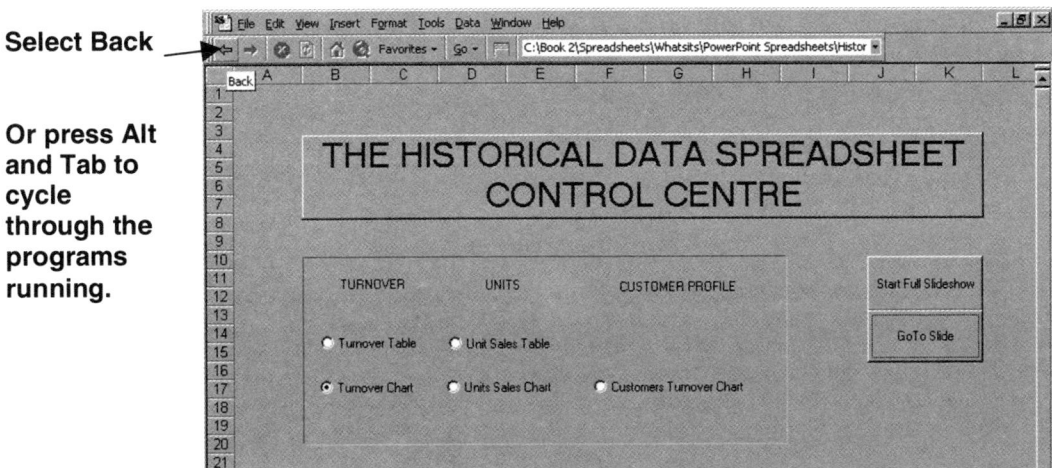

RUN THE SLIDESHOW

When setting up the slide show,

- Load Excel first. Start the spreadsheet.
- Start PowerPoint. Begin the slideshow.

The hyperlink should move to the spreadsheet, and the Web button should move to the slide show, without fuss.

When closing down the programs, end the PowerPoint presentation first, then close Excel.

RUN PROGRAM

Why did we not select Run Program instead of hyperlinking to the spreadsheet? This would allow us to automatically start Excel, but there are three problems:

- The time delay while Excel loads
- The time delay while the individual spreadsheet loads
- The spreadsheet has to be set to load automatically on starting Excel.

CONCLUSION

That concludes the section, and the tutorial. We have explored how to summarise data and present it in Excel in an effective and professional manner. We have looked at how we can use Excel VBA to enhance our control over the visual presentation of information, and how we can use Excel VBA to provide a professional, high-quality, front-ended spreadsheet wizard to non-technical users.

We have also demonstrated our strong presentational skills with PowerPoint, suitably coordinated with Excel. By the time we complete our slide show we will have impressed the senior management team with both our analytical skill and our professional presentation skills.

NEXT

The next section deals with the specific question of consolidating accounts and projections prepared in Excel.

Section Five

CONSOLIDATIONS: OVERVIEW

Sections One to **Four** are related, and draw together the knowledge required to present information to senior management in a clear and structured manner.

This section covers material that does not fit into that scenario — specifically the consolidation capabilities of Excel, and how it can be used in accounts preparation.

This section will make more sense if you have covered the material in *The Accountant's Guide to Excel*. If you have not covered it you can skip this section if desired.

Chapter Thirty-five

CONSOLIDATIONS

Coming together

Accounts consolidations are different from spreadsheet consolidations. They are the adding together of different sets of accounts, usually within a group of companies. Consolidation adjustments have to be made in order to net off inter-company debts, and other adjustments may be required. There is also the matter of including associated companies within the accounts.

From an accounting point of view, the mechanics can become quite complex. Within the spreadsheet, consolidation involves adding spreadsheets together vertically — like a three-dimensional chessboard.

First of all, we will look at the steps for consolidating data in Excel. Then we will look at how to consolidate accounts.

SPREADSHEET CONSOLIDATION

Start a new workbook.

Rename Sheet 1, Consolidated; Sheet 2, Consolidated 2; Sheet 3, Source 1; and insert a new sheet, naming it Source 2. Enter the following details into the spreadsheet:

Sheet	Cell	Data
Source 1	A1	Sale Of Goods
	A4 to A 12	Type 1, Type 2 etc.
	B4 to B12	1, 2 etc.
	D1	Sale of Goods
	D4 to D12	Type 1, Type 2 etc.
	E4 to E12	1, 2 etc.
Source 2	A1	Sale Of Goods
	A4 to A 12	Type 1, Type 2 etc.
	B4 to B12	1, 2 etc.
	D1	Sale of Goods
	D4 to D12	Type 2, Type 3 etc.
	E4 to E12	2, 3 etc.

Notice that Source 2 details in D4 are out of step by 1 with the details in Source. The spreadsheet is saved as **Consolidation 1.xls**.

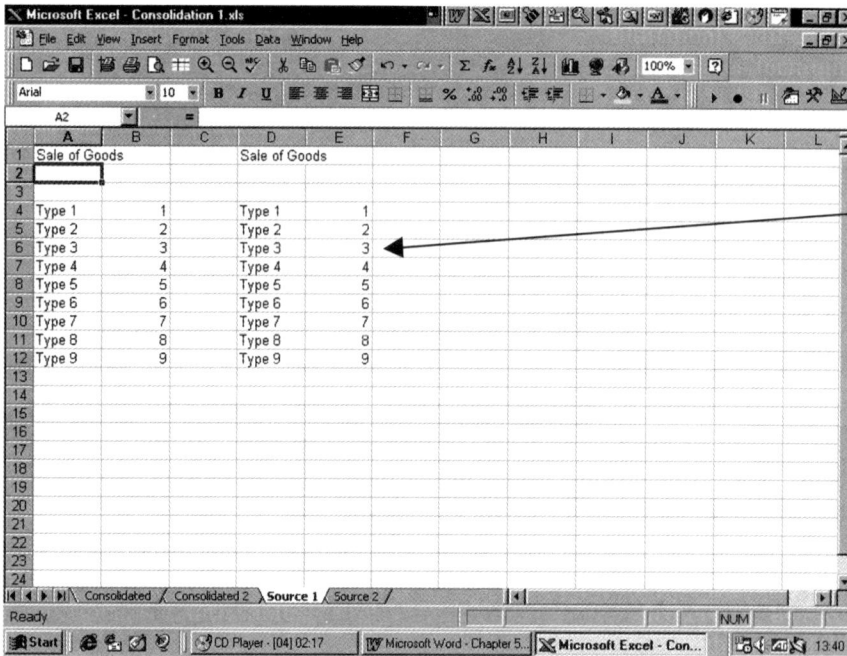

The details above are entered in the spreadsheet

Copy the heading Sale of Goods to the sheet labelled Consolidated, and enter Consolidated in cell B1.

Place the cursor at A4, and from the menu select Data, Consolidate.

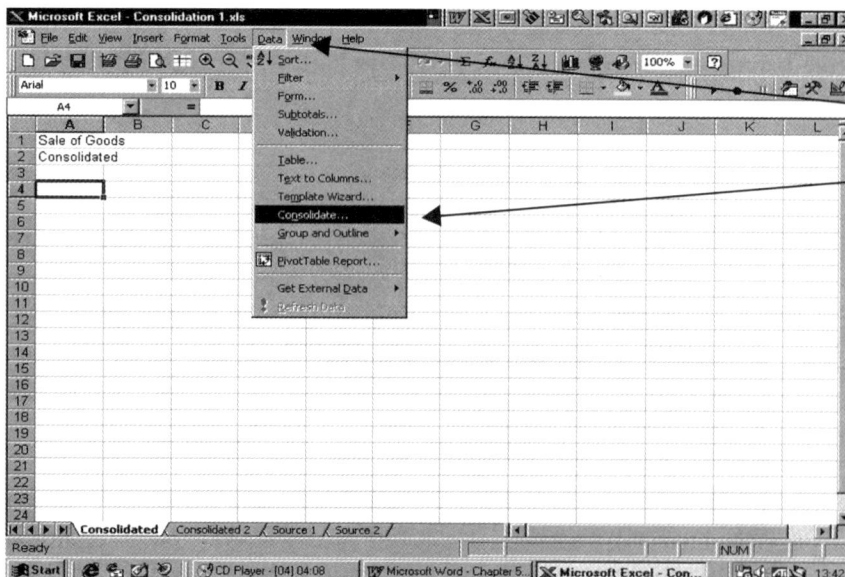

Select Data

Consolidate

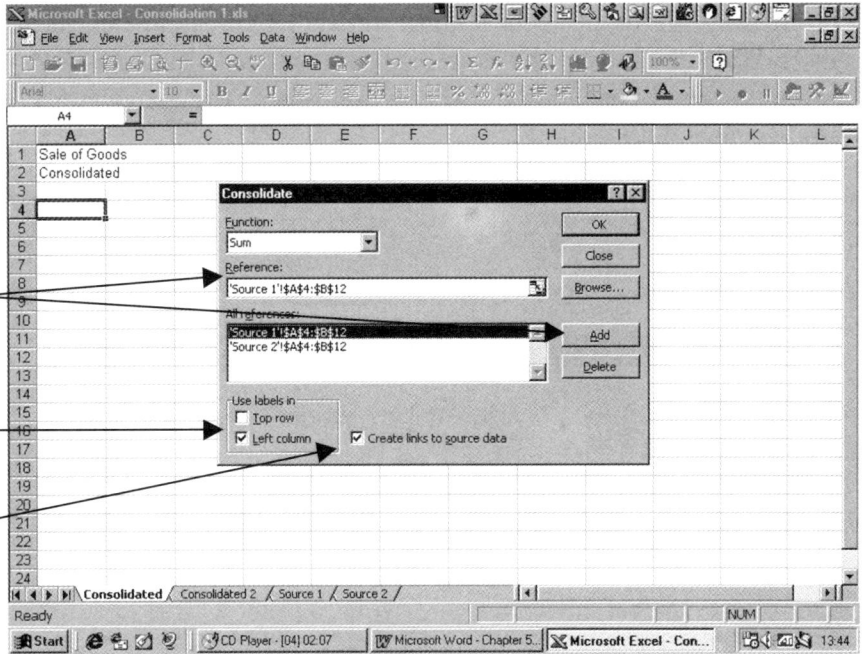

Select the cells, and click Add. Select the next set of cell references.

Tick Left Column and Create Links

The consolidated data and labels are entered on the sheet.

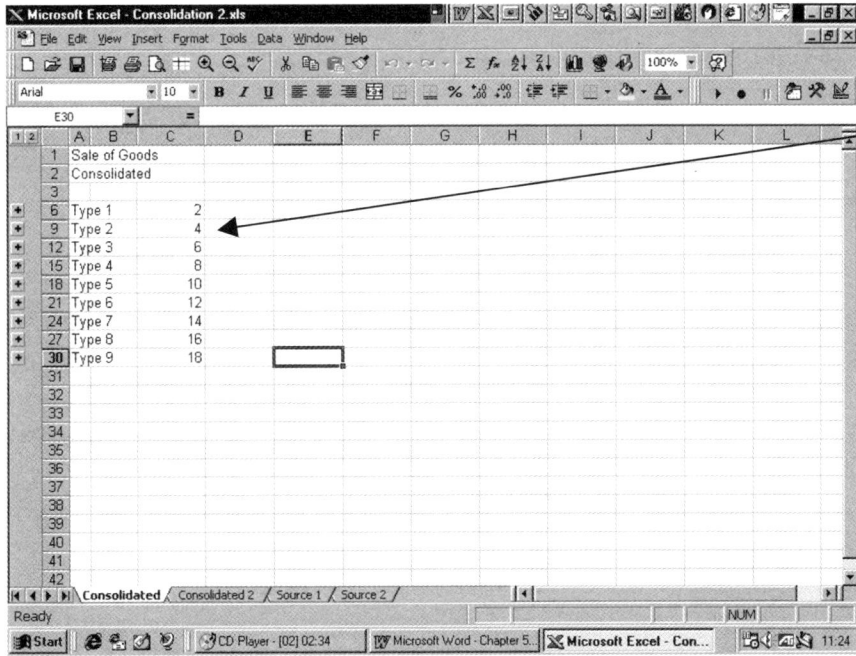

The figures are displayed

Change one of the source cells to 1000. The consolidated figures are updated.

This works well for two sets of data in exactly the same cell location in different sheets. We will now add the data from the data sets in E4 to E12.

Activate the Consolidated 2 sheet, and repeat the above steps for selecting the data to consolidate.

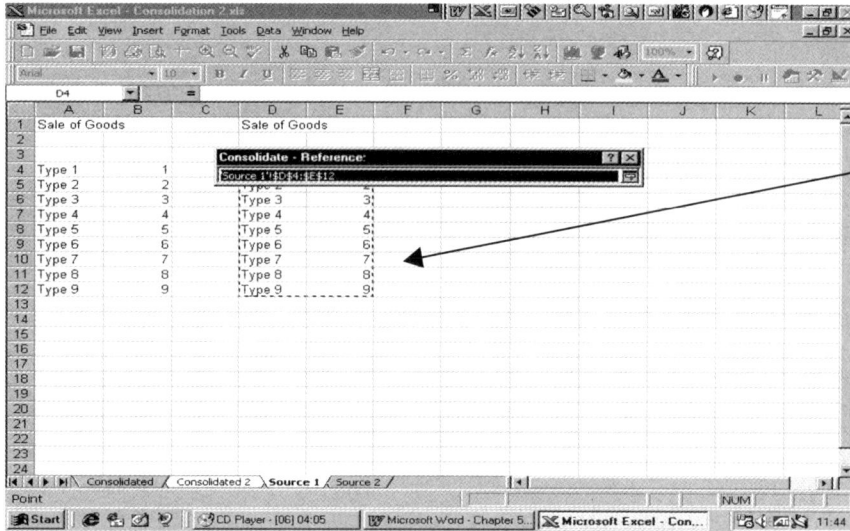

Select from the second range of data

The consolidated data is automatically adjusted to include all of the Type headings, and the figures are correctly calculated.

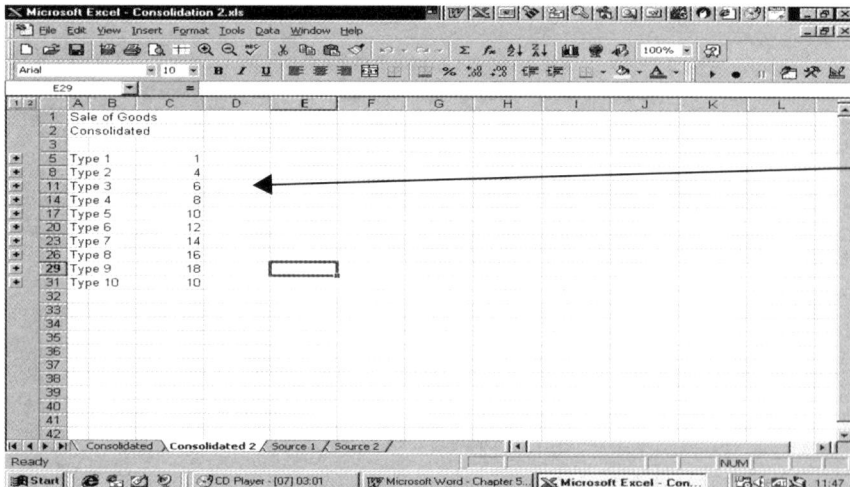

The data types are correctly picked up, and the figures are correctly shown

The consolidated figures can be totalled using Σ. The formula inserted in the spreadsheet when this is done is in the style:

=SUM(C31,C29,C26,C23,C20,C17,C14,C11,C8,C5)

This means that totals are correctly added; otherwise the detail would be added together with the Type totals.

The spreadsheet is saved as **Consolidation 2.xls**.

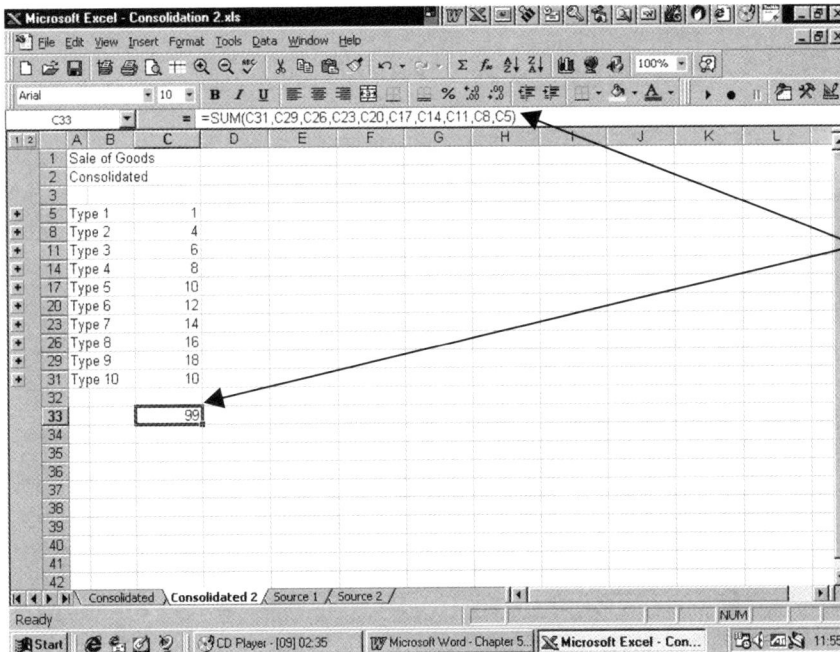

The SUM function accesses the individual cells, rather than a range

Notice that the left of the screen shows small + signs, and that the row numbers are not in numerical sequence.

The detail behind the figures is placed in the consolidation sheet, and it is then hidden. The detail can be accessed either by clicking on these + buttons, or from the menu by choosing Data, Group and Outline, Show Detail.

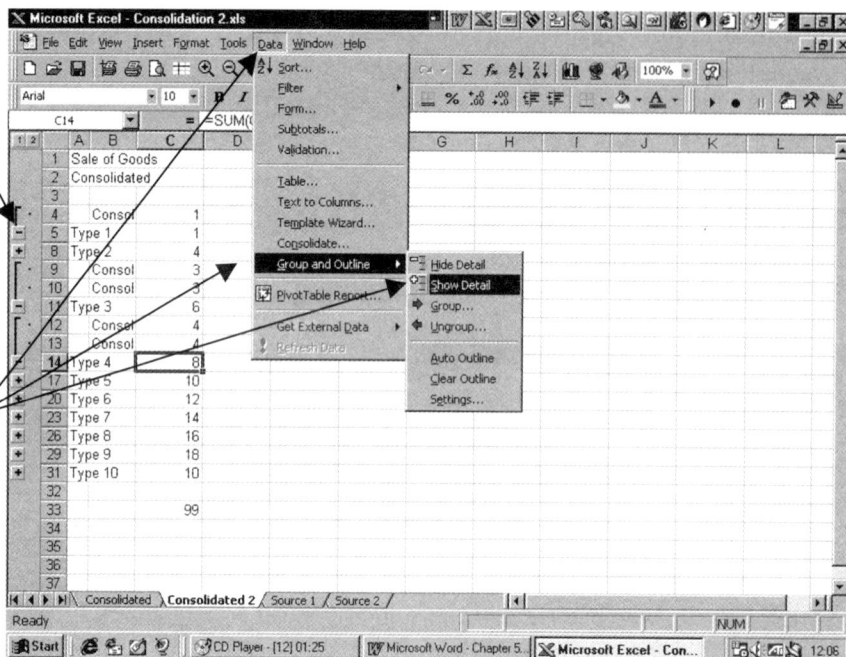

Click on the + buttons to show detail, and the – buttons to hide detail

Or, from the menu select Data, Group and Outline, Show Data

NEXT

That clarifies the steps in Excel for consolidation. In the next chapter we consider it from an accounting perspective.

Chapter Thirty-six

CONSOLIDATED ACCOUNTS

Drawing it together.

On the face of it consolidations are going to be easy. Excel consolidates subsidiary sheets, and everything is always included.

However, as the computer program does more, the ease with which errors can be found is greatly reduced.

It is therefore vital to set up a clear audit trail through the spreadsheets. Firstly, we will look at monthly management accounts for a single company, then group financial statements requiring consolidation.

MONTHLY MANAGEMENT ACCOUNTS

The reason for preparing monthly management accounts in Excel is to avoid a long list of reversing entries, such as accruals and prepayments, in the main program used by the company. Items like depreciation can also be left out of the nominal ledger until the end of the year, and they are then journalised, monthly, in Excel separate from the TB produced elsewhere.

The accounts can also be linked to projected data to see the effects of cash flow and revised budgetary analysis.

The monthly accounts of an individual company are straightforward. Use the model built in *The Accountant's Guide to Excel*, using one sheet per month.

The ETBs are **not** linked, because the TB from the system that is input into the accounts is cumulative. Depreciation, accrual, prepayments and any other adjustments that are made outside the nominal ledger are not cumulative.

The report section needs to be amended to display cumulative figures to date, monthly figures (cumulative this month minus cumulative figures from last month), last month's figures and whatever other detail is required.

Charts can be added, and the monthly management accounts report begins to take shape. If annual projections are to be included within the monthly management accounts report in order to have a projected twelve-month figure available, place the projections in a separate sheet within the spreadsheet. The monthly projected figures can then be included in the journal section — one journal for each month, is probably the easiest way to enter the figures.

As each month passes, that month's detail can be deleted from the journal section, and the journals can be amended as new information comes to light throughout the year.

ACCOUNTS CONSOLIDATIONS

When consolidating a set of accounts, the question is, "At which point should consolidation take place?" The choices are:

- Extended Trial Balance
- Rounded Trial Balance
- Profit and Loss Account.

This is irrespective of the actual mechanics of how to consolidate. The advantages and disadvantages of each are:

Advantages

Disadvantages

ETB

The detail is combined at the Trial Balance stage. The detail is therefore evident, including Accruals and Prepayments within each company.

Too much detail will increase the amount of work required in order to finalise consolidation.

Rounded ETB

The final accounts figures, net of all accruals and prepayments, are available in trial balance format. All figures are rounded off.

Work is necessary to prepare the P&L and balance sheet reports. This work must then be duplicated to produce the consolidated reports.

Inter-company adjustments for accruals and prepayments may be missed.

Profit And Loss Account

The accounts are in final format, and all expenses headings that are going to be combined into, for example, general expenses have been reviewed already.

Inter-company adjustments for accruals and prepayments may be missed.

A new sheet is necessary for each part consolidated i.e. one sheet for P&L, one for BS etc.

CONSOLIDATION STEPS

Make a duplicate of the accounts template sheet, and rename it Consolidation. Create a consolidation link with the Rounded ETBs of the companies, and bring this into the sheet at cell BA2000. If any rows are hidden as part of the consolidation process it will not affect the ETB etc. in column A.

Pick up the consolidated figures in the ETB, and then use the Journals section to make inter-company adjustments. The figures are then carried forward into the Rounded ETB, and the Report section.

Build error checking into the ETB by linking to the profits of each company and displaying this detail at the bottom of the consolidated ETB.

This approach also allows global "what if" analysis similar to that discussed for the single company management accounts discussed above.

LINKING TO SOURCE

In order to ensure the group accounts are always in agreement with the underlying sets of accounts links will be created. The question is, are the links internal within one spreadsheet, or external to workbooks set up for each company? This will depend on how you wish to organise your work.

The choice is made primarily on considerations of speed. If monthly management accounts are prepared there will be twelve sheets in the workbook for the accounts, plus cash flow workings and projections, the number of sheets can become substantial, and the workbook may be slow to work with.

Experiment, and see what you prefer.

NEXT

That completes the book. The next chapter looks at where to go from here.

Chapter Thirty-seven

SUMMARY

Looking back

The tutorial section has drawn together the various aspects covered in the first three sections, in order to practise what we have learnt and, more importantly, to give a flavour for what can be achieved.

Categorising the foundations that have been built, both here and in *The Accountant's Guide to Excel*, we have:

- Reviewed the Windows program, to understand the broader context in which we are working;

- Reviewed Excel's functionality;

- Produced a checklist of questions so that the spreadsheet is properly thought through and developed BEFORE starting on the actual program;

- Categorised spreadsheets into three broad types
  ◊ Calculation intensive (accounts and projections)
  ◊ Volume intensive (clerical processing of VAT invoices)
  ◊ Front ending for use by others (net pay to gross calculator);

- Built a robust accounts and projections preparation program, including a full and proper visual trail so that errors are easily and quickly traced;

- Reviewed advanced tools for auditing;

- Reviewed VBA, both as control tools on a spreadsheet and as a user form outside the immediate worksheet;

- Used PivotTables to summarise large amounts of data, in order to identify trends and to produce information;

- Used charting to display PivotTable information, and then used the charts to project future periods;

- Reviewed PowerPoint in order to broaden our range of presentation skills;

- Practised on a large volume of random data, so that we have new data to work with, and are not trying to learn the skills on a small data set that is unrealistic;

- Built VBA models, to demonstrate how the facility can be used constructively.

This provides a very good, solid foundation of knowledge and computer skills. Further development depends on what you want to achieve:

- **Advanced spreadsheet modelling** with Excel is worthwhile. However, it will require an in-depth knowledge of VBA and VBA programming;

- **Microsoft Access** is an excellent tool for accessing other databases. It is also an exceptional tool in itself, especially when used in conjunction with Excel PivotTable capabilities. However, Access is based around generating Forms for inputting data and, whilst there are wizards to help, a knowledge of Access VBA is a prerequisite;

- **PowerPoint** has many advanced features which, if you are making presentations in this format on a regular basis and you want to maximise their impact, would be necessary to learn;

- Having come this far, it is difficult, and probably unwise, to ignore **Visual Basic** if you want to move further forward.

Whichever subject you learn in greater depth, the cumulative knowledge will accelerate your ability to study at an intensive and professionally rewarding level.

Personally, if I had to choose one topic from the above, I think I would recommend learning Access. The use of databases is now all-pervasive and skills in this area will pay huge dividends.

In the meantime, thank you for coming through this voyage with me. The random data generator should prove to be a useful learning tool for you to practise with "live" data. My apologies for the program being so slow — this is a function of the in-built randomisation, and the number of calculations required. Perhaps a cup of tea while you wait, and then a large whiskey while you practise!

Good luck!

APPENDICES

- Whatsists Sales Data Generator
- PowerPoint Pro-forma
- The Spreadsheets on CD

Appendix 1

THE WHATSITS SALES DATA GENERATOR

The Whatsits Sales Data Generator program is designed to allow any number of sales transactions, up to a maximum of 65,000, to be produced.

The data is created randomly, but it is also flexed to allow directional trends to be inserted. Each of the data headings is discussed below:

- Invoice numbers are always generated in numerical order, starting with W1.
- Dates always begin at 1 January 1998. A minimum of 39 sales per day occurs. After that, sales are tested against a randomly generated number.
- Customers are randomly generated. However, the customer file is set to work on a "rule of 78" basis. There are 112 customers in the database.
- Growth in sales of Widgets can be flexed for each size of product, from minus 50% per annum to plus 50% per annum.
- Growth in sales of Whatsits can be flexed for each size of product from zero to plus 50% per annum.
- Selling price can be changed from minus 10% to plus 10% per annum for all products. Price changes take effect on 1 January each year.

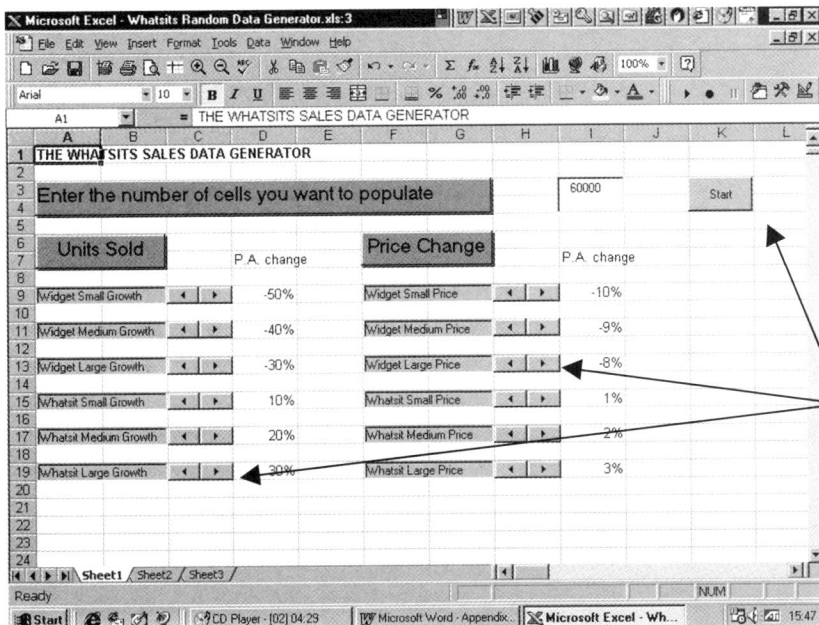

The opening screen, at cell A1

Data is generated at cell AA1

Use the spin buttons to adjust growth rates and price changes, then click Start

After start is clicked, a form opens in order to input the number of transactions to be generated.

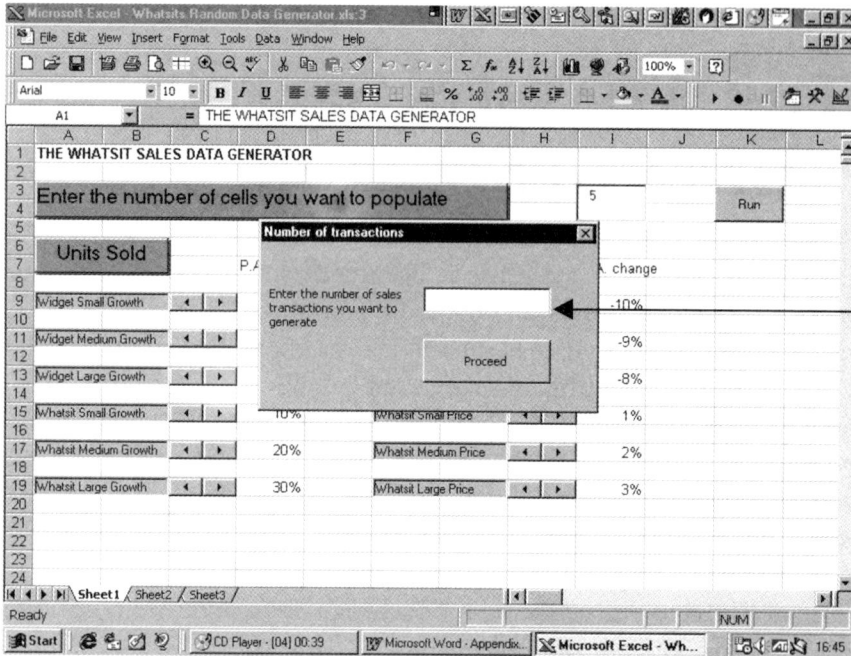

The form for input of the number of items to generate

The code has not been protected, and you are free to review the program if you wish. The same techniques have been used as were demonstrated elsewhere in the book, such as input key restriction etc.

Appendix 2

POWERPOINT PRO-FORMA*

BUSINESS PLAN (STANDARD)

[Company Name]
> Business Plan

Mission Statement
> A clear statement of your company's long-term mission. Try to use words that will help direct the growth of your company, but be as concise as possible.

The Team
> List CEO and key management by name.
> Include previous accomplishments to show these are people with a record of success.
> Summarize number of years of experience in this field.

Market Summary
> Market Past, Present, & Future
> Review those changes in market share, leadership, players, market shifts, costs, pricing, or competition that provide the opportunity for your company's success.

Opportunities
> Problems & Opportunities
> State consumer problems, and define nature of product/service opportunities create by those problems

Business Concept
> Summarize key technology, concept or strategy on which your business is based

---

* The PowerPoint Pro-forma presentations shown here and used within the book are taken from the Templates prepared by Microsoft and are included with the PowerPoint software.

Competition

Summarize competition

Outline your company's competitive advantage

Goals & Objectives

5-Year Goals

State specific measurable objectives

State Market share objectives

State revenue/profitability objectives

Financial Plan

High-level financial plan that defines financial model, pricing assumptions, and reviews yearly expected sales and profits for the next three years.

Use several slides to cover this material appropriately

Resource Requirements

Technology Requirements

Personnel Requirements

Resource Requirements

financial, distribution, promotion,etc.

External Requirements

products/services/technology required to be purchased outside company

Risks & Rewards

Risks

Summarize risks of proposed project

Addressing Risk

Summarize how risks will be addressed

Rewards

Estimate expected pay-off, particularly if seeking funding

Key Issues

Near Term

Isolate key decisions and issues that need immediate or near-term resolution

Long Term

Isolate issues needing long-term resolution

State consequences of decision postponement

If you are seeking funding, state specifics

MARKETING PLAN (STANDARD)

[Product Name] Marketing Plan
[name]

Market Summary
Market Past, Present, & Future

Review changes in market share, leadership, players, market shifts, costs, pricing, competition

Product Definition
Describe product/service being marketed

Competition
The competitive landscape

Provide an overview of product competitors, their strengths and weaknesses

Position each competitor's product against new product

Positioning
Positioning of product or service

Statement that distinctly defines the product in its market and against its competition over time

Consumer promise

Statement summarizing the benefit of the product or service to the consumer

Communication Strategies
Messaging by audience

Target consumer demographics

Packaging & Fulfillment
Product packaging

Discuss form-factor, pricing, look, strategy

Discuss fulfillment issues for items not shipped directly with product

COGs

Summarize Cost of Goods and high-level Bill of Materials

Launch Strategies

Launch plan, if product is being announced

Promotion budget

Supply back up material with detailed budget information for review

Public Relations

Strategy & execution

PR strategies

PR plan highlights

Have backup PR plan including editorial calendars, speaking engagements, conference schedules, etc.

Advertising

Strategy & execution

Overview of strategy

Overview of media & timing

Overview of ad spending

Other Promotion

Direct marketing

Overview of strategy, vehicles & timing

Overview of response targets, goals & budget

Third-party marketing

Co-marketing arrangements with other companies

Marketing programs

Other promotional programs

Pricing

Pricing

Summarize specific pricing or pricing strategies

Compare to similar products

Policies

Summarize policy relevant to understanding key pricing issues

Distribution

> Distribution strategy
> Channels of distribution
> Summarize channels of distribution
> Distribution by channel
> Show plan of what percent share of distribution will be contributed by each channel — a pie chart might be helpful

Vertical Markets/Segments

> Vertical market opportunities
> Discuss specific market segment opportunities
> Address distribution strategies for those markets or segments
> Address use of third-party partner role in distribution to vertical markets

International

> International distribution
> Address distribution strategies
> Discuss issues specific to international distribution
> International pricing strategy
> Localization issues
> Highlight requirements for local product variations

Success Metrics

> First year goals
> Additional year goals
> Measures of success/failure
> Requirements for success

Schedule

> 18-month schedule highlights
> Timing
> Isolate timing dependencies critical to success

RECOMMENDING A STRATEGY (STANDARD)

Recommending a Strategy

> Presenter's Name

Recommending a Strategy

> Ideas for Today and Tomorrow

Vision Statement

> State the vision and long term direction

Goal and Objective

> State the desired goal
> State the desired objective
> Use multiple points if necessary

Today's Situation

> Summary of the current situation
> Use brief bullets, discuss details verbally

How Did We Get Here?

> Any relevant historical information
> Original assumptions that are no longer valid

Available Options

> State the alternative strategies
> List advantages & disadvantages of each
> State cost of each option

Recommendation

> Recommend one or more of the strategies
> Summarize the results if things go as proposed
> What to do next
> Identify Action Items

THE SPREADSHEETS ON CD

All of the spreadsheets referred to herein are on the CD that comes with this book. The CD is structured so that the relevant spreadsheets are all contained in one folder.

The folders, and the heading to which each relates, are as follows.

Folder Title	**Relevant Section**
Auditing	Section 1
VBA	Section 1
Data Filter	Section 2
Data Table	Section 2
Forecasting	Section 2
PivotTables	Section 2
Scenarios	Section 2
Solver	Section 2
Charting	Section 2
Map	Section 2
PowerPoint	Section 3
Whatsits	Section 4
Sub Folders:	
Historical Data	
PowerPoint Spreadsheets	
Projections	
What If	
Consolidations	Section 5